PAPERS AND CORRESPONDENCE
OF
WILLIAM STANLEY JEVONS

Volume IV

PAPERS AND CORRESPONDENCE
OF
WILLIAM STANLEY JEVONS

Volume IV
CORRESPONDENCE 1873–1878

EDITED BY
R. D. COLLISON BLACK

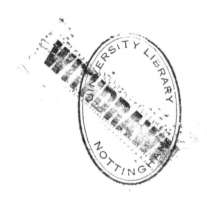

in association with the Royal Economic Society

First published 1977 by
THE MACMILLAN PRESS LTD
London and Basingstoke
Associated companies in New York
Dublin Melbourne Johannesburg and Madras

SBN 333 19977 4

Printed and bound in Great Britain by

UNWIN BROTHERS LTD
Woking and London

CONTENTS

Letter

Letter

Letter

Letter

A complete index to the *Papers and Correspondence, Lectures,* and *Papers on Political Economy* will be contained in Volume VII.

PREFACE

The letters in this volume cover the years from 1873 to 1878, when Jevons's career was at its zenith. The correspondence reflects the growth of his reputation and the spread of his interests; his interest in monetary affairs and applied economics is shown clearly through the extensive correspondence with Sir Robert Harry Inglis Palgrave, which began in these years.

On the side of economic theory, this volume contains the bulk of the letters concerned with the propagation of the doctrines of the 'marginal revolution'. Central to this is Jevons's correspondence with Walras, which has already been published in Professor William Jaffé's monumental edition of the *Correspondence of Léon Walras and Related Papers*. Nevertheless these letters are included in full here, not only because much of the other correspondence would be difficult to understand without them, but also because there are numerous differences between the actual letters from Walras received by Jevons and the drafts from which Professor Jaffé prepared his edition. Less familiar, but almost of equal significance, is the correspondence with Johan d'Aulnis de Bourouill, the Dutch economist who first drew Walras's attention to the significance of Jevons's work.

The suggestion that Jevons and his work were better known at this time on the Continent than in Britain receives support in the number of letters from other European economists and statisticians of the time such as Luigi Bodio, Falbe Hansen, Harald Westergaard and N. G. Pierson. Yet if British supporters of Jevons's theories were fewer in number during this period, there is special interest in some of their letters to him, notably those of G. H. Darwin.

Among Jevons's British correspondents, one of the most notable to emerge in this period is H. S. Foxwell. It was Jevons, as Keynes noted[1] who first kindled in Foxwell the interest in economic bibliography which was to become his ruling passion, and they remained close friends for the rest of Jevons's life. More evidence of Jevons's interest in the bibliography of economics and diligent search for earlier uses of the mathematical method in the subject is provided in this volume by exchanges of letters with W. H. Brewer and Robert Adamson. In particular, the full

---

[1] *Essays in Biography, Collected Writings of John Maynard Keynes*, vol. x, p. 140.

correspondence relating to the 'disagreeable incident' of the discovery, in 1878, of Gossen's work is here published for the first time.

Once again, I am indebted to many colleagues for help both in locating material for this volume and in dealing with the varied questions which have arisen in editing it. Mr R. D. Freeman, now of the Organisation for Economic Co-operation and Development, who is preparing an edition of the correspondence of H. S. Foxwell, kindly supplied me with copies of all the Jevons letters in that correspondence. Professor William Jaffé scrutinised all the Walras material in the Jevons Papers and compared it with the Fonds Walras texts from which he had worked, making many valuable editorial points. For assistance with material in Danish libraries and translation of Danish texts I am much indebted to Professor Mogens Boserup of the University of Copenhagen. Professor Piero Barucci and Signorina Dott. Simonetta Bartolozzi of the University of Florence, Dr Marco Brazzale of the University of Venice and Dr Giorgio E. Ferrari, Librarian of the National Library of San Marco in Venice, were generous with their help on Italian material. My thanks are due to them as also to Professor P. B. Kreukneit of the University of Leiden and Mr D de Roo van Alderwerelt of Amsterdam for help with Dutch sources. My colleague Professor Peter Froggatt gave me valuable advice concerning the background to the letter (No. 489) from Francis Galton, and I am similarly indebted to Dr W. H. Chaloner of the University of Manchester for information about W. H. Brewer and also about many aspects of the history of Manchester in Jevons's time. My thanks are also due to Professor M. W. Beresford of the University of Leeds, Mr Colin Treen, Department of Architectural Studies, Leeds Polytechnic and Mr A. B. Craven, City Librarian of Leeds, for biographical information relating to John Marshall; to Mr D. A. Collard, of the Department of Economics, University of Bristol, and the City Archivist of Bristol for similar information on T. P. G. Hallett and Mrs Elliott; to Mr Vincent Knowles and Mr G. H. Ashworth, Registrar and Deputy Registrar respectively of the University of Manchester, for information about some of Jevons's students and about candidates for the Chair of Political Economy at Owens College, vacated by Jevons in 1876; and to Mrs M. Gaskell, Librarian of Girton College, Cambridge, for biographical information about the women students at Cambridge examined by Jevons in 1875 and 1876.

I am grateful also to Miss C. England, of University College London, and Miss H. M. Young, of the University of London Library, for details of the examinerships held by H. S. Foxwell; to Mrs M. Lightbown, Curator of the Slade School of Fine Art, University College London, for information concerning the portrait of Lord Granville referred to in Letter 434; to Mr H. D. Erlam, Librarian of the Philson Library,

University of Auckland, New Zealand, for biographical details of Dr Millen Coughtrey. Similar information was kindly provided by Miss Olive Perry, of the Records Branch, Department of Education and Science, for W. H. B. Brewer; by Mr Philip James, Librarian of the Royal Archive Section of the Bank of England, for Hammond Chubb; by Mr F. P. Richardson, Librarian of the Law Society, for G. P. Allen; by Mr A. G. S. Ensor, Borough Librarian of Eastbourne, for Russell Scott; by Mr B. W. Butler, Library Information Officer of the Meteorological Office, Bracknell, for Richard Strachan; and by Rev. Brian Golland, General Secretary to the General Assembly of Unitarian and Free Christian Churches, for Harold Rylett and C. L. Corkran.

I should like to record my thanks to all these people, as also to Mr J. M. Shaftesley, Chairman of the Society of Indexers, who provided information about the early days of the Index Society, and Mr P. Spiro, Librarian of the Institute of Bankers, who supplied details concerning the Cheque Bank and its founder, James Hertz.

For permission to make use of manuscript material of which they have custody or in which they hold the copyright my thanks are due to Mrs M. Barker, Sir William Gladstone, Bt, Sir Geoffrey and Lady Margaret Keynes, Dr Wolfe Mays, the Misses E. A. and M. L. Macleod, Mrs H. A. Mettam and Mr J. D. Mettam, Mrs R. T. Sneyd, Dr C. M. Faas, Keeper of Manuscripts, Universitiets-Bibliotheek van Amsterdam, the British Library Board, the Librarian of Cambridge University Library, Mr P. Sraffa, of the Marshall Library, Cambridge, the Directors of The Macmillan Press Ltd, Dr F. W. Ratcliffe, John Rylands Librarian of the University of Manchester, the Director, Bibliothèque Cantonale et Universitaire, Lausanne, the Trustees of the National Library of Ireland, *Guardian* Newspapers Ltd, the Editor of *Nature*, the Editor of the *Spectator*, the Editor, *Indian Journal of Economics*, the Rt Hon. Lord Armstrong, the Royal Observatory, Edinburgh, Baron W. J. d'Aulnis de Bourouill and the Rt Hon. Lord Brassey.

Queen's University   R. D. COLLISON BLACK
Belfast
12 November 1975

LIST OF ABBREVIATIONS

used throughout the volumes

Relating to Jevons material

LJ   *Letters and Journal of W. Stanley Jevons,* edited by his wife (1886).

LJN   Previously published in LJ; manuscript not now in Jevons Papers, or other known location.

LJP   Previously published in LJ, but only in part; fuller text now given from the orginal manuscript in the Jevons Papers or other indicated location.

WM   From a manuscript made available by Dr Wolfe Mays, University of Manchester.

Investigations   *Investigations in Currency and Finance,* by W. Stanley Jevons. Edited, with an Introduction, by H. S. Foxwell (1884). All page references to first edition.

Methods   *Methods of Social Reform and other papers,* by W. Stanley Jevons (1883).

T.P.E.   *The Theory of Political Economy* by W. Stanley Jevons (1st ed. 1871, 4th ed. 1911). All page references to fourth edition, unless otherwise stated.

Relating to other material

BM   British Museum, (Now Library) London.

FW   Fonds Walras, Bibliothèque Cantonale de Lausanne.

HLRS   Herschel Letters, Royal Society, London

JRSS   *Journal of the London* (later *Royal*) *Statistical Society.*

KCP   Palgrave Papers in the Library of King's College, Cambridge.

LSE   London School of Economics, British Library of Political and Economic Science.

MA   Archives of Macmillan & Co. Ltd.

NYPL   New York Public Library.

RDF   From a manuscript made available by Mr R. D. Freeman.

TLJM   Isabel Mills, *From Tinder Box to the 'Larger Light'. Threads from the Life of John Mills, Banker* (Manchester, 1899).

Walras Correspondence   *Correspondence of Léon Walras and Related Papers* edited by William Jaffé (3 vols, Amsterdam, 1965).

Figures following any of these abbreviations denote page numbers.

LETTERS

351. W. S. JEVONS TO W. H. B. BREWER [1]
[LJN, 273–4]

Parsonage Road,
Withington.
15th January, 1873.

. . . I am very much obliged to you for the letter which I received at the college a day or two ago. I was very desirous of learning what attempts had been made to apply mathematics to political economy, and I carefully searched the British Museum catalogues, the Royal Society catalogues of papers, and some bibliographical books without success. Whenever the occasion shall arise, I shall hope to make proper use of information which you have so kindly procured for me. Since the *Theory of Economy* was published I discovered that I had by some unaccountable oversight omitted to notice Garnier's mention of Cournot's work, [2] *Recherches sur les Principes Mathématiques de la Théorie des Richesses*, par Augustin Cournot; Paris, 1838. I have lately procured this book without difficulty through Messrs. Ascher and Company, [3] but have not yet read it sufficiently to form a definite opinion on its value.

It evidently has little or no relation to my mode of approaching the subject through a theory of utility. The almost total oblivion into which such works have fallen is very remarkable, and not encouraging to those who attempt other works of the sort.

I shall be glad to have any other information which you obtain about the books named; I think something ought to be done to rescue them from entire oblivion.

It was a pleasure to the examiners to have a candidate to whom they could so unhesitatingly award the medal as to yourself. . . .

---

[1] William Henry Brooks Brewer (b. 1842), B.A. London University, 1870; M.A. 1872. Served as a substitute lecturer for Jevons at Owens College, Manchester (see below, Letter 364, p.oo); became an Inspector of Schools in the Blackburn area from 1874 to 1907.
[2] See Preface to the second edition of *Theory of Political Economy*, pp. xviii–xix, xxx–xxxi, and Letter 358, n. 7, below, p. 15.
[3] Ascher & Co. were at this date foreign booksellers with offices at 13 Bedford Street, Strand, London, and at Berlin.

352.   W. S. JEVONS TO THE EDITOR OF *NATURE*

Maupertuis on the Survival of the Fittest[1]

Considering that the theories of Darwin and Spencer are among the most important additions ever made to human knowledge, it seems to be a matter of much interest to trace out any occasional glimpses which previous philosophers may have had of the Principles of Natural Selection. In a long note appended by Lord Bolingbroke[2] to his fourth essay concerning Authority in matters of Religion (octavo edition of the Philosophical Works, 1754, vol. ii, p. 253; quarto edition, 1754, vol. iv. p. 255), he reviews a Memoir by Maupertuis[3] printed in the History of the Royal Academy of Berlin, for the year 1746. Speaking of the appearances of design, Lord Bolingbroke says:— "Mr. Maupertuis proceeds, and admits, but admits, as it were, for argument's sake alone, that the proportion of the different parts and organs of animals to their wants carries a more solid appearance; and he judges that they reason very ill who assert that the uses to which these parts and organs are applied, were not the final causes of them, but that they are so applied because the animal is so made. Chance gave eyes and ears; and since we have them we make use of them to see and hear. He thinks, however, it may be said that chance having produced an immense number of individuals, those of them whose parts and organs were proportioned to their wants, have subsisted, whilst those who wanted this proportion have perished and disappeared. Those who had no mouth, for instance, could not eat and live; those who wanted the organs of generation could not perpetuate their species; and thus from the present state of things theists draw an argument which will appear fallacious when it is applied to the possible original of things".[4]

I am not aware that notice has been drawn to this distinct allusion to the survival of the fittest. So far as regards the introduction of the notion of *chance* the statement is no doubt erroneous.[5]

W. Stanley Jevons

Manchester, Feb. 12

---

[1] Published in *Nature*, 6 March 1873, p. 341.

[2] Henry Saint-John, Viscount Bolingbroke (1678–1751), statesman and philosopher.

[3] Pierre Louis Moreau de Maupertuis (1698–1759), French mathematician and philosopher, follower of Newton.

[4] *The Works of the Right Hon. Henry St. John, Lord Viscount Bolingbroke*, 7 vols (1754–98), IV, 249–632 (257). The note from which this extract was taken stretched over five pages in this edition, 255–9.

[5] See below, Letter 358, p. 15.

353. W. S. JEVONS TO W. H. B. BREWER
[LJN, 274−5]

Parsonage Road,
Withington.
14th February, 1873.

. . . Best thanks for your letter, enclosing the extracts from Kroncke's economical investigations; I shall carefully preserve them for future use. I procured Cournot's other work upon economy [1] which you now mention, but have not read more than a few pages. The fact is that what time my health at present allows me to give to work is nearly absorbed by a logical work in slow progress through the press, so that I have to keep economical matters for the future.

I have, however, since your previous letter, looked a little more into Cournot's *Recherches,* and am inclined to regard it as a very able and mostly sound work, though it hardly gets anywhere to the bottom of the matter. The latter part of the book, in which he treats of the law of supply and demand, is very striking and original.

My *Theory* has been reviewed in the *Academy* of 1st April 1872, p. 131; the *Manchester Guardian* of 22d November 1871; the *Manchester Examiner* of 15th November 1871; the *Glasgow Daily Herald* of 16th December 1871; the *Evening Standard* of 17th December 1871,[2] in addition to those you mention, and a few other brief notices.

You may be interested to hear of a paper by Mr. Fleeming Jenkin in the *Proceedings of the Edinburgh Royal Society*[3] (1871−72), p. 618, in which

---

[1] In his 'List of Mathematico-Economic Books' Jevons refers to two works by Claus Kroncke and notes a third which he had not seen. Only one of these, *Das Steuerwesen nach seiner Natur und seinen Wirkungen untersucht* (Darmstadt, 1804), is now considered significant in the development of mathematical economics. Cf. R. D. Theocharis, *Early Developments in Mathematical Economics* (1961) pp. 100−3.

[2] For the text of the *Academy* review, see Vol. VII.

[3] 'On the Principles which regulate the Incidence of Taxes', loc. cit., pp. 618−31. Reprinted in *The Graphic Representation of the Laws of Supply and Demand, and other Essays on Political Economy* (L.S.E. Series or Reprints of Scarce Tracts in Economic and Political Science, No. 9, 1931) and in R. A. Musgrave and C. S. Shoup, *Readings in the Economics of Taxation* (1959).
After a summary of his representation of the law of supply and demand, Jenkin added: 'Professor Jevons has since given a much more complex algebraic representation of the same law which, however, reduces to the above simple form.' Subsequently, having outlined what is essentially the concept of consumers' and producers' surplus as given by the areas under the demand curve and over the supply curve at a given price, Jenkin wrote: 'Professor Jevons has used curves to integrate what he terms the utility gained by exchange in a manner analogous to the above; but utility, as he defines it, admits of no practical measurement, and he bases his curve, not on the varying estimates of value set by different individuals each on what he has or what he wants, but on the varying utility to each individual of each increment of goods. The above estimate of the gain due to trade, deduced from the demand and supply curves as orginally drawn in my *Recess Studies* article is, I believe, novel . . .'
The wording of these passages could be construed as an implicit claim to priority but, at least in the second passage, Jenkin was careful to point out that he and Jevons approached the problem from different angles. Cf. Vol. III, Letters 290−2, pp. 167−78.

the method of his paper in 'Recess Studies' is farther pursued. Some reference is made to my *Theory;* but as regards questions of priority, Mr. Jenkin has allowed himself to be in error.

I shall look forward with interest to any further results of your researches. . . .

354. D. M. BALFOUR TO W. S. JEVONS

Boston, February 24th, 1873.

Dear Sir,

I am in receipt of your esteemed favor of 25th ulto. and contents noted. Some important facts are developed in the table alluded to.

1. The following statement will exhibit the average price of a dozen articles, for the twelve years preceding, and the twelve years succeeding the discovery of gold in California and Australia.

Period	Beef	Pork	Cod fish	Flour	Corn	Rice	Coffee	Tea	Sugar	Hides	Cotton	W
	$	$	$	$	cents	$	cents	cents	$	cents	cents	c
1838 to 1849	9.94	11.32	2.62	6.12	67	3.60	$7\frac{1}{4}$	54	5.27	$12\frac{7}{8}$	10	
1850 to 1861	12.35	16.30	3.26	6.37	79	4.16	10	38	5.77	18	12	

Thereby exhibiting an increase of twenty per cent.

2. War is a great enhancer of prices. The following table will exhibit the average prices of a dozen articles during the decade preceding, and the decade succeeding the Civil War in the United States.

Period	Beef	Pork	Cod fish	Flour	Corn	Rice	Coffee	Tea	Sugar	Hides	Cotton	W
	$	$	$	$	cents	$	cents	cents	$	cents	cents	c
1854 to 1863	13.00	16.38	3.25	6.63	85	4.93	$12\frac{1}{8}$	41	6.59	$22\frac{7}{8}$	$19\frac{1}{2}$	
1864 to 1873	14.27	24.72	5.87	6.98	113	7.86	$10\frac{3}{4}$	51	8.40	$25\frac{3}{4}$	$41\frac{3}{4}$	

Thereby exhibiting an increase of thirty-five per cent. Between 1861 and 1865, Cotton advanced eight hundred per cent, Pork two hundred, Rice one hundred and eighty, Sugar one hundred and eighty, and Beef one hundred and thirty per cent.

3. The repeal of the British corn-laws, in 1849, enhanced the price of corn in the United States, twelve cents per bushel. The Civil War in the

United States enhanced, during the decade 1864 to 1873, twenty eight cents per bushel, as indicated above.

4. The difference in prices between 1858 and 1865, was one hundred and thirty per cent; between 1865 and 1873, one hundred and fifteen[1] per cent; the prices of 1873, are five per cent below those of 1853.

I notice that a writer in the London Economist[2] estimates the advance in prices consequent upon the discovery of gold in California and Australia, at only ten per cent., somewhat below the statement above. That writer attributes it to some other cause than the excessive production of gold. The latter has increased four hundred per cent within thirty years, whilst prices have advanced only from ten to twenty.

I think that the writer in the L.E. is in error in estimating the annual product of gold at only £20,211,000 or $89,826,666. The gold product of

the United States is	$28,000,000	
Mexico	29,000,000	
South America	3,000,000	$60,000,000
Australia		58,000,000
Europe		23,000,000
Asia		15,000,000
New Zealand		9,000,000
Africa		4,000,000
Polynesia		2,000,000
Grand Total		$171,000,000

The emigration from Ireland in 1847, and also from England and Scotland in 1852 and successive years to Australia, doubtless has had some effect in enhancing the prices of labor in Great Britain. The loss of a million of men during the Civil War in the United States, 1861; 1865 doubtless has had the same effect in this country.

Undoubtedly the cost of living in cities and large towns has greatly increased within a few years. May it not be attributed to the disposition all over the world, since the introduction of railways, of people to forsake the country and congregate in cities?

There is a typographical error in the table. Beef, in 1840, should be $12.58.

Yours truly,
David M. Balfour.

W. Stanley Jevons, M.A.

---

[1] 'fifteen' replaces 'sixty-two', crossed out in the original manuscript.
[2] *The Economist*, 25 January 1873, pp. 92–3. 'Economist' replaces 'Examiner', crossed out in the original manuscript.

355.   W. H. B. BREWER TO W. S. JEVONS

27 Grace's Road,
Camberwell,
London S.E.
26/2/73.

My dear Sir,

I trust you will excuse the liberty I take in forwarding you a copy of two works[1] lately published by a friend of mine, bearing upon the practical side of political economy. Having assisted in their preparation by reading the whole of the proofs and by making various contributions to them, a number of copies were placed at my disposal. Amongst the parts of the vols. I prepared I may mention two in which the graphical system of representation has been resorted to; viz. The Historical chart and description, prefixed to the "Growth and Vicissitudes of Commerce" and the "Appendix on National Debts with Chart", added to the other work. There is something of interest attached to the first-named chart. It was modified and enlarged, and finished with a letter press description, from a chart in an old work in my possession, written in the earlier years of the present century. The edition I have is the second, and is dated 1807. The date of the first edition would not probably be very far from that of Canard's work in which, according to Rau, mathematical economics began. The work is called "An Inquiry into the permanent causes of the decline and fall of powerful and wealthy nations". The author is W. Playfair,[2] brother of Prof. J. Playfair, of Edinburgh. He seems to have been a voluminous writer and a man of versatile if not great talents. This graphical system, which he calls "Linear Arithmetic" he employs in four charts illustrative of his work. Of the first you will get some knowledge from the work I have sent. The second is a curious one and is entitled "Chart representing the extent population and revenue of the principal nations in Europe in 1804". Circles of varying size represent the extent, and a pair of vertical lines, tangential to the circle at the extremities of the diameter, represent population and revenue. The height of the vertical tangents is determined by longitudinal lines representing millions. The third chart is a graphical representation of the amount of English imports and exports. Vertical lines divide the chart into periods of time, and horizontal lines show millions of money. Two irregular curved lines show the values of the exports and imports. When the export line is above the import, the intervening space is coloured green, é contra red. The fourth

---

[1] John Yeats, *Technical Industrial and Trade Education. The Growth and Vicissitudes of Commerce from B.C. 1500 to A.D. 1789* [and] *A Manual of Recent and Existing Commerce from 1789 to 1872*, 2 vols (1872).

[2] William Playfair (1759–1823), *An Inquiry into the permanent causes of decline and fall of powerful and wealthy nations, illustrated by four engraved charts* . . . (first edition, 1805). Cf. Vol. II, p. 427.

is a chart of the revenues of England and France and is constructed on a principle very similar to that of Chart III. In the case of England a third curved line divides the Revenue into "Interest of Debt" and "Free Revenue". There is a certain general resemblance in the last two charts to those in Mr. Dudley Baxter's "National Debts". Relative to W. Playfair I may mention that he calls himself "Author of Notes and Continuation of an Inquiry into the Nature and Causes of the Wealth of Nations by A. Smith LL.D."[3]

I think he might have got the hint of the economical application of his so-called "linear arithmetic" from Canard's work, for I find he lived many years in France just about the time Canard's work was published, and indeed was editor of Galignani's Messenger[4] there for some time.

Having mentioned Canard I may say a little more about him. Following bibliographers and linographers I find that I have got into an error relative to him. I have his "Principes de l'economie politique"and his pamphlet on the question "Est il vrai que dans un pays agricole, toute espece de contribution retombe sur les proprietaires fonciers?" as two distinct works. On examining the "Memoires de l'Institut etc.", the body which crowned Canard's work, I find there that this answer to the question was the work crowned, that it was called "Essai sur la circulation de l'impot", and that on publishing it, he made numerous and extensive additions and at the same time changed the title to "Principes etc."[5] Vol. 4 of the "Memoires" contains a short epitome of the original work. It is extremely brief, occupying only a few pages. No mention is made of the employment of algebraical formulae which perhaps only appeared in the enlarged work.

I thank you for the information you gave me in your last. I am afraid I shall be considered a troublesome correspondent by you, but I look to the interest you take in the subject of my letter to be my apologist.

I remain,
Very faithfully yours,
W. H. Brewer.
W. S. Jevons Esq., M.A.

---

[3] Adam Smith, *An Inquiry into the Nature and Causes of the Wealth of Nations*, eleventh edition, with notes, supplementary chapters and a life of Dr Smith, by William Playfair (1805).

[4] An English daily newspaper founded by the Galignani family and published in Paris under various titles from 1814 to 1904. It contained articles taken from French and English newspapers which were of interest to English people living on the Continent, and enjoyed a wide circulation. William Playfair, who had spent several years in France during the Revolution, returned to Paris after Waterloo and became editor of *Galignani's Messenger* from 1815 to 1818.

[5] Nicolas François Canard (*c.* 1750–1833), *Principes d'économie politique, ouvrage couronné par l'Institut national dans sa séance du . . . 5 janvier 1801; et depuis revisés, corrigés et augmentés par l'auteur* (1801).

P. S. I find Canard's publisher was Buisson of Paris (according to the Secretary of the "Institut"). I have sent an inquiry for the book through Messrs. Nutt & Co.[6]

356.   W. S. JEVONS TO R. H. INGLIS PALGRAVE
        [KCP]

The original manuscript of this letter has a number of observations written on it in Palgrave's handwriting. These observations are here reproduced in italics, as close as possible to the point at which they occur in the manuscript. They clearly formed the basis for Palgrave's reply to Jevons, Letter 359 below p. 16.

I think that my table dividing the country, between Agric. and Ind. Districts shows that note cir. is less wanted in the former now. These continued in the old ways of requiring notes the longer.
About 7 months writing the paper.

Parsonage Road,
Withington, Manchester.
23rd March 73.

My dear Sir,   .

I have had much pleasure in looking over the proofs of your valuable & elaborate paper,[2] as far as time would allow. It contains so great an amount of information, and so much close reasoning, that I cannot pretend to have studied it with the care requisite to anyone pretending to criticise the paper as a whole. My remarks will therefore be limited to those parts with which I am most familiar or which have most struck my attention. Col. I. Sir R. Peel was moved to the act of 1844 by the virtual bankruptcy of the bank in 1839 when the note issue was placed in peril.[3]

I do not know what estimate you quote as making the gold & silver

Daily News Oct. 21 1873

circulation of 1872 as 130 millions. In 1868 I made the *total* metallic currency to be 95 millions *as a maximum* meaning the amount of coin, and

---

[6] It has not proved possible to trace any information about either of these firms.

[1] [Sir] Robert Harry Inglis Palgrave (1827–1919), banker and writer on financial and economic subjects; knighted 1909; editor of the *Bankers' Magazine* and, from 1877 to 1883, of *The Economist*. His published works included the well known *Palgrave's Dictionary of Political Economy*, 3 vols (1894–1914).

[2] 'Notes on Banking in Great Britain and Ireland, Sweden, Denmark and Hamburg; with some remarks on the amount of Bills in Circulation', *JRSS*, 36 (1873) 28-152.

[3] Jevons's references to 'Col.' presumably relate to galleys. On page 78 of the printed paper Palgrave wrote 'In 1844 Sir Robert Peel had, besides 1839, 1819 still fresh in his memory'.

it is not likely that it has since increased so much in spite of the great coinage of the last year or two. I do not think that the

notes & coin

whole circulating medium now much exceeds 140 millions. (Statistical

R.H.I.P. estimate includes bullion.

Journal Dec. 1868. pp. 446–447).[4] Nevertheless your arguments concerning the increased proportion of metallic money must hold good on the whole, and are quite novel so far as I remember.

Statements in E Jan. 11 show it is only fractional.[5]

Col. 4. Your statements about the use of notes & coin hardly

Probably a local custom.

agree with what was told me when inquiring concerning sovereigns. –

This is Wales &/what I have observed & Seebohm – Banker's Notes.[6]

Stat. Journal. ibid p. 450–1.[7] Col. 5. Have not the usury laws a good deal to do with the early *apparent* steadiness of the rate of interest; if you go further back you will find that the rate used to be almost invariable.[8] Col. 6. *Cheques are not currency* and

I think not – the rate av. so much below 5.

when actually paid and not written off against each other *they require*

[4] Palgrave altered his figures in response to these criticisms; on p. 79 of the printed paper the metallic circulation for 1872 is estimated at 105 millions, with the note 'Estimate based on Professor Jevons' statement, *Statistical Society Journal,* 1868, p. 446, and the account of the "Coinage of Gold for Twenty-four Years", *The Economist,* 29 June 1872'. The statement that 'in this country the amount of gold in circulation is estimated at 130,000,000 l.' occurred in a Money Market review in the *Daily News* of 21 October 1872: Palgrave wrote '1873' by mistake.

[5] *The Economist* (vol. 31, no. 1, 533) 11 January 1873, pp. 29–30, contained part II of an article entitled ' Mr. Lowe on Scotch Banking' which argued that 'cheques and bills are by far the most important part of our currency'.

[6] Presumably a reference to Frederic Seebohm (1833–1912), well known in later years as an economic historian and author of *The English Village Community* (1905). Seebohm was a partner in the banking firm of Sharples & Company of Hitchin, Herts, and an advocate of country-bank note-issues. Palgrave's note might seem to refer to a publication by Seebohm on this subject, but he does not appear to have published anything on it at this date.

[7] In his 1868 paper Jevons had argued, largely on the basis of evidence drawn from North Wales, that dealers in the agricultural districts still carried cash – both notes and gold – in large amounts, and that only manufactured goods were mainly paid for by cheque. Palgrave, on the other hand, contended in this 1873 paper that 'the circulation in *gold* has increased probably as fast as the increase in retail trade and the total of wages. But the circulation in *notes* has increased very slowly indeed. The extension in the use of cheques for sums of 5l. and above has supplanted the use of notes' (loc. cit., p. 86).

[8] Palgrave argued that although the total note-issue had increased only slightly since 1844, the unregulated (country bank) portion had fallen while the regulated (Bank of England) portion had risen; corresponding in date with this 'the number of alterations in the rate of discount, and the extent of the fluctuations in that rate, tend to augment' (loc. cit., p. 87). The alternative explanation suggested by Jevons was based on the fact that prior to 1833 Bank Rate was limited to a maximum of 5 per cent by the Usury Laws.

Had been altered.

currency to pay them.

Col. 9. I have been much interested in your discussion of the fall in the country note circulation as noticed by Gladstone; But in spite of your successfully explaining away a part of it, there remains a real decrease of some amount. In the diagram prefixed to John Mills' paper,[9] which I posted a day or two ago, you will find a certain variation of the country circulation roughly indicated, and my diagram of the Bank Accts. 1844−62 shows it to the eye.[10] If you have not got a copy of this diagram, I shall be happy to present you with one. I do not say anything as to the cause or inferences to be drawn from

Have accounted for more than half.

the variation.

Col. 6. Why do you restrict the table of reduction of note

Had some thoughts of restricting the table to a shorter period.

circ. to 1855−64 and not carry it on a few years.

The reduction in the Issue make me keep to the period more corresponding in amount.

Col. 13−14. Section XIII. Here you approach the main point of the whole question. I believe it is the narrow reserves of Country Bankers & the dependence of some banks on others or the B.

Not the Country Bankers only. The subdivision.[11]

of England which leads us into trouble for the most part.

Col. 17. I fully concur in what you say as to the increasing danger of crises, & the reasons given.

Your inquiries concerning the *bill circulation* seem to be very important, & interesting in results, but it is no use my attempting to discuss them.

In conclusion, allow me to say that perhaps with the exception of Gilbart's treatise and Tooke's & Newmarch's History, I know no private publication which contains so much indisputable & valuable information about the Banking system, as your paper will. It seems to me the kind of paper which does good by supplying us with sound & original

---

[9] J. Mills, *The Bank Charter Act and the Late Panic* (1866).

[10] On pp. 95−6 of the published version of his paper Palgrave referred to a speech made by Gladstone in 1866 drawing attention to the fact that during the period of pressure on the Bank of England in the Overend, Gurney crisis country-bank issues had actually fallen. Palgrave pointed out that a seasonal drop in country-bank note-issues could be traced from May to August in every year, adding in a footnote − 'This is also clearly indicated to the eye in Professor Jevons's very careful diagram showing all the weekly accounts of the Bank of England . . . published by Edward Stanford.'

[11] i.e. the subdivision of the Bank of England into Issue and Banking Departments by the Act of 1844.

information from those who thoroughly understand the working of the system. But at the same time I am not prepared to accept all your inferences. Your advocacy of the English Country circulation seems far less strong than other parts of the paper. I more and more admire the Act of 1844, and should like to see one uniform currency for the whole Kingdom, issued from a central institution on the basis of the Issue Department. The present rather complicated state of things simply arose from concession to vested interests, & Sir. R. Peel managed very cleverly to carry out a sound principle in spite of those concessions.

Intended to refer only to requirement of gold being held against issues

I rather question the accuracy of your statement on p. 26 that no additional security is provided by law to Irish Bank note holders, for without the law we would have no guarantee against excessive issues & perpetual failures such as used to occur in England.[12]

Competition will now restrain issues.

I have made candid remarks on your paper because you requested me but of course I do not suppose that you will entertain any of them, & I merely ask you to excuse the liberty with which I have made them. I have posted a copy of Mills' paper according to your request. I consider it a very able one. Mr. Langton's paper[13] was a brief one, printed in 1857, but I have no copy of it, and I do not think one can be easily had. He is, as perhaps you know, a leading banker here of long experience, and has a great acquaintance with the subject though he has printed so little.

I return the proofs by book post which I never find to fail.

I much value your kind present of the Blue Book concerning the Finance of U.K. which forms a solid basis to my statistical Library.

I am glad to know about your article in the Quarterly Review,[14] which I believe is one that I partially read, but shall now read with much more interest. I suppose it criticised Levi's History which though useful & accurate does not seem to me to show any great excellence.

If ever I come near Yarmouth I shall have much pleasure in calling on you, but I have never been very near it as yet, & do not know when I shall.

Yours very faithfully,
W. S. Jevons

R. H. Inglis Palgrave, Esq.,

---

[12] 'Scarcely any security is really provided for the holder of any Irish note by the additional stock of coin which may be held by any bank. It is impossible to distinguish the notes which are in excess of the fixed limit, and to say these notes were issued against gold, and therefore in case the bank which issued them stops payment, the holder may claim gold for them' – Palgrave, loc. cit., p. 56.

P. S. I am glad to find my Tables have been of any use to you: no one else has seemed to see how they were requisite to disentangle fluctuations and obtain accurate results. – Gladstone evidently overlooked the seasonal variations.

357.   W. S. JEVONS TO R. H. INGLIS PALGRAVE

Parsonage Road, Withington
Manchester
1 April 73.

My dear Sir,

I think that the remark which you propose to insert concerning the bullion since 1839 is quite accurate & that the fact ought not to be lost sight of.[1]

After a few days' absence from Manchester I now send you by post a copy of my Bank diagram which you will readily observe was a work of great labour.

I enclose a post card[2] which shows the cause of delay of the paper which you sent for.

Believe me,

Yours faithfully,
W. S. Jevons.

358.   W. H. B. BREWER TO W. S. JEVONS

27 Grace's Road,
Camberwell S. E.
2nd April, 1873.

Dear Sir,

I owe you an apology for omitting to acknowledge the receipt of your charts. I have examined them with considerable care, and can admire the completeness of the information they contain in so small a compass, and appreciate the immense labour involved in their construction.

---

[13] W. Langton, 'On the Balance of Account between the Mercantile Public and the Bank of England', *Transactions of the Manchester Statistical Society*, Session 1857–8, pp. 9–22.

[14] 'History of British Commerce', *Quarterly Review*, 134 (1873) 204–25. Palgrave's article reviewed Levi's book of the same title, but did not offer any criticism of it.

[1] Attached to the original letter is the following note in Palgrave's handwriting: 'Since 1844 the bullion in the Bank of England has never approached in any degree the low level at which it stood in 1839, and thus one great element in security has been gained.' This sentence appears in Palgrave's paper 'Notes on Banking in Great Britain and Ireland . . .' *JRSS*, 36 (1873), at p. 90.

[2] This postcard is no longer with the manuscript.

I read the works of Maupertuis a year or more ago, for the sake of his principle of Least-Action, and jotted down a few passages in which the author seemed to recognise the "Survival of the fittest". On seeing your letter in "Nature",[1] I referred again to my note book and sent on some of the passages I had transcribed in confirmation of your recognition of the principle. The "Essai de Cosmologie"[2] seems to have been known to Mr. Darwin, for he refers to its contents in his "Variation of Animals and Plants under Domestication".[3] I have nowhere in his writings, however, met with anything which seemed to show an acquaintance with the "Venus physique" or the "Systeme de la Nature". Dr. Ross and Mr. Monro are a little fortunate in their communications,[4] for Mr. Darwin gives the very passage of Aristotle, which the one quotes and the other cites, in the footnote to the first page of his Historical Sketch of Nat. Sel., at least in the last edt.[5] I know nothing of Gassendi,[6] except from histories of Philosophy. I will refer to his works when I have the chance.

Have you observed that Cournot[7] in his "Principes de la theorie des Richesses" refers to another work on mathl. economy. (see note to p. 329.[8] It is a pamphlet of about 30 pp., and is in the Mus. library. Ordinary Algebra is the mathematics employed by Prof. Hagen; and the work seems very acute and thorough as far as it goes.)

By the next post you will receive the two earlier vols. of Dr. Yeats's series of works on Commerce,[9] which my friend has begged me to request your acceptance of.

I am,
Very faithfully yours,
W. H. Brewer

W. S. Jevons Esq., M.A.

[1] Reproduced above, Letter 352, p. 4.
[2] *Essai de Cosmologie*, par M. de Maupertuis (Leiden, 1751).
[3] Charles Darwin, *The Variation of Animals and Plants under Domestication*, third edition, 2 vols (1905) I, 15.
[4] *Nature*, 27 March 1873, p. 402. In addition to the letter from Brewer himself to which he refers in the text here, this page of *Nature* contained a letter from one James Ross and another from C. J. Monro; both drew attention to the fact that Aristotle had attributed the doctrine of survival of the fittest to Empedocles.
[5] Darwin, 'Historical Sketch of Natural Selection', *The Origin of Species*, sixth edition (1872) p. xiii: 'Aristotle in his *Physicae Auscultationes*, lib. 2, cap. 8, s. 2. . . .'
[6] Pierre Gassendi (1592–1655), Professor of Mathematics at the Collège de France, 1645–8. He was considered one of the leading mathematicians and philosophers of his age, and his followers included Cyrano de Bergerac and Molière. He was an influence upon Newton and Diderot.
[7] Antoine Augustin Cournot (1801–77), Professor of Mathematics at Lyons and rector of the Academies of Grenoble and Dijon; pioneer of mathematical economics.
[8] Cournot here refers to 'la critique . . . qu'un auteur allemand, M. Hagen, a faite de notre théorie dans une brochure intitulée: *Die Nothwendigkeit der Handelsfreiheit fur das Nationaleinkommen mathematisch nachgewiesen*. Konigsberg, 1844, in-8°'. Cf. below, Letter 360, p. 19.
[9] John Yeats, *The Natural History of Commerce* (1870); *On the National Exodus; its consequences and its cure* (1865).

P. S. I have failed to get a new copy of Canard, but have some hopes of succeeding in getting a secondhand one. I am promised a long letter from Germany at Easter, relative to math. eco.

359.   R. H. INGLIS PALGRAVE TO W. S. JEVONS

Gt. Yarmouth,
April 10, 1873.

My dear Sir,

I would have replied at once to your very complete and kind letter on my paper[1] which I was very much obliged to you indeed for but I have been up to this time so fully occupied that I have been unable to find leisure to do so before.

I will reply in the first place to the points mentioned in your letter.

1.   *Estimate of metallic circulation*

I had taken this from one in the Daily News. On looking into it again I feel that it is excessive and that the amount of paper circulation of the Bank of England *based on bullion* must be included – as this would introduce a further point, I have marked the fact in a note[2] – and reduced the amount to an estimate based on yours and the recent coinage which has been very great.

Use of coin and notes

I remember being struck with the remark in your paper[3] at the time – of coin and notes being held by Drovers and others. It does not correspond with what I have observed here – or with the experience of any Bankers in this neighbourhood, or in any part of *England* that I know about. Here up perhaps to 10 – certainly within 15 years all such persons have banking accounts. They *used* to carry great rolls of notes and pay for their purchases – but all that is passed away now.

I am much obliged to you for calling my attention to this, as well as to the amount of the gold circulation, and I hope you will find my amended remarks according to your own impressions.

It is a curious thing but I have sometimes thought in reading the papers that robberies in the West of England from the *person,* have appeared to

---

[1] A comparison of the points made in this letter with the text of the paper makes clear that Palgrave altered a number of passages in the proof in response to the criticisms made by Jevons in his letter of 23 March 1873. See above, Letter 356, p. 10.

[2] Loc. cit., note to p. 79.

[3] W. S. Jevons, 'On the Condition of the Gold Coinage of the United Kingdom', *Investigations*, p. 277.

produce a greater amount of *plunder* in the shape of notes or gold, than in the East. This you will say, is to regard crime from a Banking point of view. I think it supports my impression (and also yours) of the use of notes and gold – and that it is a local matter. The Bankers in the West and North of England have a practice of charging a heavyish commission on the turnover of an account, which tends to increase the use of notes. In the remainder of England a somewhat different practice prevails. This is a *private* detail of the business which of course I cannot allude to in print.

Rate of interest and usury laws

I have never thought the usury laws had anything to do with the steadiness of rate – partly because it was usually so much below the permitted maximum. But this question would require a very full treatment to make it clear. I have sometimes thought of endeavouring to elucidate it.

'Cheques' and 'currency'

I am much obliged to you for calling my attention to this – it was a slip of the pen – I meant they *had* a currency i.e. were *current*. I have altered the phrase. I had intended to alter it before seeing it was not clear, but had not completed it.

Country note circulation in 66

I admit that there was a great, and *unusual* drop – but I do not think Mr. Gladstone's inference was the correct one. I have accounted for $\frac{6}{10}$ of the whole, which is *something*. I am much obliged to you for the diagram and have called attention to it in a note.

Table of reduction in note circulation

I restricted this to the years 1855–64 because *earlier than that* the circulation was considerably larger – then the drop was periodically *more*. But I thought it not fair to compare the state of things when the circulation was regularly larger – though if *I had* done so – it would have *appeared* to strengthen my case.

Question of Reserves

I do not think the *narrow reserves of the country Bankers alone* are the main cause of the general *smallness* of the reserves. But this is a most difficult question. Speaking privately – I believe the real cause arises from the *subdivision* of British Banking. There are something like *400* separate Banks (I write from memory). What is the 400th part of any responsibility?

English Provincial circulation

I am sorry my defence of this is not to your mind adequate – I have always regretted that Mr. R. Peel did not

1. require security
2. give *every* facility for transfer of circulation.

Had this been done in /44 I believe we should long ere this have seen large and powerful Banks extended over great districts of the country. I have made some reference to this in my concluding remarks.[4]

Irish note issues

I see that my remarks on this were not clear, but I have altered them.[5]

I think that nowadays *competition* will always restrain issue and *convertability* secure the correct amount of a *solvent* circulation.

I have made some further remarks in my Paper on 1 *domestic* and 2 *general* note issues. 1 Country Bank – 2 Bank of England

I think that we ought to strengthen the *domestic* and separate it from the *general* issue.

At present if a man goes to his Banker (an issuing Banker) and says I am going to another part of England, to London, to Scotland, to France, What money shall I take with me? The Banker replies "You had better take Bank of England notes" (He must say this – his *own* notes are unknown at a town 60 miles off, much more in Scotland, or France) "or gold". Well the customer takes off his £50 – £100 – whatever it may be. You will say, what of that? But I have to answer "This process is going on all over England at the same time".

Let us attempt an estimate. Do *less* than 100,000 people go out *at one time* for the autumn holidays? You will answer at once – *many more*. Now let us go a little further. Would the 100,000 take *less* than £5 each – I cannot think less. You have at once a drain of half a million, merely to pay

    Railways
    Hotels
    Lodgings.

This process goes on for fully 2 months and what is the use of it?
None to the Bank of England.
None to any one else that I know of.

If the Domestic circulation were one generally accepted – it would provide for a great part of this needless waste of the Central Banking Reserve. I give this as one instance merely.

I believe that with a *Central* and *uniform* note circulation the fluctuation would increase and intensify in the *Bank rate* – if the *Banking reserve* remains as at present, and that subdivision between a *general* and a *domestic* issue would be of service – though I do not think this alone would meet the evil without a great strengthening of the Banking Reserve.

L. Levi's Book[6]

This *might have been better*. But it is the best recently attempted and deserved some remark on that account. *I wish all Books that deserve as much*

---

[4] Palgrave, loc. cit., p. 151.
[5] Ibid., p. 56.
[6] See above, Letter 356, p. 13.

including some that deserve more obtained it. But it is easy reading and that is a great thing.

I found your Tables of much service and was very glad to refer to them as an independent testimony.[7]

I enclose a little bit of my paper which I think was left out of the proof you saw – showing the differences of circulation in the *agricultural and industrial districts.*

I do not know if I have given you a good return for your very thorough letter – by imposing all this on you – I was really very much obliged and thought it very kind of you.

At some future time I shall hope to have the advantage of discussing these points more fully with you.

I am, yours very truly,
R. H. Inglis Palgrave.

Pray excuse a scrawl but I hope you will be able to make it out.

360.   FRAGMENT OF A LETTER FROM W. H. B. BREWER
      TO W. S. JEVONS
      [25 April 1873]
   . . ."Perceptive powers" of the Atoms themselves.

I have just completed my reading of Cournot's two works.[1]
I think they have both met with undeserved neglect. I think no one can deny that the method of the "Recherches" has brought to light much that is original. It is a work of far higher character than either Kroncke's brochure or Whewell's papers.[2] In the larger work amongst many other interesting and valuable chapters, I was especially struck with those giving a sketch of the origin etc., of money, with that on "le mécanisme économique", and with the whole of Book iv on "l'optimisme économique". An interesting speculation common to both works is that on a "Standard of Values", especially the remarks on an economical analogue to the astronomer's "mean sun".

[7] Ibid., p. 96.
[1] A. A. Cournot, *Recherches sur les principes mathématiques de la théorie des richesses* (1838); *Principes de la théorie des richesses* (1863).
[2] William Whewell, 'Mathematical Exposition of Some Doctrines of Political Economy', *Cambridge Philosophical Transactions*, 3 (1829) 191–230; 4 (1831) 155–98; 9 (1850) 128–49. In the 'List of Mathematico-Economic Books . . .' printed as appendix v to Jevons's *Theory of Political Economy* (fourth edition), three works by Claus Kroncke are cited under dates 1802, 1804 and 1810. It is not clear to which of these Brewer's comment here relates.

361.   W. S. JEVONS TO A. NEILD [1]

London
14 June 1873

Alfred Neild Esq.
    Treasurer of Owen's College

Dear Sir
    It is with much regret that I now feel obliged from a regard to the condition of my health to offer the resignation of my position in the College at the close of the agreement now existing which is if I recollect right until the end of next September. I beg to place my chair entirely at the disposal of the Council from that date so that if my connection with the College is not to terminate then, it must be in consequence of a new & distinct appointment. As however the Council may not be pleased to have so sudden notice of resignation just at the close of the session, I beg to say that I shall be happy to receive a reappointment for twelve months from the 30th of September next at my present salary, on the understanding that I be allowed to find an efficient substitute to perform the teaching duties of the chair during the session. It is only right to say at the same time that I have literary work on hand which I should in any case attempt to finish before taking the complete relaxation in travelling which is recommended by D[r] Morgan. [2] I should also regard myself as entirely free from any kind of obligation to return to my college duties at the end of the year, unless it was in my opinion suitable to my interests to do so. I am quite aware that this proposal may in many respects appear an objectionable one, but I do not wish hastily to leave the College in the progress of which I have so long been interested & from the members of which I have received so much kindness. Believe me dear Sir
                                        Yours faithfully
                                        W. Stanley Jevons.

[1] Alfred Neild, son of Alderman William Neild (1789–1864), friend of Cobden and Chairman of the Owens College Trustees, 1858–64; succeeded his father as Chairman of the Trustees, 1864; Treasurer of Owens College and Chairman of the Council, 1871–89.

[2] John Edward Morgan (1829–92), Professor of Medicine at Owens College, Manchester, 1873–91; B.A., Oxon., 1852; M.A. 1860; M.D. 1865; M.R.C.P. 1861; F.R.C.P. 1868; author of *The Danger and Deterioration of Race from the Increase of Great Cities* (1866); *Town Life Among the Poorest, the Air they Breathe and the House they Inhabit* (1869); *The Victoria University, Why Are There No Medical Degrees* (1881). Cf. Thompson, *Owens College*, pp. 518–20, 526–7.

362.   J. G. GREENWOOD TO W. S. JEVONS

20 June 1873

The Owens College, Manchester

My dear Jevons,

I have barely time before post goes out to tell you that I read your letter at the Council today. As there was of course no notice on the paper, and moreover no *quorum*, the Council did not feel qualified to pass a formal resolution on the subject; but a minute was made to the effect that your letter to the Chairman and me had been read and that the Council while receiving with great regret the announcement of your temporary withdrawal was so fully convinced of the value of your service to the College that they had no hesitation in recommending that at the next meeting your second alternative should be accepted.

The next meeting of Council falls on Friday 4th July. Can you before that date procure us any further assurance of Mr. Brewer's qualifications[1] & if so I think we might close the negotiation at once. It would be better for him and you and us, as it seems to me.

I need not say that I was exceedingly sorry to get your letter both on our account and yours. You have of course no choice but to obey D.ʳ Morgan on such a matter. Shall I see you again before you go? I think your proposed arrangement in financial matters very liberal.

In great haste I am
              Faithfully Yours
              J. G. Greenwood

Nicholson[2] will send you a copy of the minute or quasi-resolution of the Council.

363.   W. S. JEVONS TO HERBERT JEVONS
       [LJN, 277−8]

Parsonage Road,
Withington,
25th June 1873.

. . . We leave for a long tour in Norway the day after to-morrow,[1] and I write a few lines to say that I hope you are now much better in

---

[1] See above, Letter 351, n. 1, p. 3.

[2] James Holme Nicholson (1825−1901), Registrar of Owens College, 1853−84; Librarian, 1853−71. His original appointment was as Clerk and Librarian of the College: the title was changed to that of Registrar in 1867. A Unitarian and native of Westmorland, he was an accomplished antiquary and founder of the Lancashire and Cheshire Antiquarian Society.

[1] Jevons and his wife spent the summer of 1873 in Norway. See LJ, pp. 278−88.

consequence of the bold step you took. [2] Your correspondence has again dropped off, but in the meantime I take no news to be good news.

I have also taken a bold step, in asking the college to give me a session's leave of absence, offering at the same time my resignation as an alternative. Though there has been no opportunity yet of giving me leave formally, I understand that there is no doubt about it. I have to find a substitute at a cost of £200, but have got a good one for that. You must not suppose that my health is any worse; on the contrary, it is better, but there is so much leeway yet to make up, and so little reason why I should at all endanger my ultimate complete restoration, that I feel sure it is wise to make the sacrifice, and both Harriet and myself will enjoy the tours we intend to make.

We begin with Norway again, where I intend to do much execution on the salmon and trout, having laid in some fine tackle.

In September we hope to have Tom and his family here; in the new year we hope, if all goes well, to spend many months in Italy, the Tyrol, Germany, or other parts of the Continent.

All that I suffer from now is nervous and muscular weakness, which it takes some time to recover from; but having improved during a session of work, I trust there is little doubt of thorough restoration during a session of play.

I know too little of your present affairs to discuss them as I should like.

I am much occupied with final arrangements for our departure, and so must say farewell. . . .

364.   W. S. JEVONS TO W. H. B. BREWER
        [LJN, 283–5]

Udvick, Nord Fiord,
Norway.
5th August 1873

. . . I was glad to receive your letter a few days since, and to hear that the council had, as I expected, appointed you as lecturer for the following session. As I have now an opportunity of posting a letter by the steamboat to-morrow, I will answer your questions as fully as I can.

1.   Your classes will be four in number. (a) Logic and mental and moral philosophy three hours per week throughout the session. The logic is taken first, and has usually occupied the course till the end of January, but if you prefer you can terminate it at Christmas. In this part of the

---

[2] Probably a reference to Herbert Jevons's appointment as manager of the branch of the Bank of New South Wales at Grahamstown, New Zealand. See Vol. I, p. 9.

course I have always given exercises – at least twice a week. Mental philosophy begins when the logic is concluded, and occupies the time till about the end of April; and the remaining four or five weeks are then given to moral philosophy; occasional essays are required in mental and moral philosophy.

2.   You will not need to give any formal introductory lectures. Certain of the professors will give public introductories[1] at the opening of the new buildings, but we are much opposed to admitting the public to the opening of each class. You can, therefore, start with your subject at once; but as the class is not always complete the first day or two, it is well not to get into any important part of the subject.

3.   All the lecturers hold examinations of their classes at Christmas and I think also at Easter, of which you will be fully informed; but you can also appropriate a lecture hour to a brief examination whenever you think fit. I find I have overlooked the greater part of my answer to (1) and therefore return to it. (b) The political economy day-class is held for one hour weekly throughout the session, and you can count the number of lectures in the calendar. In this class occasional essays or written answers to questions may be required at your discretion, but you will not get as full answers as you might desire. I have generally followed somewhat the order of subjects in Mill's *Political Economy,* in perfect independence, however, of his views and methods when desirable. In the subject of currency I have always abandoned his book altogether; although it would of course be desirable to include in your lectures more or less reference to all the parts of the subject, especially those named in the prospectus, yet the relative amount of attention given to the different parts must be left to your own discretion, and it has in my own case varied much from year to year. (c) The evening logic class consists of twenty weekly lectures. It may consist of the day lectures condensed and slightly simplified; but you will find a considerable proportion of the students able to enter pretty fully into the subject. Weekly exercises should be given out, though many will not give satisfactory answers. (d) Evening political economy. This may consist of the day lectures condensed, and some of the less important parts omitted. A few essays may be expected, and directions for reading may be given. (e) Pupil teachers' class. In this class rudimentary instruction in political economy is given. My usual method has been to begin with a *viva voce* cross-examination and discussion on the subject of last week's lecture for about a quarter of an hour or twenty minutes; and then to proceed to the DICTATION of a simple lesson, interspersed with explanations and illustrations. I find that the pupil

---

[1] See *Essays and Addresses, by Professors and Lecturers of the Owens College, Manchester. Published in commemoration of the Opening of the new College Buildings, October 7th, 1873* (1874).

teachers are mostly too young to take down proper notes of an ordinary lecture, and therefore, I have dictated the more important parts slowly.

Having had so much experience in teaching, you will of course be able to choose your own way of instruction, and I only mention my own way for sake of suggestion. Brief essays should be required from the pupil teachers. You will have to select your own style of lecturing. Some of our professors write their lectures complete and read them off; others give them entirely extempore, as in chemistry especially. My own mode is to have full notes, extracts, and written propositions of importance, and to dictate important statements verbatim and slowly, interspersing them with extempore discussions. The lecture is much relieved by occasional questions to the class generally, and I also use the blackboard upon every possible opportunity, especially in logic. You will, I hope, take these suggestions founded on my own practice for what they are worth, and your own experience will probably lead you to the best mode of instruction.

I shall hope to be at home in England before the middle of September, when I will write again to you; and we may perhaps have the pleasure of seeing you in Manchester shortly after that. We are having very bad weather at present, every day rainy and cold; but still there is enjoyment in the continual succession of splendid scenery through which we are slowly travelling by land and water.

Thanks for your kind wishes concerning my health. I think Norway is doing me much good on the whole, though the slight hardships we have to put up with are sometimes rather trying to those whose digestion is not very good. Nothing, however, can exceed the perfect idleness and freedom from business or anxiety which we enjoy here: we have not had any news at all since we left England five weeks ago. . . .

365.   G. H. DARWIN[1] TO W. S. JEVONS

Down
Beckenham
Sat. Sept 27 1873

Dear Sir,

I thank you for your courteous letter which I have read & thought over with much interest. I fear I may be involved in some radical muddle about the nature of interest, but I venture nevertheless to trouble you with another letter on the Subject; I beg however that you will not

[1] Sir George Howard Darwin (1845–1912), F.R.S., second son of Charles Darwin, the naturalist; called to the Bar in 1874, but returned to Cambridge to devote himself to mathematics; Plumian Professor of Astronomy and Experimental Philosophy, Cambridge University, 1883.

consider yourself bound even to acknowledge the receipt of it, as your time must be valuable to you.

If interest is defined as ∂ (produce)$/ \partial$ (invest!) your result of course follows. But I fancy that if it is so defined, you define interest to be what is usually called '*amount*'. Let PM denote the total am! of produce due to

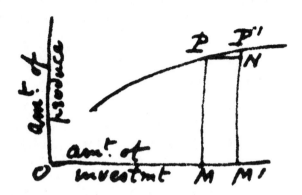

the am! of invest! OM +let P be the p! at wh. any increase will just yield the current int!; – then the further invest! MM′ will yield the produce P′N – the total produce of the whole investmt OM′ being however P′M′ . Now d(produce)/d(invest!) at the point P , translated out of the language of the Diff.Cal. is the produce due to a unit invest! (i.e. to the invest! of unit capital for unit time); Surely then unit capital invested for unit time yields unit capital × int. on unit capital for unit time – for one must suppose that the unit of capital is completely uninvested at the end of the unit of time. Thus ∂ (produce)$/ \partial$ (invest!) is the '*amount*' of unit capital fructifying for unit time & *not* the interest thereon. A numerical case will perhaps give further illustration of my meaning. Let a month pound be the unit investment. Then it seems reasonable to suppose that produce of such an invest! w! be worth £ $1.0.3^d$, -3^d is however the interest on the £ 1 for the month & not £ 1.0.3 as w! be given by your law. It is incredible that any one w! lend the £ 1 if the total yield were onle 3^d, for we sh! have to assume that the present value of £ 1 due a month hence was only 3^d Thus I take it that your idea (not your quasi definition) of interest leads to the law

Interest $= \dfrac{f'(t)}{f(t)} - 1$ or in my notation $\dfrac{1}{P} \dfrac{dP}{dT} - 1$.

This result bears a considerable resemblance to mine.

I have always considered interest as the reward of the abstinence of the invester in not spending his capital; such a reward must clearly increase as its period of fruition is deferred, & the increased amount of invest! must also be a factor in its constitution. But to discover the law of the reward one must, I think, have recourse to its origin viz. the value of the product, & I cannot see that the manner of distribution of this value is so obvious that the law is given as a mere matter of definition.—

I quite see that "the aggregate earnings of capital will almost always exceed the amount which must be paid for borrowing the capital", & that the difference *may* be looked on as of the nature of rent. I however have always looked on this difference as of the nature of insurance. Supposing that I invest my money in a manufacture, & that the *average* rate which it returns (after paying my manager or myself the wages of management) is 15% — the first doses returning me possibly 30% & the last only 5% & that 5% is the current rate of int!. — Then I consider the 10% $(15-5)$ will represent my reward for risk. If the current rate had been 4% there w^d be a tendency for myself or others to invest in the same line, until the value of the products was so reduced that the total yield was only 14%, wh. w^d still return me reward for risk & reward for abstinence. Thus on the average the total returns from each manufacture may be divided into two parts, the first varying with the nature of the business and the second constant for all. It surely then *does* matter what rate the earlier doses of capital have earned — for if they earned so much as to more than cover the reward for risk, there will at once arise a greater inducement for abstinence, & men will become more abstinent, until the reward for abstinence has been reduced to a state of equilibrium. And if the earlier doses returned a large excess above the current int!, it seems probable that it might continue profitable to continue dosing a considerable amount, when the rate returned was only just that current for int^t.; for since the earlier doses return more than a reward for the risk of themselves, they would cover the risk of a considerable increment of investmt. I may illustrate this by the subjoined curves

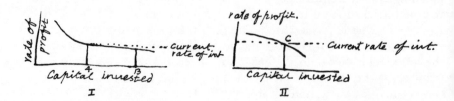

In I I might continue invest(ing) from A to B, but in II I sh^d be bound to stop at C. In I I sh^d not gain by transferring the capital AB to a new manufacture, since I sh^d then have to cover a new risk, but in II I sh^d certainly lose by continuing after C.

The view I take seems identical with that of Mill (from whom I suppose I derived it)B^k II ch. 15.[2]
Mill says §4 "The rate of int. on equally good security does not vary according to the destination of the capital("), and he also says (§7) that the only two elements to determine the rate of int. are the value of the produce & the proportion of that produce obtained by the labourers themselves "i.e. the ratio which the remuneration of the labourers bears to the amount they produce. These two things form the data for determining the gross amount divided as profit amongst all the capitalists of the country; but the *rate* of profits, the percentage on the capital, depends only on the second of the two elements, the labourer's proportional share, & not on the amount shared . . . the rate of profits depends on wages" (i.e. cost of labour) "rising as wages fall and falling as they rise".

It seems then that Mill takes no account of dP/dT, & you, I conceive, take no account of f(T)/P, - does not my method by taking both into account, perhaps present a truer theory?

In the letter which I wrote you, I assumed that the value of the product *less the reward for risk* must be such as to reimburse me my several investments and give me the current reward for abstinence. After reading your letter I must slightly modify what I then said. If p is the chance of receiving a sum P, pP is the value of the expectation. Then I sh^d now say that the value of the *expectation* of the produce must reimburse outgoings & return the current interest on each of them, irrespectively of the rates actually earned by them or of the rates at wh. I may have borrowed. I will suppose that I am not my own manager, so that the wages of management have to be deducted from the value of the product & form in fact a part of the outgoings. Then if p be the chance of success & P the nett value of the product by like reasoning as I employed before

$$Pp = \int_0^T f(t)e^{R(T-t)}dt$$

$$\&\quad p\frac{dP}{dT} = f(T) + RPp$$

$$\therefore\quad R = \frac{1}{P}\frac{dP}{dT} - \frac{f(T)}{Pp}$$

---

[2] J. S. Mill, *Principles of Political Economy*, II, xv, § 4: 'The rate of interest, on equally good security, does not vary according to the destination of the principal, though it does vary from time to time very much according to the circumstances of the market' (Ashley's edition, 1909, p. 411). Ibid. § 7: 'It thus appears that the two elements on which, and which alone, the gains of the capitalist depend, are, first, the magnitude of the produce, in other words, the productive power of labour, and secondly, the proportion of that produce obtained by the labourers themselves; the ratio which the remuneration of the labourers bears to the amount they produce' (loc. cit., pp. 418–9).

If the outgoings consist partly of a lump sum W at starting & partly of uniform outgoings for wages of w per unit of time, we have

$$Pp = We^{RT} + \int_0^T w\, e^{R(T-t)}dt \quad \& \quad R = \frac{1}{P}\frac{dP}{dT} - \frac{w}{Pp} \tag{A}$$

Thus the lump sum W does not appear explicitly in the result & if

$$w = 0, \quad R = \frac{1}{P}\frac{dP}{dT}$$

If only simple interest is allowed

$$Pp = W(1 + RT) + \int_0^T w(1 + R(T - t))dt$$

$$p\frac{dP}{dT} = R(Pp - W) + w \quad \textit{when if the square of R is very small}$$

$$R = \frac{p\dfrac{dP}{dT} - w}{Pp - W} \quad \& \text{ if } W = 0, \ R = \frac{1}{p}\frac{dP}{dT} - \frac{w}{Pp} \quad \text{identical with (A)}$$

$$\& \text{ if } w = 0, \quad Pp = W(1 + RT) \qquad R = \frac{p\dfrac{dP}{dT}}{W} \quad [3]$$

It appears however more proper to allow compound interest & the result is simpler.[4]

If my principles accord with your idea of interest, surely the results should be compatible – or at least one sh^d be able to explain the discrepancy by the difference of data. I cannot see that the greater complication of my method is any objection to its accuracy, if, as I conceive, the state of facts is more complicated than you imagine & that the rate returned on the earlier doses does affect the current rate of interest. It does not seem to me that the theory of rent is open to similar objections to those which I find with your theory of interest; for the excess earned by the earlier doses does not affect the level of cultivation and does not pass into the hands of the farmer but into those of the landlord. The landlord gets all he can & the rate of int. for the farmer's capital & his remuneration for his risk & labour are otherwise determined.—

I hope you will excuse the great length at which I have written & into which my desire to make myself clear has led me. If I have been betrayed

---

[3] In the original letter, all this part has been stroked out.
[4] For a discussion of the issues in the theory of interest raised by this letter, see K. H. Hennings, 'Darwin, Jevons, and the Rate of Interest', *History of Political Economy*, 9 (1977) No. 4.

into an apparent positiveness in any place pray attribute it to the countervailing desire for brevity.

If as is not impossible, I sh.^{d} on further reflection write a paper for publication on the subject, you w.^{d}, I presume, have no objection to my utilizing the remarks in your letter.

 Believe me yours very faithfully

G. H. Darwin

P.S. My address after the end of next week will be Trinity College, Cambridge, if you sh.^{d} feel sufficient interest in the subject to have anything to say in answer–wh. however I hardly expect.

366. W. S. JEVONS TO J. MILLS
  [TLJM, 337–8]

November 18, 1873.

Dear Mills—

 I have read the article on Herbert Spencer which you mentioned to me.[1] It is an able one, and is written, as I have heard, by Moulton, a recent Senior Wrangler. I am afraid that there is a good deal of truth in his criticism, and on the whole, it is damaging as regards Spencer's conception of physical science. When I read the First Principles I was occasionally puzzled to know exactly in what sense he spoke of the persistence of force. I daresay that a great many of the details & illustrations of Spencer's philosophy will not stand examination, and I think it is a pity that he has attempted to produce a complete system of philosophy.

 Nevertheless, I do not think that any criticism will shake the general truth and value of his fundamental ideas, which, especially as applied to mental and moral matters, are most fruitful.

Yours etc.
W. S. Jevons

367. J. B. SMITH TO W. S. JEVONS

Kings Ride,
Ascot. Staines.
Dec. 23, 1873.

My Dear Sir,

 Your letter dated Oct. only reached me here a week ago. I am obliged by your Book on the Coal question which I shall doubtless find at my

---

[1] 'Herbert Spencer', *Quarterly Review*, 135 (1873) 509–39. Jevons's attribution of authorship was incorrect; the article was written by the naturalist St George Mivart (1827–1900). *Wellesley Index to Victorian Periodicals*, 1, 756.

house in Town. I have read the substance of your lecture[1] on coal with much interest. This is one of the most important questions of the day and you will see by my speech[2] on the Budget which I sent you that I take very much the same view of this question as yourself. The Government however are so bent on temporary popularity that instead of applying the larger surplus revenue we are likely to have at the end of the financial year to the reduction of the National Debt it is reported that the surplus is to be applied to giving the people a free breakfast table.

I have just rec[d] the report of the American Iron and Steel Association from which it appears that the production of pig iron has risen from 736,218 tons in 1854 to 2,880,070 tons in 1872!! The Iron and Steel production of America for 1872 was as follows

Iron and Steel Daily	941,992 tons
Other rolled and hammered iron	1,000,000
Forges and Bloomaries	58,000
Cast Steel	32,000
Bessemer Steel	110,000
Pig iron	2,830,070

The increased production of Coal then in two years from this time will startle us.

Truly Yours
J. B. Smith

Production of Pig iron in 1862.   787, 662
,,   ,,   ,,   ,,   1872.   2,830,070
Increased production per annum in 10 years 2,042,408 tons.

368.   R. H. INGLIS PALGRAVE TO W. S. JEVONS

11, Britannia Terrace,
Gt. Yarmouth.
March 20, 1874.

My dear Mr. Jevons,

I have been wishing to write to you for some little time past, and I therefore take the opportunity, which the sending a copy of my 'Analysis

---

[1] The last lecture which Jevons had given on this topic was 'On the Probable Exhaustion of our Coal Mines' at the Royal Institution on 13 March 1868, and this is presumably the lecture referred to by Smith.

[2] *Hansard's Parliamentary Debates*, third series, Vol. 215, 678–81 (7 April 1873).

of the Transactions of Bank of England 1844 to 1872' gives me to do so. I
am aware that you will have my paper[1] which I have thus republished in
the transactions of the Statistical Society, but it may be convenient to you
to have it in this separate, and I also hope somewhat clearer form. When
you have time to look at it I should be much obliged if you will give your
consideration to the point mentioned on the paper which I enclose.[2]

The periodical fluctuation in the rate of interest to which it refers is a
curious thing. I had been aware, from experience, that the autumn was
the highest, or rather generally included, the highest time, but I was not
sure before, though I had expected to find, that a similar course was
experienced in the spring, and culminated of late years in May. I cannot
feel at all certain that this is to be attributed to any effect which the Scotch
circulation may produce, but it is remarkable that the *spring* as well as the
autumn maximum of interest would coincide with the maximum of the
Scotch circulation in May as well as in November. I should be much
obliged by any remarks which you may make on this point. The gradual
diminution of the proportion of the Bank of E. reserve to the liabilities is
also a striking thing, coupled as it is with the increase in the Bankers
Balances. But it is the former point to which I wish now to direct your
attention. The reason for which I had wished to write to you, was to
express the very great pleasure which your Book on the 'Principles of
Science' has given me. To say that I can fully understand the whole of it,
is not what you will expect from any of your readers, but it has been a
great pleasure, and will I hope be also a service to me, to have read so very
careful and powerful a statement of the course you feel to be that which
inquirers should follow. Some time I hope that Mrs. Jevons and yourself
may be persuaded to pay us a visit, and then perhaps I may ask you some
questions about your Book. For the present I shall content myself with
enquiring whether the attempt which I enclose at the solution of the
problem on p. 370 of Vol. II is the correct one, as I hope it is.[3] I suppose
that you intend the division to be into 4 equal groups in number. If it is

---

[1] R. H. Inglis Palgrave, 'On the Relation of the Banking Reserve of the Bank of England to the
Current Rate of Interest, with an Inquiry into some of the Causes which have led to the higher rates
charged in Recent Years', *JRSS*, 36 (1873) 529–64. This paper was published separately in 1874
under the title *Analysis of the Transactions of the Bank of England 1844 to 1872*.

[2] The notes, which are reproduced below, were written on a separate sheet and are not in
Palgrave's handwriting.

[3] This was an inductive problem, of which Jevons wrote on p. 126 of the second edition of *The
Principles of Science*: 'In the first edition (vol. II. p. 370) I gave a logical problem involving six terms,
and requested readers to discover the laws governing the combinations given. I received satisfactory
replies from readers both in the United States and in England. I formed the combinations
deductively from four laws of correction, but my correspondents found that three simpler laws,
equivalent to the four more complex ones, were the best answer; these laws are as follows: $a = ac$,
$b = cd$, $d = Ef$.'

correct would you mind the trouble of signing it and returning it to me, and then I will fasten it into the Book.

March 24. I have delayed sending this for a few days as I have expected to receive the copies of my pamphlet every day, but I hope to send it you now in a day or two.

I am my dear Mr. Jevons,

Yours very truly,

R. H. Inglis Palgrave.

If you thought that Prof. Cairns,* whom I believe that you are acquainted with, would be interested to have a copy of my analysis of the 'Transactions of the Bank' I should have pleasure in sending him one. In that case would you be so good as to let me know his present address.

Prof. Jevons.

One object of the Bank Act of 1844 was to make the circulation of notes follow the fluctuations of the Bullion in the Bank of England.

(Sir R. Peel's Speech, May 6, 1844)

(Ld. Overstones "Thoughts on the Separation of the Departments of the Bank of England").

Mr. Tooke, Mr. Wilson considered that hence greater fluctuations in the value of money would arise.

"Inquiry into the Bank Charter Act of 1844" and

"Capital Currency – Banking" [4]

In this case, the influence of any periodical fluctuations in the circulation would probably be reflected in the rate of interest.

A periodical fluctuation takes place in the Scotch circulation which, under the provision of the Bank Act, produces the same effect as a fluctuation in the circulation of the Bank of England.

By the statement on page 21 it will be observed that the highest rate of interest, when calculated month by month, coincides with the highest periods of the Scotch circulation, and that this state of matters has become more marked since 1856.

Does this fact bear out Mr. Tooke and Mr. Wilson's anticipations?

Or, may the higher rates at these periods (May–November) be attributed to other causes?

---

[4] Thomas Tooke, *On the Bank Charter Act of 1844* (1856); James Wilson, *Capital, Currency and Banking* (1847).

369.   W. S. JEVONS TO T. E. JEVONS
    [LJN, 299–301]

Withington, Machester,
19th April 1874.

. . . Although I have a great many other letters requiring answers, I must defer them until I have written at least a short letter, although it is but to tell you what you must know, that I have been grievously distressed about poor Hebert's death.[1] The fears I had entertained about the nature of his illness had been somewhat removed by his later letters, so that I was quite expecting to see him in England within a few weeks from this time, and I was planning how we could best arrange for his comfort and restoration. The letter therefore which I received in Paris[2] from John was quite a shock, and joined to a rather disquieting report of Lucy's health led us to travel to Ludlow with much speed. . . .

Of poor Herbert's end I have tried to take the most cheerful view, that it was probably not a *very* painful one, and that the sudden termination undoubtedly relieved him from much suffering. Judging from his letters, I cannot suppose that he had felt any very acute pain, which must have earlier convinced him of the hopeless nature of his illness.

. . . I have been reading over with painful interest the letters which I had from him for years back, which are not many. I am inclined to find some comfort in the belief that the later years of his life, in spite of disappointments and misfortunes, were his happiest. . . . I do not think that he was ever really solitary and purely unhappy. I feel sure he was the most sociable of us all, possibly excepting Lucy, and his days were occupied between bank work during the morning and afternoon, and music, theatres, games of whist, billiards, etc., or occasional dances in the evening. No doubt, as he said in one letter, his life was a dull routine, but so it is for a great many people, and I have little doubt that the free and easy society which arises in new colonial towns may have suited him better than the slow heavy society of English towns.

There is probably sufficient difference of age between us to prevent you from having as long a recollection of him as myself. My recollections, indeed, are not very vivid, in especial before 1850, when I lodged with him in London. Ever since that time I have felt constant sorrow for his state of health, and more or less anxiety as to what might come of

---

[1] Herbert Jevons died on 24 January 1874, apparently of cancer, while staying at Waiwera, near Auckland, where he had probably gone in the hope of obtaining benefit from the hot springs. See Vol. I, pp. 9–10.
[2] Jevons, accompanied by his wife, toured France and Italy from January to April 1874. See LJ, pp. 292–301.

it. . . . But there is one most pleasant feature in his recent letters. They all show with what courage and strength of mind he was bearing disappointments and misfortunes of various kinds, and at last encourtering the certainty of a painful death. All his fickleness of mind seemed to have gone, and he stuck to his post until it was too late to see us again, though we may hope that he had no idea how suddenly his end would come. . . .

370.   W. S. JEVONS TO A. MACMILLAN

> Parsonage Road,
> Withington,
> Manchester.
> 19th April 74.

Dear Mr. Macmillan,

. . . .

As regards a logic Primer I have been much interested by Mr. Reade's proposals on the subject, but I had myself previously occasionally contemplated a little work of the same kind, though I had been far too much engrossed of late upon the "Principles" to allow of my making any proposal. As you now mention the matter I must say that I shall be happy to devote myself to the preparation of the Primer as soon as a previous engagement for the International series is off my hands, which if my health continues good, ought to be in about six months.

Such a primer will require much thought and very careful writing to make it perfectly untechnical and very easy yet precise and scientific at bottom, but I think it will not be found impossible to apply to Logic the general method and style of the other science Primers. As a first rough suggestion I would propose as a title the following

The Logic Primer

or

First Exercises in the
Art of Thinking

. . . . [1]

> I remain,
> Yours very faithfully,
> W. S. Jevons.

(Copy)

---

[1] These indications of passages omitted appear in the copy made by Jevons.

371. W. S. JEVONS TO G. H. DARWIN
[LJN, 301–2]

Parsonage Road,
Withington,
Manchester,
22d April 1874.

... For more than three months past I have been travelling on the Continent. Your letter of 12th February[1] was forwarded to me, and I was very glad to find that you now allow the correctness, in a certain point of view, of my mode of representing the rate of interest. You will remember that I never denied the correctness of your own formula, which arises from the supposition of different conditions. The question really is, therefore, which conditions most accurately correspond to those of actual industry, and though I have still a prejudice in favour of my own, and like very much the simplicity of the result, I do not propose at present to attempt to decide the question, but shall preserve your solution for the time, if ever, when I approach the subject anew.

Let me also now thank you for the copy of your paper[2] in the Contemporary Review on Mill's views of capital. I read it, when received, with great interest, and agreed with it cordially. I hope we may see many contributions to the theory of economy from you, for I think I could count on the fingers of one hand those in England who really give any contributions of the sort.

When I reached home a few days ago I was sorry to find that your circular concerning the marriages of cousins[3] had been lying here quite unnoticed. I need hardly say that if I had been at home it would have been promptly returned. I now send it in the hope that it is not altogether too late. Although I am sufficiently acquainted with the genealogical details of a very great number of relatives, either of my own or of my wife's, I cannot find that there has been more than one marriage of cousins, that included in the accompanying return from my wife. There has *been no marriage at all of two persons with similar surnames, so far as I can ascertain.* At first sight I did not perceive the purpose of the return and the method of inquiry, but I presume you intend to count up in newspapers, or other lists of marriages, the comparative number of marriages of similar names to whole number of marriages, and thus by a double ratio to obtain proportional frequency of cousins' marriages. It seems a happy device. . . .

[1] This letter is not among the Jevons Papers.

[2] G. H. Darwin, 'Commodities *versus* Labour', *Contemporary Review*, 22 (1873) 689–98.

[3] See G. H. Darwin, 'Marriages between First Cousins in England and their effects', *JRSS*, 38 (1875) 156.

372.   W. S. JEVONS TO W. E. GLADSTONE

> Parsonage Rd.
> Withington
> Manchester
> 29 April 74.[1]

Dear Sir,

Having lately, after much labour, completed a book upon Scientific Method, called the 'Principles of Science', I cannot refuse myself the pleasure of offering a copy for your acceptance, and I take the liberty of forwarding it herewith by book post.

I can hardly hope that it will receive much of your attention, being indeed to a considerable extent occupied with technical logical or scientific matters. But I have ventured to add a chapter at the end on the Limits and Results of Scientific Method bearing upon subjects which you have treated in your address at Liverpool and in a subsequent published letter.[2] The work therefore may not be altogether without interest to you.

I should like to add however that in venturing upon theological subjects I have been very much embarrassed to know how to express in a sufficiently strong and clear manner my own positive convictions on the subject without seeming to imply more than I mean. The fact is that I am by descent a Unitarian and as regards my own convictions am not perfectly clear. I should have a strong objection to being thought to mean either more or less than I actually say.

I have the honour to remain, dear Sir, with ever growing admiration and respect —

> Yours faithfully
> W. Stanley Jevons.

The Right Hon. W. E. Gladstone M.P.
        etc.   etc.   etc.

373.   L. WALRAS[1] TO W. S. JEVONS

> Lausanne, 1 Mai, 1874[2]

Monsieur le Professeur,

J'ai l'honneur de vous adresser aujourd'hui par la poste un Mémoire[3] dont je suis l'auteur et sur lequel je prends la liberté d'appeler votre attention bienveillante.

---

[1] The original manuscript of this letter is now in the Gladstone Papers, BM Add. MS 44443, f. 184.

[2] See below, Letter 374, p. 38.

[1] Marie Esprit Léon Walras (1834–1910), Professor of Political Economy at the University of Lausanne, 1870–92, and creator of general equilibrium economics. Walras maintained a vast correspondence with all the economists of his time, which has been meticulously edited by Professor William Jaffé and published under the auspices of the Royal Economic Society and the Royal

Je suis sur le point de commencer la publication d'un *Traité d' Economie politique et sociale* dont le premier Volume, consacré à l'*économie politique pure*,[4] contient une *théorie mathématique de l'echange* que m'a coûté plusieurs années de recherches et à laquelle j'attache, pour cette raison, quelque importance. J'ai communiqué le principe de cette théorie à l'Institut de France l'été dernier, et c'est de cette communication que j'ai l'honneur de vous adresser un exemplaire.

La théorie dont il s'agit étant, comme vous le reconnaîtrez sans peine, d'un caractère particulièrement abstrait, je ne puis espérer la faire pénétrer dans le public que si elle obtient prealablement l'assentiment des hommes compétents. Votre haute position scientifique en Angleterre et la nature speciale de vos beaux travaux me feraient attacher le plus grand prix à votre jugement, et le but de la présente démarche est d'en solliciter la faveur. Soyez donc assez bon, je vous prie, pour jeter les yeux sur mon mémoire: s'il vous paraît dénué de valeur je n'aurai pas à me reprocher d'avoir trop abusé de vos instants; et que si, au contraire, le sujet vous semble mériter un examen plus approfondi, je m'empresserai de vous adresser, dès que je le pourrai, un exemplaire de mon ouvrage.

Veuillez agréer, Monsieur le Professeur, l'expression de mes sentiments de profond respect et de sincère dévouement.

Léon Walras.

374. W. E. GLADSTONE TO W. S. JEVONS

Hawarden Castle,
Chester.
May 10.74

My dear Sir

I have this day in a quiet hour read with attention the closing Chapter of your Book: and I cannot resist paying you the very indifferent compliment of saying how greatly I am impressed and pleased with it.

Netherlands Academy – *Correspondence of Léon Walras and Related Papers,* 3 vols (Amsterdam, 1965). Hereafter cited as Jaffé, *Walras Correspondence.*

[2] This is the only letter in the correspondence between Walras and Jevons of which Walras did not keep a draft, but the text given here has been published as an appendix to Jaffé, *Walras Correspondence,* III, 445.

[3] Léon Walras, 'Principe d'une théorie mathématique de l'échange', *Journal des Economistes* third series, 34 (1874) 5–21). The paper had originally been read before the Académie des Sciences morales et politiques on 16 and 23 August 1873. Cf. Jaffé, *Walras Correspondence,* I, 326.

[4] Walras's *Elements d'économie politique pure* appeared in two instalments, in 1874 and 1877. At this time Walras had it in mind to publish two other volumes, one on 'économie politique appliquée' and the other on 'économie sociale'. Cf. Jaffé, op. cit., I, 319 and 321.

I am not indeed altogether an impartial witness: for in several points of great importance it indicates or asserts what have very long been favourite points with me, amidst those speculative disturbances of the present age which have reached me even in the sphere of politics.

That there is gross ambiguity and latent fallacy in much that we hear about 'uniformity of laws'.

That we are not warranted in predicating, of time & space themselves, that they are necessarily adhering conditions of all existence

That there is real insoluble mystery in some of the formulae of mathematics—

That we are in danger from the precipitancy and intellectual tyranny of specialism—

That the limits of our real knowledge are (if I may use the word) infinitely narrow.

That we are not rationally justified in passing over our inward perceptions of things inward, and confining the sphere of knowledge to things outward—

Are my old convictions which I live in the hope of doing something before I die to sustain and illustrate: and they are I think all, nearly in these terms, supported by your authority.

But I hope I have a better reason for admiring this Chapter: I find it in the true and high philosophic spirit, in which it seems to me to be conceived. I hope you will not be shocked if I designate it by an epithet which to my mind conveys the highest commendation: it seems to me eminently *Butlerian*.[1]

With respect to evolution and to Darwinism I had never formed any opinion, when Mr Spencer criticised me, except that the results assigned to them were unwarrantable.[2] Since that time I have a little examined

---

[1] Joseph Butler (1692–1752), theologian and philosopher; Bishop of Bristol, 1738; Dean of St Paul's, 1740; Bishop of Durham, 1750. His *Analogy of Religion, Natural and Revealed, to the Constitution and course of Nature* (1736) was widely read during the nineteenth century. Gladstone published an edition of Butler's *Works* in two volumes (Oxford, 1896).

[2] The controversy between Gladstone and Herbert Spencer had arisen over Spencer's *The Study of Sociology*, which was first published in sixteen instalments in the *Contemporary Review* from April 1872 to October 1873. After the publication of chapter II, 'Is there a Social Science?' in May 1872 (*Contemporary Review*, 19 (1871–2) 701–18), Gladstone twice made public statements which Spencer interpreted as a denunciation of the evolutionary theory of creation. Accordingly, in his 'Conclusion' (*Contemporary Review*, 22 (1873) 663–77), Spencer described Gladstone as 'the exponent of the anti-scientific view' and stated that 'he regards as irreligious any explanation of Nature which dispenses with immediate divine superintendence'. Gladstone replied on 3 November 1873 with a letter to the editor of the *Contemporary Review*, 23 (1873–4) 162–3, in which he defended his opinions on the ground that ' . . . my complaint is that the functions of the Almighty as Creator and Governor of the world are denied upon grounds, which . . . appear to me to be utterly and manifestly insufficient to warrant such denial'. See *The Study of Sociology*, third edition (1874) pp. 392–5, 423–6; also Duncan, *The Life and Letters of Herbert Spencer*, II, 162–4. Cf. above, Letter 372, p. 36; and below, Letter 376, p. 42.

them, not as propositions of natural philosophy, but in their moral and speculative aspects. Having done this, I entirely subscribe to what you say of them. Indeed I must say that the doctrine of Evolution, if it is true, enhances in my judgment the proper idea of the greatness of God: for it makes every stage of creation a legible prophecy of all those which are to follow it.

What you said of your own theology inspired me with great respect, although I am myself much addicted to what I may call historical Christianity, and profoundly disbelieve the notion of some, and of some eminent and able men, that it is to be overthrown in its old historic form, and to revive and flourish in a new form, simplified as they say, but as I think attenuated. The true religious difficulty lies I think where you have pointed to it in your p. 463.

As one interested in such matters I must cordially thank you for this most able Chapter, which I shall be very desirous to assist in making known to any persons likely to appreciate its distinguished merits

I remain my dear Sir
Very faithfully yours
W. E. Gladstone

375. W. S. JEVONS TO L. WALRAS
     [LJN, 302 – 4][1]

Manchester, 12th May 1874

My dear Sir,

Pray, accept my best thanks for your kindness in sending me a copy of your Memoir[2] and for the very courteous letter in which you draw my attention to it. When your letter came I had, indeed, already noticed in the *Journal des Economistes* your very remarkable theory. I felt the greater interest in the subject because my own speculations have led me in the same direction, now for the last twelve years or more. It is satisfactory to me to find that my theory of exchange, which, when published in England, was either neglected or criticized, is practically confirmed by

[1] The original manuscript of this letter, which Walras presumably lent to Mrs Jevons when she was preparing LJ, is not now to be found either in the Jevons Papers or in Fonds Walras, and the version printed in LJ contains certain obvious omissions and mistakes. Professor William Jaffé has produced a more accurate interpretation by collating the LJ text with that contained in Ludwig von Winterfeld's translation of Walras, *Mathematische Theorie der Preisbestimmung der Wirtschaftlichen Guter* (Stuttgart, 1881). Cf. *Walras Correspondence*, I, 393 – 5. This interpretation is followed here, except that Mrs Jevons's spelling of 'rarity' has been retained as more probably corresponding to the original manuscript.

[2] 'Principe d'une théorie mathématique de l'échange', *Journal des Economistes*, third series, 34 (1874) 5 – 21.

your researches. I do not know whether you are acquainted with my writings on the subject. All the chief points of my mathematical theory were clear to my own mind by the year 1862 when I drew up a brief account of it, which was read at the meeting of the British Association at Cambridge,[3] as you will learn from the Report of the meeting (Reports of sections, p. 158). A very brief abstract was then alone inserted in the report, but the original paper was printed in the Journal of the London Statistical Society in 1866, vol. XXIX, p. 282. I beg to forward you, by book post, a copy of this paper. Finally, in 1871, I caused to be published by Messrs. Macmillan & Co. an octavo volume called the *Theory of Political Economy* in which is given a full explanation of the theory with the aid of mathematical symbols. I shall be glad to learn whether you are yet acquainted with this work, since, if you are not, I shall be happy to present you with a copy.

You will find, I think, that your theory substantially coincides with and confirms mine, although the symbols are differently chosen and there are incidental variations. You will see that the whole theory rests on the notion (section 8 of [my][4] paper) that the *utility* of a commodity is not proportional to its quantity; what you call the *rarity* of a commodity appears to be exactly what I called the *coefficient of utility* at first, and afterwards the *degree of utility*, which, as I also explained, was really the differential coefficient of the utility considered as a function of the quantity of commodity.

The *theory of exchange* is given in section 14 of my paper, and may be considered to be contained in one sentence: "An equation may thus be established on either side between the utility gained and sacrificed at the ratio of exchange of the whole commodities, upon the last increments exchanged."

Now, in my book of 1871, I show fully how this theory may be expressed in symbols. If there be two persons, A and B, of whom A holds the quantity a of one commodity, and B holds b of another, then I give the equation of exchange in the form

$$\frac{\phi_1(a-x)}{\psi_1 y} = \frac{y}{x} = \frac{\phi_2 x}{\psi_2(b-y)}.$$

in which x is the unknown quantity which A gives to B in exchange for y. It follows that $\frac{y}{x}$ is equivalent to your p_a or p_b, namely, the price current or ratio of exchange. Again $\phi_1(a-x)$ means the degree of utility of the first commodity remaining to A, and $\phi_2(x)$ means the *degree of utility* of so

[3] Cf. Vol. I, p. 188.
[4] LJ version here reads 'your paper'.

much as he has handed over to B.[5] Now these degrees of utility are

exactly equivalent to your *rarities*, and your equation $\quad P_a = \dfrac{r_{a,\,1}}{r_{b,\,1}}$ [6]

is identically the same in meaning with my own form of statement. Indeed, when the meaning of the terms are explained, your proposition "Les prix courants ou prix d'équilibre sont égaux aux rapports des raretés" is seen to coincide precisely with my theory, except that you do not point out how many equations are requisite or how many unknown quantities there are.

The publication of your paper as it now stands is very satisfactory in so far as it tends to confirm my belief in the correctness of the theory, but it might lead to misapprehensions as to the originality and the priority of its publication. I shall therefore take it as a favour if you will kindly inform me whether you are sufficiently acquainted with my writings or whether you would desire me to forward a copy of my *Theory of Political Economy*.

With many thanks for your kindness in bringing the Memoir to my notice, and with much admiration of the clear manner in which you have treated the subject, believe me etc.

W. Stanley Jevons

376.   W. S. JEVONS TO W. E. GLADSTONE

Parsonage Road,
Withington,
Manchester.
13 May 74.[1]

My dear Sir,

I have been very pleased to learn from your letter that I was not altogether wrong in supposing that the closing chapter of my 'Principles' would have some interest to you. I shall much value the remarks which you have made upon it and shall feel all the more encouraged to do what

---

[5] LJ version here reads 'Again, $y_1\,(a-x)$ means the degree of utility, of so much as he has handed over to B'. This, as Professor Jaffé says, 'makes sheer nonsense'. Apart from the fact that the printer has substituted y for ø throughout the LJ version it seems possible that a full line of the text was omitted here.

[6] LJ version here reads $\quad P_a = \dfrac{z_{a,\,1}}{z_{b,\,1}}$,

[1] The original manuscript of this letter is now in the Gladstone Papers, BM Add. MS 44443, f. 235.

has been my previous intention, namely to expand this chapter at some future time, if health allows, into a separate essay, in which I may more freely discuss difficult questions on which I have as yet only entered negatively, that is, as disputing the logical validity of supposed insuperable objections to Divine existence or interference.

About the doctrine of evolution I really feel no difficulty at all, except that of understanding how men of the genius and intellect of Darwin and Spencer can suppose for a moment that it sufficiently explains all the forms of living beings *without any arbitrary disposition of causes*. I fear that Spencer does go to such a length, but I do not call to mind any expressions of Darwin which commit him to opinions of the kind. However the doctrine is now in the possession of many thousands besides the discoverers, and many of their followers undoubtedly imagine the doctrine of evolution to be inconsistent with design, a simple logical blunder as it appears to me.

> Believe me my dear Sir,
> Yours faithfully,
> W. S. Jevons.

The Right Hon. W. E. Gladstone   M.P.

377.   W. S. JEVONS TO T. E. JEVONS
        [LJN, 304–5]

> Parsonage Road, Withington,
> Manchester, 14th May 1874.

. . . I agree with you that it is not well to think much of the past, which is for us in many ways so melancholy. We have enough to think about and do in the present. You will, however, wish to hear the details of poor Herbert's death, which I have now received in a letter from Dr. Coughtrey,[1] of which I enclose a copy. It is quite evident that he died almost instantaneously. . . .

Thanks for the copy of the *New York Tribune*. I have received two other copies of the same from other people. I have also the *Times* and *Post*. I like the *Tribune* notice very well, and that in the *Times* is not bad.[2] The

---

[1] Probably Millen Coughtrey (1848–1908); graduated M.B., C.M. at Edinburgh, 1871; held teaching posts in Liverpool before emigrating to New Zealand, arriving in Auckland in December 1873; first Professor of Anatomy and Physiology at the University of Otago, Dunedin, 1874–6; subsequently entered general practice in Dunedin.

The letter from Coughtrey is no longer among the Jevons Papers, but it seems probable that he was known to members of the family. Herbert Jevons's death within a short time of Coughtrey's arrival in New Zealand makes it appear unlikely that he was Herbert's regular physician.

[2] These references are to reviews of *The Principles of Science*, which was published in February 1874.

reviews here are very slow in speaking, if they mean to speak at all. Having sent a copy to Gladstone, I have had a very pleasant and interesting letter on the theological part.

... I have been rather troubled about my professorship and monetary arrangements, but shall probably continue, on condition of having no evening lectures this next session. I very nearly resigned. I am at present commencing in a very leisurely way my book for the International Scientific Series, upon the subject, *Money, and the Mechanism of Exchange.* As I look forward to an American demand, I must show some knowledge of the American markets and currency. There was a book I once presented to you, or lent, upon the New York Money Market. Can you post it back to me, or at all events give me the title, since it is essential to me, containing an account of the New York Clearing House?[3] I am ordering Sumner's *History of the American Currency,*[4] but if you can come across any other books relating to American money and banking, I should much like to have them or the titles. I should also be glad if you would explain to me the exact position of the American currency at the present moment, and the relation between the greenbacks and the National Bank currency. Of course I have noticed and rejoiced over the veto of the Inflation Bill,[5] which has saved America from a gigantic job and blunder. . . .

378.   V. FALBE HANSEN[1] TO W. S. JEVONS

Statistisk Bureau.
Kjobenhavn den 18 May 1874.

My dear Sir,

I was very delighted with your kind letter and with the advice that you intend to make a trip in Norway this summer visiting Christiania and other places there.

[3] James Sloan Gibbons (1810–92), *The Banks of New York, their dealers, the clearing house, and the panic of 1857* (New York, 1859).

[4] William Graham Sumner (1840–1910), *A History of American Currency, with chapters on the English bank restriction and Austrian paper money* (New York, 1874).

[5] 'A Bill to provide for the redemption and re-issue of United States notes and for free banking', 43rd Congress, 1st Session, S 617. This Bill, which would have increased the maximum 'greenback' circulation from $383,000,000 to $400,000,000 and provided for an issue of a further $46,000,000 of bank notes, was passed by Senate and Congress, but vetoed by President Ulysses S. Grant. See Carlton Jackson, *Presidential Vetoes, 1792–1945* (Athens, Ga, 1967).

[1] Vigand Andreas Falbe-Hansen (1841–1932), Danish statistician; joined the staff of the Statistical Office of the Danish Government, 1870, served as its Director, 1875–7 and again from 1902 to 1904; Professor of Political Economy at the University of Copenhagen, 1877–1902; member of the lower house of the Danish Parliament, 1881–4, and of the upper house, 1909–18.

I have been unwell for a long time (congestions to the head and nervousness caused by over-work) and have also spent the two last summers in Norway for the sake of my health, on the bath "Grafsen" near Christiania.

I intend together with my wife and my little daughter to visit "Grafsen" again this summer, to start from Copenhagen in the last days of June and stay in Christiania about 6 weeks. It should be very pleasant if I could meet you in Norway, we could have a discourse on the "gold-question" and make a little tour together in the beautifull surroundings of Christiania.

You understand now Danish (or Norwegian, that is quite the same language) and I will speak Danish then![2]

Vi kunne gjøre en Tour i Kristianias smukke Omegn, besøge "Maridalen", Sæteren[3] paa Thyvandsaasen, spise en engelsk Beuf paa "Egeberg" eller paa det Norske Tivoli "Klingenberg".[4] Jeg skal vise Dem Kristianias Mærkværdigheder, præsentere Dem for dets berømte Mand, o.s.v. Deres navn er ikke ganske ukjendt i Norge, thi i det danske "Nationaloekonomisk Tidsskrift",[5] som jeg er en af Udgiverne af og som laeses en Del i Norge har vi flere Gange havt Lejlighed til at omtale Deres videnskabelige Virksomhed, naemlig Deres Sidste Vaerk om den "politiske Oekonomis Theori". Jeg skal en af dagene sende Dem et Hefte af dette Tidsskrift, hvori der findes en længere Afhandling, der staaer i naer berøring med Deres Vaerk. Nu har De maaskee Ondt ved at forstaa det, men jeg haaber at De i den kommende Sommer vil laere godt "Norsk". Jeg skal gjøre mit til at De kan blive en complet Normand.

My adress in Christiania is "Grafsen Bad" only ½ english mile from the city – not longer than Withington from Manchester – you can take a Trille (a cab) for it, every Kudsk (cab-man) know that place, or you can send to me an epistle by the post and I will go to you in your hotel.

Falbe-Hansen used Jevons's index-number methods in a dissertation on *Changes since the Discovery of America in Danish Prices and Wages*, written in 1869 in a professorial competition. He visited Jevons in Manchester in 1870 and again in 1871.

[2] 'We might make an excursion in the beautiful surroundings of Kristiania, visit "Maridalen", the seter on the Thyvandsaas, eat an English beefsteak at "Egeberg" or in the Norwegian Tivoli "Klingenberg". I shall show you the marvels of Kristiania, introduce you to its famous men, etc. Your name is not quite unknown in Norway, for in the Danish "Nationalokonomisk Tidsskrift", of which I am now one of the editors, and which is fairly widely read in Norway, we have several times had the occasion to mention your scientific activity, especially your most recent work on the "Theory of Political Economy". One of these days, I shall send you an issue of this periodical, in which there is a long dissertation closely connected with this your work. Perhaps you find it hard to understand now, but I hope that in the coming summer you will learn good "Norwegian". I shall do my best to make you become a complete Norwegian.'

[3] saeter, the characteristic Norwegian summer grazing.

[4] A comparison with the Tivoli Gardens in Copenhagen.

[5] F. Bing and J. Petersen, 'Bestemmelse af den rationelle Arbejdsløn samt nogle Bemaerkninger om Økonomiens Methode', *Nationaløkonomisk Tidsskrift*, 1 (1873) 296–320.

Hereby I send you a Danish "parliamentary paper" on the rise of prices in the last 6 years, which I wrote last January and February for our Government; the main result of my researches is that the value of gold is depreciated about 20% from the years 1867–70 to 1873.

The publications of our statistical office which you have received was sent to you last winter through the Manchester Statistical Society.

Hoping to meet you among the "Fjelde & Fjorde" I beg you to bring my best compliments for Mrs Jevons and I remain my dear Sir

Yours very truly
V. Falbe Hansen

To Professor W. Stanley Jevons.

379. L. WALRAS TO W. S. JEVONS

Lausanne, 23 mai 1874[1]

Cher Monsieur,

Lorsque j'eus l'honneur de vous écrire, le 1er de ce mois, en vous envoyant mon' Mémoire sur le *Principe d'une théorie mathématique de l'échange,* je vous connaissais de réputation, mais seulement comme auteur de travaux estimés sur la question de la variation des prix et de la dépréciation de la monnaie. Je vous savais mathématicien, mais je me figurais que vos applications mathématiques étaient plutôt statistiques qu'économiques. Quelques jours après, M. d'Aulnis de Bourouill, étudiant en droit à l'Université de Leyde, ayant lu mon travail dans le *Journal des Economistes,* m'écrivit, en date du 4 mai, pour me signaler la direction commune de nos recherches et me fournir le titre exact de votre ouvrage. Dès lors, je fus détrompé, et j'attendais en quelque sorte votre lettre lorsqu'elle m'est arrivée.

[1] The version of this letter published here is an exact copy of the original manuscript received by Jevons and now in the Jevons Papers. Jaffé, *Walras Correspondence,* I, 397–9, publishes a version based on the rough draft in Fonds Walras. There are only minor differences between the two, as indicated below:

	Walras Correspondence.	*Jevons Papers*
para 2	je vous prie très – instamment	je vous prie instamment
para 3	vous me permettrez quelques observations	vous me permettrez quelques explications
para 3	il suffit de passer	il n'y a qu'à passer
para 3	que de permettre de discuter	qu'à permettre de discuter
para 4	et me mis	et je me mis
para 4	que vous fussiez entré dans la même voie	que vous fussiez entré déjà dans la même voie

La coincidence de nos deux théories sur le point que vous m'indiquez est éclatante. Il est évident que votre *coefficient* ou *degré d'utilité*, qui est le *"coefficient différentiel* de l'*utilité* considérée comme une fonction de la *quantité* des marchandises", est identique à mon *intensité d'utilité* ou à ma *rareté* qui est "la *dérivée* de l'*utilité effective* par rapport à la *quantité possédée"*; que votre *raison d'échange* n'est autre chose que mon *prix courant*; et qu'enfin votre *équation d'échange* se confond avec mon *équation de satisfaction maximum*. En lisant très-attentivement votre "Brief Account", et notamment les §§ 13 à 20, j'ai cru reconnaître une certaine différence dans la manière dont nous introduisons cette équation, et surtout dans la manière dont nous en usons. Je ne vois pas que vous la fondiez sur la considération de *satisfaction maximum*, qui est pourtant si simple et si claire. Je ne vois pas non plus que vous en tiriez l'équation de *demande effective* en fonction du *prix*, qui s'en déduit si aisément, et qui est si essentielle à la solution du problème de la détermination des prix d'équilibre. A vrai dire, je crains que nos deux théories ne soient, en dehors de ce point de contact, quelque peu divergentes. Mais c'est là une question que je n'ai pas à examiner pour le moment. Puisque vous voulez bien m'offrir un exemplaire de votre "Theory of Political Economy", je vous prie instamment de me l'envoyer; je vais vous envoyer moi-même les épreuves de mes *Eléments d'économie politique pure* où la *théorie mathématique de l'échange* est exposée *in-extenso*. Après que nous aurons pris connaissance de nos doctrines respectives, nous pourrons, si vous le voulez, les discuter entre nous. Pour aujourd'hui, je dois surtout répondre à votre observation touchant la forme de mon mémoire. Cette observation est fondée, et je suis prêt à y faire droit. J'espère seulement que vous me permettrez quelques explications de nature à mettre ma bonne foi hors de doute.

Les deux seuls hommes des travaux antérieurs desquels je me sois aidé sont ceux que je·me suis fait un devoir et un plaisir de citer dans mon Mémoire: A.-A. Walras, mon père, et M. Cournot. Mon père est connu comme auteur d'un ouvrage intitulé *De la nature de la richesse et de l'origine de la valeur*, publié en 1831, et dans lequel la théorie qui fonde la *valeur d'échange* sur la double condition de l'*utilité* et de la *limitation dans la quantité* est aussi solidement établie qu'il est possible de le faire avec les seules ressources de la logique ordinaire. Au Ch. XVIII de cet ouvrage, mon père énonce et développe cette proposition que "l'économie politique est une science mathématique", et il indique même l'analogie du rapport qu'il y a, d'une part, entre la *vitesse*, le *temps* et l'*espace* et de celui qu'il y a, d'autre part, entre la *rareté*, la *quantité* et l'*utilité*. Il est vrai qu'il ne songe qu'au mouvement uniforme; mais, pour peu qu'on soit mathématicien, il n'y a qu'à passer de la considération du mouvement uniforme à celle du mouvement varié pour saisir immédiatement l'analogie des conditions mathématiques de l'échange avec les conditions mathématiques du mouvement. Quant à M. Cournot, ses *Recherches sur les principes mathéma-tiques de la théorie des richesses* sont de 1838. Il explique dans sa Préface, avec une netteté qui ne laisse rien à désirer, comment l'application des mathématiques à l'économie politique est une application du calcul des fonctions, et comment cette application a moins pour but de conduire à des calculs numériques qu'a permettre de discuter des relations entre grandeurs. J'ai songé, dès le début de ma carrière d'économiste, à faire l'application du calcul des fonctions indiqué par M. Cournot à la théorie de la valeur d'échange de mon père, qui m'a toujours paru la théorie vraie et définitive; et tout homme qui prendra la peine d'examiner les choses de près reconnaîtra que c'est bien là le but auquel je suis arrivé. Je pense, au surplus, que la conclusion de mon Mémoire est, à cet égard, suffisamment décisive.

Mes premiers efforts en ce sens datent de 1860. La nécessité de me livrer à des occupations pratiques me força de les interrompre pendant dix ans; mais je ne cessai jamais de rapporter à ce point de vue toutes mes observations et toutes mes études économiques. Ayant obtenu, en 1870, la chaire d'économie politique de l'Académie de Lausanne, mon premier soin fut de reprendre mes recherches, et, malgré l'obligation où je fus alors de mettre en train plusieurs cours sur les diverses parties de l'économie politique et sociale, j'arrivai à un assez prompt résultat. Je fus, en effet, dès le milieu de 1871, en possession de la solution du problème de l'échange de deux marchandises et de celle du problème de l'échange de plusieurs marchandises entre elles, que j'introduisis dans mon enseigne-ment pour l'année scolaire 1871–72, et que j'exposai dans des con-férences publiques faites à Genève en janvier 1872. Dans le courant de cette même année 1872, j'achevai d'établir en détail la théorie mathéma-tique de l'échange et celle de la production, et je me mis à la rédaction de mon traité élémentaire d'économie politique pure. En 1873, ayant trouvé un éditeur, je commençai l'impression de cet ouvrage et communiquai le principe de ma théorie à l'*Académie des sciences morales et politiques*. Si votre nom n'a pas été mentionné dans cette communication, c'est qu'au moment où je la fis, j'ignorais absolument que vous fussiez entré déjà dans la même voie; mais je suis tout disposé à réparer cette ommission involontaire.

Si l'on ne considérait l'état de la question qu'en France et en Angleterre nous n'aurions guère à nous partager, Monsieur, d'après ce que vous me dites vous-même de l'accueil fait, dans votre pays, à vos idées, qu'une réputation de rêveurs assez chimériques; et ce partage ne vaudrait peut-être pas la peine d'être effectué si soigneusement. Mais je suis heureux de pouvoir vous apprendre qu'il en est autrement ailleurs, notamment en Italie où la méthode nouvelle a été saisie dans son esprit et dans sa portée, avec une intelligence et une promptitude merveilleuses, et où des hommes éminemment distingués, avec lesquels je ne saurais trop vous engager à vous mettre en rapport, Messieurs les professeurs Alberto Errera,[2] de Padoue, Boccardo,[3] de Gênes, Bodio,[4] directeur général de la statistique du royaume, à Rome, Zanon,[5] de Venise, lui ont donné leur assentiment. Dès lors, il importe essentiellement que l'opinion publique soit mise en mesure de vous attribuer, sur le point capital dont vous me parlez, la priorité que vous réclamez et qui vous appartient incontestablement en vertu de l'antériorité de vos publications de 1866 et de 1871 sur les miennes. A cet effet, je vous propose de demander à M. Joseph Garnier, rédacteur en chef du *Journal des Economistes,* qui a bien voulu reproduire mon Mémoire, de vouloir bien aussi insérer votre lettre et la présente reponse dans son prochain numéro; je ferais tirer ces deux lettres à part et les distribuerais à toutes les personnes qui ont recu mon Mémoire. Pour l'avenir, vous pouvez compter qu'après avoir lu votre ouvrage, que je vous prie de nouveau de me faire parvenir, je saisirai toutes les occasions qui s'offriront de le faire connaitre. La parfaite courtoisie de votre lettre m'est un gage assuré que, de votre côté, si vous trouvez que le mien intéresse tant soit peu le progrès de la science, vous voudrez bien le signaler à vos élèves et à vos lecteurs, et non-seulement, il va sans dire, en empruntant celles de mes idées qui vous paraîtraient bonnes pour le fond ou pour la forme, mais aussi en critiquant en toute liberté celles qui se trouveraient opposées à votre manière de voir.

Croyez, Cher Monsieur, à mon vif désir de me conduire en tout ceci de la manière la plus propre à m'acquérir votre amitié, et recevez, dès à présent, la sincère assurance de mes sentiments d'estime et de sympathie.

Léon Walras

380.   J. G. GREENWOOD TO W. S. JEVONS

The Owens College,   27 May
Manchester   1874

My dear Jevons

At the last meeting of the Council your letter of the 5th inst. was read but no final action taken upon it. I cannot but regret very greatly that you should resign your chair, especially when we had hoped that you would

---

[2] Alberto Errera (1842–94), economic historian and statistician; Professor of Political Economy at Venice and subsequently at Milan and Naples.

[3] See Vol. V, Letter 590, n. 1.

[4] See below, Letter 392, n. 4, p. 68.

[5] Giovanni Antonio Zanon (1845–1920), physicist; Professor of Naval Architecture and Mechanical Engineering at the Nautical Institute, Venice. Author of 'Sulla teoria matematica dello scambio del Professore M. L. Walras – Lettera del Professore Giovanni Antonio Zanon al Professore

have returned with your health repaired, and ready for a fresh term of academic vigour. I have therefore a proposal to make which, I trust, will be acceptable both to you and to the Council: viz. that your letter of the 5th. should be regarded as not written, and that you should renew your engagement for another year on the same terms as before, but with the understanding that you are again at liberty to place the Evening Classes in Political Economy in the hands of a deputy, the Council guaranteeing that the total emoluments of these classes, fees and the class – stipends included, shall not be less than £60 for the evening session.

In the course of the year the Council will proceed to make the formal appointments so long postponed, when, of course, both the Council and you will approach the consideration of the conditions absolutely unfettered.

Believe that I am
Very sincerely Yours
J. G. Greenwood

381. W. S. JEVONS TO L. WALRAS
[FW]

Owens College, Manchester
[May] 30, 1874[1]

My dear Sir

I have now been in possession for two or three days of part of the proofs of your work on the "Theorie de la Richesse Sociale",[2] which you have been so good as to send me, and I have already read a considerable portion of them with much admiration. Before attempting to form any final opinion as to whether there are important points of difference between our views or not, I should like to have more time to study and reflect upon your printed chapters, and also to see the remainder of the work. But I cannot delay expressing the pleasure with which I find that

---

Alberto Errera', *Rassegna di Agricoltura, Industria e Commercio*, 2 (1874) 217–23; and of numerous articles on physics and engineering.

In the letter to Errera referred to above, Zanon explained his position thus: 'Poichè volete ch'io vi esponga il mio debole parere sulla memoria scritta dal sig. prof. Leone Walras, la quale porta il titolo: *Teoria matematica dello scambio*, io aderisco a questo vostro desiderio solo per questo, che essa si fonda su principii matematica; altrimenti io mi chiamerei affatto incompetente giudice di economia politica.'

[1] The date of this letter is '30 June 1874' in the original manuscript, but this appears to have been a slip, as Walras had crossed it out and written 'May' under it in red ink, also pencilling in '31 Mai' as the date of its receipt. However, in the Jevons Papers there is what appears to be some form of copy of the original letter. This is dated '30 June 1874' and does not have the postscript.

[2] As Jaffé explains (op. cit., p. 403) this refers to the proofs of the first instalment of the first edition of Walras's *Eléments d'économie politique pure*.

we have by independent paths reached conclusions which are nearly if not quite the same. I flatter myself with the hope that the unity of our results arises from the best cause, namely that we have both reached the truth, which must be one.

After receiving your very friendly letter of 23rd May and after seeing a full statement of your mode of arriving at the equations of exchange, I cannot for a moment entertain the least doubt of the entire independence of your own researches as regards my own.

As to the question of priority of publication, it is of course of less importance than that of the truth of the theory itself. But I confess that I have always in my own mind attached much importance to this mathematical theory of economy, believing it to be the only basis upon which an ultimate reform of the science of political economy can be founded and a solution of many difficult problems effected. I cannot therefore help accepting your very kind offer to make known in the *Journal des Economistes* or otherwise the fact that I had already gone over part of the same ground as yourself altho in a different manner. I must add that I feel it to be most honourable in you after seeing merely the brief sketch of my theory as printed in the *Statistical Journal* for 1866, to acknowledge at once my priority on some points, and I shall be glad to learn your opinion of the much fuller statement of my views contained in the "Theory of Political Economy" of which I have lately posted you a copy.

For my own part I shall have much pleasure in doing what I can to make known in England your own excellent statement of the theory of exchange, and to show my high estimation of your friendly conduct. I trust that the theory of exchange will thus become the origin of the exchange between us of many friendly letters.

Believe me to be, my dear Sir,

Yours very faithfully,

W. Stanley Jevons

Postscript – If you have to pay anything to the postal office either for this, or for the previous letter papers or book, please inform me, as I find that mistakes are made in the English post office about the rates of postage. I sent a second copy of the paper because I thought I had perhaps broken the foreign postal regulations in wrapping up the first.

382. T. BRASSEY[1] TO W. S. JEVONS

4 Great George Street,
Westminster, S. W.
June 2nd, 1874.

Dear Sir,

I am much gratified by your kind observations upon the publication which I ventured to send you.

I cannot but think that the general rise of wages in this country, which will have the effect of increasing the price of English goods in foreign countries, must necessarily impose a considerable check upon our export trade. We have had a flourishing trade, of late years, with foreign countries, though the rates of wages have been higher here than abroad; but the British workman, though receiving a higher nominal amount of daily wages, has performed a greater amount of work in the day. A fair day's wages must of course be regulated by the market rate, that is to say by demand and supply. Wages are not determined by philanthropy, but by the proportion of workmen seeking employment in any particular trade.

I regret that considerations as to space prevented me from saying more of the scheme of Messrs. Fox Head & Co.,[2] of which I entertain the highest opinion.

I am, Dear Sir,
Yours faithfully,
T. Brassey.

To Professor W. S. Jevons.

383. W S. JEVONS TO MRS LUCY HUTTON
[LJN, 306]

122 Gower Street, London, W.C.
[5th June 1874][1]

. . . We are settled in comfortable lodgings at the above address, and shall probably be here for a week longer. I think we shall have a good time

[1] Thomas Brassey, first Earl (1836–1918); M.P. for Devonport, 1865 and for Hastings, 1868–85; Civil Lord of the Admiralty, 1880–4, and Secretary to the Admiralty, 1884–5; Governor of Victoria, 1895–1900. Publications include *Work and Wages* (1872) and *Foreign Work and British Wages* (1879).

[2] A profit-sharing scheme, which is referred to on p. 226 of Brassey's article 'Co-Operative Production', *Contemporary Review*, 24 (1874) 212–33. It may have been an advance proof of this which was 'the publication' referred to in this letter; there is no mention of Fox, Head and Co.'s scheme in Brassey's *Work and Wages*. Cf. Vol. III, Letter 278, p. 151.

[1] The letter as printed in LJ bears no date, but this can be inferred from the record of the meeting of the Political Economy Club – see n. 2 below.

of it, and I combine a little business with a good deal of pleasure. This evening I go to dine with the Political Economy Club for the first time since they made me an honorary member, but the subject is one about India, on which I do not see how I can have anything to say. [2] To-morrow I am going to the annual visitation of the Greenwich Observatory, when one has a good opportunity of seeing the place. . . .

The worst of coming to London is that it makes me wish to live here altogether, the libraries are so attractive. I have already been once to the Royal Academy, and like the show of pictures much on the whole, including the celebrated picture of Miss Thompson. [3] I am probably going again this afternoon. . . .

383A.   W. S. JEVONS TO H. S. FOXWELL[1]
         [RDF]

122 Gower Street
London WC
5 June 74

My dear Sir

I am much obliged to you for your letter received this morning & think we shall have no difficulty between us in arranging the Pol. Econ. exam[n]. I am so deplorably ignorant of Cambridge affairs that I look to you & Mr Pearson[2] to ensure the papers being in proper form, and of course it is undesirable to diverge much from the customary manner and standard. Otherwise I should agree with you that questions specially directed to particular books are not so good as those more freely given. As the University prescribes certain books for reading I suppose we had better give a few distinctly out of them.

[2] On 5 June 1874, William Newmarch proposed the question 'To what extent is it true that, on economical grounds, the Administration of the Government of India by this country is becoming impracticable?' at the Political Economy Club. See *Political Economy Club . . . Proceedings, . . . and Questions Discussed, 1821–1900*, 6 (1921) 96.

[3] Elizabeth Thompson (1846–1933), more sidely known as an artist of military subjects by the title Lady Butler, after her marriage in 1877 to Lt-General Sir William Francis Butler. Her famous painting, 'Calling the Roll after an Engagement in the Crimea', caused a sensation when it was exhibited in the Royal Academy in 1874 and was subsequently purchased by Queen Victoria. Cf. below, Letter 431, p. 118.

[1] Herbert Somerton Foxwell (1849–1936), one of Marshall's first pupils, was appointed a Fellow and Lecturer in Moral Sciences at St John's College, Cambridge, in 1875; succeeded Jevons in 1881 as Professor of Political Economy at University College London, while retaining his Cambridge fellowship. From Jevons Foxwell acquired the interest in economic literature which made him the most noted bibliophile in the history of the subject.

[2] Josiah Brown Pearson (1841–95), Fellow of St John's College, Cambridge, 1864–80; Bishop of Newcastle, New South Wales, 1880–90; Examiner with Jevons and Foxwell in the Moral Sciences Tripos, 1874.

To mark a single long essay properly has always appeared to me very difficult, but the difficulty is less with three or four long answers, and I should propose to give a paper of 4 or 5 important questions to be treated in the essay-like manner. This also seems to me fairer than a single subject for an essay, as there is less chance of the subjects having been accidentally overlooked or misunderstood by a candidate otherwise well read.

I do not know why Mr Pearson wants to make up his papers so soon, but I supposed that there might be some custom or regulation to that effect I quite concur in deferring the making up of the papers until the Autumn, supposing that there is no reason to the contrary, & I will write to you again (after the vacation) or say some time in September.

Believe me
Yours very faithfully
W. S. Jevons.

H. S. Foxwell Esqe.

384.   W. S. JEVONS TO R. H. INGLIS PALGRAVE

Withington, Manchester
17 June 74

My dear Palgrave,

I have again been away from home for two weeks and on my return find your agreeable letter & enclosed present unforwarded – I thank you very much for the little book of your brother's[1] hymns which are full of deep feeling & thought. The one which you point out upon the Reign of Law seems to me remarkably good.[2] It entirely expresses in a brief form my own reflections on the subject laboriously explained in my book. I suppose the same views were stated by the Duke of Argyll in his "Reign of Law"[3] but it is now several years since I saw the book, and at the time I did not think his views were very clearly explained.

I am glad I have had an opportunity of becoming acquainted with your Brother's beautiful hymns. I have long felt grateful to him for his

---

[1] Francis Turner Palgrave (1824–97), Professor of Poetry in the University of Oxford, 1886–95; best known as editor of the *Golden Treasury of English Lyrics* (1861).

[2] *Original Hymns by Francis Turner Palgrave* (1867). The hymn referred to in this letter is 'Faith and Sight in the Latter Days' (pp. 25–7) which includes the verse

Unchanging law binds all and Nature all we see
Thou art a star far off, too far,
Too far to follow Thee.

[3] George Douglas Campbell (1823–1900), eighth Duke of Argyll, *The Reign of Law* (1867).

admirable Golden Treasury which has from time to time given me much pleasure.

I am commencing a more extended enquiry into the course of prices, which will require a good deal of labour. I find statistical work quite refreshing after so much logic.

I dare say the opening of the Spring trade to the Northern ports may exercise some influence on the Money Market but I should think there must be something more in the background to occasion so distinct a fluctuation: & why are the two pressures in May and November at almost exactly 6 months' interval.[4] Believe me,

Yours very faithfully,
W. S. Jevons

385.   W. S. JEVONS TO T. E. JEVONS
      [LJN, 306–8]

Parsonage Road, Withington,
19th June 1874.

. . . Your agreeable letter of 14th June was received a few days since. I need hardly have said that it was agreeable, as yours are always so, and serve to cheer me.

Thanks for sending the books. . . . I think you are quite right in deferring any remarks on *American Currency* until there is something fixed. It will be next year before the book is done, I feel sure. In the meantime there are many little points you might inquire into, quite useful in any case. I want to know—

1.   What is the nature of a certified cheque as used in New York?

2.   Are they much used, and are they used in other towns of United States?

3.   When a cheque is certified, is the banker justified or obliged to retain a sufficient deposit on the part of the drawer to provide for it; or is it merely a kind of general acceptance of a bill upon himself, that is, the banker?

It might be very useful if you could get access to the banker's clearing house in New York, and send me a few notes as to how they do the business – especially whether they still make payments in coin or notes. If you could get copies of the paper forms employed, it would be very valuable.[1]

---

[4] Cf. above, Letter 368, p. 31.

[1] *Money and the Mechanism of Exchange* contains a general account of the New York Clearing House (fourth edition, p. 278) and of the system of certified cheques (ibid., p. 243) but does not cover the points of detail mentioned in this letter. But cf. Letter 458, below, p. 155.

I have lately visited the London clearing house by the aid of Sir John Lubbock, and have been much interested both in that and the small Manchester one. I should also like to know whether any, and if so, what coins circulate in the States now?

We spent nearly two weeks in London pleasantly for the most part. . . .

I am going again into the subject of mortality, and the effect of the Irish population on mortality in English towns.[2] The volume of the *United States Census* which you gave me has just supplied some data quite countenancing my theory. Thus in the States of higher mortality the proportion of Irish deaths to all deaths is 8 per cent. In the States of lower mortality the proportion of Irish deaths is only 2 per cent, a very striking difference, which quite accords with other facts. Applying the same kind of calculation to German deaths the proportions are 4·4 per cent and 3·0, showing little evidence of any connection.

I hope your estimate of the *Principles of Science* may prove true in some degree. I have seen a letter from a scientific old lady, Miss Wedgwood,[3] the niece of Charles Darwin, who seems greatly pleased with it. The reviews hang fire very much. I quite agree with you that the *Saturday Reviewer*[4] failed to see the connection between the parts of the book altogether.

I will consider what you urge about a tax on coal. It is much the same as the proposal of Sir Rowland Hill in a paper read to the London Statistical Society, December 1873, vol. xxxvi. p. 565.[5] The paper was not favourably received, and it would be worth your while to read the discussion if you can meet with the journal. I do not feel quite sure about the matter, but must make up my mind, as I proposed the point for discussion at the Political Economy Club, and suppose I shall have to argue it some time next session.[6]

[2] Jevons did not, however, publish anything further to his 1870 address to the British Association on this subject. Cf. *Methods*, pp. 213–16.

[3] Julia Wedgwood (1833–1913), great-granddaughter of Josiah Wedgwood (1730–95); authoress of *Life of John Wesley* (1870); *The Moral Ideal* (1888); *The Message of Israel* (1894) and *The Personal Life of Josiah Wedgwood the Potter* (1916). Owing to close intermarriage between the two families, she was both a niece and a cousin of Charles Darwin: Darwin's mother was a daughter of Josiah Wedgwood; his wife, who was also his cousin, was a granddaughter, and a sister of Hensleigh Wedgwood (1803–91), lawyer, mathematician and philologist, father of Julia. Cf. N. G. Annan, 'The Intellectual Aristocracy', in *Studies in Social History: a Tribute to G. M. Trevelyan*, edited by J. H. Plumb (1955) pp. 243–87. It is not clear why Jevons assumed that Miss Wedgwood was 'an old lady' at this date.

[4] An unsigned review of Jevons's *Principles of Science* appeared in the *Saturday Review*, 23 May 1874, pp. 654–6.

[5] Rowland Hill, 'High Price of Coal. Suggestions for Neutralising its Evils', *JRSS*, 36 (1873) 565–70.

[6] Jevons did not introduce any question relating to coal at the Political Economy Club. In the autumn of 1875 he did read his paper 'On the Progress of the Coal Question' to Section F of the British Association, but the abstract of this in *Transactions of Sections*, p. 216, contains no mention of a possible tax on coal. See Vol. VII.

I think I can detect a gradual improvement in my health. I still frequently knock myself up, but recover much more rapidly than before, which seems to me a good sign.

At present I feel overwhelmed with things to do, and our frequent absences from home waste so much time. I have arranged with the college to continue for a session without evening work, leaving future arrangements unsettled. . . .

386.   W. S. JEVONS TO T. E. JEVONS
       [LJN, 308–9]

Withington, Manchester,
29th June 1874.

. . . We sail for Norway on 3d July, and I must write a note to say goodbye before we go.

I have been enjoying much some volumes of music I bought lately, being the trios, quartettes, and violin duets of Beethoven, arranged for the piano, and published in Litolf's* edition of his works. [1] You should buy them by all means, and after a little practice you will find them, as might be expected, full of delightful music, not more difficult than his pianoforte sonatas, and of a lighter character in general.

As regards the book on money, I have now partially promised to have it done by Christmas, so that I should like to know something about American currency, say by October. I have noticed what is said in the papers of recent Bills in Congress. So far as I can make out, they are going to withdraw greenbacks, and leave National Bank currency almost unrestricted. [2] Unless I misunderstand the matter, I can hardly imagine a worse solution. I should like to know why these banks should have the right of issue? What constitutes a national bank? Is there any limit to what they can issue? Unless there be some careful restriction, there will probably be a repetition of what happened in 1830–40. Does the profit of bank issues go in any way to Government? . . . [3]

---

[1] Henry Charles Litolff (1818–91), French pianist and composer, settled in Brunswick in 1851 and took over the business of the music publisher Meyer. The well known *Collection Litolff*, a cheap, accurate edition of classical music, was begun in 1861: a collection of Beethoven's arrangements for the piano was published in 1862.

[2] After the veto of the Inflation Bill, Congress had produced compromise legislation, which freed the national banks from the requirement of a reserve against note circulation, but limited the total issue of greenbacks to $382 million. See Unger, *The Greenback Era* (Princeton, 1964) pp. 245–8.

[3] By an Act of January 1863 any group of five people possessing a specified capital could form a banking corporation and upon deposit of Federal bonds with the Comptroller of the Currency would be issued national bank notes to the extent of 90% of the value of the bonds. The effect of the act was to impose a limit of $300 million on this note issue. See A. Davies, *The Origins of the National Banking System* (Washington, D.C., 1910); A. Bolles, *Financial History of the United States from 1861 to 1885* (New York, 1894).

387. J. D'AULNIS[1] TO W. S. JEVONS

Leyde 29 Juin 1874

Monsieur!

Mon nom vous sera déjà connu par la lettre de M. Léon Walras, publiée dans le Journal des Economistes de Juin 1874. Etant ainsi introduit chez vous j'ose prendre la liberté de vous écrire quelque chose, qui peut être vous sera de quelque intérêt, et de faire appel à votre bienveillance.

Je suis occupé d'une dissertation sur quelques principes d'économie politique, et c'est sur l'avis d'un de mes compatriotes, un économiste de la plus haute autorité dans les Pays-Bas, M. N. G. Pierson, [2] directeur de la Banque Néerlandaise à Amsterdam, que je me suis mis, en Février, à étudier votre "Theory of political economy". A présent je me propose de populariser aussi bien qu'il me sera possible votre théorie admirable sur la valeur. Avant de mettre mon manuscrit sous presse, je profiterai de la bienveillance de M. N. G. Pierson, qui le lira. Ainsi j'ai l'espoir que le désir d'être populaire ne porte aucun préjudice à la rigueur scientifique. De plus j'ai l'avantage de pouvoir compter sur le secours d'un de mes amis, qui est mathématicien. [3]

J'ai lu avec regret dans votre lettre à M. Walras, que votre théorie est négligée ou contestée en Angleterre. Comme je suis moi-même sur le

---

[1] Johan, Baron d'Aulnis de Bourouill (1850–1930) received his doctorate from the University of Leiden in 1874 for a thesis entitled *Het Inkomen Der Maatschappij* ('The Income of Society') based on Jevons's theory of value. In the preface to this thesis d'Aulnis wrote:

'I had made much progress remodelling the new theory when the number of April 15, 1874, of the *Journal des Economistes* came to my hands. In this issue, Léon Walras, Professor of Political Economy at Lausanne, expounded a mathematical theory of exchange, and soon I found that this author, although he had used a method and a terminology differing from Jevons', arrived at conclusions fundamentally identical with those of the English Professor. My surmise that the work of the latter was unknown to the French economist was soon confirmed by a correspondence with him which I entered into in May.' (Cf. Jaffé, *Walras Correspondence*, I, 388, 390–1.) d'Aulnis continues:

'In August of this year a work by the hand of Walras, entitled *Elements d'Économie Politique Pure*, appeared. In this the theory, as it was developed by this Professor and already partially published in the *Journal des Economistes*, was fully unfolded. But, although I have the highest appreciation for the great penetration and originality that shine in this book, I reached the opinion that Jevons' work should be preferred, as to philosophical spirit of conception, simplicity of form and terminological correctness.'

After a period of legal practice in Amsterdam d'Aulnis served in the Finance Department of the Netherlands Government until 1878, when he became Professor of Political History, Statistics and Economics at the University of Utrecht, from which chair he retired in 1917.

[2] Nicolaas Gerard Pierson (1839–1909), Dutch economist, banker and statesman. Began his career in banking and in 1868 was appointed one of the directors of the Bank of the Netherlands. After 1877 he combined this with the professorship of economics and statistics at the University of Amsterdam, until he became President of the Bank in 1885. Minister of Finance of the Netherlands 1891–4, and Prime Minister 1897–1901.

[3] This was Dr I. de Jong of Leiden.

point de publier sur elle un livre, je voudrais bien volontiers que vous me donneriez des renseignements sur les critiques *valables*, qui sont publiées sur votre livre. Celle de M. Cairnes ("Some leading principles of pol. economy." pag 11 – 16.) m'est connue. Il me semble que cet économiste n'a absolument rien compris de toute la théorie. Ensuite j'ai lu la critique, dénuée du sérieux, que l'on doit aux problèmes de la science, d'un anonyme dans le numéro du Saturday Review de 11 November 1871.[4] En dernier lieu la remarque superficielle et arrogante de M. Carey[5] "Unity of Law". Si toutes les critiques, portées à votre égard, sont du même genre que les nommées, je vous prie de me dispenser de la lecture. Il s'agit pour moi seulement de celles, qui m'instruisent, qui m'indiquent un point réellement obscur ou incomplet.

Comme M. Walras a écrit que le théorie mathématique a du succès en Italie, je suis heureux de vous dire que dans les Pays-Bas non seulement M. N. G. Pierson, mais, selon mes informations, aussi M. W. C. Mees,[6] président de la Banque Néerlandaise à Amsterdam, économiste très renommé dans ma patrie, et M. Quack,[7] Professeur en écon. pol. à Utrecht ont donné leur assentiment à votre livre. Et je vous assure que j'enverrai ma dissertation à tous les économistes de profession, que me sont connus en Hollande, et peut être aussi à un Allemand, que vous connaîtrez sans doute, M. E. Laspeyres, qui sait le Hollandais.

J'ai vu que vous avez publié votre théorie dans le Journal de Société Statistique de Londres, en 1866. vol. xxix. p. 282. Si vous aviez publié là quelque chose d'intéressant, que vous avez omise dans votre livre de 1871, vous me rendriez un grand service en m'envoyant un extrait de ce numéro. Car j'éprouve quelque difficulté dans l'exposition de l'échange de commodités indivisibles, un problème que vous avez traité pag 122 – 126. Je voudrais en faire analyse mathématique et montrer scientifiquement dans quelles limites les termes du rapport sont indé-

[4] *The Saturday Review*, 11 November 1871, pp. 624–5. For the text of this review and notes on its authorship, see Vol. VII.

[5] H. C. Carey, *The Unity of Law, as exhibited in the relations of Physical, Social, Mental and Moral Science* (Philadelphia, 1873) p. 10. Carey characterised Jevons's conclusion that 'value depends entirely upon utility' as 'arrived at in face of the greatest of the facts of our age, to wit: that as the *utility* of electricity has been more and more developed, its *value* has so steadily declined as to have already brought its services within reach of the common labourer desirous of communicating with his wife and children.'

[6] Willem Cornelis Mees (1813–85), Secretary of the Rotterdam Chamber of Commerce, 1843–9, Secretary of the Netherlands Bank, 1849–63, President, 1863–85. His published works included *A History of the Banking System in the Netherlands* (Rotterdam, 1838) and *Leading Chapters of Political Economy* (Amsterdam, 1866).

[7] Hendrik Pieter Godfried Quack (1834–1917), Professor of Political Economy at Utrecht, 1868–77; Secretary to the Board of Directors of the Netherlands Bank, 1877–85, and Managing Director after 1885; Extraordinary Professor of Political Economy at Amsterdam, 1885–94. Quack's approach to economic problems was sociological; his main work was *De Socialisten, Personen en Stelsels*, 4 vols (1875–97).

terminés, puis éclaircir l'opération de telles raisons d'échange indé-
terminées dans le cas de grands agrégats d'individus commerçants.[8] Je
suis convaincu qu'alors la loi de l'échange se manifeste de nouveau,
comme s'il n'était question que de quantités infiniment petites, au moins
qu'on trouvera des données moyennes, qui correspondent aux résultats
du calcul infinitésimal. Mais je ne voudrais pas volontiers faire une faute
dans cette supposition, parceque je crois qu'il n'y a rien de plus
dangereux pour une théorie nouvelle, que de la publier d'une manière
incorrecte. Ainsi je donnerais des armes à ceux, qui voudraient attaquer
la théorie, et qui peut-être la condemneraient entièrement parceque
j'aurais commis une faute dans un point accessoire.

Je vous serais infiniment reconnaissant si vous voudriez avoir la bonté
de m'instruire un peu sur la difficulté nommée. Quelques petits
renseignements peut-être suffiront. Je n'ai non plus trouvé la lumière
suffisant dans les épreuves, que M. Léon Walras a eu la bienveillance de
m'envoyer, et dans lesquelles il traite la question pag 135–136.

J'ai introduit ensuite quelque chose de nouveau dans la théorie, savoir
la variation de la courbe d'utilité elle-même que vous traitez comme
invariable. Par cette variation le degré d'utilité peut devenir plus grand
ou plus petit, sans variation de quantité. La methode graphique s'y prête
fort bien; vous trouverez le problème traité par M. Courcelle Seneuil[9]
(traité théor. et prat. ed. 1858. I chap viii). Ainsi j'obtiens le résultat
évident que les degrés d'utilités et en conséquence les prix, dependent des
besoins des individus et des quantités des marchandises, en somme de 4
variables.

Je ne puis terminer cette lettre, Monsieur, sans l'expression de ma
profonde reconnaissance envers vous. Vous avez jeté une lumière
brillante sur la question cardinale de la science économique, et sans votre
livre je n'aurais pu écrire mon petit livre san être moi-même très mal
satisfait. Avant la lecture de votre livre je voyais dans la science presque
partout une confusion inextricable d'idées. Je suis heureux d'être un des
premiers, qui aient pu profiter de votre découverte.

Ma dissertation sera prête en Septembre, et j'aurai l'honneur de vous
offrir un exemplaire. Probablement vous ne saurez pas la langue
Hollandaise. Mais j'espère de vous envoyer avec mon livre une missive,
dans la quelle vous pourrez au moins voir la déduction populaire et les
illustrations pratiques, dont je me suis servi.

[8] Cf. Letter 405, below, p. 90.

[9] Jean Gustave Courcelle-Seneuil (1813–98), *Traité Théorique et Pratique de l'Économie Politique*,
2 vols (1858–9) vol. I, chap. VIII, 'Des Variations Subjectives d'Utilité', pp. 182–3.

Veuillez agréer, Monsieur, l'assurance de mon haut respect.
Votre humble serviteur
J. d'Aulnis de Bourouill

étudiant en droit

Mon adresse sera à Boisleduc, province Brabant Septentrional, Pays-Bas.

388.   W. S. JEVONS TO J. E. CAIRNES[1]

Manchester.
1 July 74.

Dear Cairnes

As I am just starting for abroad I write a few lines to say that I have heard that your treatise on Pol. Econ. is to be reviewed for the Manchester Guardian by Mr W. H. Brewer M A lately my substitute lecturer. As I have previously noticed your two vols of Essays for the same paper I should like you to know that I am not responsible for what the same paper says of your new book, but Brewer is a very able man & will no doubt do justice in some degree to your treatise.

I am glad to see what a very flattering reception your book is having generally.

Thanks for your last letter.[2] I see that I had very stupidly written *valuable* at first instead of variable, so that you could hardly fail to read it *valuable*.

The objection which you make that you do not pay more for your dinner because you are hungry, nor part with the rest of the meat in the larder when you have satisfied your appetite, is an ingenious & apparently strong one. The requisite answer would be too long for me to trouble you with, but the materials for it are given in several parts of the "Theory of P. E."

p. 72.

Utility is *prospective* as well as immediate[3] & you keep as much meat in your larder as is requisite for a few days. But if there is a greater supply of a perishable article than can be[4] consumed at the usual price in time, it is sold off at any requisite sacrifice as in the case of an over abundant fish market.

---

[1] The original manuscript of this letter is in the Cairnes Papers, MS 8954, National Library of Ireland.

[2] This letter has not been traced.

[3] In the first edition of *T.P.E.*, the section of chapter III (Theory of Utility) entitled 'Actual, Prospective and Potential Utility' commences on p. 72.

[4] 'sold in time' is deleted here in the original manuscript.

The objection that you do not pay more for dinner because you are very hungry is met by the principle that there cannot be *two prices* for the same article in the same market (p. 91)[5]

You pay the current market price and if you were charged for hunger at one place you would go somewhere else. But in fact when there are many hungry people unsatisfied, holders of food who know this take advantage of it & raise their prices as in all cases of famine.

When I began this note I had not intended, however, to get into controversy & so beg that you will not trouble yourself to read it & certainly not to answer it, as I should not receive the answer for two months.

Believe me

Yours very faithfully

W. S. Jevons.

389.   W. S. JEVONS TO J. D'AULNIS
       [LJN, 309–11]

Christiania, 7th July, 1874.

... I received your very agreeable letter one hour before leaving Manchester for a journey in Norway, and was therefore unable to answer it before arriving here. I sent by post from England a copy of the brief paper on the mathematical theory of political economy printed in the *Statistical Journal* in 1866, to which you referred in your letter. You will find, however, that it contains nothing but what is much more fully described in my book on the theory, and there are some parts of the paper, especially section 15, which I now regard as erroneous.[1]

Allow me to thank you very much for the kind expressions which your letter contains, and to say how gratified I am that you approve of my efforts to trace out a mathematical theory. It is quite true that what I have written on the subject has received little or no attention in England, and by those who have noticed it the theory has been generally rejected, or

[5] 'When a commodity is perfectly uniform or homogeneous in quality, all portions may be indifferently used in place of equal portions: hence, in the same market, and at the same moment, all portions must be exchanged at the same ratio' – *T.P.E.*, first edition, p. 91.

[1] 'Brief Account of a General Mathematical Theory of Political Economy', § 15: 'When the useful object on one side only is infinitely divisible, we shall have only one unknown quantity, namely, that of the divisible commodity given for the indivisible object, and also one equation to determine it by, namely, that on the part of the person holding the divisible commodity, and able to give more or less for it. But this does not apply to unique objects, like a statue, a rare book or gem, which do not admit of the conception of more or less. When both commodities are indivisible as first supposed (Section 13), we have neither unknown quantities nor equations.'

even ridiculed. This has not shaken my conviction of its substantial truth, though I have feared that it would take a long time to obtain for it any reception. Until the last few months I was not aware that any attention had been given to my book abroad, and you may therefore believe that I was gratified with what you tell me.

As to the reviews in the English periodical journals, that in the *Saturday Review* of 11th November 1871 is the most important, and indeed the only one requiring any attention. There was indeed a review in the *Academy* of 1st April 1872, but though more fair than that of the *Saturday Review*, it contained no criticism worthy of your notice.[2] Mr. Cairnes, as you truly say, has failed to seize the idea of the theory, and his objections are consequently of no weight, though he is usually a most able economist. He has, indeed, stated, both in print and in private letters to myself, that his want of mathematical knowledge prevented him from reading a large part of the book, but that being so, I regret that he has thought proper to controvert the foundation of the theory on false grounds.

With the remarks of Mr. Carey referred to by you, I am quite unacquainted.

I am most happy to hear that you propose in a forthcoming work to illustrate the principles of political economy, and present them in a popular form while preserving the scientific form, which is necessarily a mathematical form. I have felt great difficulty in conveying the fundamental ideas of the theory in at all a popular form, and I shall therefore look with much interest to the book, of which I feel the importance. I am sorry indeed that it will be printed in a language of which I can read nothing, but I may suggest that after completing the edition in Hollandaise you may undertake another edition either in French or English. I shall myself have much pleasure in making known, as much as I can, your opinions on this subject.

I can only regard my own work as a bare and imperfect outline of some of the more important theorems of political economy, and there can be no doubt that a hundred points still of importance remain to be cleared up by yourself or others. The question of the variation of the curves of utility is one of evident importance and I shall much wish to see how you treat it.

As to the exchange of indivisible commodities, I feel myself quite unable at present to add anything to what I have said in the book. The conclusion which I adopted in one case, that the ratio of exchange was indeterminate, seemed unsatisfactory, but I could find no other answer to give. If you can suggest a better result, it will remove what may well be regarded as a difficulty in the way of the theory. I am not even yet sure

---

[2] The review in the *Academy* was written (and signed) by Alfred Marshall; see Vol. VII.

that my statement of the theory is free from errors. Objections have been made even to the fundamental equations of exchange, but the fact that M. Walras has arrived at substantially the same equation makes it very probable that my statement was correct.

While I am not aware that my views have been accepted by any well-known English economist, there are a certain number of younger mathematicians and economists who have entered into the subject, and treated it in a very different manner. Among these I may mention Mr. George Darwin, the son of the eminent naturalist; he is a very good mathematician and an acute economist; and his only important objection was to the expression for the *rate of interest*, $\dfrac{ft}{ft}$ but after proposing one or two more complicated expressions himself, he at last allowed that my expression was satisfactory and simple.

In conclusion, I must say that I am very sorry that your letter should have remained so long unanswered, but the delay is due to the fact that I was just setting out on a journey when your letter came. . . .

390. L. WALRAS TO W. S. JEVONS
[FW]

Lausanne,
29 Juillet, 1874[1]

Cher Monsieur,

Votre volume et l'excellente lettre dont vous l'avez fait suivre me sont parvenus tous deux en leur temps. J'ai été fort occupé depuis lors, d'abord, pendant tout le mois de juin, par l'impression de mon ouvrage qui a paru[2] et que je m'empresse de vous adresser aujourd'hui, puis, en juillet, par des examens de fin d'année. Mais je profite de mes premiers jours de vacances pour entamer la correspondance amicale que vous me proposez et que j'accepte de grand coeur avec la ferme intention de l'entretenir fort exactement.

---

[1] Here, as in Walras's letter of 23 May 1874 (above, Letter 379, p. 45), there are minor differences between the version given here, reproducing the original letter in the Jevons Papers, and that published by Jaffé from the draft in Fonds Walras (FW 1, 278/2):

	Walras Correspondence	*Jevons Papers*
para 2	de m'expliquer	de m'en expliquer
para 2	ce qui serait le mieux	(ce qui serait le mieux)
para 3	sur mon terroir	sur mon terrain
para 3	que nous tenons la verité	qu' on tient la verité
para 3	combien d'autres choses	combien d'autres choses
	y a–t–il à trouver	à trouver encore

[2] *Elements d'économie politique pure*, part 1.

La première et rapide lecture que j'ai faite de votre beau livre serait tout-à-fait insuffisante s'il s'agissait d'accuser les points accessoires sur lesquels nous pouvons différer et de discuter ces différences. Dès que j'aurai terminé quelques travaux urgents, je me propose de faire de ce livre une traduction littérale en français; [3] cela me permettra d'en saisir et d'en critiquer tous les détails; et, cette opération faite, je serai en mesure de m'en expliquer avec vous et aussi de faire connaître vos idées aux lecteurs français, soit *in-extenso* (ce que serait le mieux), si les circonstances le permettent, soit tout au moins par des articles. En revanche, cette lecture m'a permis de constater avec un plaisir infini notre complet et merveilleux accord sur tous les points capitaux. Nous avons bien conçu et entrepris, chacun de notre côté, la même révolution à opérer dans la science en lui restituant son caractère et sa méthode véritables. De plus, en introduisant les courbes ou fonctions d'utilité, les degrés ou intensités d'utilité et en établissant la relation mathématique de ces degrés ou intensités avec le prix ou la raison d'échange, nous avons posé tous deux la point de départ de la science nouvelle avec une similitude dans la manière de procéder qui demeurera, je crois, comme un curieuse exemple de ces sortes de rencontres, fréquentes du reste dans l'histoire de la science.

Comme je n'ai nullement la prétention d'être supérieur aux faiblesses de la nature humaine, je vous avouerai franchement que j'ai été tout d'abord un peu dégrisé en perdant la priorité de l'équation dont il s'agit et qui est bien la pierre angulaire de toute la théorie mathématique de l'échange et de la richesse sociale. Mais ce simple énoncé que vous en faisiez dans votre première lettre était décisif pour un homme aussi au courant de la question que je l'étais. Or quand il n'y a plus qu'à s'exécuter, autant faut il le faire de bonne grâce. J'estime qu'avant même d'être un grand savant, il convient d'être un homme comme il faut, et j'ai toujours déploré qu'on pût voir des hommes ayant assez de génie pour inventer le calcul infinitésimal et n'ayant pas assez de savoir-vivre pour les partager décemment cette invention. D'ailleurs à la lecture de votre ouvrage, le léger désappointement que j'avais éprouvé en vous trouvant déjà installé sur mon terrain a été largement compensé par la vive satisfaction de voir mes résultats si remarquablement confirmés. J'ajouterai que c'est une circonstance qui avance, selon moi, singulièrement l'état de la question que celle de notre rencontre si spontanée et si complète dans la même voie. Dans de telles conditions, nous pouvons, je crois, si nous savons nous entendre, voir changer d'ici à quelques années la face de l'économie politique. Assurément, il eût été agréable et flatteur d'être le premier; mais n'est-il pas plus important d'être deux et de trouver dans cet accord une preuve qu'on tient la vérité et un moyen de la

---

[3] See below, Letter 533, n. 6, p. 261.

faire réussir? Enfin, comme je l'ai dit dans ma Préface,[4] tandis que vous vous attachiez à exposer la méthode nouvelle et à poser les bases de son application non seulement à la théorie de l'échange, mais encore à celles du travail, de la rente et du capital, je m'efforçais, quant à moi, d'approfondir spécialement la première de ces théories, celles de l'échange. Dans cette direction j'ai établi quelques points qui, je pense, me resteront acquis, par exemple le théorème de l'équilibre général et son corollaire, les lois d'établissement et de variation des prix d'équilibre. Et combien d'autres choses à trouver encore! Ainsi mon amour-propre peut espérer des consolations.

Je vais m'occuper de répandre mes *Eléments d'Economie politique pure* et de solliciter quelques articles de revues et de journaux en France et à l'étranger. Bien que le sujet soit difficile je ne désespère pas de trouver quelques juges. S'il s'en rencontrait d'assez consciencieux pour consentir à faire la critique de votre livre en même temps que du mien, ne pourriez vous disposer d'un petit nombre d'exemplaires en leur faveur? Le cas échéant, je vous indiquerais les noms de quatre ou cinq personnes peut-être auxquelles vous auriez à les adresser. Et je mettrais en tête de ma liste M. le Professeur Alberto Errera, à Venise, rédacteur de la *Rivista Europea*. Pour moi, je vous ferais reconnaissant de vouloir bien me signaler ainsi quelques écrivains compétents dans votre presse anglaise si active et si autorisée.

Je suis, Cher Monsieur, bien sincèrement
Tout à vous,
Léon Walras

391.   W. S. JEVONS TO L. WALRAS
[FW]

Parsonage Road,
Withington
Manchester
13 September 1874

My dear Sir,

I have now been at home for a few days since my return from a long journey in Norway, and I have received with much pleasure both your letter and the copy of your work accompanying it.

I have begun to read your work, especially the part on Money which happens to be of much interest to me because I am engaged upon a book

---

[4] Op.cit., pp.vii–viii: cf. Jaffé, *Walras Correspondence*, I, 414.

having the same subject, in which I hope to profit by some of your theories and most luminous expositions. My little book is, however, of a semi-popular character so that I cannot enter into the question in the profound manner in which you have treated it.

I will not attempt on the present occasion to express my feelings concerning your book as a whole, except to say that it strikes me as throughout most scientific and original. I have been thinking how I could make it known in this country, but am sorry to say that there are only one or two publications which I could ask to admit an article on so unpopular a subject.

Nor can I readily indicate to you any persons who would take any interest in it except a few that I mention below—

> George H. Darwin Esq.
> Down
> Beckenham
> Kent
>
> Professor W. B. Hodgson
> The College
> Edinburgh
>
> Professor Leonard H. Courtney[1]
> 8 Queen's Square
> Westminster
> London SW.
>
> Prof. F. Bowen
> Harvard University
> Cambridge
> United S.A.
>
> Professor Fleeming Jenkin
> 3 Great Stuart Street,
> Edinburgh.
>
> Hr. Falbe Hansen
> Det Statistiske Bureau
> Kjobenhavn

I will send further names if I can think of any suitable ones.

In the mean time I shall be happy to distribute five or six copies of my

---

[1] Leonard Henry Courtney (1832–1918), from 1906 Baron Courtney of Penwith; Professor of Political Economy at University College, London, 1872–5; M.P. for Liskeard, 1875; Secretary of the Treasury, 1882–4.

In the original manuscript the names of Hodgson and Courtney have been stroked through, presumably by Walras.

"Theory" as you suggest and shall be happy to receive some names in addition to that of the Venetian Professor whom you mention.

Believe me
Yours very sincerely
W. Stanley Jevons

Please be so good as to tell me the *price* of your book as I think of ordering some copies.

392.   L. WALRAS TO W. S. JEVONS

Lausanne,
24 septembre 1874[1]

Cher Monsieur,

J'ai reçu ces jours-ci votre lettre du 13 courant par laquelle j'ai appris avec plaisir que mon volume vous etait bien parvenu. Croyez que je suis sensible à ce que vous m'en dites et particulièrement de mes leçons sur la monnaie. Je crois, en effet, qu'il s'y trouve quelques germes d'idées susceptibles de fructifier dans un esprit tel que le vôtre; mais je dois vous faire remarquer que les fondements principaux de cette théorie se trouvent dans celle de l'échange: ainsi le principe de la proportionnalité des valeurs aux raretés (20e et 23e Leçons), la distinction du numéraire et de la monnaie (25e Leçon), et surtout la discussion des changements de valeur absolus et relatifs (28e Leçon). Il faut que je vous avoue à cette occasion que la tâche de populariser l'économie politique et sociale de la manière dont on l'entend aujourd'hui me paraît bien difficile. Moi qui ne me suis donné que celle de la faire, je ne la trouve déjà pas fort aisée. On m'a demandé, à moi aussi à plusieurs reprises, de faire des conférences ou des articles sur cette question si complexe et si délicate

---

[1] As with previous letters from Walras, slight differences exist between the wording of the original letter in the Jevons Papers and the draft in Fonds Walras, and these are specified below:

	Walras Correspondence	*Jevons Papers*
para 1	la distinction entre le numéraire et la monnaie	la distinction du numéraire et de la monnaie
para 1	pour les très compétents	pour les hommes compétents
para 1	mécanique, cela avec les seules ressources	mécanique céleste avec les seules . . .
para 1	dépourvus	et dépourvus
para 2	je me suis imposé	je me suis empressé
para 2	article critique	article de critique
para 2	Ce sont les Messieurs	Ce sont ceux de MM.
para 2	Ministère Agriculture, Industrie, Commerce, Rome	Ministère de l'Agriculture et du Commerce, Rome
postscript	mon éditeur	mes éditeurs

de la monnaie. J'ai toujours répondu que cela ne m'était pas possible, que la théorie de la monnaie se trouvait dans l'économie politique telle que je l'enseigne, comme le binôme de Newton dans l'algèbre, c'est-à-dire qu'elle était la 25e Leçon du cours pour l'intelligence de laquelle la connaissance des 24 Leçons précédentes, était absolument necéssaire. Cette réponse n'a pas paru très satisfaisante et je m'attends à des instances nouvelles. S'il m'était tout-à-fait impossible de décliner ces propositions, je crois que je prendrais le parti de populariser l'économie politique comme on popularise l'astronomie, c'est-à-dire de passer par-dessus les démonstrations supposées faites pour les hommes compétents, et d'affirmer purement et simplement des conclusions claires et précises. Mais ce n'est pas cela qu'on veut aujourd'hui: on exige que nous traitions comme une science facile une science des plus compliquées: on veut que nous exposions le système de la mécanique celeste avec les seules ressources de l'arithmétique élémentaire. Faute d'y consentir, nous sommes déclarés hostiles à la démocratie et dépourvus de sentiments philanthropiques et humanitaires.

Merci, Monsieur, pour les adresses que vous m'avez données. Je me suis empressé de faire les envois. Puisque, de votre côté, vous voulez bien disposer sur mes indications de cinq ou six exemplaires de votre ouvrage, je vous en demanderai un pour le vénérable M. Cournot, ancien inspecteur général des études, 10 carrefour de l'Odéon, à Paris (en ce moment, je crois, et pour jusqu'à la fin de la saison, au château de Vellexon, par Fresne-St. Mamès, Haute-Saône) – et un pour M. Auguste Langel,[2] Ingénieur des Mines, publiciste, 19 rue de la ville l'Evêque à Paris. Je m'adresse à M. Langel pour lui demander un article de critique dans le *Temps,* qui est un de nos meilleurs journaux. Quand j'aurai trouvé quelqu'un pour en faire au *Journal des Débats* et à la *Revue des Deux Mondes,* je vous demanderai deux autres exemplaires. Maintenant, voici les noms de trois savants italiens que je vous signale, le premier comme singulièrement bien disposé en faveur de notre méthode et les deux autres comme économistes et mathématiciens également distingués. Ce sont ceux de MM:

Comm. Prof. Luigi Bodio,[3] Directeur de la statistique générale du
royaume, Ministère de l'Agriculture et du
Commerce, Rome

         ,,   ,, Messedaglia[4]) Députés au Parlement italien,
)
         ,,   ,, Ferrara[5]   ) Chambre des Députés, Rome.

[2] I have been unable to trace any biographical information concerning Auguste Langel (Editor).

[3] Luigi Bodio (1840–1920), permanent secretary, and, from 1878 to 1898, director of the Central Statistics Office of the Italian Government (Ufficio Centrale di Statistica del Regno). Served on the Council of State, 1898–1909, and acted as director of the commissariat-general for emigration, 1901–4.

Lorsque vous aurez l'occasion de m'écrire, voudrez-vous me dire, je vous prie, si les deux mémoires de W. Whewell, mentionnés dans votre livre (p. 15) ont été reproduits dans quelqu'édition de ses oeuvres, et sous quel titre. [6] Je pense qu'ils pourraient bien se trouver dans les 2 volumes intitulés Scientific Ideas; mais je voudrais en être sur avant de les faire venir.

Je suis, Cher Monsieur, toujours tout à vous
Léon Walras

Le prix de mon volume pour le public chez mes editeurs, est de 3fr. 75.

392A.   W. S. JEVONS TO H. S. FOXWELL
[RDF]

Parsonage Road
Withington
Manchester
4 Oct 1874

My dear Sir

I have been drawing up a few questions for our examination in Pol. Econ. but I find myself much hampered by my lamentable ignorance of the usual form & character of the Cambridge papers.[1] I doubt if I could obtain any copies of previous papers in pol. econ in Manchester, nor do I think that it is easy to meet with them elsewhere. If you happen to have any old copies by you I should be much obliged if you would send them by book post as a loan for a few days.

My own inclination is quite to agree with what you said in your letter June 4th namely that in Political Econ. at least it is not desirable to restrict ourselves closely in the choice of questions from the books or to make any precise division, but in choosing questions myself I am afraid of going quite out of the ordinary course & getting into technical points

---

[4] Angelo Messedaglia (1820–1901), Professor of Political Economy and Statistics at Padua from 1858, and at Rome from 1888; deputy for Verona in the Italian Parliament, 1866–83.

[5] Francesco Ferrara (1810–1900), Professor of Political Economy at Turin, and later at Pisa and Venice; initiator of *Biblioteca dell'Economista* and editor of the First and Second Series therein.

[6] W. Whewell, 'Mathematical Exposition of some Doctrines of Political Economy', *Cambridge Philosophical Society Transactions*, 3 (1830) 191–230; 'Mathematical Exposition of some of the leading doctrines in Mr. Ricardo's "Principles of Political Economy and Taxation" ', ibid. 4 (1833) 155–98. These papers were not reprinted in Whewell's *History of Scientific Ideas* (Cambridge, 1858).

[1] Jevons had been appointed External Examiner in the Moral Sciences Tripos examination held at Cambridge on 3 and 4 December 1874. The other examiners were Josiah Brown Pearson, Percy Gardner and H. S. Foxwell. See *Cambridge University Calendar* (1875) pp. 98–101, 194.

which happen to have attracted my own attention. I am willing enough to suggest any number of questions & to judge the answers but I must certainly look to your discretion in deciding upon the selection of questions & the form of the papers.

If I understand aright we are to set two papers in political economy; if so I should prefer not to take up one with a single essay but with a moderate number of difficult general questions to be treated as Mr Pearson suggested in an essay like manner. I agree with him that the difficulty of marking single essays comparatively is very great, though we always have one such essay in the London M A exam^s.

Believe me
Yours faithfully

H. S. Foxwell Esqe MA.   W Stanley Jevons.

393.   W. S. JEVONS TO J. D'AULNIS
        [LJN, 320–1]

Parsonage Road, Withington,
Manchester, 9th October 1874.

. . . I hope that you safely received my former letter, written from Norway, in reply to your letter of 29th June, and also the copy of a printed paper which I posted from Hull when on the point of leaving England.

I have now returned from Norway, and am again engaged in my usual work. I am about to prepare a memoir, to be read at the Statistical Society of Manchester, upon the subject of the mathematical theory of political economy,[1] and if the book which you are proposing to publish is sufficiently advanced, I should much like to draw the attention of the Society to it.

You have stated that your dissertation would be ready in September, but I presume that some of those unavoidable causes of delay, which so often occur in publication, have hitherto prevented its appearance. I look forward with much pleasure to becoming acquainted with your improvements and additions to the theory.

Since receiving your letter I have reflected much upon the point which you mentioned, namely, the exchange of indivisibles; but I cannot say that any mode of improving what I have said in the book has occurred to me, and I await your criticisms on the treatment of it with interest.

---

[1] 'The Progress of the Mathematical Theory of Political Economy, with an explanation of the Principles of the Theory.' Paper read before the Manchester Statistical Society, 11 November 1874 See *Transactions of the Manchester Statistical Society* (1874–75) 1–19. Reprinted in *JRSS*, 37 (1874) 478–88, and in Vol. VII of the present work.

While it is no doubt necessary to work out the theory with fulness and correctness by degrees, yet I think that we need still more at present to make known its simple principles, and show that the notions of value, utility, price, etc., may be made more precise, and may be explained thereby.

I have now received a copy of the first part of M. Walras' treatise, and find that it has been very ingeniously thought out and written. He has, I think, discovered the true principles of the science with the greatest insight and ability, and I shall be truly sorry if he experiences any disappointment at not being quite the first in the field. But, as he remarks, his formulae and general mode of treating the theory are complementary to mine, and both books serve remarkably to confirm and supplement each other. What I mainly regret about the form of M. Walras' book is, that it is in no way adapted to make the principles of the theory more popularly known: it seems almost worse in this respect than my own book. Therefore I feel sure that there is the greatest need of a book to illustrate and explain the new view of the science, and this, as I understand your letter, will be accomplished by your work. I hope, however, that your treatise will not appear only in Hollandaise, but will be translated into French, if not into English, so that it may have a wider range of readers. . . .

394. J. D'AULNIS TO W. S. JEVONS

Bois le Duc. 11 Octobre 1874

Cher Monsieur!

Je vous suis extrêmement reconnaissant de l'envoi de votre mémoire de Juin 1866 et de votre aimable lettre du 7 Juillet.

Ma dissertation est sous presse. Elle va paraître dans un mois, sous le titre: "le Revenu social, un essai d'économie politique théorique." Mon but a été de formuler deux notions économiques; la production et la consommation. Comme vous dîtes, (p. 1. de votre livre) il ne s'agit en économie principalement que de notions élementaires. J'ai donc élaboré les dites notions. Pour cela votre théorie d'*utilité*, de l'*échange*, et aussi en quelque porte du *travail*, et du *capital* m'étaient indispensables. Comme mon livre est une dissertation, pour obtenir le titre de docteur en droit, je devrai la défendre en public contre tous ceux qui voudraient faire opposition, principalement contre les professeurs de la faculté en droit à Leyde. Je vous communiquerai ce que les professeurs, desquels deux sont de bons philosophes, bons économistes, et avec lesquels j'entretiens une amitié assez intime, en diront. D'avance ils m'ont déjà dit qu'ils étaient extrêmement curieux de la nouvelle théorie de la valeur. Et ils ont même déjà reconnu la méthode, comme vraiment philosophique et bonne.

Je me suis efforcé principalement à populariser les théories. C'est pourquoi je suis immédiatement commencé la théorie d'utilité par faire appel à la nature humaine. L'homme est satiable. De là l'utilité de différentes portions varie: ensuite la distinction entre *utilité totale* et *degré d'utilité* (votre "final degree of utility" que vous nommez aussi quelques fois "degree of utility" tout court. pag. 83.128.160.191.) La variation du degré d'utilité par la variation de la *quantité* et de la *courbe de besoin*. Alors vient la théorie de l'échange. Elimination du mot "valeur". Une polémique contre M. Bastiat.[1] (En parenthèse, j'ai entremelé à la théorie quelquefois quelque polémique. C'est le meilleur moyen pour se faire lire.) La théorie elle même, démontrée par la géométrie analytique.

1e Application. La vraie signification de la loi de l'*offre* et de *demande*. Elle n'est que l'expression de la vérité que les variations dans la quantité (offre) et dans les besoins (demande) causent les variations dans le rapport d'échange.

2. Comment on démontre qu'une extension de consommation parmi de classes nouvelles de population est un empêchement d'une baisse excessive des prix.

3. Les prix des grains. Leur variations. Données statistiques de Davenant, de Cordier,[2] de Tooke. Expérience de l'année 1874.

4. Description d'un marché, théoriquement parfait. J'y ai laissé la parole à vous.

5. La vérité $\dfrac{x}{y} = \dfrac{dx}{dy}$ (la méthode mathématique me dispensait de la mettre en avant de la théorie d'échange, comme vous dans le calcul différentiel $\dfrac{x}{y} = \dfrac{dx}{dy}$). Cette vérité cause les grands gains de l'échange.

Si on achète 5 kilogrammes de pain on voudrait peut-être donner

pour le 1er kilogramme	—	1000 florins
2me	,,	—	100
3me	,,	—	50
4me	,,	—	10
5me	,,	—	0.20

[1] Claude Frédéric Bastiat (1801–50), the best-known French advocate of free trade and *laissez-faire*, through his *Sophismes Économiques* (1846) and *Harmonies Économiques* (1850).

[2] Joseph Louis Etienne Cordier (1775–1849), French civil engineer; member of the Chamber of Deputies for Ain, later for the Jura, from 1827. The statistics to which d'Aulnis here refers are given on pp. 495–526 of Cordier's *Mémoire sur l'Agriculture de la Flandre française, et sur l'économie rurale* (1823). Cordier was also author of *La France et l'Angleterre, ou Recherches sur les causes de prosperité et les chances de décadence des deux nations et propositions de reformes* (1843), and numerous works on engineering topics.

Somme 5 kilogrammes. Le prix n'est pas f.1160.20, mais il est
5×0.20=f1.00.

6.   Surrogats ("equivalence of commodities")

7.   Comment un individu tient ses provisions toujours en telle quantité
que les degrés d'utilité sont en raison inverse des rapports d'échange du
marché.

8.   Pour le riche et pour le pauvre sur le même marché au même instant
la *proportion* entre les degrés d'utilité est la même.

9.   Explication théorique comment le "prospective supply" ou le
"prospective demand" influent sur les prix actuels.

10.   Preuve qu'il ne s'agit pas en économie de connaître les *motifs* du
désir, qui constitue l'utilité. Voir MacLeod.[3] "Principles of economical
philosophy." pag. 337.

Théorie d'overproduction

1.   Consommation de materiaux. Une théorie quelque peu nouvelle,
mais bien simple.

2.   Mauvaise distribution du travail.

3.   Mauvaise distribution du capital.

Polémique contre M.W. Roscher, Professeur à Leipsig. Celui-ci a
critiqué en 1874 votre théorie très superficiellement (en six lignes!!) et a
dit que le tout était plus curieux que d'intérêt scientifique.[4] Maintenant
j'ai demontré que Roscher n'a jamais compris quelque chose du
phenomène d'overproduction. Ce qu'il en dit se resout en absurdités. Et
je lui enverrai mon livre! Je crois qu'il sait le Hollandais. Je regrette
beaucoup, Monsieur, que vous ne connaissez pas le Hollandais. Nous
avons dans notre langage des essais précieux d'économie politique. M.
Mees a écrit un "*recueil de quelques chapitres d'économie politique*"[5] un chef
d'oeuvre, qu'on pourrait comparer avec les ouvrages de Ricardo et
Stuart Mill. C'est le meilleur livre sur la distribution des richesses, qui me
soit connu. Il parut à Amsterdam 1866. Ensuite nous avons le traité de M.
v. Houten sur la Valeur.[6] Un petit chef d'oeuvre, d'originalité, de
profondeur, et de critique.

[3] H. D. MacLeod, *The Principles of Economical Philosophy* (1872) 1, 337:
'Some persons indeed consider that it is an inadequate account to say that value originates in
demand, but that the economist should go further, and investigate the causes of demand. But this
would be a great error. This would introduce the whole of psychology into economics.'

[4] Wilhelm G. F. Roscher (1817–94), *Principles of Political Economy,* translated from the thirteenth
German edition by John J. Lalor (Chicago, 1878) v, 22, 103: 'Jevons has recently endeavoured to
give Political Economy a mathematical basis by reducing the objects of which it treats to the feelings
of pleasure (+) and pain (−). The duration of a feeling is treated as an abscissa, its intensity as the
ordinate of a and its quantity as the areas. Future feelings are reduced to present ones, by allowing for
their distance, and the uncertainty of their occurrence. All this, however, is rather curious than
scientifically useful.'

[5] See above, Letter 387, n. 6, p. 58.

[6] Samuel van Houten (1837–1930), *Verhandeling over de Waarde* (Groningen, 1859).

En dernier lieu, des essais fort beaux de M. van Houten en de M. Pierson, dans une Revue scientifique.

Les Hollandais connaissent tous l'Anglais, le Français et l'Allemand. Par cela ils peuvent lire presque tous les ouvrages sur la science. Ils peuvent choisir sans préjudice national ce qui est bon. Ils glanent la vérité chez tous leurs voisins. Et ils se distinguent en général par un eclectisme heureux. Surtout les dissertations des Académies sont quelquefois des monographies très-remarquables. Un étudiant consacre une année spéciale à écrire un essai sur quelque chapitre préféré: ensuite il obtient le titre de "docteur".

Quant à moi je vais m'appliquer après ma promotion, spécialement à l'économie et à la statistique. J'espère de pouvoir compter dans mes études sur l'assistance de M. Pierson et de M. Mees. M. Pierson m'a dit que votre essai "on the coal question" était un modèle de la manière, par laquelle il faut traiter les questions d'Ec. politique appliquée. Quand j'aurai le temps, je vais le lire.

Un de mes amis, le mathématicien, qui m'a aidé à lire votre livre, et à populariser la théorie mathématique; m'a écrit de ces jours que vous aviez édié un "Logic". J'espère que la lecture ne soit pas au dessus de mes forces. Je me sens plus à l'aise dans la logique appliquée que dans la logique théorique.

En somme, comme vous ne savez pas le Hollandais, ce qui est bien natural, nous verrons si je pourrais faire paraitre une traduction française. En tout cas je ne ferai pas cette traduction, qu'après la critique des économistes compatriotes.

Veuillez agréer l'assurance de mon respect.

J. d'Aulnis.

The preceding letter had evidently been written before d'Aulnis received Jevons's letter to him of 9 October 1874 (Letter 393). The first sheet of the following letter is now missing, but the enquiry in the last paragraph about the meeting of the Manchester Statistical Society makes clear that it was written in response to Letter 393. Some of the points made in it were taken up by Jevons in his letter of 25 November 1874 to d'Aulnis (Letter 400). Hence it would seem that it must have been written between 11 October and 25 November 1874.

394A.   J. D'AULNIS TO W. S. JEVONS

[October/November 1874]

Démonstration que le *contrat d'échange* n'a pas une *force productive* par lui même comme prétendait Condillac. La production consiste à créer de l'utilité. Par l'échange on obtient un *droit* sur les choses utiles. Utilité est la *cause*, non *l'effet* de l'échange.

Après avoir demontré ce que c'est que *produire*, le revenu social n'est que la somme de tous les produits.

Ce que c'est que consommer. Le vrai sens des paroles d'Adam Smith: "Consumption is the sole end and purpose of production."

Comment on finit par votre théorie d'*utilité* l'éternel combat entre les économistes, sur la question, si les consommations sont bonnes ou mauvaises pour un peuple. Je démontre qu'il y avait ici confusion de mots. Ceux qui ont prétendu que la consommation était indispensable pour la richesse, avaient la vue que les choses doivent toujours être *utiles*, *désirées*. Mais ça ne conduit pas à la proposition, que les consommations créent les richesses. Par la consommation les richesses (les choses désirées) s'en vont. Le consommation implique toujours un appauvrissement. La nature a lié la consommation à la jouissance humaine. Plus l'homme réussit à jouir de ses richesses, sans les consommer, tant mieux.

Polémique contre Roscher. J'ai démontré que sa fameuse théorie d'un *"équilibre entre les consommations et la production"* nécessaire pour un peuple, répose sur une confusion de mots. Si cette théorie était littéralement vraie l'humanité serait aussi pauvre que dès son existence. La production était presque toujours plus forte que la consommation.

Le contrat d'assurance: comment il rend les consommations inattendues, et extraordinaires, – ordinaires et prévues.

Appendix. Théorie d'échange de commodités indivisibles.

———————

Voici, Cher Monsieur, la table des matières de ma dissertation. Partout je me suis efforcé de démontrer votre mérite envers la science; Comme vous êtes parvenu à ériger un système sur l'idée d'utilité nouvelle. Chez nous, nous avons un prédécesseur de votre théorie dans un M. van Houten, membre des états généraux à la Hage. Il a écrit en 1859 une dissertation sur la Valeur. "La valeur répose sur l'utilité. L'utilité est le même que desirableness." L'atmosphère n'a pas de valeur, parce que *une quantité distincte* "n'est jamais l'objet du désir d'un homme, n'a pas d'utilité!" N'est ce pas remarquable? M. v. Houten est un des hommes les plus éminents de notre petit pays. Il a un influence énorme.

Maintenant je vais vous dire encore une chose. Les meilleurs économistes de notre pays sont M. Mees, président de la Banque Néerlandaise à Amsterdam, et M. Pierson, Directeur de la même Banque. (Ce dernier a déjà lu mon manuscrit.) Ils ont vivement applaudi à votre théorie. Soyez en sur, chez nous son succès est hors doute.

Quant à la théorie de quantités indivisibles je détermine le prix d'une maison (par exemple), par la quantité d'argent que veut donner la plus pauvre homme sur le marché. C'est pour ça que dans une ville le prix des maisons peut baisser si vîte par une augmentation de la quantité. L'architecte doit vendre bientôt ses maisons à des familles pauvres. Celles-ci ne donnent jamais beaucoup. Eh bien, ils dépressent les prix aussi pour les plus riches, car $\dfrac{x}{y} = \dfrac{dx}{dy}$. Que pensez vous de ce mode de détermination?

Comme vous le dites, le livre de M. Walras est moins populaire que le votre. Sa méthode mathématique est un peu compliquée: elle n'est pas assez simple. M. Walras a envoyé son livre à beaucoup d'économistes de ce pays, dont je lui avais fourni l'adresse. M. Pierson était de la même opinion, que vous, sur ce livre. Néanmoins l'originalité en est grande; il y a des idées vraiment nouvelles, et de la plus grande importance pour le progrès de la science.

Veuillez m'écrire quand aura lieu la conférence du "Statistical Society of Manchester." S'il m'est possible, je vous enverrai les épreuves, dans lesquelles la théorie est traitée. Vous pourrez voir par les figures la simplicité de l'exposition.

Croyez moi, en attendant

Cher Monsieur

votre très dévoué

J. d'Aulnis de Bourouill

395.   W. S. JEVONS TO R. H. INGLIS PALGRAVE

Parsonage Road,
Withington, Manchester.
2 Nov 74

My dear Palgrave,

I have read the proof of your article[1] with much interest and am obliged to you for letting me see it. I am sorry however to say that I do not agree with it as much as I usually do with your writings on currency.

[1] 'The Effect of Superseding the Existing English Country Note Issue with the Notes of the Bank of England', *Bankers' Magazine*, 34 (1874) 877–87.

I may be heterodox but I agree with Gladstone & not with Tooke & Newmarch. The dictum of the latter that a banker cannot increase his issues beyond a certain point is quite opposed to truth. It is true that he cannot at any one moment force an unlimited amount of paper into circulation, but every additional note which he puts out acts as if there were so much more gold; prices thus tend to rise, & the exchanges turn against the country so that gold is exported – thus there is room for a further issue of notes and a renewal of the process – All the while the notes may be perfectly convertible into gold, & it is the whole mass gold & notes which are depreciated in company. In this way supposing all the bankers or many to have the power of unlimited issue, the notes will go on gradually driving out the gold so that a larger & larger circulation will be maintained on a narrower basis.† Of course if those bankers were perfectly wise they would stop at a certain point, but this is hardly in human nature so that, as often occurred both in America & England, the very convertibility of the notes was ultimately endangered.

I perfectly agree therefore with the restriction placed on the country bank issues, and only regret that Peel could not carry out the measure perfectly, by constituting the Issue dept. of the B. of Eng. as the sole note issuer.

The stringency of the money market is not a question of note circulation only, because everyone is at liberty to use gold and the notes are only a temporary substitute for gold, partly to save the trouble of carrying gold & partly to save the interest on that part which is issued upon securities.

As to the general question of the sensitiveness of the money market I think it entirely arises from the competition between English bankers obliging them to work with the smallest possible reserves and make a profit upon every pound they can. It is a want of reserve capital not a want of money and nothing will save us from trouble but more caution & more reserves. It is impossible that the B. of Eng. or any one bank can keep reserves for the whole country the bankers must look to their own reserves, and the fact that they habitually work so very closely is the strongest possible argument against allowing them to have any discretion in the issue of notes.

I dare say you are right about the country issues not coinciding with the districts where business is active but my answer would be that there is no reason why the population should not use B. of Eng. notes & gold to any extent they like, because anyone who has the requisite balance at his bankers can get either he likes.

Your paper is full of the most useful information & it puts the views to which I am opposed in the most distinct light, but I am none the less opposed to those views. I fear the Currency question is fated to produce divisions of opinion until Doomsday. I return the proofs as you have not requested me to keep them.

Yours very faithfully,
W. S. Jevons

†This argument must be somewhat modified since the prohibition of £1 notes – since of course a certain proportion of sovereigns must be maintained as change for the £5 notes.[2]

396.   R. H. INGLIS PALGRAVE TO W. S. JEVONS

Private

Great Yarmouth
11th Nov. 1874.

My dear Jevons,

Thank you for your letter. Fortunately there are a great many subjects on which we do agree – of course I should have been most glad if you, whose scientific training and insight are so far beyond mine, could have agreed with me on 'Currency' also – but I cannot help holding the opinions I do – I fully agree with you on the question of 'Reserves' – but as Bagehot has very clearly pointed out in his 'Lombard Street' we must be content with attempting to improve the system that exists. To *set up* another new, quite fresh one, however perfect, would be impossible.

We happen in this neighbourhood to experience an annual and large demand for 'money' – by which in this case I mean coin or note. When the fishing boats at this and a neighbouring port are paid off very few 'cheques' are circulated, or can be circulated among the crews who now receive their 'wages' – which are whole pay for the entire fishing voyage handed over to them in one lump sum. That is to say the men on one day receive the reward for some 3 months labour. By far the larger part of this sum, which is in the aggregate very considerable, is paid to the men in 'coin' or 'notes' – and is at once then put into 'circulation' – but it does not ever stay in 'circulation' more than a very few days. Besides a large sum in gold the payments in our notes last year were fully 30-m. I enclose you the copy of our Gazette returns from the commencement of Dec. 73 to the close of Feb. 74 – you will see by it how our circulation immediately rose about Xmas, when the herring voyage is concluded – and how rapidly it returned to its former level. We could, I admit, put this amount into circulation but we have no power to retain it in circulation – and I take it that the position of all other Bankers is really similar to our own.

---

[2] In the original manuscript this comment is written in the margin of the sheet on which the argument appears.

We cannot force one single coin into circulation more than the wants of our customers require.

I have marked this 'private' merely because, though it gives very little information beyond what any person may obtain from the published Returns, it goes a while into some business questions – and I shall be obliged by your keeping it to yourself – except of course so far as it is a quotation from the Gazette returns [1] – which are at everyone's disposal. I mention it as one instance, and a curious one, of the manner in which the matter works.

I think of continuing my last paper [2] – and if you care to see what I have said I shall have much pleasure in sending you the proofs to work on, as I sent you the last – not that I at all hope to induce you to agree with me – but you may like to know what I have said on the subject. I do not wish at all to write on the question from a 'Banking' point of view only, but from a general one. The advantage of the privilege of note issues is now rather the convenience of it than as a source of profit. If I felt it opposed to the real welfare of the country I should not hesitate to hold that opinion – but it is the manner in which the existing arrangements aggravate the fluctuations in the Central Reserve which I have decided to write about.

I am yours very truly,
R. H. Inglis Palgrave

Circulation of notes of Y. & S. Bank [3]
for the weeks ending with the
dates stated. [4]

1873

Dec.	6	£34,865
	13	35,854
	20	53,360
	27	60,575

1874

Jan.	3	47,480
	10	43,481
	17	42,529
	24	38,490
	31	37,045
Feb.	7	35,413
	14	34,235
	21	33,685

[1] The *London Gazette* each week published 'An Account, pursuant to the Act 7 & 8 Vict. c. 32, of

397.   W. S. JEVONS TO L. BODIO
        [LJN, 323–4]

The Owens College, Manchester,
12th November 1874.

. . . . I have been informed by my correspondent, M. Léon Walras of Lausanne, that you take an interest in the mathematical treatment of the science of political economy, and that you are inclined to look favourably upon attempts to reform the science. I have, therefore, been encouraged to forward to you by book post, registered, a copy of my work on the *Theory of Political Economy*, published in 1871. This work was very unfavourably received in this country, and almost the only English economist of importance who noticed it, namely, Professor J. E. Cairnes, repudiated it altogether.

Nevertheless I am quite convinced of the substantial truth and importance of the view put forward, and am much gratified to find that the profound and ingenious researches of M. Walras, pursued as they have been in an independent manner, lead to the same conclusions.

This remarkable coincidence of results emboldens me to bring the book to your knowledge, in the hope that it may receive the approval of yourself and of some of the other distinguished representatives of the science in Italy. . . .

398.   W. S. JEVONS TO MRS LUCY HUTTON
        [LJN, 324]

Parsonage Road, Withington,
19th November 1874.

. . . My books are beginning to pay at last. The little *Lessons* sells 2500 copies a year, and is now paying about £70 a year. Three other books pay about £3 : 10s. between them. I think I am going to write more school or college books. I hear that my *Theory of Political Economy* is going to be translated into Italian.[1] I am much oppressed with the too abundant exercises of my logic class. . . .

---

the average amount of Bank Notes of the Several Banks of Issue in England and Wales, in circulation during the week ending . . .'

    [2] See above, Letter 356, n. 2, p. 10.

    [3] The Yarmouth and Suffolk Bank, under Gurneys Birkbeck & Co., in which Palgrave was a partner.

    [4] On this sheet of the original manuscript there is a note in the handwriting of W. S. Jevons – 'Palgrave – Circ. at Grt Yarmouth'.

    [1] See below, Letter 409, p. 94.

399. W. S. JEVONS TO G. H. DARWIN
     [LJN, 324–5]

Parsonage Road, Withington,
24th November, 1874

. . . I shall be very happy to read anything you have written about the theory of political economy though it would be more to satisfy my own curiosity than because I should be likely to suggest any alterations.[1]

It is very gratifying to hear that you are so clearly in favour of the mathematical treatment of the subject, as it would be difficult to meet with any who join mathematical and economical knowledge and ability in a manner better calculated to allow of forming a sound judgment than they are joined in you, as I am well assured.

I much regret that Cairnes should have raised such absurd objections to the theory, proceeding entirely from misapprehension. His remarks may temporarily prejudice the theory, and it would be a great advantage if you would thoroughly refute them, without using too many mathematical symbols, so as to frighten readers away. I am more afraid of this with English readers than of Cairnes, and I think his objections may serve as a good opportunity for explaining the principles of utility.

I do not know whether you have seen my paper on the subject, read to the Manchester Statistical Society, but in case you have not, I send a paper containing a copy of it.

Walras' method may be rather intricate, but it is ingenious, and I think sound. There are also certainly some valuable novelties in his book, but I have not studied them very closely yet.

P.S. I now have a Dutch treatise on the theory of political economy, by d'Aulnis de Bourouill of the Leyden University. . . .

400. W. S JEVONS TO J. D'AULNIS
     [LJN, 325–7]

Parsonage Road, Withington,
Manchester.
25th November 1874

. . . I received the very welcome copy of your dissertation about two days ago, and write to say how much pleased I feel that you have thought it worth while to treat so fully of the mathematical theory of political economy

[1] This letter foreshadows the review of Cairnes's *Some Leading Principles of Political Economy newly expounded* (1874) which G. H. Darwin wrote under the title 'The Theory of Exchange Value', *Fortnightly Review*, 17 (1875) 252. See below, Letter 403, p. 87.

I regret very much that I am quite unable to read the book or follow the argument to any extent. Fortunately the Dutch and English languages are very closely akin, and the Norse is evidently closely related to both, so that I can here and there gather the meaning of a few sentences. I am intending to borrow a Dutch dictionary, which will enable me to go farther. However, the notes, diagrams, and other indications show me very often the nature of the discussion, independently of the statements in your last letter. Your work is written, I should think, in a manner well calculated to secure attention to the subject, and I wish that I could study the additions and improvements which you have made.

I am particularly curious to know your theory about the exchange of indivisibles treated in the appendix. If you have now more leisure time, could you give me a slight sketch of your way of treating the subject?

I feel what an advantage it must be to have a command of so many languages as your countrymen. Those whom I have met in travelling were often remarkable linguists.

I have sent you a copy of a newspaper containing a report of a paper I read to the Manchester Statistical Society, and I will send you a formal copy when printed.

I am desirous of offering for your acceptance a copy of my book on logic, the *Principles of Science*, but should like to know exactly to what address it should be sent, and whether you will be in Leyden to receive it.

Is the work of M. Van Houten written in French? If so, and in fact in any case, I should like to have its exact title. I hope some time or other to form an historical sketch of opinions bearing on utility and value, and it would be necessary to introduce his views.

Would it be too much trouble if I were to ask you to send me the exact addresses and names of a few of the most eminent economists of your country, to whom I might with advantage send copies of any papers referring to the theory of political economy?

In asking you to explain your theory of exchange of indivisibles,[1] I did not overlook the brief explanations which you have already given, that it is the poorer purchasers which determine the price for the rich. But this can only apply where there are many articles of a similar character, and it will not, as far as I can see, overcome the difficulty alluded to in p. 122 of my book, of an isolated exchange of indivisible objects of value.

In sending a copy of my book on logic, can it be delivered at Bois le Duc by railway, or will it not be better for me to send it to some address at Leyden? It will be too heavy to go by post. . . .

[1] In LJ, p. 326, this word is given as 'divisibles', but this is contrary to the whole sense of the passage and is evidently a misprint.

401.   J. D'AULNIS TO W. S. JEVONS

Boisleduc, ce 25 Nov. 1874

Cher Monsieur,

Je vous remercie bien cordialement de l'envoi du "Manchester Examiner", dans lequel j'ai lu avec le plus grand intérêt votre adresse à la Société de Statistique de Manchester. Aussitôt que je vais à Amsterdam je ferai lire votre adresse aux économistes, M. W. C. Mees, et M. N. G. Pierson.

Comme je suppose, que vous aurez déjà reçu ma dissertation sur le Revenu de la Société, je m'empresserai de vous envoyer si tôt que possible la note explicative en Anglais ou en Français, que je vous ai promise. Mais à présent je manque le temps, que la composition d'une telle note exige d'une personne, qui, comme moi, n'est pas assez linguiste pour écrire facilement en langages étrangères. Je vous prie donc de vouloir attendre un peu. Je m'acquitterai de mon devoir.

M. Land,[1] Professeur en logique à Leide, m'a parlé avec la plus grande distinction de votre ouvrage récemment publié: "Principles of Science, etc." Il ne savait point, que vous aviez publié un livre sur l'Economie politique, et en recevant ma dissertation, il était bien surpris de trouver votre nom sur le premier page, avec l'annonce que vous aviez découvert une nouvelle théorie sur la valeur; – il s'est mis à lire ma dissertation et je suis heureux de vous dire, que M. Land a applaudi vivement votre théorie. Aussi il m'a assuré qu'il a pu lire coulamment tout mon opuscule, quoiqu'il était étranger à la science d'Economie politique. De plusieurs personnes distinguées j'ai reçu l'assurance qu'ils étaient vivement intéressés à la question et qu'ils ne tarderaient point à lire le livre avec attention et intérêt. Il est donc probable que votre théorie sera critiquée sans préjudice et d'une manière purement scientifique.

Veuillez agréer, cher Monsieur, l'assurance du plus haut respect de
votre très dévoué
J. d'Aulnis de Bourouill

---

docteur en droit

[1] Jan Pieter Nicolaas Land (1834–97), philosopher, theologian and musicologist; Professor of Philosophy at Leiden from 1872.

402.   L. WALRAS TO W. S. JEVONS

Lausanne, 28 novembre 1874[1]

Cher Monsieur,

J'ai reçu ces jours-ci le no. du *Manchester Examiner* que vous avez eu la bonté de m'envoyer et dans lequel se trouve votre mémoire sur *l'application des mathématiques à l'économie politique*. Ce morceau m'a paru tout à fait de nature à faire faire à la question quelque chemin dans l'opinion publique et je ne doute pas que vous ne soyez disposé à le répandre. Aussi profité-je de mon premier moment de loisir pour vous donner quelques indications à cet égard.

Vous l'aurez envoyé, je pense, à ceux de nos amis d'Italie que vous citez ainsi qu'à MM. Messedaglia et Ferrara. Ce dernier est tout à fait capital. Vous pourriez joindre à ces noms les suivants:

Professeur Vito Cusumano, Université de Palerme.[2]

      ”   Cognetti de Martiis, Institut royal technique, Mantoue.[3]

M. Antonino Basile, rédacteur de l'*Economista d'Italia*, 42 via Fontanella di Borghese, Rome.[4]

Je n'ai pas encore recueilli d'adhésions bien positives et bien explicites en Suisse et en Allemagne. Cependant j'ai de ce côté quelques relations

[1] In Jaffé, *Walras Correspondence*, 1, 455, the date of this letter is given as '29 novembre', because the figure in the draft in Fonds Walras is overwritten and ambiguous: the original letter in Jevons Papers is clearly dated '28 9bre 1874'. There are also more differences between the text of this letter and the draft than in previous instances, as noted below:

	Walras Correspondence	*Jevons Papers*
para 1	mes premiers moments de loisir	mon premier moment de loisir
para 2	Fontanella di Borghi	Fontanella di Borghese
	Basile's name precedes	Basile's name follows
	Cognetti de Martiis	Cognetti de Martiis
para 3	comme vous verrez	comme vous le verrez
	je connais [bien]	je connaissais
	la prochaine occasion	la première occasion
para 4	pour faire	pour nous faire
para 6	écrire à M	écrire aussi à M
	je vous engage	je vous ai engagé
para 7	que en somme nos affaires	que nos affaires, en somme
para 7	Mémoires, revues	Mémoires, résumés
para 7	nos correspondances	notre correspondance
para 7	que les bons goûts interdisent	que le bon goût interdit

[2] Vito Cusumano (1843–1908), Professor of Political Economy at Palermo, an adherent of the German historical school.

[3] Salvatore Cognetti de Martiis (1844–1901), served as a soldier with Garibaldi; Professor of Political Economy at Mantua, 1868–79, and subsequently at Turin; continued *Biblioteca dell'Economista* initiated by Franceso Ferrara.

[4] Antonino Basile, author of *Della Due Scuole Economiche in Italia* (Rome, 1875).

entamées que je mets à votre disposition. Ce sont les suivantes:
Professeur Gustave Vogt, Université de Zurich. [5]

,,	Hanssen,	,,	de Göttingen. [6]
,,	Carl Knies,	,,	de Heidelberg.[7]
,,	Schmoller,	,,	de Strasbourg.
,,	Friedrich Knapp,	Chef au bureau de statistique,

Leipzig. [8]

M. Julius Faucher, rédacteur en chef du *Volkswirtschaftlichen Vierteljahr-schrift*, Berlin.[9] M. Edouard Pfeiffer, 10 See Strasse, Stuttgart.[10]

Pour ce qui est de la France, j'espère que vous n'aurez pas oublié M. Joseph Garnier, rédacteur en chef du *Journal des Economistes*, 14 rue Richelieu, Paris, ni M. Langel du *Temps*. Ce dernier nous a fait, dans sa *Causerie scientifique* du 14 octobre, un article qui vaut peu comme discussion, mais qui vaut beaucoup comme publicité.[11] Je ne sais si vous avez eu cet article. A tout hasard je vous l'envoie ainsi qu'un autre no du *Temps*, du 10 novembre, où il est encore question de nous dans le feuilleton. Comme vous le verrez, notre idée commence à paraître assez bonne pour valoir la peine de nous être disputée. Je connaissais le mémoire de M. Dupuit dont il est ici question. M. Dupuit y a effectivement abordé le problème de l'expression mathématique de l'utilité; mais il ne l'a nullement résolu. Je n'ai pas jugé à propos d'engager cette discussion avec le *Temps* dès à présent, mais je me réserve d'établir le fait à la première occasion favorable.

Je n'ai encore trouvé personne pour nous faire un article dans la *Revue des Deux Mondes* et dans le *Journal des Débats*. Ces deux organes seraient décisifs; mais précisément à cause de cela, je ne veux rien précipiter. En voici, par exemple, deux autres auxquels le moment me paraît venu de s'adresser.

L'un est la *Critique Philosophique* dirigé par M. Ch. Renouvier.[12] M. Renouvier m'a promis un article sur la question de méthode. Il vous

[5] Gustav Vogt (1829—1901), Professor of Public Law at the University of Zürich, 1870—1901.

[6] Georg Hanssen (1809—94), specialist in German rural economy.

[7] Karl Gustav Adolf Knies (1821—98), Professor at Marburg and Freiburg until 1865 and at Heidelberg from 1865 until 1896; one of the 'older generation' of the German Historical school and early exponent of its methodology.

[8] Georg Friedrich Knapp (1842—1926), a disciple of Schmoller, best known for his *Staatliche Theorie des Geldes* (1905); Professor Extraordinarius at Leipzig, 1869—74; Professor at the University of Strassburg, 1874—1907.

[9] Julius Faucher (1820—78), a leader of 'Manchesterismus' in Germany; editor of *Vierteljahrsschrift für Volkswirthschaft und Cultur geschichte* (Berlin, 1863—93) from 1863 until his death.

[10] Eduard Pfeiffer (1835—1921), a leader of the German consumer co-operative movement and Walras's first correspondent outside French-speaking countries. See Jaffé, *Walras Correspondence*, I, 300.

[11] Langel's unsigned review in *Le Temps* drew largely on a letter which Walras had written to him on 25 September 1874, and which is reproduced in Jaffé, *Walras Correspondence*, I, 433—4.

[12] *La Critique philosophique, politique, scientifique, litteraire* was edited at this time by Charles Bernard

faudrait lui écrire, à La Verdette, près Avignon (Vaucluse) pour lui dire que je vous ai informé de ses dispositions et que je vous ai engagé à lui envoyer votre volume et votre mémoire que vous joindriez à votre lettre.

L'autre est la *Revue Scientifique* dont le rédacteur en chef est M. Emile Alglave.[13] Cette revue, assez importante, et qui a succédé à l'ancienne *Revue des Cours Scientifiques* publie, comme sa devancière, des leçons de professeurs français et étrangers. A ce titre je lui ai demandé l'insertion d'un résumé de mon ouvrage que j'ai fait moi-même avec le plus grand soin. Vous devriez, ce me semble, écrire aussi à M. Emile Alglave, 36 rue Gay-Lussac, à Paris et lui dire, comme à M. Renouvier, que je vous ai engagé à lui envoyer vos publications. A votre place mis, je lui demanderais la reproduction du Mémoire dans sa Revue. S'il n'avait personne pour faire la traduction je m'en chargerais volontiers. Il pourrait ainsi, par la publication de vos deux documents, donner à ses lecteurs une première idée de la question. Après quoi il serait libre de faire, s'il le voulait, un article de critique. Pour ne pas allonger cette lettre outre mesure, je me bornerai à vous dire que nos affaires, en somme vont bien sur le continent selon moi. Pour qu'elles continuent à aller de mieux en mieux, je crois que nous devons, pendant quelque temps encore, payer de notre personne en multipliant les explications soit dans des Mémoires, résumés, analyses, soit dans notre correspondance avec les professeurs et publicistes. Je suis également convaincu que rien ne nous sert mieux que de nous appuyer moi sur vous et vous sur moi. On ne saurait croire combien on est peu prophète en son pays et combien un nom étranger a du prestige. Mais je craindrais, en insistant sur ce point, de paraître trop vouloir vous faire comprendre combien il est spirituel et ingénieux de nous faire l'un à l'autre les compliments que le bon goût interdit à chacun de nous de se décerner à lui-même.

Très cordialement tout à vous

Léon Walras

Renouvier (1815–1903), a mathematician who had turned to philosophy. The anonymous review which he published in the issues of 28 January 1875 (Vol. 3, II, 405–11) and 25 March 1875 (Vol. 4, I, 122–9) dealt with the work of Walras and is summarised in Jaffé, *Walras Correspondence*, I, 449.

[13] Emile Alglave (1842–1928), Professor of Public Finance at the Paris Faculty of Law.

403. W. S. JEVONS TO G. H. DARWIN
    [LJN, 327–8]

Parsonage Road, Withington.
29th November 1874

. . . I have read your article[1] with much interest, and am glad to find that you almost perfectly agree with me. I have made a few marks upon the paper, but none of any consequence. All that I have to say about the form of the article is that it can hardly be called, as it stands, a review of Cairnes' book, but rather a defence of mine. If you publish it as a review of Cairnes' it would clearly be desirable to say something more, in fact much more, at the beginning about the excellence of other portions of his book. There can be no doubt of the value of Cairnes' discussions of many questions, though on the theory of value I think him so unfortunate.[2]

As regards the channel of publication, you know quite as well as I do what is best, and I should hardly like to make suggestions.

I have been reading your article in the *Contemporary*[3] with much interest, and am glad to find the puerile style of Max Muller's reasoning (as it has always struck me) so well shown up. It is impossible not to admire his flow of learning, and his agreeable and instructive style. He has done an immense deal for linguistic study in England, but when he approaches theory or argument he makes the most extraordinary blunders.

It is curious you think your handwriting bad. I think I have seldom or never read a more legible paper. It is almost as easy to read as type.

When you have time, I wish you would consider the mathematical nature of the equations (*Theory of Political Economy*, pp. 99–101, etc.) I have a standing difference with my friend Barker, who says they are (or at any rate ought to be) differential equations demanding integration, whereas I hold that, though deduced by the use of differentials, they are simple algebraic equations. The problem, as I regard it, is a statistical one, closely analogous to that of the lever as treated according to virtual velocities.[4]

---

[1] See above, Letter 399, n. 1, p. 81.

[2] Cf. R. D. Collison Black, 'Jevons and Cairnes', *Economica*, 20 (1960) 231.

[3] G. H. Darwin, 'Professor Whitney on the Origin of Language', *Contemporary Review*, 24 (1874) 894–904. And see Friedrich Max Muller, 'My Reply to Mr. Darwin', *Contemporary Review*, 25 (1875) 305–26.

[4] The equations to which Jevons was referring were his well known equations of exchange set out in the section headed 'Symbolic Statement of the Theory' of the chapter on the Theory of Exchange in *T.P.E.* In the first edition this appeared on pp. 99–103 and was immediately followed by the section headed 'Impediments to Exchange'. In the second edition Jevons inserted a new section between these two, headed 'Analogy to the Theory of the Lever' in which he justified his view of the nature of the equations more fully. See *T.P.E.* (fourth edition) pp. 102–6. Since in *T.P.E.* Jevons

I have to be in Cambridge at the end of the week for the Moral Science Tripos examination,[5] and may perhaps have the pleasure of making your acquaintance. . . .

404.   W. S. JEVONS TO MRS LUCY HUTTON
       [LJN, 328]

Bull Hotel, Cambridge,
6th December 1874.

. . . We spent about two days in London, rather successfully, and came here on Saturday afternoon. We have not yet been out into the streets, but the town looks very interesting from the window. We have had a great many visitors already, and they seem to come at all hours. We have invitations already for most of the days we shall be here, and are not likely to be dull. The examination work is fortunately much lighter than I expected, as there are practically only thirteen men and two women candidates. . . .

405.   J. D'AULNIS TO W. S. JEVONS

Amsterdam le 8 Dec. 1874
Cher Monsieur,
    Bien volontiers je vais vous répondre aux diverses questions, que vous m'avez faites dans votre dernière lettre; mais en premier lieu, je vous remercie de tout mon coeur à cause de l'aimable offre de votre ouvrage important sur la Logique. En étudiant l'économie politique j'ai éprouvé vivement la nécessité de faire étude de la Logique, une science qui est trop négligée non seulement dans ma patrie; mais aussi ailleurs. Vous comprenez donc comment je suis charmé de votre offre; et que je l'accepte avec la plus grande complaisance. Mon adresse, à laquelle vous pourrez expédier le paquet par chemin de fer, est toujours encore à *Boisleduc.*
    La dissertation de M. van Houten est publiée en 1859 à Gronigue. Elle est intitulée "*Verhandeling over de Waarde*" (treatise on value). L'auteur a

---

abstracts from the problem of integration by considering only what he calls the 'purely statical problem' rather than the 'problem of dynamics', it seems likely that the word 'statistical' on p. 328 of LJ was a misprint for 'statical'.
    [5] See above, Letter 392A, p. 69.

emporté en 1858 le prix d'argent à l'occasion d'un concours scientifique que la Faculté de Droit à Leyde avait proposé sur la question de la Valeur. Les idées les plus remarquables de M. van Houten sont:

1. En économie pol. Utilité ne peut être que "desirability, desirableness".

2. L'air n'a pas de la valeur, parce qu'une *quantité distincte* n'est pas l'objet du désir de l'homme.

3. Pour trouver la loi de la Valeur il faut analyser un seul contrat d'échange: car la loi, qui se manifeste par une série d'échanges, se trouve dans chaque échange en particulier.

4. Le problème de la Valeur doit finalement se résoudre par une bonne solution de la loi d'offre et de demande.

De plus les critiques de M. van Houten contre divers auteurs sont ingénieuses et tranchantes. La dissertation est, à mes yeux, le meilleur traité sur la Valeur, qui ait paru avant votre livre, quoique s'y trouvent encore beaucoup de passages obscurs et confus. Nil mirum! Si vous auriez plaisir à recevoir la dite dissertation, je tâcherai d'en acquérir un exemplaire et de vous l'offrir.

Je vous donnerais bien volontiers une liste des principaux économistes de ce pays, mais je ne crois pas que vous auriez beaucoup de satisfaction par l'envoi des papiers, que vous avez mentionnés. Je crains que ces économistes, qui n'ont peut être pas encore entièrement lu ma dissertation, et qui n'ont pour la plupart point étudié votre "Theory of P.E.", ne se soient pas rendus assez familiers avec la théorie, en calcul differentiel, en terminologie nouvelle, pour comprendre et apprécier les expositions courtes et abstruses d'une petite note. Quant à moi j'ose vous confesser que j'ai eu beaucoup de peine à saisir entièrement la théorie, et que si je ne l'avais pas connu par votre "Theory of P.E." je n'aurais presque absolument rien compris de la note, que vous m'avez envoyée en Juillet. Je vous conseille donc (si j'ose vous donner conseil) de ne pas envoyer les notes, concernant la théorie, aux économistes Hollandais, et d'attendre en tout cas jusqu'au moment, où l'opinion du public compétent Néerlandais se sera manifestée plus clairement.

Cependant si vous voudriez envoyer la note à M. N. G. Pierson, à Amsterdam, vous lui feriez sans doute beaucoup de plaisir. C'est lui qui a fixé mon attention sur votre ouvrage, en m'écrivant en Février 1874, que votre ouvrage était le seul bon quant aux questions fondamentales de la théorie économique. En outre cet économiste, qui sait parfaitement l'Anglais et connaît presque tous les ouvrages de quelque renommée sur la science, a adopté votre méthode de diagrammes pour représenter les *quantités distinctes* desquelles il s'agit dans presque toutes les questions théoriques de la science. Il a publié de ces jours un petit traité fort intéressant sur le "Wagefund-theory" et d'autres questions, concernant la condition sociale des travailleurs;[1] et il a illustré ses idées par un diagramme, que repose sur la géométrie analytique. Je lui ai donné le numéro du "Manchester Examiner", qu'il lirait avec le plus grand intérêt.

Quant à la théorie de l'échange de commodités indivisibles, je conviens que je n'ai point réussi à déterminer le Rapport d'échange dans le cas d'un échange isolé d'une chose indivisible. Mais serait il de haut intérêt pour la science, à déterminer les prix de telles choses indivisibles et isolées? Une loi d'économie ne s'y manifeste point distinctement. Vous même avez fait l'objection à W. T. Thornton,[2] qui a nié l'existence d'une loi d'offre et de demande, parcequ'il ne l'apercevait point "in retail trade or in Dutch auction"! Quel interêt y a t il donc à determiner le prix pour lequel la Russie a vendu Alaska? Je me trouve aussi incapable que vous à determiner le prix dans des échanges parfaitement isolées, de commodités indivisibles. Mais je crois avoir le droit de me consoler de l'idée, que le problème n'est pas de haut interêt pour une science, qui s'occupe plus d'échanges de quantités divisibles, et d'échanges non-isolées.

Je me suis fait installer comme avocat à Amsterdam, et je me propose de vouer mon temps libre à l'étude de l'Economie politique. Pour cela je vais étudier en premier lieu avec soin l'ouvrage de Stuart Mill; je vais en faire une critique rigoureuse, afin d'en retenir ce qui me paraît bon et de rejeter ce qui me paraîtra mauvais. Mais je me souviendrai pendant cette étude de votre belle remarque, que toute théorie nouvelle doit être constructive, destructive et conservative. D'un côté hérétique, je me sens d'autre côté conservateur en matière scientifique. J'ai taché par toute ma dissertation de rattacher les idées nouvelles aux anciennes. Voici la traduction de la première page du Préface de ma dissertation: Quelques mots me paraissent nécessaire pour informer le lecteur sur une nouvelle théorie, que j'ai développée dans cet opuscule.

La théorie concerne la question de la Valeur et fut publiée en 1871 par W. Stanley Jevons, Professeur en Logique et en Economie à Manchester. Le défaut d'idées claires sur la Valeur a donné naissance à une discussion vive sur les questions les plus graves de l'Economie, depuis le commencement de la science jusqu'à nos jours; cette discussion a presque perpétuellement offert le spectacle d'une confusion à peu près immense.

[1] In 1874 Pierson published a translation of P. Leroy Beaulieu's *La Question Ouvriere au dix-neuvieme siècle* into Dutch. To this he added three original articles of his own, on Trade Unions, Strikes and Wages, and Co-operative Societies. The article on Strikes and Wages was published in *Zeitschrift für die gesamte Staatswissenschaft*, 32 (1876) 216–42 under the title 'Arbeitseinstellungen und Arbeitslohne'. In this German version the diagram referred to by d'Aulnis appears on p. 223: it is a simple Ricardian rent diagram designed to show that if workers combine to raise wages the resultant increase of costs will cause the least fertile land to be thrown out of cultivation, producing a reduction of employment.

[2] See W. T. Thornton, *On Labour* (second edition, 1870) chapter 1, 'Of Supply and Demand, and of their Influence on "Prices and Wages"', especially pp. 56–8.

On aurait donc rendu à la science un service éminent par une bonne solution du problème de la Valeur. Stanley Jevons croit avoir découvert la solution. Je laisse au public compétent la décision, jusqu' à quel point Jevons a heureusement accompli sa tâche importante. De mon côté je tiens à constater que la théorie excelle par une méthode rigoureusement logique; qu'elle est en pleine harmonie avec les faits, qu'elle veut expliquer; qu'elle met en état d'apprécier ce qu'un Ricardo, un Stuart Mill, un Senior ont écrit sur le sujet; tandis qu'elle suit la direction plus philosophique, désignée à la science par Courcelle Seneuil,[3] Macleod et van Houten, et même confirme et, à ainsi dire, couronne beaucoup d'idées originales de ces auteurs plus récents. Bien loin donc de débuter par la protestation arrogante que tout ce qui est écrit antérieurement sur la Valeur est totalement dénué de fondament, et bien loin de nier ainsi le développement nécessaire de vérités scientifiques, cette théorie mène à une appréciation juste de beaucoup de résultats d'investigation scientifique antérieure.

Alors suit le petit roman qui a eu lieu en Mai et en Juin à l'égard des théories de M. Léon Walras à Lausanne.

Agréez, Cher Monsieur, l'assurance du parfait dévouement de
J. d'Aulnis de Bourouill

406. W. SUMMERS[1] TO W. S. JEVONS

Sunnyside,
Ashton under Lyne.
December 12th, 1874

Dear Sir,

I take the liberty of sending you a copy of a letter which I sent to the Examiner immediately after the publication in that Journal of the article entitled 'Mr. Stanley Jevons on Political Economy',[2] but which I need hardly say the Examiner refused to publish. My letter ran as follows:—

[3] Cf. above, Letter 387, n. 9. This linking of Courcelle-Seneuil's approach with that of Macleod accords with the view given by Jevons in *T.P.E.* (second edition) p. 275: 'There are valuable suggestions towards the improvement of the science contained in the works of such writers as Senior, Cairnes, Macleod, Cliffe Leslie, Hearn, Shadwell, not to mention a long series of French economists from Baudeau and Le Trosne down to Bastiat and Courcelle-Seneuil.' In the first edition this list read 'Senior, Banfield, Cairnes, Jennings and Hearn, not to mention such original foreign authors as Courcelle-Seneuil or Bastiat'.

[1] William Summers (1853–93): educated at Owens College, Manchester, and afterwards at University College London; awarded the Prize and First Certificate in Logic and Mental and Moral Philosophy, and the Second Certificate in Political Economy in Jevons's classes at Owens in 1871–2; M.P. for Stalybridge, 1880–5, and for Huddersfield, 1886–93.

[2] *The Examiner*, 28 November 1874, pp. 1294–5. The article was an attack on Jevons's address to the Manchester Statistical Society. See above, Letter 393, n. 1, p. 70.

To the Editor of the Examiner.

Sir,

I write to protest against the entire spirit of the anonymous article in your last issue entitled 'Mr. Stanley Jevons on Political Economy'. The language which its author has thought fit to adopt would be natural enough in the mouth of a bigot, but we have a right to expect better things from a journal whose chief boast would seem to be that it exists for the expression of free-thought. The article of which I am speaking deals largely in a method of controversy which one had fondly hoped was dying out, and furnishes another example of that style of criticism (if such it can be called) of which the chief point lies in the imputation of interested motives. That a man cannot come forward to defend his own writings from the criticisms that have been passed upon them, or to express his dissent from some prevailing views on confessedly difficult subjects in Political Economy, without having cast in his teeth the imputation that he is doing all this merely to exalt himself and put down another, and not for truth's sake, does not bespeak a very advanced state of public morality; and that a liberal journal should (as far as I am aware) be the first to throw out such mean insinuations is not very creditable to its spirit and conduct. Surely a journal of free thought should welcome all criticism even on the works of those whom it has every reason to honour and respect, and when such criticism comes from the lips of a man who like Mr. Jevons; has devoted a large portion of his life to the study of the subject about which he speaks and whose views have not been formed in an hour or a day but are the results of the severe and patient thought of many years; and when, moreover, he is a man of European reputation and (as all who have any acquaintance with Mr. Jevons know him to be) so far removed from any passionate or petulant outburst of feeling as to seem to them the very impersonation of 'dry light' itself—such a man's criticisms I say deserve at least respect even from those who may differ from him on essential points. To imagine that Mr. Mill (or anybody else) has said the last word on such perplexing subjects as Capital, or Value, or the Theory of Wages is to imagine what is foolish and absurd; and those are not among the least rational of mankind who believe that many of the peculiar views of that great man are destined to be overthrown by the conclusions of a more profound philosophy and by the researches of a more comprehensive science. At all events all honest

The description of the style of the article given by Summers is not unfair; its author combined unqualified praise of Mill with unqualified condemnation of Jevons. The utility theory, the author declared, 'has been examined and rejected more than once, and, we venture to think, would not bear reproduction at all were it not for the garnish of mathematical formulae with which Mr. Jevons delights to surround the simplest propositions'.

criticism ought to be heralded with delight and not with arrogant scorn; and the man who sets himself to oppose such criticism in a passion is not likely to arrive at any trustworthy conclusion, or even to see the real issues, of the problem before him.

I am, etc.
William Summers.

University College,
Oxford. Nov. 30th.

I should not have ventured to obtrude this letter upon your notice, had I not found it impossible to obtain for it publicity by means of the press.

Believe me,
Yours very truly,
Wm. Summers

407. W. S. JEVONS TO MRS LUCY HUTTON
       [LJN, 328]

Withington, 16th December 1874.

. . . Thanks for your letter received at Cambridge. We were so busily employed there that I had no time to answer. We only returned last night, having had perhaps the pleasantest visit to a place that I can remember. Not only were the college buildings and chapels very interesting, but the people were exceedingly kind, and we made a great number of new acquaintances, chiefly among the college tutors and lecturers, with two or three of the professors. I think we were at a breakfast or luncheon or dinner party almost every day, and sometimes two, and I was greatly pleased with dining in the college halls several times. Harriet, of course, could not accompany me there, but she went one evening to Trinity College Hall to see the dinner from the gallery. We were also greatly pleased with the college chapels, which we frequently attended. . . .

408. W. S. JEVONS TO W. SUMMERS
       [LJN, 329]

Parsonage Road, Withington.
16th December 1874

. . . On returning home after a few days' absence I am pleased to receive your letter containing a copy of a letter which you addressed to the

Examiner newspaper. I have read the latter with much interest, and am naturally gratified to find that you consider the remarks of the *Examiner* ill-considered and erroneous, to say the least. I fear it is impossible to criticise Mr. Mill's writings without incurring the danger of rousing animosity, but I hope and believe you are right in saying that I have said nothing from petulance or passion. Whatever I have said or shall say of Mr. Mill is due to a very long consideration of his works, and to a growing conviction that, however valuable they are in exciting thought and leading to the study of social subjects, they must not be imposed upon us as a new creed. We may profit by their excellences, and there is no fear on this point; but we may also suffer from their defects. . . .

409.   W. S. JEVONS TO J. D'AULNIS
       [LJN, 329–30]

Withington, Manchester,
23d December 1874

. . . The Messrs. Macmillan inform me that they have forwarded a copy of my book on logic, *The Principles of Science*, addressed to Bois le Duc. I directed that the cost of conveyance should be paid to the destination, and I hope that you will duly receive the book.

I am much gratified to hear M. Land, the professor of logic at Leyden, approves of the work, which cost me far more labour than the *Theory of Political Economy*.

Having recently seen Mr. George H. Darwin, a son of the well-known Charles Darwin, and a very clever mathematician and economist, he expressed a great desire to see your dissertation, as he can, in some degree, read your language. I have therefore lent him my copy for a time. I wish that there were more people in England able to read it.

I am informed by Professor Boccardo of Genoa that he proposes to translate my *Theory* into Italian.[1] I shall in the course of two or three months draw up some little alterations and improvements, and I should be very glad to know whether you will point out the places which need alteration most.

The paper for the Manchester Statistical Society is in course of being printed in the *Transactions*, and when finished I shall have the pleasure of sending you a copy.

Please do not put yourself to any inconvenience concerning the note of

[1] The translation, prepared under Boccardo's supervision, appeared in 1875 in *Biblioteca dell'Economista*, 3 serie, ii, 175–311, under the title 'La Teorica dell'Economia politica, esposta da W. Stanley Jevons'.

the contents of your dissertation, which you kindly offered to send. It will be very interesting to me when you are able to write it, but I fear it is taxing you too much to expect it. Such a statement would, however, enable me to refer more fully to your work in England. . . .

410. W. S. JEVONS TO L. BODIO

> Parsonage Road
> Withington
> Manchester
> 29 Dec. 74.

My dear Sir

I write a few lines to express my regret that I see no prospect of being able to meet you in London before the 4th of January when you say you are leaving. On reaching Manchester from Cambridge on the day I mentioned, I called at the Queen's Hotel within ten minutes of getting to the railway station, but found that you had left. I am glad however that you visited the Owens College and saw two of my colleagues. I regret very much that I should not have had the honour of meeting you & the pleasure of discussing particularly the application of mathematical reasoning to the economical sciences in which I am so much interested. I find that many distinguished Italian economists are disposed to look with favour upon attempts to extend the application of mathematical method. In France the tendency in the same direction is also marked. In England there is on the contrary a marked prejudice against any step beyond the methods of Adam Smith & Ricardo.

As you are hardly likely to be acquainted with my book upon the mathematical theory of Political Economy, I should like to have the pleasure of forwarding you a copy if I hear that you are in London as you expected to be.

Believe me to be my dear Sir yours very respectfully & faithfully
> W. Stanley Jevons.

411. W. S. JEVONS TO A. MARSHALL

> Parsonage Road,
> Withington,
> Manchester.
> 7 Jany. 75.[1]

Dear Mr. Marshall,

Ever since our most agreeable visit to Cambridge I have been intending to write to you and say how much I was interested in the

---

[1] The original manuscript of this letter is now in the Marshall Library, Cambridge. For the details

answers in political economy. While at Cambridge indeed, I called at your rooms in hope of seeing you but found you had gone down, or rather to be strictly accurate I was on the way to do so when informed that you had gone down.

I thought that nearly half the candidates gave very intelligent answers, showing that they had not merely crammed up a little of Mill but had been induced to enter more into the subject as a study of their own. What interested me most of all however was the way in which some of them applied the graphical method no doubt according to your views. I did not understand the particulars of all the figures as some of the men in the hurry of writing seemed to think the examiners must know all about the figure if they merely sketched it out. I understood enough however to think that the way in which you had applied curves to questions of taxation and the like was very successful. I have no doubt that there is a great field open for the investigation of economy in this way and I wish that you could be induced to print what you have already worked out on the subject. I do not know whether your proposed articles or books were to touch on this subject.

I am reading Sidgwick's book[2] with much interest. It is exceedingly acute and full of novelties, but cannot be said to be easy reading. It cannot have very many readers, but no one who pretends to be well read in moral philosophy can pass it over without careful study.

Believe me,
Yours faithfully,
W. S. Jevons.

412.   J. D'AULNIS TO W. S. JEVONS

Amsterdam 8 January 1875.

My dear Sir,

Before two days I received the copy of your work on Logic, and I express you my most kind thankfulness for offering me a work of such great learning and such high importance. Professor Land has promised me his aid, when there would arise difficulties in studying the book. Now I am convinced that the lecture will not be an easy one.

Much pleased also I felt by the communication in your last letter, that Mr. George H. Darwin, who knows in some degree the Dutch language, has undertaken to read my dissertation. By this way you will

---

of Marshall's life and intellectual development at this period, when he was a Fellow and Lecturer of St John's College, Cambridge, see J. M. Keynes, 'Alfred Marshall, 1842–1924' in Pigou, *Memorials of Alfred Marshall* (1925) pp. 13–18.

[2] Henry Sidgwick, *The Methods of Ethics* (1874).

possibly soon be informed with its contents in a more complete manner, than a note of my hand can do. I propose to write this note in a series of brief theses, in French language. But I have hitherto not had the leisure time to draw up this note; for I must devote myself to the study of Law, because I now am advocate at Amsterdam, and must at least repeat the "elementa juris" which I almost totally have neglected writing my dissertation.

Believe me to be

my dear Sir
Your very faithful and thankful
J. d'Aulnis de Bourouill

My address is Amsterdam, Leidsche Straat. x. 730.

413.   L. BODIO TO W. S. JEVONS

Ministero D'Agricoltura, Industria e Commercio,
Rome le 9 janvier, '75

Monsieur le Professeur,

Je vous demande pardon si j'ai tardé trop longtemps à vous remercier de votre savant ouvrage The Théorie of political Economy, dont vous avez bien voulu me faire cadeau.

J'ai été malade pendant plus d'un mois, et ensuite j'ai été tellement accablé de travail routinier que je ne suis pas encore en état de vous dire que j'ai lu en entier et medité votre ouvrage ainsi qu'il mérite.

Permettez moi pourtant de vous féliciter pour cet essai qui me parait heureux et sur lequel j'aurai l'honneur de m'entretenir avec vous encore une fois prochainement; essai de donner la précision de la formule mathématique au raisonnement purement logique. Je suis avec beaucoup d'interêts les progrès de cette science qui se manifestent aujourd'hui par deux voies, celle de la recherche historique et statistique, c'est à dire par la voie de l'expérience, et celle de la déduction mathématique, qui, si elle est bien assise sur ses prémisses et [si elle est][1] appuyée sur ses flancs par les coéfficents[2] des milieux et des résistances accidentelles, est la plus propre à satisfaire un esprit scientifique.

---

[1] Deleted in the original manuscript.
[2] So spelt in the original manuscript.

Je vous prie de vouloir agréer un exemplaire de l'*Italia economica* en 1873,[3] que j'ai eu l'honneur de vous expédier il y a quelque semaine.

Votre serviteur,
Louis Bodio

Je crois que vous êtes déjà informé qu'on va traduire bientôt votre ouvrage dans la *Biblioteca dell'Economista*.[4] Sans doute on a du obtenir votre consentement pour cela. C'est une collection très intéressante et très répandue en Italie.

414.   W. S. JEVONS TO R. H. INGLIS PALGRAVE
[KCP]

Parsonage Road
Withington
Manchester
26 Jany 75

My dear Palgrave

I have for some time past been working hard at a book on Money for the International Series & have from time to time put off answering your last interesting letter. I am just going to touch upon the point you discuss of the power of expanding the note circulation, and I should like to be allowed to allude to your paper on the subject.[1] I do not however know in which number of the Bankers' Magazine it would appear and shall be much obliged if you can spare the time to inform me. I do not mean to say that any one private banker could put notes afloat *ad libitum,* but I think many bankers acting all over the country in a period of prosperity may so swell the apparent quantity of the currency as to raise prices, turn the exchanges against the country, cause the export of specie, fill up the space with more notes until they have unduly reduced the specie basis. It could only be done by a slow and gradual process.

This is no doubt a point on which much discussion is possible and as my book will be only of moderate size & have to touch on many parts of the subject of money I can only make concise allusions to it.

[3] An annual official publication of the Ufficio Centrale di Statistica del Regno.

[4] Cf. above, Letter 409. p. 94.

[1] Palgrave's articles in the *Bankers' Magazine* entitled 'The Effect of Superseding the Existing English Country Note Issue with the Notes of the Bank of England' appeared in November and December 1874 (see above, Letter 395, n. 1, p. 76) and were continued in April, May and June 1875 – *Bankers' Magazine*, 35 (1875) 277–82, 357–64 and 453–9. However, the reference which Jevons gave in *Money and the Mechanism of Exchange* (p. 314) was to Palgrave's 'Notes on Banking' – a short title for his Statistical Society paper of 1873 (see above, Letter 356, n. 2, p. 10).

What you told me about the peculiar circumstances of the banking business in Yarmouth is interesting. I will of course not use it in any way to which you could object, but I suppose the facts are to a certain extent patent to any one & may be so far alluded to if I ever have need. No doubt under such peculiar circumstances the power of expanding your paper issues would be very convenient, but knowing that the pressure is a temporary & regular one I suppose you can arrange so as to meet it.

Believe me

Yours very faithfully

W. S. Jevons.

415. W. S. JEVONS TO G. H. DARWIN
      [LJN, 330]

Portico Library, Manchester,[1]

2d February, 1875

. . . At the earliest possible moment after reading your article in the *Fortnightly*,[2] I write to say how warmly I thank you for so boldly taking up the cause of the *Theory*. Not only must your article give new courage to those already believing in the possibility of applying mathematical methods to economy, but it must go far towards silencing those who have hitherto ridiculed the notion, and opening the eyes of those who have been entirely blind. It seems to me just the kind of article likely to do most good in counteracting the ill-considered criticisms of Cairnes.

I quite agree with you that Cairnes' own speculations on value are probably much more sound than his objections to other people's speculations, but I have of late been so much occupied in other reading that I have really not read his book properly, and look forward to the pleasure of studying it with care. I expect to find it confirmatory on the whole of the mathematical theory.

The Dutchman[3] seems to read the *Fortnightly* much more regularly than I do, and will be pleased to see that you favourably mention his book.

I have posted a copy of my paper to Beckenham, not knowing whether you are there or at Trinity College.

I hope to see before long your paper on production,[4] a new theory of

---

[1] Jevons was elected a member of the Portico Library on 7 March 1867, and presumably went there to read periodicals such as the *Fortnightly*.

[2] G. H. Darwin, 'The Theory of Exchange Value', *Fortnightly Review*, 17 (1875) 243–53.

[3] Johan d'Aulnis de Bourouill, whose work was mentioned by Darwin on p. 253 of the article in question.

[4] I have not been able to trace any paper by Darwin on this subject [Editor].

This is the last letter from Jevons to G. H. Darwin of which any record now survives, but from

which will be a true novelty. I cannot say I have hitherto been able to conceive the line you take. . . .

416.   A. MARSHALL TO W. S. JEVONS

S.J.C.
4 Feb. 1875.

Dear Professor Jevons,

I thank you for your paper on the Mathematical Theory of Political Economy which I have just received. I read it with interest some time ago in a newspaper.

I incline to think that the substantive difference between us is less than I once supposed.

We appear to be held apart more by the divergence of our views with regard to Mill than by any other cause. As a result of many courses of lectures on Mill I have been convinced that his work instead of being full of plausible sophistries, appears at first sight and perhaps even more at second sight to contain fallacies where really there are only incomplete truths.

I admit however that the Theory of Political Economy is in its infancy; that Mill was not a constructive genius of the first order, and that, generally the most important benefits he has conferred on the science are due rather to his character than to his intellect.

Believe me,
Yours faithfully,
A. Marshall.

I am glad Mr. George Darwin has attacked the first chapter of Mr. Cairnes "Leading Principles".

---

correspondence between G. H. Darwin and his father Charles Darwin, now preserved in Cambridge University Library, it seems likely that there was at least one later letter. On 12 October 1875 G. H. Darwin wrote to his father 'Jevons' letter is very pleasing to me and encourages me to believe that I perhaps may do something, health notwithstanding' and on 13 October Charles Darwin replied: 'Stanley Jevons' letter has pleased me more than anything which I have read for many a long day.'

417. W. S. JEVONS TO H. S. FOXWELL
    [RDF; LJP, 331-2]

> Parsonage Road
> Withington
> 7 Feb. 75

Dear Foxwell

I have been very much interested in your letter concerning my paper. It has told me much which I had no previous means of knowing concerning the ideas current on philosophical subjects in Cambridge. I was not aware that Marshall had so long entertained notions of a quantitative theory of P. E. & think it a pity he has so long delayed publishing something on the subject.[1]

It is of course open to him or you or others to object to the special way in which I have applied mathematics, and I should like to see other attempts in different directions, but what I contend is that my notion of utility is the correct one & the only sound way of laying the foundations for a math. theory.

In regard to what I have said of Mill I must allow that I should not have expressed so strong an opinion had I been thinking only of his political economy. There is much that is erroneous in his 'Principles' and he never had an idea what *capital* was, but the book is not the maze of self contradictions which his Logic undoubtedly is. If you have not examined his logical theories very critically you will hardly be aware that upon the principal points he usually holds from three to six inconsistent views all at the same time. It is to this I allude in reality and in the course of a year or two I hope to make it apparent.

I have not yet read enough of Cairnes book to form any opinion about it as a whole, & though I cannot think much of the beginning I did not suppose it was as shallow as you say.

Mʳˢ Jevons joins me in kind regards—

> Believe me
> Yours faithfully
> W. S. Jevons.

P.S. To give you a slight clue to Mill's logical maze I may mention that in regard to the nature of geometrical science he states in one place or other the following opinions
1. It is entirely inductive.
2. It is the type of a deductive science.

[1] On the background to this letter, see Keynes's comments in *Memorials of Alfred Marshall,* pp. 18–28. Regrettably, the manuscript of Foxwell's letter to Jevons, which must have contained an interesting account of the state of economic ideas at Cambridge, has not survived.

3.   That though usually called inductive it is improperly so-called.[2]
4.   That there is no opposition between deduction & induction.
5.   Geometry is deductive as opposed to experimental.
6.   Nevertheless geometry is experimental & all the truths of geom. can be verified & proved by actual trial.
7.   As the experiments of geometry cannot be perfectly performed we substitute mental experiments.

W. S. J.

418.   W. S. JEVONS TO L. WALRAS

14 February 1875

My dear Sir,

I have been very much occupied for some months past in writing a book upon the subject of money, and trust that you will excuse the delay which has occurred in answering your last agreeable letter.

Much time was taken by the Manchester Statistical Society in printing my paper upon your book and the theory, but it has now been printed. It has also been reprinted partially in the Journal of the London Statistical Society[1] which has a large circulation and the three Manchester newspapers which circulate over a considerable part of the country also printed most of it. Thus it has been widely read and I am sending about 150 copies of the full paper to the principal economists and others interested in the subject. I have had a considerable number of letters upon the subject, and much more assent to the theory is now apparent.

The last number of the Fortnightly Review (February) contains an article on the subject entitled "on the theory of Exchange Value by George Darwin".[2] It is a defence of our theory against Cairnes and will have considerable effect, owing to the reputation of the name of Darwin, George Darwin being the son of the celebrated Charles Darwin. The writer mentions your book very favourably, saying that in some respects you have treated the subject more profoundly than myself.

I have arranged to introduce the theory as the subject of discussions at the Political Economy Club of London, of which I am an honorary member. This club consists of the principal economists and professors of the science in the kingdom, and you may rely upon my bringing the merits of your work before the society.[3]

[2] In the version published in LJ, the second and third points were reversed in accordance with an alteration to the original manuscript, presumably made by Mrs Jevons.

[1] See above, Letter 393, n. 1, p. 70.

[2] See above, Letter 415, n. 2, p. 99.

[3] The published records of the Political Economy Club do not record Jevons as the proposer of any theoretical question in 1875, although on 4 June he brought forward the issue of railway reform. On 2

A german resident of Manchester Hildebrandt[4] is the correspondent of a German newspaper, the Polytechnische Zeitung. He has already briefly noticed my paper therein, and I have supplied him with copies of your and my books which he is going to review.[5] Some months since I sent four copies of my book to professors Boccardo, Errera, Zanon, and Bodio,[6] I addressed that for Zanon to Venice, and have since heard from him that he was not a professor of political economy, but of naval architecture.[7] Apparently the professor of political economy had gone to Padua. M. Bodio has very courteously answered my letter and also sent a copy of the fine publication *Italia Economica*. Boccardo sent a prospectus of the third series of the Biblioteca della Economista and has also written to say that he intends to translate your and my works into Italian. I have undertaken to make the requisite corrections and improvements. As the book will then be in the reach of all nations in a short time I do not propose to send any more copies to Italy. I am exceedingly obliged to you for the trouble you have taken in giving me a list of correspondents in Germany[8] and France, but I have been so much engaged as to neglect sending the copies hitherto. Moreover I have been a little discouraged by the result of those which I have sent. Perhaps I shall forward copies of my paper; but it would not be well for you to depend upon my sending copies, although I am always glad to hear of correspondents.

I think that a considerable change of opinion is taking place in England. Various correspondents express their acquiescence and some of the professors are beginning to bring the theory before their students. When I was in Cambridge two months ago I found the subject was much better understood there than I supposed, and I have little doubt about its gaining ground gradually.

In one of your letters you inquired whether the memoirs of Dr. Whewell on the mathematical treatment of political economy are reproduced elsewhere than in the transactions of the Cambridge Philosophical Society. I do not think that they have been anywhere reprinted, and they could hardly be purchased except by buying the

---

February 1877 he did introduce the question 'What is the relation of value to utility and labour?' *Political Economy Club . . . Questions Discussed . . .* 6 (1921) 97, 99.

[4] Albert Hildebrandt, civil engineer and surveyor; recorded as living in Manchester from 1874 to 1881; a member of the Manchester Statistical Society, 1873–81, before which he read a paper entitled 'On Coroners' Juries' on 15 November 1876; correspondent of the *Deutsche Allgemeine Polytechnische Zeitung*.

[5] Cf. below, Letter 480, p. 188.

[6] See above, Letter 379, nn. 2, 3 and 5, p. 48; and Letter 392, n. 1, p. 68.

[7] Cf. above, Letter 379, n. 5, p. 48.

[8] Jevons does not appear to have approached any of the German or French economists whom Walras had suggested in his letter of 28 November 1874 (see above, Letter 402, p. 85); he certainly had no correspondence with any of them.

expensive volumes of the transactions in which they are embodied. They are not in my opinion of much value,[9] but I am told that Mr. Todhunter of Cambridge is likely to edit them among a series of volumes of Whewell's miscellaneous works.[10] He seems to be slightly interested in the mathematics of political economy and has made some inquiries from me about Cournot's work. You might like to send a copy of your book; his address is

> Isaac Todhunter Esqe. F.R.S.
> Brookside
> Cambridge

I have managed to insert a reference to our theory in my book on "Money"[11] for the "International Series" which may have a considerable circulation in England, America and possibly in other countries where some of the volumes are reprinted.

I still hope to be able to bring forward the subject for discussion at the meeting of the British Association in August which will give it much publicity. You may rely upon my always loyally joining our names as the authors of the theory, regard being had to the relative dates of publication, and I shall always entertain a warm appreciation of the highly satisfactory way in which you have referred to my labours.

I have no doubt whatever about the ultimate success of our efforts, but it will take some fighting, the disciples of J. S. Mill being bitterly opposed to any innovation upon his doctrines. I have already been very severely criticized for what I said about him, by the London *Examiner* which

---

[9] Professor Jaffé has suggested (*Walras Correspondence*, 1, 422) that this represented a change of view by Jevons. In the first edition of *T.P.E.* (pp. 15–16) Jevons did say that Whewell's papers 'possess considerable interest and are remarkable for clearness of style', while in the second edition he placed them among 'mathematical treatises, which must be pronounced nonsense' (Preface, p. xxiv). Even in the first edition, however, Jevons went on to say that Whewell's papers 'fail to lead to any satisfactory results'.

[10] I. Todhunter, *William Whewell . . . An Account of His Writings with Selections from his Literary and Scientific Correspondence* (1876).

[11] In *Money and the Mechanism of Exchange* Jevons's approach, which was so widely copied by later writers as to become almost a cliché, was to begin with an account of barter, proceed to exchange, and hence to show the functions of money in relation to exchange. In chapter II, 'Exchange', he included 'a very brief discussion concerning the nature of value' which contained the following passage (p. 10):

'Regarding utility, then, as constantly varying in degree, and as variable even for each different portion of commodity, it is not difficult to see that we exchange those parts of our stock which have a low degree of utility to us, for articles which, being of low utility to others, are much desired by us. This exchange is continued up to the point at which the next portion given would be equally useful to us with that received, so that there is no gain of utility: there would be a loss in carrying the exchange further. Upon these considerations it is easy to construct a theory of the nature of exchange and value, which has been explained in my book called "The Theory of Political Economy". It is there shown that the well-known laws of supply and demand follow from this view of utility, and thus yield a verification of the theory. Since the publication of the work named, M. Léon Walras, the ingenious professor of political economy at Lausanne, has independently arrived at the same theory of exchange, a remarkable confirmation of its truth.'

upholds his views, but I am going to criticize J. S. Mill without the least fear of the final result.

Yours faithfully,
W. S. Jevons

419. W. S. JEVONS TO R. H. INGLIS PALGRAVE
[KCP]

Parsonage Road,
Withington
19 Febr. 75

My dear Palgrave,

Mrs. Jevons and I feel much pleased at your so kindly repeating the invitation to Yarmouth which you gave us some time ago. I am tied by my College duties at present & sorry not to see my way in that direction, but if all goes well I quite expect to live much more nearly in your neighbourhood before long when it would give us much pleasure to have a glimpse of a place which is always associated in my mind with the best of Dickens' works.[1]

Poor Cairnes was bad enough when I saw him last & I hope he is no worse but I fear improvement is out of the question.[2]

I shall probably be able to send you the proof of the part where I deal with your views about the note currency but I do not think I shall need in the present book to mention the Yarmouth case. I referred to possible future use.[3]

I lately obtained the Bankers' Almanac for 1875 & was interested to find you had become editor.[4] It is vastly improved since I last had a copy many years ago – and is now full of information interesting to me. I shall be much obliged by your allowing me to send you a small portion at least of my proofs. Believe me,

Yours very faithfully,
W. S. Jevons

---

[1] i.e. *David Copperfield.*

[2] Cairnes was suffering from a rheumatic disease which produced almost complete paralysis: he died on 8 July 1875. See below, Letter 428, p. 113.

[3] *Money and the Mechanism of Exchange*, pp. 314–21.

[4] The correct title of this work was *The Banking Almanac and Directory*. According to the *Bankers' Magazine*, 35 (1875) 67, 'this familiar book of reference for bankers, in its thirty-first year of publication, has passed into the editorial hands of Mr. R. H. Inglis Palgrave, and now contains, in addition to the more formal matter which we are accustomed to, a great deal of useful information, amongst which may be mentioned a table of cardinal numbers and commercial terms, applicable to bills of exchange, in ten different languages; statistics of bank-note circulation; fluctuations in bank rates of discount in England, France and Prussia, and a deal of other matter interesting to bankers and others which, we think, cannot fail to be duly appreciated.'

420.   C. R. WILSON TO W. S. JEVONS

National Debt Office.
22 Feb. 75.

My dear Sir,

Part V of the enclosed act[1] contains the Law regulating Stock Certificates and will I think give you the information you request as to the way in which they are issued and paid – as to the amount of such certificates issued the Bank would not give the information unless required for official purposes so I hesitate to ask the question – but it would doubtlessly be given at once if you requested any M.P. to move for a Return – and you would then have it as a Parliamentary Paper – I believe however that you are quite right in your supposition that the scheme has been practically a failure the number of certificates issued being very small – you will see that the certificate has coupons.

Very truly yours,
C. Rivers Wilson

The original act was passed in 1863.[2]

421.   W. S. JEVONS TO MRS LUCY HUTTON
        [LJN, 332]

Parsonage Road, Withington.
[February or March 1875].

. . . I am getting on very fairly on the whole, but incline to be rather overworked, and sometimes have neuralgia in my neck, which comes on in my lectures, and makes me very nervous. The proofs of my new book on money are coming very fast, and I have two or three more books in my head. I suppose I shall write as long as I live, but how long that will be I cannot tell.

. . . I am very sorry I have not more time for writing, but I have had a good deal of correspondence lately with other people that I am obliged to attend to somewhat; and with my book and lectures, I feel hardly able to find sufficient time and strength. But you must not suppose I am unwell, as on the whole I gradually become better, and Morgan told me the last time I saw him that I could now insure my life. . . .

[1] 33 & 34 Vict., c. 71, referred to by Jevons in *Money and the Mechanism of Exchange*, p. 247: 'The English government has rendered the National Debt as transferable as possible by authorising, in terms of the Act of 33 and 34 Victoria, chap. 71, the issue of stock certificates . . . But it is understood that a comparatively small amount of such certificates has ever been applied for.'

[2] 26 & 27 Vict., c. 28, An Act to give further facilities to the Holders of the Public Stocks (8 June 1863).

422.　W. S. JEVONS TO A. NEILD

Grand Hill House
Ludlow
3rd March 1875

Dear Mr Neild

In reply to your letter requesting me to renew my temporary engagement with the College for another year, I regret to say that I feel the time has come when I must bring to a close the connection with Owens' College which I have enjoyed for twelve years past. It has cost me much pain to come to this conclusion, and I have time after time anxiously reconsidered the motives which make me wish to remove from Manchester to London. These motives resolve themselves mainly into a desire to devote my time under the most advantageous circumstances, to the library and scientific work which presses upon me more and more urgently. I know that I shall have reason to regret parting from the many good friends whom I have known at Owens' College. I shall enjoy however for the rest of my life the memory of my occupations and friendships in Manchester and it will be a source of gratification that I have had some share in the second foundation of a College which is sure to have a great future.

The Council will justifiably desire that I should complete the work of the session, and I shall therefore be happy to receive a reappointment to the close of the Academical year.

I beg to remain
Yours very faithfully
W. Stanley Jevons

423.　W. S. JEVONS TO R. H. INGLIS PALGRAVE
[KCP]

Parsonage Road
Withington, Manchester
5 March '75

My dear Palgrave,

I enclose a copy of the Manchester Bankers' Memorial which Mr. Langton handed me for you.[1] I presume it is the document you inquired for.

---

[1] This memorial, together with another from the Cumberland and Westmoreland Banking Company, was presented to the Chancellor of the Exchequer on 15 June 1874. Both memorials represented the view of English provincial bankers that the legislation of 1844 and 1845 placed them at a disadvantage by comparison with Scottish and Irish bankers, who were not prevented from

I am interested to hear that you are translating Roscher's Pol. Econ.[2] I do not know much of the book but it has a great reputation, and being different in character from our treatises would be a welcome addition to our libraries.

I will make some inquiries about the Schuster you mention but I do not know him.[3] He has never attended my classes and I do not see how he can know anything of pol. Econ. His brother is now away upon the Eclipse Expedition. I presume you only want a good German Scholar who would correct errors of translation, and not a pol. Econt. There would be no difficulty in meeting with some young German well acquainted with English, but it would resolve itself into a question of remuneration. Our lecturer on French is a German, called Breymann,[4] of great intelligence with a capital knowledge of modern languages. I do not know whether he would undertake anything of the kind.

I am sorry that my almost entire want of knowledge of German precludes me from forming any opinion as to the accuracy of a translation.

> Believe me,
> Yours faithfully,
> W. S. Jevons

423A. J. ROBSON TO W. S. JEVONS
       [RDF]

> Univ. Coll.
> London
> March 8ᵗʰ 1875

Dear Prof. Jevons,

On the reading of your last letter to the Council last Saturday, the following resolution was unanimously adopted:

"That the Senate be informed that the Council propose, in view of Mr. Jevons' eminence as a Political Economist, to appoint him, without again

---

making additional note issues against gold coin nor from opening branches in London. The question had come to the fore when the Clydesdale Bank established branches in Cumberland and proposed to open others in London. A Bankers Act Amendment Bill, which would have applied the same restrictions to Scottish and English banks, was introduced into the Commons by Goschen, but not pressed when the Chancellor of the Exchequer agreed to set up a Select Committee. See *Bankers' Magazine*, 34 (1874) 571–3; Fetter, *Development of British Monetary Orthodoxy*, pp. 221–4.

² There is no evidence that Palgrave completed this translation; a translation of Roscher's book by John J. Lalor was published in Chicago in 1878. Cf. above, Letter 394, n. 4, p. 73.

³ Presumably Felix Schuster (1854–1936), created first Baronet 1906, third son of F. J. Schuster and brother of Arthur Schuster. See below, Letter 491, n. 4, p. 204.

⁴ Hermann Breymann, Ph.D., Lecturer in French Language and Literature and German Language and Literature, Owens College, Manchester, 1871–5.

advertising the vacancy, as Professor of Pol. Econ., his duties not to commence until next Session".

Our Bye Laws render it necessary to make such a communication to the Senate, which will certainly express its entire concurrence in the Council's proposal; & then on Dec! 4th the appointment of yourself will be completed.

With respect to M! Foxwell, the Council were of opinion that it would be more regular & less objectionable, if his appointment as Lecturer for the current Session were made directly by the Council itself; & this the Council accordingly did; but I was directed to inform you of this step, before I wrote to M! Foxwell on the subject. Will you, then, kindly inform me whether you see any objection to the course adopted by the Council; in order that I may as soon as possible communicate with M! Foxwell? The plan suggested by you as to that gentleman's Lectures was in the main approved by the Council.

I remain

Yours v. truly

John Robson

Prof. W. S. Jevons, M.A.

424.   W. S. JEVONS TO R. H. INGLIS PALGRAVE
       [KCP]

Parsonage Road

Withington, Manchester

7 April '75

Dear Palgrave,

With reference to your proposed translation of Roscher's works, I am very sorry to find that though I made inquiries about Schuster whom you mentioned, I forgot to write to you at the time.[1] I am afraid I am a very bad correspondent, but it mainly arises from causes beyond my control.

I was told that the younger Schuster is at some German university at present (Leipzig if I remember aright). His father is very well off & he in no want of money, so that it is hardly likely he would undertake work except such as was congenial to him & I cannot learn that he knows anything of P.E. I do not think it likely he would suit. The elder Schuster is observing the eclipse in India & would also be too much in the scientific line.

I do not know anyone likely to suit myself unless it be our lecturer in

---

[1] See above, Letter 423, p. 108.

modern languages Dr. Breymann, a young German of great intelligence, author of a French grammar just published by MacMillan.[2] He does not know pol. econ., but his knowledge of languages and of things in general would doubtless enable him to revise a translation with much success if he would undertake it. There are however many Germans in Manchester and if you like I could easily make further inquiries.

I have more than once hinted at a change in my affairs. I am now resigning my professorship with the intention of residing in London but I do not want it mentioned until the Council have accepted the resignation & announced the vacancy.

Yours very faithfully,
W. S. Jevons

425.   T. B. MOXON[1] TO W. S. JEVONS

12 Royal George St
Greek St
Stockport
10 Apl'75.

W S Jevons Esq

Dear Sir

I thank you for your kind note and place my pamphlet entirely at your disposal for as free extracts as you may desire

There is a clerical error on page 12. I therefore send you a corrected copy.[2]

The "populus" have an idea that investments in Government Stocks are the panacea against all Banking panics – perhaps such investments give confidence but they are not available to relieve a panic once raised for what one sells another must buy so that it is only an exchange not a creation of currency and currency is what is needed at such times.

The germ of panics seems to be the desire for rapid accumulation of wealth which fosters unreasoning confidence, recoils before unanticipated impediments and ends in universal distrust

Is it possible to regulate a system (!!) so dependent upon the emotional part of human nature?

[2] Hermann Breymann, *A French Grammar, based on philological principles* (1874).

[1] Thomas Bouchier Moxon (d. 1923), Manchester banker, who spent most of his career with the Manchester and County Bank and from 1897 to 1919 with the Lancashire and Yorkshire Bank. A founding Fellow of the Institute of Bankers, he was a member of the Council, 1905–19, and Deputy Chairman in 1915. President of the Manchester Statistical Society, 1886–8; author of *English Practical Banking* (1886), which went into twenty-five editions, and of many pamphlets and papers on banking.

[2] *The Banks of the United Kingdom. Their Resources and Reserves. A Statistical Research* (1875).

An Article in the New York Commercial Chronicle (the leading American Financial Organ) for 27 March '75 upon the New York Banks and the panic of '73 & another on 27 Feb '75 on the position of the Banks of the U.S.A.[3] would interest you, if you have not seen them & if you will send a note or call at the County Bank, York St. Manchester, I shall be happy to lend them to you.

Yours truly
Thos B. Moxon

426.   W. S. JEVONS TO R. H. INGLIS PALGRAVE

Withington.
19 April, 75.

My dear Palgrave,

I am immensely obliged to you for the full criticisms and corrections which I have received this morning.[1] I am giving them the most careful attention and hope to introduce all the more important points but you will understand that it is hardly possible to make alterations which tell against one's general argument without re-writing the thing which it is too late to do. I do not mean to say that I abandon my position at all but you suggest difficulties which it would take much space to answer, but which I think may be answered.

For instance the convertibility i.e. safety of the bankers reserves in the B. of E. is no doubt a point of growing importance but I do not see that it has anything to do with the question of Bank notes. The bankers can if they like gradually draw out these balances and hold them in notes and then the Bank Act secures their convertibility. If they like to risk them it is a totally different matter and one with which it is difficult to deal by legislation.

Your figures about the decrease of notes 1844−47 and 1852−7 seem plausible but you will observe that the whole period 1844−7 was one of inflation and that the increase would be from 1842 to 1844. Accordingly we find that in 1848−50 there was a small circulation which up to 1853 had increased about 5 millions or 20 per cent!! and had not the bank act

---

[3] 'The Banks and Monetary Ease', *New York Commercial and Financial Chronicle*, 27 February 1875, pp. 195−8; 'The New York Banks and the Panic of 1873', *New York Commercial and Financial Chronicle*, 27 March 1875, pp. 300−1.

[1] Some of these criticisms survive in the Jevons Papers in the form of notes on the proofs of chapter XXIV of Jevons's *Money and the Mechanism of Exchange*, 'The Bank of England and the Money Market'. The notes underline the difference of view on this subject between the two men which is apparent in this letter and Letter 356, above p. 10, Jevons supporting the 1844 Act as ensuring effective control of the note issue, Palgrave objecting 'that it places, or at least appears to place, the convertibility of the *notes* before the convertibility of the *Deposits*'.

restrained the increase I believe it would have gone much further. It is a long question but I have at various times carefully gone over the evidence.

My diagram of the bank accounts down to 1861 [2] shows clearly that there is an increase of circulation coincident with a rise of speculation. By the bye do you happen to have a copy of my diagram? If not I will at once send you a copy.

I shall of course take care to alter the proof so that you will not be classed with the Free Banking School. [3]

It is at present quite uncertain whether I shall leave Manchester for London, as the College are negotiating with me as to an alteration of arrangements.

I must alter the remark that *bills are paid in notes*. I was quite aware that usually no notes are really used and that they merely become a matter of clearing. What I meant was that legal tender notes would be a valid payment for meeting a bill. This makes a deep distinction between the two.

> Believe me,
> Yours very faithfully,
> W. S. Jevons.

427.   J. G. GREENWOOD TO W. S. JEVONS

The Owens College,   7th May
   Manchester   1875

My dear Jevons

At the Council today the matters relating to your letter of resignation were again brought forward. I narrated the substance of the conversations that had passed between you and me in pursuance of the resolution of the Council at its last meeting. I was further able to report to

---

[2] *Diagram showing all the Weekly Accounts of the Bank of England since the passing of the Bank Act of 1844* . . . (1862). It seems evident from Palgrave's Notes on Banking, *JRSS*, 36 (1873) 96, that Jevons had sent him a copy of this diagram after writing Letter 356.

[3] In the notes referred to above, Palgrave had written: 'I do not think that I ought to be classed with the "currency *theorists*" or the "Free Banking School" as I have never advocated "discretionary reserves" in their sense and have never yet published anything on that point. If you like to class me with Ricardo and Tooke, whom I strive to follow, I do not mind *that*.' In the published version the passage in question reads – 'There is also a school of currency writers, formerly represented in England by Ricardo and Tooke, who hold that it is impossible to over-issue convertible paper money. Arguments to this effect have been recently urged with great ability by Mr. R. H. Inglis Palgrave . . . But there is, to my mind, an evident flaw in their position'. – *Money and the Mechanism of Exchange,* p. 314.

the Council – not, as I had hoped, the addition of a capital sum large enough to provide a *permanent* addition to the income of the chair (though this I believe to be only *delayed*) but – the presentation by an anonymous donor of such a sum as will allow of our making the augmentation named between us for a period of six years. The Council therefore unanimously passed a resolution that for a period of six years from September next the fixed stipend of the Professor of Logic and Political Economy be raised to £300 per annum.

The limitation to six years was of course necessary with the fear of our Treasurer and his deficit before our eyes; but I have no shadow of doubt that long ere that term is out we shall have the means of replacing this temporary sum.

I should add that neither I nor, as I believe, any other member of the Council has any knowledge who our anonymous friend is.

I did not read your and my letters entirely for obvious reasons; but I communicated what you said about the Evening Classes, and the substance of your remarks about the comparative assessments of work involved in different Professorships.

I suppose the next formal step will be the withdrawal of your letters?

Ever (and today with additional satisfaction)   Yours
most truly
J. G. Greenwood

428.   J. E. CAIRNES TO W. S. JEVONS

Rasay,
Kidbrook Park Road,
S.E.
9 May 1875[1]

My Dear Jevons,

I received your letter some days ago and should not have delayed so long in returning you my warm thanks for the very kind and flattering terms in which you have spoken of my recent publications, if it had not been that my health has, of late, been so miserable that for days together I have been unequal to the exertion of dictating a letter. There are few persons living for whose judgment on a question of logical method I have a higher esteem than for yours; and as I was far from feeling certain that I should have your adhesion to even the main ideas of my doctrine, I am the more gratified and encouraged by the very frank adhesion you have

---

[1] This, the last letter written by Cairnes to Jevons, was discovered by the late Professor A. N. Agarwala in a second-hand bookshop in Calcutta, and published by him in the *Indian Journal of Economics*, 25 (1944–5) 80–2.

given. Of course, I am quite prepared for a good deal of dissent on subordinate points, not to speak of our unfortunate disagreement as regards the feasibility of mathematical treatment. But, in accepting my views as I understand you to do, that the premisses of Political Economy are not "unverified hypotheses" (as some professors now are industriously seeking to make the world believe), but well-established facts of man's moral and physical nature and of his environment in [the][2] world, and in holding that the science is to be developed deductively from these premisses with such aid as induction, in the circumstances of the case can afford, in accepting these two positions you accept everything that I much care to contend for. You will find a new chapter on Definition,[3] and I shall feel particularly glad to know how far you can agree with me in the view I take of this question. It has been quite latterly discussed in the Political Economy Club,[4] and from what I hear without throwing much light upon the subject. Thornton's Essay in the Fortnightly on the Definition of Wealth[5] (which by the way, was highly praised in the debate at the Club) seems to me to illustrate nearly every fallacy into which it is possible to fall in connection with this question.

I am very glad to hear that your inquiry into prices is making progress. The results analysed and discussed by you cannot fail to throw much light upon the whole subject. I trust you mean to carry the inquiry beyond the year '66. The most surprising feature to me in the figure you have kindly sent me is the slight advance of prices in New South Wales – considerably less, it would seem, than 50 per cent. I have no knowledge of the special influences acting on the Newfoundland markets.

Again thanking you for your very kind letter, I remain

Very truly yours,

J. E. Cairnes.

[2] Omitted in the original manuscript.

[3] The second edition of Cairnes, *Character and Logical Method of Political Economy*, published in 1875, contained a new Lecture 'Of the Place and Purpose of Definition in Political Economy', pp. 135–48.

[4] On 7 May 1875 W. T. Thornton posed the following question at the Political Economy Club: 'Political Economy being commonly regarded as the science which treats of national wealth, in what sense should the word Wealth be understood when used in politico-economical discussions?', *Political Economy Club. . . . Proceedings . . . and Questions Discussed, 1821–1920*, VI, (1921), 97.

[5] W.T. Thornton, 'Economic Definition of Wealth', *Fortnightly Review*, 17 (1875) 566–74.

429. H. D. MACLEOD[1] TO W. S. JEVONS

17 Gloucester Terrace,
Campden Hill, W.
May 11, 1875.

My dear Sir,

I send you an article of mine in the *Contemporary*,[2] which is the substance of a lecture I gave at Christ [*sic*] Hospital to the Grecians or sixth form: about 50 or 60 boys came: it being quite voluntary: and shewed much interest: of course being intended for young men and boys it was as simple as could be; and of course very far from exhausting the subject.

I wish to make up a list of Economists of the different schools:[3] I wish to know if I may place you in what I call the *third* school? The distinctive features of it are these: that Pure Economics is the Science of Exchanges: or the Theory of Value: that the Principle of Wealth and Value consists exclusively in exchangeability: that every thing which is exchangeable is wealth whatever its form. That there can be only a *single* General Theory of Value; or a *single* general Equation of Economics which must contain all phenomena of Value.

These are the fundamental principles of the 3rd school. Do you agree to these generally? Of course not binding as to all matters of detail.

Believe me,
Yours very truly,
H. D. Macleod.

430. W. S. JEVONS TO H. S. FOXWELL
[RDF; LJP, 334]

36 Parsonage Road
Withington
Manchester
23 May 1875

My dear Foxwell

The arrangement which you propose with respect to the examinations quite suits my inclinations. I should have, of my own accord, chosen Logic and Political Economy. I will therefore consider the selection to be

[1] Henry Dunning Macleod (1821–1902), Scottish lawyer and bank director; author of *Theory and Practice of Banking* (1855–6); *A Dictionary of Political Economy*, vol. 1 (1863); *The Principles of Economic Philosophy* (1879); *Elements of Economics* (1881) and *History of Economics* (1896). Cf. Vol.II, Letter 166, n. 2, p. 456.

[2] H. D. Macleod, 'What *is* Political Economy?', *Contemporary Review*, 25 (1875) 871–93.

[3] In the article cited Macleod distinguished three schools of economists; the first was the Physiocratic and the second and third were defined in terms of his statement that 'One half . . . of Smith's work is based upon labour and materiality as the essence of wealth and the other half on

settled unless I hear to the contrary. I think it will be time enough to make up the examination papers about the end of September, but perhaps it will be well for me to communicate with the other two examiners before the long vacation begins.

I have thought a good deal about what you said with reference to Mill. It seems to me very undesirable that the world generally should look upon him as the soundest logician, when as I feel pretty sure, his system as a whole is unsound. But I [am][1] too much engaged in other matters at present to write any criticism just now. I have heard several other men connected with the London University speak like you as if the recognition of the Moral Sciences hung by a thread, so they might be thrown over altogether in consequence of the least indiscretion. But I trust that the authorities of the universities are not quite so narrow minded. Moreover Mill's eccentric, and in many ways, as I believe, really hurtful opinions, do much to prejudice people against the sciences which he is supposed to represent. I shall hope however to have further opportunities to discuss such matters with you – so believe me

Yours faithfully
W. S. Jevons.

Mrs Jevons desires me to send her kind regards.

431.   W. S. JEVONS TO HARRIET JEVONS
        [LJN, 335–6]

Scientific Club,
7 Savile Row, 5th June 1875.

. . . The discussion went off very fairly last night.[1] I got on without any difficulty, and was quite fluent most of the time. I tried particularly to wind up so that the club should know when I had done, but failed entirely. When I left off there was a dead silence of several minutes, and Leslie,[2] sitting next me, remarked that he thought I was going to begin

---

exchangeability and two classes of writers have followed who have adopted either half – Ricardo and his followers who have adopted labour as the essence of wealth, and Whately, who has adopted exchangeability' (loc. cit., p. 883).

   [1] Omitted in the original manuscript.

   [1] On 4 June 1875 Jevons proposed the following question for discussion at the Political Economy Club: 'Is any great reform in the administration of the Railways of the United Kingdom necessary and practicable?', *Political Economy Club . . . Proceedings*, vi, 97. Jevons presumably put forward the same view as he had in 'The Railways and the State' (1874, reprinted in *Methods*, pp. 353–83) which was unfavourable to any state purchase of the lines.

   [2] See below, Letter 539, n. 1, p. 272.

again. The discussion was somewhat spirited, though tending to become conversational at times. The preponderance of opinion was strongly in my favour, though the chairman, old Edwin Chadwick, was much riled at my ideas, and answered them at much length and as strongly as he could.[3]

Sitting next me was a Mr. Horace White, a well-known American,[4] who seemed to be editor or proprietor of the *Chicago Tribune*, and spoke of the Mr. Lloyd[5] who writes as a young man in his office; opposite was another American guest whom I thought I knew the face of, and he turned out to be MacCulloch, the former treasurer of the United States, whose portrait is on the greenbacks.[6] Another guest was Lord Fortescue,[7] a pleasant man, but poor speaker. The debate was much interrupted by a great noise outside the window in the yard, and by Newmarch, who every now and then blew up the waiter and rushed about calling for the proprietor to stop the noise.

This morning I got to the Academy soon after nine, when the rooms were quite cool and nearly empty, and had a long comfortable look at the pictures for nearly three hours. The greater number of the pictures strikes me as being almost worse than ever, and there are very few really good ones. There is, however, one very wonderful one, the Assyrian Marriage Market, representing the sale of a number of young women, who are ranged in the front of the picture in order of beauty. The whole details and idea are perfectly worked out, somewhat in the manner of Holman Hunt, but I believe that the artist (A. Long)[8] beats Hunt altogether. Miss Thompson's picture may have some signs of cleverness in it, but is

---

[3] Sir Edwin Chadwick (1800–90), Bentham's assistant and disciple, architect of the English Poor Law and public health systems. See S. E. Finer, *Life and Times of Sir Edwin Chadwick* (1952).

Chadwick favoured direct state control of enterprises requiring large capital outlay, such as railways, gas supplies and telegraphs, in opposition to Jevons's *laissez-faire* ideas. See Vol. VII.

[4] Horace White (1834–1916), one of the leading American journalists of his day; editor-in-chief of the *Chicago Tribune*, 1865–74; later financial and economic editor for the *New York Evening News* and the *Nation*.

[5] Henry Demarest Lloyd (1847–1903), financial editor of the *Chicago Tribune*, 1872–85; campaigned throughout his career against the growth of monopoly in American industry, becoming known as one of the first 'muck-raking' journalists; later devoted himself to political activities in support of the labour movement.

[6] Hugh McCulloch (1808–95), manager and president of the State Bank of Indiana, 1856–63; Comptroller of the Currency, 1863–5; Secretary of the Treasury, 1865–9. At this date McCulloch was a partner in a London Banking House.

[7] Hugh, third Earl Fortescue (1818–1905); M.P. for Plymouth, 1841–52; and for Marylebone, 1854–9; a Lord of the Treasury, 1846–7; Secretary to the Poor Law Board, 1847–51. An earnest social reformer, he was author of a number of pamphlets and addresses on such topics as local government, health and education.

[8] Edwin Longsden Long (1829–91), Associate of the Royal Academy, 1876; Academician, 1881. This painting, of which the correct title was 'The Babylonian Marriage Market', was one of his first important pictures, subsequently purchased by Thomas Holloway. It is referred to again by Jevons in his *Principles of Economics*, chapter XXVIII, p. 137.

very disagreeable, and not much worth looking at. [9]

This club is a convenient sort of place, and I am glad I joined it.

I have spoken a little about the University College, London, professorship both to Robson, the Secretary of the college, and to Courtney. It is quite evident that I have the refusal of it, and they want me to apply. . . .

432.   W. S. JEVONS TO R. H. INGLIS PALGRAVE
        [KCP]

                                            36 Parsonage Road,
                                                    Withington,
                                                    Manchester.
                                                20 June 75.

Dear Palgrave,

Thanks for two papers from the Bankers' Magazine [1] which I received a little time ago. I have read them with much care. They contain very valuable information especially the tables showing the annual fluctuations of the English country note issues.

I am sorry that I am still quite unconvinced that bankers can never extend their issues. This is a complete fallacy, trust me. The possibility of expansion is no doubt kept somewhat in check in England by the prohibition of one pound notes, so that a large part of the currency will always consist of gold. But you seem to me to fail to perceive that though when convertible notes and gold will always be of equal value, both may be lowered in value compared with other commodities. Prices in short may be raised in certain states of trade – the exchange turned against us, *gold exported* – not *notes* so that there is a vacuum to fill up with notes. In this way notes come to form a large percentage of the whole currency and this process might be repeated.

However when my book comes out you will see this view more fully explained. It is now just finished but will not appear till September.

Papers like yours in the Bankers' Magazine are always valuable to me and kept for reference and use in the future.

                            Believe me,
                            Yours faithfully,
                            W. S. Jevons

[9] This painting, entitled 'Quatre Bras', depicted the Twenty-eighth Regiment of British Foot at the battle fought on 16 June 1815. Cf. above, Letter 383, n. 3, p. 52.

[1] Presumably the April and May 1875 articles in the series which Palgrave wrote on 'The Effect of Superseding the existing English Country Note Issue with the Notes of the Bank of England'. See above, Letter 414, n. 1, p. 98.

433.   J. CAZENOVE[1] TO W. S. JEVONS

No. 47, Pevensey Road,
Eastbourne.
13th July 1875.

Dear Sir,

I have among my books *one* entitled *A survey of Political Economy* by *John Macdonell M.A.*[2] printed at Edinburgh in 1871. The author, in his preface, lays it down that J. S. Mill is the *greatest of Economists.* This however does not, it appears, preclude him from differing from the writer he so much admires on some important points. He says (page 50) "There is another truth regarding capital, which a distinguished expositor, J. S. Mill has not perhaps *fenced round with due limitation.* No explanations are required to shew that, while producing any article, a workman is not supported by the money, or rather the money's worth of food etc. given by the purchaser for the completed article. Manifestly a shoemaker while making a pair of boots does not subsist upon what has not yet been paid to him. His capital must have been supplied by another than the purchaser. This truth Mill expresses in the formula *a demand for commodities is not a demand for labour. This proposition in the above naked form is ambiguous.* Of course it is true that the demand for a certain number of shoes is not a demand for a certain number of shoemakers. In the one case the results of labour are bought, in the other case labour itself is bought. But when Mr. Mill proceeds to add that a demand for commodities *determines the direction of the labour, but not the more or less of the labour itself, or of the maintenance or payment of the labour,* he draws *an unwarrantable inference.* For imagine demand for all manufactures to cease, would the direction of labour *alone* be affected? would there be no less demand for labour? Why, all demand for it would cease, except in the case of mere attendants. Returning to the primary conception of capital, we shall perceive, without any laborious search, the limitations to this truth. Capital is not distinguished from other kinds of wealth by any material peculiarity, but *by the intention of the owner.* The opposite idea, sanctioned by McCulloch, leads to confusion. It is not certain things that always constitute capital (as he thought) but things put to a certain use viz. to the production of other wealth. Consequently, by a mere change of mind, a man may increase or diminish his capital, or the amount of wages to be distributed. He may increase it within limits, or may diminish it indefinitely. The motives

[1] John Cazenove (1788–1879), a London merchant who was one of the original members of the Political Economy Club and author of a number of economic works of a somewhat unorthodox stamp including, *Considerations on the Accumulation of Capital* (1822), *The Money Crisis* (1847) and *Thoughts on a Few Subjects of Political Economy* (1859).
[2] John Macdonell, *A Survey of Political Economy* (Edinburgh, 1871). The book was based on a series of articles in the *Scotsman*. The passages quoted by Cazenove are from pp. 50 – 2; the quotation is not a literal transcription but follows the original text closely.

which induce a Capitalist to alter his mind may be summed up in the state of demand for commodities. *If demand be small and there is no hope of profits, he will perhaps spend unproductively what otherwise might have been capital. If the demand be great, he may do the reverse."*

(I may here take occasion to observe that if Mill were alive, he would demur to this; for he had embraced the doctrine put forth by Monsieur Say and his own Father James Mill, that production *itself creates demand.* James Mill says, *Every producer goes to market both with a demand and a supply.*)

"Thus we see that demand for commodities may increase the amount of capital; and consequently the amount to be expended in wages. Although therefore a demand for commodities may not have given or created the actual physical articles constituting the capital which supported the fashioners of the commodities, that demand may have caused the creation by others of capital, and indirectly of a demand for labour. Most productions are now carried on with a view to a future demand; and the purchasing of commodities is the only reason why fabricators of them continue to be hired."

In these remarks of Macdonell on Mill's doctrine that a demand for commodities is not a demand for labour I fully agree with him. I hold that it is not the production of commodities which is the cause of demand for them, but the demand for them which is the cause of their production. No doubt commodities are sometimes produced in expectation of a demand for them which is disappointed. The commercial failures that annually take place may mostly be attributed to an oversupply of commodities that were not wanted; but this very fact itself proves that production itself does not ensure a demand for what is produced.

When Mill first put forth his doctrine that a demand for commodities was not a demand for labour he employed it to express that the purchaser of commodities had not maintained the labour that had produced them, which is, no doubt, true. But by some more recent authors who profess themselves to be his disciples, a very different interpretation has been given to the proposition. They have represented it as implying that the purchaser of commodities in no way contributes to the *future* maintenance of labour; and if such was the meaning that Mill himself meant to attach to it, it is in flat contradiction with what he has elsewhere stated (Bk. 1 Ch.5 ff 9) where he says "If I expend £*1000* in buying velvet, I enable the manufacturer to employ £*1000* in the maintenance of labour; and if I change my purpose and hire labourers myself instead, I undoubtedly create no new demand for labour."

There must however have been some confusion in Mill's mind on this subject, for in my quotation from him, (page 14 of my Remarks)[3] if an

---

[3] Cazenove would here appear to have been referring to one of his own publications, but the reference cannot be identified precisely. The only work with such a title which Cazenove published

adequate portion of Revenue had been applied to the purchase of the unsold commodities therein referred to, it would, *upon his own shewing,* have created as great a demand for labour, as by accumulating it. Moreover the capital employed in producing them would not have been wasted.

In another respect, Mill has employed the term capital in a sense not in accordance with what has been taught us by Adam Smith, or with the meaning that is usually attached to it. He says (Bk. 1 Chs. 8 & 9) "Manufacturers and their labourers do not produce for the pleasure of their customers, but for the supply of their own wants; and having still the Capital and labour which are the essentials of production, they can either produce something else which is in demand, or if there be no other demand, *they themselves have one, and can produce the things they want for their own consumption.*" Now manufacturers, like most other capitalists, employ workmen to produce something from the sale of which they expect to derive a profit. If their commodities do not suit their customers, they will get no customers, and their goods will be unsaleable. The idea of employing their workmen to produce all the variety of different articles they might want for their own consumption is really absurd. It is scarcely within the bounds of possibility; and even were it possible it would be a conversion of their capital into revenue, which would be expanded by their consumption of it.

It is somewhat remarkable that Ricardo should have fallen into this same mistake of confounding capital with Revenue. In his chapter 21 (Edit. 3) on Accumulation he says "Some would consume more wine, if they had the ability to procure it. Others, having enough of wine, would wish to increase the quantity or improve the quality of their furniture. Others might wish to ornament their grounds or enlarge their houses. Nothing is required but the means, and nothing can afford the means but an increase of production. If I had food and necessaries at my disposal, I should not long be in want of workmen who would put me in possession of some of the objects most useful or desirable to me."

Now any one who had those means at his disposal might purchase some of these objects he wished to have of capitalists who produced them, or might himself employ workmen to produce them for him, but in either case it would be an expenditure of his *Revenue* and not of his *Capital.* Before the establishment of a distinct order of Capitalists, the direct employment

---

was a new edition of Malthus's *Definitions in Political Economy* 'with a Preface, Notes and Supplementary Remarks' (London, 1853), but no relevant quotation from J. S. Mill appears on page 14 of these Remarks, or elsewhere in the volume. Cazenove's *Thoughts on a Few Subjects of Political Economy* does, however, contain a critique of Mill's doctrine that 'demand for commodities is not demand for labour' along lines similar to those developed in this letter; see especially pp. 34–42, 'On the Natural Limit of Demand'.

of labour was the only means our ancestors had of procuring what they wanted over and above the means of subsistence of which they were in possession. The same practice is adopted in our own days by those who employ Artists to paint pictures for them. The late Duke of Devonshire maintained, during a certain period of his life, a Sculptor in Italy to make copies for him of some of their choicest pieces of Statuary that are now to be seen at Chatsworth.

If we take a glance at the shops of any of our large towns we shall find that, with the exceptions of those of the Butcher and Baker, and Fishmonger, very few of them contain anything else but luxuries; that is, of articles which can only be *unproductively* consumed, and for which consequently there can be no demand except on the part of those who are able to expend their Revenues in the purchase of them. Such being the case, it is obvious that the amount of Capital that can be profitably employed in the production of any one or more of the those commodities, must be limited by the Revenues that are thus given in exchange for them, and by means of which the capital expended on them is replaced.

If the whole disposeable* Revenue of a Country were to be appropriated to production which is the doctrine preached by Monsieur Say, by Ricardo, by James Mill, by J. S. Mill and by their successors Professors Fawcett and Cairnes, no luxuries of any kind could be produced, for there would be no surplus fund for the replacement of the Capital that had been expended on their production.

My dear Sir, the greater part of what I herewith send you was written before I read in my paper of the melancholy and premature death of poor Cairnes, [4] who from the account given respecting it, has, I fear, been for some time past a great sufferer. I trust and hope that he has left his family in comfortable circumstances.

I had begun my letter to you chiefly to call your attention to Macdonells book, and to say that if you cared to see it, I could at any time forward it to you, by Book Post. Pray believe me meanwhile,

> With great regard,
> Your most obd. and humble Servant,
> John Cazenove.

To Professor Jevons,
M.A. F.R.S.

---

[4] An obituary notice of J. E. Cairnes appeared in *The Times*, 9 July 1875.

434. W. S. JEVONS TO J. ROBSON

2 Church Walks
Llandudno
13 July 1875

My dear Sir

It is not solely on account of my engagement with Owens College that I failed to send in any application for the professorship. The fact is that I cannot just at present feel it wise to sacrifice the income I receive from Owens College however much I wish to find myself in connection with University College & residing in London.

If I were now to apply for the vacant professorship & find myself appointed I might be obliged to resign it again almost before entering on the duties. This would not be fair to the College nor desirable in any point of view.

In six months from the present time I should probably be in a position to decide definitely whether I shall remain in Manchester or remove to London. I have no right to ask anything of your College in this matter but if it were possible to defer any decision for six months I should then in all probability be much better able to decide wisely whether I would apply or not.

The only other suggestion which I can make is that your council without making any definitive appointment should name me as a temporary lecturer for the session. I should in this case have to obtain the concurrence of the Council of Owens C.

To receive some post in University College is a thing to which I have always looked forward and I do not like to see this opportunity pass. At the same time I have strong reasons for hesitating and Owens College by giving me most liberally leave of absence during the greater part of two years and by lately increasing my salary has made it more difficult than ever to leave Manchester. You will understand how difficult it is sometimes to do what one likes & excuse my apparent want of decision. If there were any real hope of a small endowment for your professorship, it would so far remove difficulties.

I had long felt much regret at poor Cairnes' state of health. His state was such a painful one that we can hardly regret his death so far as he is concerned but he is a great loss, for no one had the same power of following out the consequences of economical conditions. His last work was a wonderful production for any one, and especially for one in his condition.

I shall be glad to be named on the com^ee for Lord Granville's portrait. [1]

---

[1] It has not proved possible to trace any information concerning this portrait. On Granville, see Vol. III, Letter 176, n. 1, p. 13.

I was intending to make a small contribution.

Believe me
Yours faithfully
W. S. Jevons

John Robson Esqe
University College

435.   W. S. JEVONS TO J. ROBSON

2 Church Walks
Llandudno
3 August 1875

Dear Mr. Robson

I have received your letter of the 2nd stating that the Council of your College have decided to act on my suggestion that I should be named a temporary lecturer in political economy for the ensuing session. You will remember however that in making this suggestion I added that it would have to receive the concurrence of the authorities of Owens College.

I am therefore writing to day without the least delay to Mr. Neild the Treasurer of O. C. to request him to bring the matter before the Council at the earliest possible opportunity, and to procure me permission so to rearrange my lectures in Manchester that I may be free to spend May and if necessary part of June in London. You kindly say that I may choose the time most convenient to myself, and as I have a course of evening lectures during the winter it would be very difficult for me to get away then. I should propose to give a course of about 20 lectures, three days a week, treating the principal problems of the Science in an elementary manner, including a discussion of the "Leading Principles" of Prof. Cairnes.

This is such a dead time at Owens College that I do not know exactly when I can get the opinion of the Council but as soon as I have it I will send the particulars you want. In the mean time I shall be glad to hear in case you see any difficulty in my proposal about the months of May & June.

I shall be happy to act as Examiner for the Ricardo Scholarship.[1] Believe me

Yours faithfully
W. S. Jevons.

---

[1] Jevons and Walter Bagehot were Examiners in the Ricardo Scholarship in Political Economy held in November 1875. See *University College, London, Calendar for the Session 1876–77*, pp. 63, xi – xii. The scholarship, of the value of £60, was awarded annually on the basis of an examination held in Michaelmas Term. Jevons had himself won the scholarsiip in 1860, and was again to examine for it with Foxwell in 1881. Cf. Letter 148, Vol. II, p. 422, and Letter 696A, Vol. V.

436. W. S. JEVONS TO J. ROBSON

36 Parsonage Road
Withington
Manchester
13 Aug. 75

Dear Mr. Robson

I have been anxious to lose no time in arranging for the proposed lectures, but, as you will learn from the enclosed extract,[1] the Council have not felt able to come to any decision on the subject. I have heard that there were only four members of the Council present, and in the absence of the principal and all the professors it was naturally difficult to sanction a change of lecture courses. I will write again as soon as anything can be settled.

Believe me
Yours faithfully
W. S. Jevons

437. W. S. JEVONS TO SIR ANTHONY MUSGRAVE[1]

21st August 1875
Withington
Manchester.

Dear Sir,

The letter with which you have favoured me arrived when I was away from home, during our college vacation, and I trust that you will excuse the delay which has thus arisen in answering it.

[1]
Enclosure accompanying letter of
W. S. Jevons to John Robson,
13 August 1875.

The Owens College.

At a meeting of the Council held at the College on Friday the 6th August 1875.
It was Resolved
That in the absence of a quorum of the Council, and also of the Principal and the Senate, the members of the Council now present do not feel competent to sanction an alteration in the Courses of lectures already fixed and advertised, but they assure Prof. Jevons that they will give a friendly consideration to any course which he may think it proper to adopt.
True copy
J. Holme Nicholson
Registrar.

[1] Sir Anthony Musgrave (1828–88), colonial administrator; Colonial Secretary of Antigua, 1854; Lieutenant-Governor of St Nevis, 1862; Governor of Newfoundland, 1864; British Columbia, 1869;

I was perfectly aware of the part which you had taken in recent discussions in political economy. What I may call your celebrated article in the Contemporary Review[2] excited more attention among economists than you may perhaps have heard. When I was in Cambridge last December engaged in the Moral Science Tripos Exam[s] I heard it discussed, and it even found its way into some examination papers which I have seen somewhere or other. I am bound to say that most who spoke of your ideas objected strongly to them, but, as I suffer under the same inconvenience myself, I do not regard their objections as conclusive.

I cannot pretend myself to accept all your views, but your criticisms on Mill seem to me most proper and well timed, and I hope you will not let the ball of discussion stop now that you have once put it so well in motion.

I beg to thank you for the pamphlet on Economic Fallacies[3] which you have been so kind as to send. I have found it interesting, and I like what you say about money, but am not prepared to agree with your discussion of Cairnes criticisms on Alby.[4] I think that Cairnes is in no danger of refutation in that part of his work.

On the subject of money, I am glad to find myself apparently quite in agreement with you. When writing my book on Money from 9 to 15 months ago I was not aware of your writings on the subject, or I should have been glad to avail myself of some of your suggestions. My book has now been in the publishers hands for 7 or 8 months & has been completely in print for some three months. It will now appear I hope in about four weeks.

I have treated gold as one out of many commodities which may & have been used for money, and I think I carry out pretty closely the doctrine you urge that it always remains a commodity or merchandise, though token money, & paper currency obscure the matter.

As regards Professor Bonamy Price's opinions[5] which you discuss, I fear I have not paid the attention I ought to have done if they are consistent either with themselves or with fact.

I take the liberty of sending by book post with this letter copies of several of my papers on economical subjects. The one last published on

---

South Australia, 1873; Jamaica, 1877, and Queensland, 1888. He was the author of a number of papers on economic subjects, mostly reprinted in his *Studies in Political Economy* (1875). For a full account of his economic thought see C. D. Goodwin, *Economic Enquiry in Australia* (Durham, North Carolina, 1966) pp. 518–43.

[2] 'Capital: Mr. Mill's Fundamental Propositions', *Contemporary Review*, 34 (1874) 729–49.

[3] *Economic Fallacies: Free Trade v Protection* (Adelaide, 1875). This was republished in the *Contemporary Review*, 29 (1876–7) 310–34.

[4] L. Alby, in an article in *Revue des Deux Mondes*, 15 October 1869, had defended the doctrine of protection: Cairnes had attacked his argument in *Some Leading Principles of Political Economy newly expounded* (1874) pp. 379–82.

[5] See Vol. III, Letter 186, p. 32.

the "Theory of Political Economy"[6] gives a better description of my proposed way of regarding utility than you will have found in my larger book of which you speak.

It must take some time to test the soundness of what I put forward but I hope to give a much fuller statement of the theory in the course of a little time.

Believe me to be
        Dear Sir,
            Yours faithfully
                W. Stanley Jevons.

To his excellency
A. Musgrave Esqe.
Governor of S. Australia.

438.   W. G. ARMSTRONG[1] TO W. S. JEVONS

Newcastle upon Tyne,
24 August 1875.

My dear Sir,

Since receiving your letter this morning I have considered, so far as my time and opportunities would permit, your criticism of the figures given in my B.A. address as to the increase in the annual consumption of coal.[2] I have not at this moment Mr. Hunt's tables[3] before me so as to examine more closely into the matter but I certainly cannot dispute your conclusion that the correct mode of determining the average of the series of years which I took was to divide by the seven intervals instead of by the 8 years. It appears however that the apprehensions which I expressed have so far been more than realized by the result though I can hardly suppose that the same prodigious rate of increase could be indefinitely continued. No one is more competent than yourself to form a just opinion

---

[6] Presumably 'The Progress of the Mathematical Theory of Political Economy', which contained a reference to Musgrave's views on Mill's theory of capital. See above, Letter 393, n. 1, p. 70.

[1] Sir William George Armstrong (1810–1900), engineer-entrepreneur; invented a hydraulic crane in 1846 and a breech-loading gun in 1855. He devoted much attention to the problem of efficiency in steam engines, which led him to take up the question of wasteful use of coal.

[2] In his Presidential Address to the British Association in 1863 at Newcastle, Armstrong discussed statistics of coal production and the probable duration of British coal reserves. Cf. Jevons, *The Coal Question*, chapter II, pp. 32–6.

[3] Robert Hunt (1807–87), Keeper of the Mining Records Office, 1843–83, was responsible for the system of Mining Records and Statistics from its institution in 1854; both Jevons and Armstrong had referred to his statistics of coal production.

upon this subject, and any remarks you may make upon it at the ensuing meeting of the B.A.[4] are sure to be received with interest and attention.

Believe me,

Yours very truly,

W. G. Armstrong.

Professor Jevons.

439.   W. S. JEVONS TO HARRIET JEVONS
[LJN, 340]

Bristol, 29th August 1875.

... I am probably going for a short drive this afternoon with my old college friend Hallett,[1] who wrote lately to me, as you will remember; but I must first write my usual daily note. Thanks for your letter, which was very pleasing to me. I am glad you get on better, but am not quite sure whether I ought to be away from you.

... I am writing in the section room, having just finished my second paper. I got into rather a mess about the reporting, as I found that the reporters had got my abstract and telegraphed it everywhere, though I did not purpose to read the paper fully. However, I gave a free statement of the purpose and nature of the paper, which seemed to excite considerable interest. I took great care to make it plain that I did not assert the truth of the connection.

I may be deluded, but my impression is that my speaking is much improved. My nervousness seems to have disappeared to a great extent, and when I know the subject I seem to get on without difficulty. . . . I have seen a good many old friends, especially to-day, such as Whitaker, Clifton, Foster,[2] Guthrie,[3] and I have made some new acquaintances. . . .

[4] Jevons's paper 'On the Progress of the Coal Question' was read to Section F of the British Association at Bristol on 26 August 1875. See his letter to his wife of this date published in LJ, p. 339.

[1] Probably Thomas George Palmer Hallett (d. 1919), who had been a student in the Faculty of Medicine, University College London, 1860–4; M.A. 1871; F.S.S. 1878. Details of his career are obscure: he passed the East India Company's Civil Service examination in 1862 and appears to have been appointed Lecturer in Political Economy in University College, Bristol, when it opened in 1876. The appointment was not renewed after Marshall's arrival in 1877. Hallett spent most of his life in Somerset, latterly settling in Bath. He was the author of an influential paper on taxation: see F. Shehab, *Progressive Taxation* (Oxford, 1953) pp. 165–72; J. K. Whitaker, 'Alfred Marshall: The Years 1877 to 1885', *History of Political Economy*, 4 (1972) 4–5.

[2] [Sir] Michael Foster (1836–1907), at this date one of the general secretaries of the British Association. Educated at University College School, 1852–3, and University College London; B.A. 1854; M.D. 1859; Instructor in Practical Physiology and Histology in U.C.L., 1867–9; Praelector in Practical Physiology in Trinity College, Cambridge, 1870–83; Professor of Physiology, Cambridge University, 1883–1903; F.R.S. 1872; K.C.B. 1899; M.P. for the University of London, 1900–6; President of the British Association Meeting held at Dover, 1899.

[3] See Vol. II, Letter 38, n. 5, p. 72.

440. W. S. JEVONS TO HARRIET JEVONS
[LJN, 340–1]

Bristol, 30th August 1875.

. . . I brought Mrs. Elliott[1] over this morning to the economic section, where several ladies, Mrs. Grey,[2] Miss Carpenter,[3] Miss Becker,[4] etc., were to hold forth. I have no objection myself to women speaking in public, but it makes a good deal of bother at present, perhaps by being unusual. If this passes over in time, I think there will be no reason why they should not.

. . . This morning Mrs. Elliott and I went to St. Mary's, Redcliffe, which I found to be a superb church inside and well worth seeing: yesterday I saw Bath Abbey Church very well, as, however, I think I told you yesterday.

In the *Daily News* today I find the abstract of my sun-spot paper given in full as a 'singular paper,' but I do not think it much matters. I am thinking of going on with the subject and trying to get something out of it. . . . I spent most of the morning in Stewart's[5] section of physics (which Stewart presides over), and entered into a little discussion. . . .

441. W. S. JEVONS TO HARRIET JEVONS
[LJN, 341]

Bristol, 31st August 1875.

. . . I have been attending the economic section all day, half the day being occupied with a long discussion on trades unions, which was partly interesting and partly tedious. I made a rather long speech on the

[1] It has not proved possible definitely to identify the Mrs Elliott mentioned by Jevons. She may have been the wife of Dr Christopher Elliott, M.D., a member of the British Institution for the Advancement of Science, Literature and the Arts at this period, who is recorded as living in various parts of Bristol from 1874 to 1921.

[2] Maria Georgina Grey (1816–1906), promoter of women's education, widow of William Thomas Grey (1807–64), nephew of the second Earl Grey; founder, with her sister Emily Shirreff, of the Girls' Public Day School Trust; also, in 1878, of the Maria Grey Training College for women teachers; a strong advocate of women's suffrage. She presented a paper entitled 'The National Standard of Education'.

[3] Mary Carpenter (1807–77), daughter of the Unitarian divine Russell Lant Carpenter. She had been involved for many years with the development of ragged and industrial schools and reformatories in the Bristol area and had become well known throughout the country for her work. She had made several visits to India, the United States and Canada, and had presented many papers at meetings of the Social Science Association. Her paper was entitled 'Industrial Schools'.

[4] Lydia Ernestine Becker (1827–90), founder of the Manchester Women's Suffrage Committee, 1867, and the Manchester Ladies' Literary Society, 1868; a member of the Manchester School Board from 1870 until her death; editor of the *Women's Suffrage Journal*, 1870–90. She attended the annual Meetings of the British Association over many years, and took part in discussions.

[5] i.e. Balfour Stewart.

subject,[1] and again this afternoon I spoke on the subject of competitive examinations.

There is to be no economic section to-morrow, so I think I will spend most of the day in seeing something of Bristol and its manufactures, which I have hitherto been unable to do for the most part.

I have booked myself for the excursion to Wells and Cheddar which was assigned to me, the Avebury one, I suppose, being previously full. This evening I shall attend the *soirée* – the first evening meeting I have been at. To-morrow evening I shall go for a short time to a glee concert, a ticket for which has been presented to me, and afterwards to the *soirée* at Clifton College.

Your letter received this morning is satisfactory, so that I shall stay over Thursday, and hope to get home in good time on Friday . . .

442.   R. O. WILLIAMS[1] TO W. S. JEVONS

1501 Jones St.,
San Francisco, California.
September 11th, 1875.

Professor W. Stanley Jevons,

Dear Sir,

The satisfaction I have had in reading your Theory of Political Economy has been so great, that I cannot keep from expressing some of it to the author. (I assume that writers upon economical subjects are not overwhelmed, like popular novelists and poets, with epistolary admiration.)

I had been feeling about darkly for some more coherent statement of economic principles than any I was acquainted with, when I came across your Theory recently. I have just read it twice – once hastily, and again carefully. It seems to me, beyond all doubt, that it marks an era in the science. It is the substitution of simplicity and order for intricacy, discrepancy and confusion. You intimate (p. 255) that the results attaching to your system may be traced out by you with a nearer

[1] There are no reports of this speech. The discussion in which Jevons took part followed the presentation of the *Second Report on Combinations of Capital and Labour* to Section F on 31 August 1875. See *Report of the Forty-fifth Meeting of the British Association . . . held at Bristol in August, 1875,* Transactions of Sections, pp. 146–55; *The Times,* 1 September 1875, p. 8.

[1] Ralph Olmstead Williams (1838–1908) graduated from Yale in the class of 1861 along with Edward R. Sill, who became Professor of English in the University of California (see below, Letter 448, n. 3, p. 000). Williams migrated to California also, but failed to find academic employment there. After working in New York as a compiler for *Webster's Dictionary,* he finally became Librarian and Curator of the New Haven Historical Society, 1900–5.

approach to completeness at some future time, when the views you insist upon have received some recognition and acceptance.[2] The new crop of economists, I am certain, will make its principles their starting-point. Any work which you may hereafter publish, carrying out your views to further conclusions, will be studied by the careful, unbiased readers of the present volume with the greatest interest.

The truth of your Theory happens to be corroborated in my understanding of it, by what seems to me to be an easy disposition of the difficulty which you acknowledge on pages 119 to 124. The difficulty arises "because we cannot contemplate the existence of an increment or a decrement to an indivisible article."[3]

I make the following suggestion with great diffidence, as you may have already rejected it in studying the problem. It is this:

Almost every commodity or service (whether divisible or not) gratifies more than one want. The principal use may be called *primary*, all the others *secondary*. The primary uses of food, clothing, houses, horses etc. are subsistence, warmth, shelter, speed, strength; the secondary uses, gratification of taste, smell, love of beauty, display etc. etc. Whenever selection can be made from many objects (divisible or indivisible) having the same primary use, a minute differentiation is effected by a *comparison* of their fitness for secondary uses. The house-market in large cities gives a wide range for selection, according to what the purchaser is willing to pay; besides *shelter,* he will get, if he pays for it, commodiousness, convenience of location, durability, elegance of proportions, beauty of finish, desirability of neighbourhood. In the country the choice is very limited; but there is always the potential house which the purchaser could build instead of the one under consideration.

Divisible objects admit of *double* differentiation – primary, by an actual reduction or increase of quantity – secondary, by a comparison of equal quantities as to fitness for secondary uses. In individual and household management, I think, discrimination is usually made in quality before a reduction of quantity is submitted to. In times of embarrassment, the superior, but higher priced articles, which minister most perfectly to secondary uses, are displaced by others of the same class answering the primary want perhaps equally well, but less effectual for the secondary ones.

This idea of primary and secondary differentiation, if true, leads to some important qualifications of economic laws – e.g. as to scarcity prices (pp 150–3)[4] when carried beyond certain limits.

---

[2] *Theory of Political Economy,* chapter VIII; first edition, p. 255; fourth edition, p. 266.

[3] Op. cit., first edition, p. 120; fourth edition, p. 121. The section referred to by Williams is that on 'Failure of the Equations of Exchange'.

[4] Section entitled 'Variation of the Price of Corn', fourth edition, pp. 155–8.

But I have trespassed too far upon your patience. I have ventured to do so at all, only because to the scientific *all* approval or disapproval has *some* importance.

With great respect,
your obedient servant
R. O. Williams

I thought I was through, but I must add an expression of admiration at the clearness, brevity and force with which your Theory is explained. The extraordinary mis-statement of it by Prof. Cairnes (Some Leading Principles of Political Economy newly Expounded – Chap. I. s, 4.) is perfectly unaccountable.[5]

W.

443.   W. S. JEVONS TO J. ROBSON

36 Parsonage Road
Withington
Manchester
3 Oct 1875

Dear Mr. Robson

At a recent meeting of the Council of Owens College my proposal to rearrange my lectures so as to be able to lecture in University College in May was again considered. It was thought that the change would involve too much inconvenience to our students here. I am not prepared to find fault with their decision, & rather blame myself for making the suggestion without sufficient consideration.

I am now thinking of sending in a formal application for the professorship without much more delay, but should first like to have answers to a few questions.

1. In the event of my appointment, would the Council of your College, in your opinion agree to the nomination of a substitute lecturer for the present session.

I am quite unwilling to inconvenience the College here by any sudden resignation even if I could legally do it, which is by no means clear.

2. Can you let me know the general regulations affecting the engagements of professors in University College?

3. Is it requisite according to your rules that testimonials should be submitted and if so would old ones do in this case.

Believe me
Yours very faithfully
W. Stanley Jevons.

[5] 'Relation of Value to Utility', loc. cit., pp. 16–21.

444. W. S. JEVONS TO H. S. FOXWELL
[RDF; LJP, 342]

36 Parsonage Road
Withington
Manchester
3 Oct 75

Dear Foxwell

I am glad you like some parts of my Book on Money. Even if I could have got more into the allotted space I do not know that I could have ventured to touch the subjects you mention. Have you seen Crump's Theory of Stock Exchange Speculation?[1] It is not altogether a good book, being written altogether from a business point of view, but it contains some useful hints.

I have often speculated on the lowness of interest on money at call, but presume that it arises from the large quantity seeking employment, and the fact that it cannot be safely employed at a higher charge. Consols would certainly not allow of a higher rate for if the money be invested say for a fortnight, the interest wd be only $\frac{3\frac{1}{4}}{26}$ or just 1/8 per cent which might any time be lost by a forced sale, not to speak of expenses. He who invests other peoples money in Consols or indeed in most other funds will on the average have to sell when the price is depressed. This subject was much discussed last session in connection with the National Debt Com^{rs} holding the funds of the Savings Bank which is money at call.

I have just received questions in pol. econ from Mr West,[2] which I am going to make up into papers.

I *shall be obliged by your informing me how I ought to address the papers* in order to get them printed at the Univ. Press. or ought I to send them through you?

Believe me
Yours faithfully
W. Stanley Jevons.

445. W. S. JEVONS TO J. ROBSON

Withington
5 Oct 75

Dear Mr. Robson

Thanks for your reply and for the printed regulations.

You must have overlooked most of my lectures in the Owens College

[1] Arthur Crump, *The Theory of Stock Exchange Speculation*, fourth edition (1875).
[2] Alfred Slater West (1846–1932), educated at University College London, and Trinity College, Cambridge; B.A. 1870; M.A. 1874; Headmaster of Amersham Hall School, 1876–92; Senior Fellow

Calendar, as I lecture four days a week throughout the first two terms and three days during the last term. If I had only had one lecture a week I should probably have proposed to travel up to London weekly but that you will see is impracticable under the circumstances.

I will at once take steps to find a right sort of man to propose as substitute during this session. I have in my eye Mr. Alfred Marshall of Cambridge but do not know whether he can be induced to act.[1]

Yours faithfully
W. S. Jevons.

446.   W. S. JEVONS TO E. J. BROADFIELD
       [LJN, 342–3]

Withington, 6th October 1875.

. . . Whether wisely or not I declared war against Mill's crotchets some years ago now, simply because I know them to be untrue, and I shall have to fight it out. I have little or no doubt about success, if only health and opportunities favour me; but you will see that in such matters one labours under disadvantages in not living, like most of the political economists and literary men, in London. You can hardly fail to see the need of my being there. It is more easy to imagine than describe. Take only the case of the Political Economy Club, of which I was made an honorary member a year or two ago. This dines and debates once a month privately, and includes every leading economist. Mill's opinions were all disseminated and discussed there many years ago, indeed he was a very prominent member.[1] I have only been able to attend the club two or three times altogether; last May I opened one discussion, but it is clearly of great importance to have such an opportunity of discussing and urging my own opinions. There are several other societies, the Statistical, Social Science, Royal, etc., from which I am practically cut off.

It is a very momentous change to me, and the necessity for deciding comes at a most inconvenient time, when I am occupied with other anxieties.[2] The professorship in University College has now been left at my disposal practically for three months, which is a very civil thing of

of University College London, 1926–32; Examiner with Jevons and Foxwell in the Moral Sciences Tripos, 1875.

[1] There is no definite evidence that Jevons approached Marshall before writing to Foxwell (Letter 448A, below, p. 142). Marshall at this time would have been just returning from his four months tour in the United States. See Keynes, in Pigou, *Memorials of Alfred Marshall*, p. 18.

[1] J. S. Mill was a member of the Political Economy Club from 1836 until his death; 'for a very long time, it was the only society that he frequented'. – A. Bain, *Life of James Mill*, p. 199, quoted in *Political Economy Club . . . Proceedings . . . and Questions Discussed, 1821–1920* VI, 304.

[2] Jevons's eldest child, Herbert Stanley Jevons (1875–1955), was born on 8 October.

them to do; but you may now consider, I think, that I have finally decided to take it, and the only difficulty is in providing for the lectures at London during the present session.

You will also see that my going to London is wholly unconnected with questions of salary at Owens College, though it is a serious matter giving up some hundreds a year, as I am going to do, at my time of life. However, I expect that the sacrifice need not be permanently a great one if I want the money. . . .

447. W. S. JEVONS TO R. H. INGLIS PALGRAVE

36 Parsonage Road,
Withington,
Manchester.
25 Oct. 75.

My dear Palgrave,

The lecturer whom you kindly promised to search for would have, between now and the end of May, to give from twelve to twenty or twenty five lectures on political economy in University College, London.[1] The lectures are usually given once a week in the latter part of the afternoon but the days and hours could to a great extent be made convenient to the lecturer in all probability.

The subject treated might be any important branch of political economy with which the lecturer happened to be particularly conversant, but he might give if desired a simple course on the elements of the subject.

The remuneration of the Professors and lecturers in University College depends in most cases on the fees of the students and is sometimes almost nominal. In this case the remuneration which I could propose would be two pounds ten shillings per lecture up to a maximum of fifty pounds. The number of lectures would have to be a matter of agreement, as I am not warranted in assuming that the College would accept less than twenty. But if you could find some man specially well acquainted with some important branch like finance, or taxation, a series of 10 or 12 lectures in it might be sufficient. The requirements are thus to a considerable degree dependent upon what can be got.

If we had more time for discussion yours and my ideas of currency would I think have been found not so far apart.

I do not wish my intended removal to London to be needlessly

[1] The lecturer ultimately appointed was H. S. Foxwell, but there is no evidence that this was a result of Palgrave's enquiries. Cf. Letters 448A and 448B below, p. 142–3.

mentioned in connection with this lectureship as I am not really appointed and am acting on my own responsibility at present.

Yours faithfully,
W. S. Jevons.

448.   R. O. WILLIAMS TO W. S. JEVONS

San Francisco, Oct. 27/75

Professor W. Stanley Jevons,

Dear Sir:
Your letter of the 4th inst and your interesting paper on "the Progress of the Mathematical Theory of Political Economy" reached me day before yesterday. Please, accept my thanks for both favors.

I cannot get over my surprise that the Theory has not attracted more attention and enlisted more adherents.

I quite failed to express my meaning as to the house.

Let me explain more at length my idea as to the primary and secondary uses of commodities.

Take first, if you please, an illustration of the *primary* use of a commodity, with increments or decrements of consumption depending on the price.

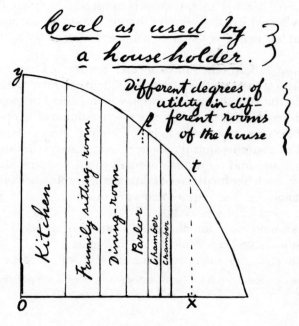

Line OX = all the coal he can use. Price being at p, he economises somewhat by having fires only occasionally in the chambers. If p should rise to y, some other fuel would be substituted, or fire be dispensed with entirely, i.e. (in the latter case) he has dropped out of house and home.

If p goes below t, no more coal than OX will be used, because that is enough.

Here only the primary use of coal – its effectiveness for supplying heat – has been considered. It would be easy to show some secondary uses attaching to coal, or any fuel, consumed by the householder, but the secondary uses are so inconsiderable, as compared with the primary, that I prefer to take a better example.

Tobacco may sell at fifty cents or fifty dollars per pound according as it may be a coarse flavored kind prepared for the pipe, or something exceptionally fine flavored, and made up with exceptional care into segars. The primary use of it in either case is the same – namely, stimulus – and the fifty cents judiciously invested would get as much of *that* in the one case as the fifty dollars in the other. Why then does not every man who intends to buy a pound of this kind of stimulus pay fifty cents for it, instead of $2. $10. $25. $50., as the case may be? There can be only one answer, viz, – there are other – secondary – uses attaching to tobacco besides stimulus.

Pounds of different kinds of tobacco prepared as segars or for the pipe.	
Gratifies inordinate vanity	$50.
Gratifies vanity, and very pleasant to the senses.	$30.
Unobjectionable, pleasant, convenient	$20.
Poor, but being segar, more convenient than pipe	$10.
Good flavored pipe - tobacco	$3.
Rank, nauseating.	$.50ᶜ

Secondary uses of tobacco.

Plainly in times of general business depression the high-priced kinds will suffer most. About the usual quantity of tobacco will be consumed, but most persons will descend to a lower grade.

This effects a reduction in the amounts consumed by the community of all tobaccos above a certain price, while there results an increased demand for the inferior kinds.

Tea and alcoholic drinks obviously "jump with" tobacco.

Less obviously, but not less certainly, the same principles apply to clothing. A person who kept an analytical account of his expenses would charge part of his clothing-bill to *Warmth* (primary use), part to *Respectability* (secondary use.) In hard times there is probably but very little increase of bodily suffering from insufficient clothing, but *Respectability* is in agony. It has "nothing to wear." People use their old clothes longer than in other times, and when obliged to buy new ones, select goods somewhat inferior to those which they wore before. The result is a reduction of demand for cloth above a certain price, and usually a reduction in the total amount of cloth sold. I have been told by a manufacturer, that there has been no falling off in the United States, since the panic of '73, in the demand for low priced cloths.

The same principles apply with different degrees of force to about all commodities. Coal and alcoholic drinks are at the two extremes of the scale.

I should distrust, therefore, the progression indicated in the table on page 150, [1] when carried beyond the point where it stops. The consumers of wheat would drop out very fast, and in rapidly increasing numbers, when the price passed that line. Of course, everything would depend upon there being a sufficiency of other cereals at hand to take the place of wheat. The preference for wheat, I believe, is nowhere else so strong as in England; but even Englishmen would succumb doubtless to high prices and descend to some other grain, of which the primary use was identical with that of wheat. Brandy for a time was almost wholly displaced by whiskey in America, in consequence of the high prices resulting from the war and the raising of the tariff.

Now as to the house. – Two houses of the same dimensions, equally weather-proof, equally durable, and equally accessible, are on a par as to their primary use – shelter. Yet one may be worth $5,000 and the other $50,000. The difference lies in their fitness for secondary uses. Suppose, if you please, that the head of a family has $30,000 which he proposes to lay out in a house, and that the two houses already spoken of answer his wants

---

[1] Davenant's table of the proportions in which a 'defect' in the harvest would raise the price of corn: *Theory of Political Economy,* fourth edition, p. 155.

exactly as to *size*. He will buy neither of them. The first will not do, because he is looking for something besides shelter, and the other is too expensive. It is not impossible, that, after looking at many, his attention will rest upon two in the same block which are like each other in all respects, except that one has (e.g.) plate-glass windows, and the other has not. If the price of the two be the same, he will take the one with plate-glass windows.

In fashionable street, — expensively decorated	$50,000
Ditto, but less expensively decorated —not in the best part of the street	$40,000
In good neighbour-hood — still expensively decorated	$25,000
Ditto, less decoration	$20,000
Indifferent neigh-bourhood — little decoration	$12,000
Neighbourhood not so good	$9,000
Objectionable neighbourhood	$5,000

(Higher priced houses are usually better built and more durable than cheaper ones — but they are not necessarily so.) Houses on a par as to shelter — i.e. as to their primary use they are equally desirable.

The man who buys a $15,000 house buys less marble, French plate-glass, ornamental wood, and decoration of all kinds, than a $50,000 purchaser. He may get as much land, but it is in a less desirable location. He has economised in the secondary uses of a house.

When a general necessity for economy sets in, the house-market, although it responds slowly to business changes, nevertheless feels at last the depressing influences. People who move go into inferior instead of better houses, rents fall, beginning with the higher priced dwellings. The movement is the same as with cloth, only it is slower in starting and it is not so easily arrested.

If now we refer to your law of exchange (p 95),[2] it seems to me to be equally applicable to houses as to coal or cloth. The whole body of house-builders and house-vendors – in fact the general public – can be regarded as a single individual who has at his disposal a quantity of house-utility, either actual or potential. This utility cannot be measured by cubic-feet, but there may be more or less of it, and the sale of a portion takes that part out of the market. It is (or will be) "put up in parcels to suit" the varying wants of different buyers. Evidently the prices of the different parcels will conform more or less closely to a general opinion existing at the time and place as to the relative utility of a certain quantity of gold and the aggregate house-utility in any one parcel. The exchange of these utilities can be illustrated by the following example.

Let us suppose that a great capitalist, having confidence in the future of some city, begins buying houses in it for speculative purposes; and let us also suppose, that, having in view a certain class of tenants, he limits his purchases to $10,000 houses or those whose prices are approximately near that sum.

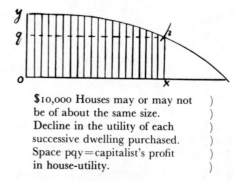

$10,000 Houses may or may not   )
be of about the same size.   )
Decline in the utility of each   )
successive dwelling purchased.   )
Space pqy = capitalist's profit   )
in house-utility.   )

If the city be large, many purchases can be made before a disturbance in the market is produced; but eventually the houses which he will get for $10,000 each will be inferior to those first bought, and as the market rises upon him at a rapidly increasing rate, a point (p) will be reached at last, where it will not be to his advantage to give $10,000 for any house purchaseable at that price. He then stops; an equilibrium (as he looks at the matter) has been reached. If an influx of buyers purchasing one house each be substituted for the single capitalist, the result will be the same.

----

[2] 'The ratio of exchange of any two commodities will be the reciprocal of the ratio of the final degrees of utility of the quantities of commodity available for consumption after the exchange is completed' – op. cit., p. 95 (first and fourth editions).

This or a similar series of exchanges could be illustrated from various points of view.

The noticeable thing in these transactions is the fact (I think), that it is not necessary to regard each house as an infinitesimal quantity. The differentiation is in their respective utilities, which may be more or less by infinitely small gradations, like the logarithms of a series of numbers. And in all kinds of intelligent bargaining is it not the more or less of the utility of a commodity which is had in view, instead of the more or less of the commodity itself?

The theory of "equilibrium", as applicable to cases of "the proper distribution of the same commodity," can be applied where the utilities of a house are under consideration. The commodity (if we may call it so) which is to be distributed is the total utility of the dwelling, the several parts of which total should be so apportioned by the occupant, that these partial utilities shall be as nearly as possible in equilibrium with various desires.

To generalise the argument. Every commodity, besides its primary use, has some which are secondary. These uses vary relatively with each other in different parcels of what (judged by its primary use) is the same thing. Hence the net utility of any parcel compared with another parcel is not wholly dependent on its mass. When, thus, there are several kinds of the same commodity, divided into numerous parcels, from which selection can be made, a differentiation may be effected as to these parcels (even if of the same mass) by a comparison of their net utilities; and it is not necessary that these parcels should be infinitesimal as contrasted with the whole commodity. When these parcels differ in mass as well as in other respects, the differentiation of net utilities may reach the last degree of minuteness, although the differences between the masses of the parcels be not minute.

My only reason for doubting the solution of the problem offered here is, that you have not applied it yourself to the difficulty. Under the circumstances that is a grave objection indeed. I seem to be discoursing of war to Hannibal.

Very respectfully yours
R. O. Williams

Should anything in this very long letter seem worth your comment be so kind as to address me, *Care of Prof. E. R. Sill,*[3] *Oakland, California* — North Am. Review (Oct 75) has an able article supporting application mathematics to P.E.[4]

[3] Edward Roland Sill (1841–87), Williams's classmate at Yale; poet and essayist, Professor of English, University of California, 1874–82.

[4] Simon Newcomb, 'The Method and Province of Political Economy', *North American Review*, 249 (1875) 241–70.

448A.   W. S. JEVONS TO H. S. FOXWELL
      [RDF]

Private

36 Parsonage Road
Withington
Manchester
29 Oct 75

Dear Foxwell

I expect to be shortly appointed to the vacant professorship of political economy at University College London, and in that case should remove to London in the autumn. In the meantime I should not be able to undertake the lectures in London during the present session, & wish to find some lecturer who will take the work temporarily. I fear that Cambridge extension lectures or other engagements may prevent your thinking of the proposal which I venture to make that you should allow yourself to be named the intermediate lecturer.

I believe that a course of 20 elementary lectures would be quite sufficient given at some time between 4 & 7 pm, on one or two days of the week. The details could no doubt be arranged to suit you in most points, & you could readily go to & return from London the same day.

The professorship will be almost an honorary one the professor receiving only the fees of about £2. 2. from each student. The lecturer will I fear have to consider the work in an honorary light also. He would receive of course the whole of the fees and I would undertake to guarantee that the amount should not fall below fifty pounds, but the travelling would absorb a considerable proportion of the sum.

I do hope[1] that you will be able to see your way to do this. You will probably have an intelligent class, and barring the travelling may find the work pleasant.

The Council of University College want to nominate the lecturers on Nov 6th and I should be much obliged if I could have your answer with the least possible delay, so that if it is unfortunately a negative one I may try elsewhere.

As nothing is absolutely settled please be so good as not to mention my approaching resignation of the professorship in Owens College.

Yours faithfully
W. S. Jevons.

---

[1] Altered from 'wish'.

448B.   W. S. JEVONS TO H. S. FOXWELL
      [RDF]

                                                      36 Parsonage Road
                                                           Withington
                                                          31 Oct 75

Dear Foxwell

I am really glad that you are favourable to the idea of these lectures and will at once propose you to the Council of University College, so that by the end of next week I hope it may be settled. The only drawback I find in your letter is that you begin

"So far as I now see I shall be able &c." I suppose however that this has no special meaning, & you afterwards say that you can "venture to take the post." About your ability to do it I entertain no doubt whatever, & I should prefer to leave the choice of subject mostly to yourself if not entirely.

I fancy a plain course of the elements of the subject out of Mill as much as you like (with all his errors) will be the thing that will suit best.

I think that they have previously found elementary courses most successful. Ricardo & Cairnes can always be introduced but I have lately been reading Malthus' Principles of Political Economy & can recommend it to you as a book not sufficiently estimated as far as I can see.

The exact times for the lectures had better be settled by yourself directly with Mr John Robson the Secretary of the College as soon as you are appointed. The times lately were 6 to 7 pm Tuesdays & Thursdays, but in former years they were 5 to 6 pm once a week. I dont think there ought to be any difficulty about these details.

I quite concur in the proposed exam^n of women this year[1] & have sent Mr Sidgwick's[2] letter to Mr West to be forwarded on as desired.

If you wish to leave Cambridge you would find this place of mine an easy berth with £350 a year or so and some advantages, plenty of society of Cambridge men &c &c; but this is anticipating.

                                          Yours faithfully
                                             W. S. Jevons.

---

[1] The Tripos Examinations were not formally opened to women students until 1881, but since 1873 the Cambridge University authorities had consented to their admission to the Examinations on an informal basis, under the same conditions as those applying to male undergraduates. This privileged arrangement was made privately with the examiners and depended entirely on the approval and consent of the individuals concerned, though in practice few declined. See John Roach, *Public Examinations in England 1850–1900* (Cambridge, 1971) pp. 122–7.

[2] Henry Sidgwick (1838–1900), philosopher; Praelector in Moral and Political Philosophy in Trinity College, Cambridge, 1875; Knightbridge Professor of Moral Philosophy in the University of Cambridge, 1883–1900; a pioneer of the higher education of women in Cambridge.

449.   W. S. JEVONS TO J. ROBSON

36 Parsonage Road
Withington
Manchester
2 Nov. 1875.

John Robson Esqe
    University College[1]

Dear Sir

Understanding that the professorship of Political Economy in University College is now vacant, I beg that you will inform the Council of my desire to be appointed to that chair. It is my intention, in the event of receiving such appointment, to remove to London as soon as can conveniently be done, that is in the autumn of next year. I should be prepared to make the success of the political economy class the first claim upon my attention, and to give the remainder of my time, as I have done during the last twelve years in Manchester, to studies and occupations suitable to the chair.

I should propose, as an experiment, to extend the course of lectures considerably, giving from 40 to 50 in the session, instead of about 24 as has hitherto been the custom, and I would endeavour to make political economy, & connected portions of the social sciences a more important feature in the curriculum of the college. I must add, however, that my own experience here, & that of other teachers in London & elsewhere, forbid me to be very sanguine as to the success of any extended courses of this kind, and I presume it will be understood that in the absence of sufficient encouragement to continue numerous lectures, the Council would consent after two or three years to a return to the old number of lectures if desired by the lecturer.

My engagement with Owens College extends until nearly the end of April next, and considering all the circumstances, I feel that it would not be right for me to put the Owens College to any inconvenience by retiring before the close of the working session. In the event of my appointment, I must therefore request the Council of your college to allow me to nominate a substitute lecturer to take my duties in University College during the present session. I have the less hesitation in asking this, as I am able to propose for this temporary appointment, a gentleman, Mr. Herbert Somerton Foxwell, M.A. Fellow of St. John's College Cam-

---

[1] Written in another hand on the back of the letter:
    'Prof. Stanley Jevons
    re Profship Pol. Economy
        Nov. 1875.'

bridge, who is sure to give satisfaction. Mr. Foxwell took his degree in 1870 at the head of the Moral Science Tripos, and has since been constantly engaged in preparing other students for the same examinations, many of whom have taken high places in honours. Political economy forms one of the principal branches of the Moral Science Tripos at Cambridge. He recently acted as one of the provincial lecturers in Political Economy of the Cambridge Extension System, and Mr. Alfred Marshall of St. John's College writes of him as follows: — "He has given elementary lectures in Political Economy at Leeds with great success, and great benefit to himself. He has a clear and easy style, and is remarkably successful in interesting beginners in their work."

Mr. Foxwell is comparatively a young man and has not yet had an opportunity of showing his powers, but my personal acquaintance with him has enabled me to form a very favourable opinion both of his special abilities & general character.

My proposal to Mr. Foxwell was that he should give a course of twenty lectures of one hour each, at some time between 4 and 7 p.m. on either one or two days per week as might be arranged for the convenience both of the College and himself. Professor Courtney I observe gave 24 lectures, but as Mr. Foxwell will have to travel up from Cambridge I thought the Council would perhaps sanction a reduction to 20 for this session. If this should be decided to be undesirable I can no doubt modify the arrangement with Mr. Foxwell. The pecuniary part of the agreement would I suppose lie between him and me, and I should I presume receive the whole of the fees, which will in any case be handed over to Mr. Foxwell.

I will add in conclusion that I have for many years looked forward to the honour of becoming some day a professor in the College, where I was so long a student, and it will always give me pleasure to contribute any slight aid I can to the progress of a college which I owe everything.

I beg to remain
Yours faithfully
W. Stanley Jevons.

P.S. Mr. Foxwell is an examiner in the Moral Science Tripos at Cambridge.

450.   W. S. JEVONS TO MRS LUCY HUTTON
    [LJN, 343–4]

36 Parsonage Road, Withington,
9th November 1875.

. . . I daresay you will be glad to hear a few things from me, especially as I am able to say that Harriet and Herbert Stanley are getting on well. . . . It is wonderful what interest one feels in the little fellow, though he has not yet shown any consciousness of his relation to me, except to cry when I touch him. . . . I have just received a letter from University College, stating that the Council propose to elect me professor, so that it is really settled, though the final ratification cannot be made until 4th December. I do not begin my work in London until next session in October 1876, and for the present a temporary lecturer will be appointed. I trust I shall never regret the important step I have taken. It involves a loss of something like £300 a year, though part of this may be made up by other appointments or gains in London. . . .

451.   W. S. JEVONS TO H. S. FOXWELL
    [RDF; LJP, 344]

36 Parsonage Rd
Withington
16 Nov. 75

Dear Foxwell

    I quite concur in the proposal about the Girton students, understanding of course that there is no objection on the part of the University.

    I have sent a new question to Mr West to be substituted for that on banking.

    I do not think the "so-called Ricardian theory" &c much matters one way or the other but am quite willing it should be altered to Ricardian theory.[1] I cannot recollect whether it was one of my questions or not. Certainly I cannot see that Ricardo has the slightest claim to the theory, as it was quite as well stated by Malthus if not by Anderson long before. I am beginning to think very strongly that the true line of economic science descends from Smith through Malthus to Senior while another branch through Ricardo to Mill has put as much error into the science as they have truth.

    I can hardly suppose that your College will object to your going to London for a few lectures.

    [1] The question appears to have remained unaltered: 'Specify the objections which have been urged against the so-called Ricardian theory of Rent, by Dr. Whewell and Professor Rogers . . . ', *Cambridge University Examination Papers*, Michaelmas Term 1875, pp. 46, 162.

I have sent the Logic papers to the Pitt Press. If I recollect rightly it is usual to submit the proofs to each examiner so I will send them to Mr Mansel[2] who will perhaps send them to you and Mr West.

Yours faithfully,

W. S. Jevons.

452. W. S. JEVONS TO H. S. FOXWELL
[RDF; LJP, 344−5]

36 Parsonage Road
Withington
20 Nov.75

Dear Foxwell

I return the revises without alteration. The question about rent was not mine but I cannot remember whether or not I inserted the "so called". I think you might as well speak of Laplace's Theory of Gravitation as of Ricardo's Theory of Rent or Airy's Undulatory Theory of Sight.

I was pleased to hear that it is definitely settled for you to lecture at London. It is not likely to do you any harm, but you must not be disgusted if you have not a very brilliant class. None of your predecessors so far [as][1] I can learn have ever been able to infuse much spirit into the class, but still the work must be done and it is worth doing, and I suppose I shall do it after you for the rest of my life.

If you have occasion to write again in a short time I should be glad to know whether it will be possible to send me down here any of the answers to read. & about what time the decision must be made. I should like to be in Cambridge for a few days, but as Mrs Jevons cannot come with me I do not wish to be long away. Moreover College work should not be neglected.

I seal my letters containing exam^n papers with a ⌒⌡ letter J. on an engine turned ground.

Yours faithfully

W. S. Jevons.

P.S. I do not care about seeing the papers in Ethics.

---

[2] Spencer Mansel (1838−75), Fellow of Trinity College, Cambridge, 1867; vicar of Trumpington, 1870−5; Examiner with Jevons and Foxwell in the Moral Sciences Tripos, 1875. He died on 2 December 1875. Cf. below, Letter 459, p. 156. Jevons wrote to Mansel two days later, enclosing proofs of the examination papers, which he requested Mansel to forward to Foxwell and West.

[1] Omitted in the original manuscript.

453.   W. S. JEVONS TO HARRIET JEVONS

36 Parsonage Road,
Withington.
Thursday
[9th December] 1875.

My dearest,

Here I am home again. I never in my life had such a hurry scurry as in the last 48 hours. I left here about 4 pm on Tuesday after deciding that it was impossible to conclude the exam on Wednesday. I reached Euston after 11 at night and found a packet of papers and various telegrams and letters requesting me to try and settle the next day. I read papers till 1 o'clock and woke the next morning at 7 and read again, then went into the city and saw one of the Kings[1] partners – left for Cambridge at noon – spent the afternoon in Foxwell's rooms finishing the reading and settling the list. Then we had a pleasant dinner party at 7, and an evening party at Marshall's rooms. Here I saw Miss Clough[2] and gave your message, Wright,[3] Dr. & Mrs. Bateson,[4] Miss Kennedy,[5] who passed 2nd class, Miss Paley[6] the lecturer on Pol. Econ. who pleased me very much, and various others. I slept as was intended at Venn's.[7] He was very kind and pleasant and I liked Mrs. Venn very well. She looks a great invalid though she is said to be better than she was.

I left Cambridge at 11 this morning and as Miss Borchardt[8] happened

[1] P. S. King & Son, the publishers of the 'International Scientific Series' in which Jevons's *Money and the Mechanism of Exchange* appeared.

[2] Anne Jemima Clough (1820–92), sister of Arthur Hugh Clough, the poet; a founder of the North of England Council for Promoting the Higher Education of Women, 1867; Secretary, 1867–70, President, 1873–4. She became head of the first house for women students at Cambridge, which opened with five students at 74 Regent Street in October 1871, moving to Merton Hall the following year. Principal of Newnham Hall, which opened in October 1875, and of Newnham College from 1880 until her death. See B. A. Clough, *A Memoir of Anne Jemima Clough* (1903).

[3] Probably William Aldis Wright (1831–1914), Librarian of Trinity College, Cambridge, 1863–70; Senior Bursar, 1870–95; Master of Trinity, 1888–1912. As a nonconformist he was ineligible for Fellowship before 1878; joint editor of the *Journal of Philology* from 1868.

[4] The Master of St John's College and his wife. William Henry Bateson (1812–81) became a Fellow of St John's in 1831, was Master from 1857 to 1881 and Vice-Chancellor of Cambridge University in 1858.

[5] Mary Kennedy, one of the five women students who went up to Cambridge in 1871 under Miss Clough's supervision, and a particular friend of Mary Paley. She married R. T. Wright, a Fellow of Christ's College, Cambridge.

[6] Mary Paley (1850–1944), who was to marry Alfred Marshall in 1877, had been invited by Henry Sidgwick to come into residence at Newnham in 1875 and take over from Marshall the lectures on economics to women students. See Mary Paley Marshall, *What I Remember* (Cambridge, 1947); Keynes, 'Mary Paley Marshall', *Economic Journal*, 44 (1944) 268–83.

[7] John Venn (1834–83), Fellow of Gonville and Caius College, 1857–83; author of *The Logic of Chance* (1866) and *Symbolic Logic* (1881).

[8] Malvina Henrietta Borchardt (d. 1916), daughter of Dr Louis Borchardt of Manchester, was a student at Girton College from 1873 to 1877; a successful candidate in the Mathematical and Moral

to be coming to Manchester I travelled with her and we had much conversation about the theory of equations, quaternions, Taylors theorem etc. I do not know what place she will take in the tripos but she is certainly an intelligent girl. Girton College is disappointed at Miss Maynard[9] being put in the second class. Keynes[10] (with the large hand writing) was a very good first as was generally anticipated. I had a good deal of talk with Kings partner. They will make an alteration if I wish but do not like or advise it. I have not settled what to do. About the foreign editions they think there is no difficulty and I have substituted a few wholly indifferent words. I am naturally very tired so excuse more.

Ever your affectionate husband,
W. S. Jevons

454. W. S. JEVONS TO J. ROBSON

36 Parsonage Road
Withington
10 Dec. 1875

Dear Mr. Robson

I have just received your letter informing me that the Council of University College on the 4th inst. appointed me Professor of Political Economy, the appointment to take effect from the beginning of next session. I beg that you will on the next opportunity convey to the Council my sense of the honour they have done me, and my desire to occupy the office with advantage to the students and the College,

Believe me
Yours faithfully
W. Stanley Jevons.

Sciences Triposes in 1877; taught in London girls' schools before becoming headmistress of Devonport High School, 1880–4. She opened a hostel for women students in Gower Street, London, in 1885 after studying women's education in Germany, and later ran a private boarding and day school for girls in Hampstead from 1890 to 1902.

[9] Constance Louisa Maynard (1849–1935), had studied at Girton since 1872 and was the first student of the College to take the Moral Sciences Tripos, in which she obtained a Second in 1875. She devoted her career to pioneering women's education and from 1882 to 1913 was Mistress of Westfield College, London, which was opened largely through her efforts. Her publications included *Between College Terms* (1910).

[10] John Neville Keynes. See Vol. V, Letter 654.

455.   W. S. JEVONS TO HARRIET JEVONS

36 Parsonage Road
Withington
Manchester
10 Dec 1875

My dearest

I was glad to get your letter though a brief one, & am particularly pleased to hear that the dear little baby is well & good.

Thank Fred [1] for his letter very much but say that I really cannot make up my mind tonight whether to go or not. There is a professors meeting tomorrow night which I do not want to miss and if I went on Sunday & came back on Monday for my class it might tire me more than if I staid* here. Perhaps he will allow me to leave it uncertain but I shall write again tomorrow. Do not expect me. I have just received a letter telling me of my appointment to University College, so that is all straight. By the same post I have a PRIVATE LETTER from Dr Hodgson saying that he hoped I might become his successor in Edinburgh, in a little time, so that I dare say if the action for libel [2] ruins us we can fall back on £600 a year at Edinburgh.

I am glad to say my last letter to the French publishers had the desired effect & has brought a civil answer with a proof sheet of the desired page & a promise to alter it if desired. This is very lucky as I find the sentence more pronounced in the French than the English. I have seen George Allen [3] today and have got a likely proposal for smoothing things down. There has been a review of my telegraph article in the Pall Mall & a brief correspondence since. [4] No doubt I am tired enough to night but Mondays class is the last as the Christmas exams then begin & I feel the term is almost over.

Ever your affec Husband
W. S. Jevons

[1] Frederick Jevons. See Vol. II, Letter 56, n. 20, p. 132. Harriet Jevons was staying with her sister and brother-in-law while Jevons was in Cambridge.

[2] The implication of this passage and Letter 453 above is that some sentence in *Money and the Mechanism of Exchange* had given rise to a threatened libel action. Since no such action took place the 'likely proposal for smoothing things down' was presumably successful. It is impossible to identify the offending sentence.

[3] George Peter Allen (1835–1905), solicitor; admitted, Trinity Term 1860; practised in Manchester from 1865 to 1905 as a member of the firm Partington & Allen.

[4] A review of Jevons's article 'The Post Office Telegraphs and their Financial Results', *Fortnightly Review* (New Series 78) 1875) 826–35, appeared in the *Pall Mall Gazette*, 7 December 1875, p. 10. The author argued that in purchasing the Suez Canal shares for political rather than commercial reasons, the Tory government was repeating the mistake made by the Liberals in 1870 with the purchase of the Post Office telegraphs, which Jevons, in his article, showed to have been a financial blunder. This gave rise to two letters published on 8 and 9 December, from 'A Liberal M.P.', who blamed Disraeli's government for the purchase of the telegraphs. In a rejoinder on 8 December the Editor pointed out that the actual transfer took place a year after Gladstone came to power.

456. R. O. WILLIAMS TO W. S. JEVONS

Oakland, California, U.S.
December 14th, 1875.

Professor W. Stanley Jevons.

Dear Sir,

Upon reconsidering my letter about the house, it has struck me that it was somewhat vague just at the point where explicitness was perhaps of the most importance.

Your law of exchange (Theory p. 95) I understand to be the statement of a *tendency* which the ratio of exchange obeys; the exact fulfillment of the law would occur only in that equilibrium (p. 98)[1] which causes a cessation of exchange. Hence (as I understand it) the impossibility of inferring from a series of exchange rates the comparative *total* utilities of the two commodities as to either party, – or of inferring the relative profit of the parties in *total* utility (vide. p. 134).[2] The corn-community (p. 96) might have *begun* the traffic by giving only one pound of corn for one of beef, but conceded more and more to the beef-community as the degree of utility of corn to the latter declined.[3]

The problem of the £(900.1100) house (p. 124)[4] seems to involve a comparison of *total* utilities, and an adjustment of *total* profits between buyer and seller. Such an inquiry would seem not to admit of any answer, according to the principle laid down on page 134. What I wanted to show in my other letter was that your law of exchange-rate applied equally to houses, horses etc. as to beef and corn, as a law of *tendency*. My attention at the time was almost wholly directed to the idea of variation in house utility apart from any differences of quantity in houses themselves, so that I barely hinted at the part such variations of utility would play in house-traffic. It is unnecessary to say anything further about such variability, except to mention the fact, that increments of house-excellence can be measured with some degree of exactness, since they command increments of money, – and that quantities of it may properly be represented by a straight line, if quantities of money may be.

---

[1] In the *Theory of Political Economy*, Jevons actually stated the criterion of equilibrium on p. 96: 'that an infinitely small amount of commodity exchanged in addition, at the same rate, will bring neither gain nor loss of utility'.

[2] Section entitled 'The Gain by Exchange', p. 134, first edition; p. 142, fourth edition.

[3] In the example here cited by Williams, Jevons, while conceding that 'the question must involve both the ratio of exchange and the degrees of utility' had assumed the ratio of exchange to be fixed throughout the transactions.

[4] 'Supposing . . . that A is really willing to sell at £900, and B is prepared to buy at £1100, in what manner can we theoretically determine the price? I see no mode of solving this question' (Jevons, *T. P. E.*, p. 124, first and fourth editions).

I do not recollect your pointing out that increments of excellence in anything have no tendency to produce satiety, but seem rather to stimulate desire. A man who limited himself to a half-pint of Burgundy at dinner might drink daily a better and better quality until he reached a priceless brand, if his resources were unlimited. The degrees of utility of increments of excellence seem also to rise at a rapidly increasing rate. A horse which trots a mile in 2.25 may sell for twice as much as one that trots the same distance in 2.30.

Now how shall a man of limited resources – as all people are – and surrounded by a circle of temptations, apportion his purchasing fund so as to procure the most happiness? The question, if not distinctly stated in your work, is constantly suggested by similar ones in it, and I suppose the answer to be, that he ought to apportion his fund so that he cannot give more to a single gratification without reducing some other to a greater extent. People, I think, follow this rule, so far as they know how, and misjudge their resources and the nature of the temptations which surround them.

Keeping, then, in mind this principle of apportionment, and that increments of excellence coincide with an ascending series of degrees of utility, let us imagine, if you please, a man setting off successive portions of his fund (consisting entirely of gold) for the purchase of a quantity of house-utility measured on a scale of excellence. This scale could be of long range and fine gradations, owing to the varying quantities of such excellence embodied in different houses.

The mental operation might be illustrated by this diagram, where rps represent the curve of utility of the fund, and qpt the curve of utility of house-excellence. Increments of excellence are measured from o toward x; increments of apportionment (amount subtracted from the fund) are measured on the same line in the same direction.

The diagram seems to show that the imaginary exchange would be interrupted whenever a further increment of appointment would

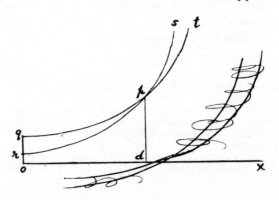

involve a greater loss of fund utility than was gained in utility of house-excellence. It would be possible also for the exchange to be pressed to such a point that no increment of house-excellence, however large, would compensate for the loss of another portion of the fund, however small. The *tendency* on the part of the prospective buyer would be to set off, for each increment of excellence, a sum of gold *approximately* in the inverse ratio of the final degrees of utility of the gold set off and the excellence gained.

But each *owner* of a house is also the centre of a circle of wants clamoring for gratification; he keeps his house only by denying or restraining some of them. Shall he not make a new distribution of his fund (he asks himself) by using an inferior house and selling the one he is in? He can be imagined surrendering mentally portions of house-excellence in exchange for coveted sums of money. The tendency in his case also will be to give up portions of house-excellence for portions of money approximately in the inverse ratio of their final degrees of utility. Will the views, however, of buyer and seller meet, so that a lump exchange can be made between money and house? Not necessarily. But where many who want to buy and many who want to sell are brought into communication, the chances of exchange are greatly increased, both because a common standard of excellence begins to be recognised, and because there is more likelihood among a large number that two persons will meet, one of whom slightly prefers to surrender a certain sum of money for a certain sum of house-excellence, while the other having that sum of house-excellence, slightly prefers to surrender it for that sum of money. In case a purchase and sale be effected on the part of two such persons, portions of house-excellence and portions of money would seem to have been exchanged in ratios inversely as the final degrees of utility of the respective quantities of each available for use after each contemplated exchange occurring in the imaginary series. – or rather approximately so; the approximation being closest in the exchange of the last portion of house-excellence for the last portion of money. The range of house-excellence available for traffic, and the minuteness of gradation in measuring it, depend upon the completeness of the market. In a perfect house-market, such a case as that supposed on page 124 could not arise. A would sell his house to some one who was just willing to give £900 for it, and B would buy a better one for £1100. A perfect house-market would conform with the conditions mentioned on pp. 85.6.[5] I would say that the difficulty in the Alaska case[6] was in the

[5] 'By a market I shall mean two or more persons dealing in two or more commodities, whose stocks of those commodities and intentions of exchanging are known to all. It is also essential that the ratio of exchange between any two persons should be known to all the others' (Op. cit., pp. 85–6, first and fourth editions.)

[6] 'When an island or portion of territory is transferred from one possession to another, it is often

restricted conditions of the market rather than in the indivisibility of one of the subjects of exchange.

Perhaps I have an exaggerated idea of the importance of my suggestion, even if it be sound; but it seems to me to have a wide application outside the house-market.

I have shown your Theory to my friend, Prof. Sill, in the state University here, who will make good use of it, in case instruction in Political Economy should be assigned to him.

Respectfully yours,
R. O. Williams.

457.   W. S. JEVONS TO L. BODIO
       [LJN, 345]

The Owens College, Manchester,
23d December 1875

. . . Allow me to return you my sincere thanks for the copies of your statistical publications which I have duly received, including the admirable treatise on the 'Casse di Resparmio',[1] which I also received some time since. They will all be valuable and highly-esteemed additions to my library.

I am much pleased to think that my book on *The Theory of Economy* is about to appear in Italian, and I cannot but be flattered by your remarks upon it.

My address will be at Owens College, Manchester, until about August 1876, when I hope to remove to London, having been lately elected professor of political economy in the University College at London. I hope by this change to enjoy greater advantages and leisure for further economical studies.

I beg you to accept the copies of pamphlets which I send by book post.

Your treatise on savings banks seems to me a most admirable work, to which we have nothing corresponding in England. It gives data for comparing the providence and progress of nations nowhere else to be found. The differences shown to exist between North and South Italy are strangely marked, and seem to show that the regeneration of South Italy will be as difficult a task for the Italian Government as Ireland has been and is for the English Government. . . .

---

necessary to take the whole, or none. America, in purchasing Alaska from Russia, would hardly have consented to purchase less than the whole' (Ibid., p. 120, first edition; p. 121, fourth edition.)

[1] Ufficio Centrale di Statistica, *Statistica delle Casse di resparmio,* 1864–76.

458.   E. B. WILLETTS[1] TO W. S. JEVONS

> No. 77 Columbia-Heights,
> Brooklyn.
> December 31, 1875.

Dear Sir,

I have the pleasure to own receipt of your valued favor of 12th, which reached me yesterday. I suppose the only object of getting a check certified is that the drawee may be satisfied that the money to meet it is actually lodged in bank. By the certification, the bank assures him that such is the case, and the possibility that the funds may be withdrawn before the check, in the ordinary course through the Clearing House, reaches the bank, precluded. As regards the certification of checks, we have recently had, what appears to me to be, a very curious decision.[2] The facts are, briefly: A.B. & Co. draw a check on the Marine Bank, which is raised, skilfully, from, say, $18 to $18000; and, after such alteration, mind you, certified. The check, thus raised and thus certified, finds its way into the City Bank, whence it goes back to the bank on which it is drawn, through the Clearing House. The Marine Bank, discovering the fraudulent character of the check, promptly declines to honor the document which it has already stamped as good, and returns it to the Marine Bank.[3] The latter bank demurs at this and enters suit, with defeat as a result. The argument is that the bank certifies the signature of the maker of the check and that it is good for the amount originally drawn for. It seems to me that this is carrying the principle of fraud vitiating everything a little too far. Perhaps your larger experience may see some reason in this; but I as yet cannot. In re-reading the passage in your book to which I have taken exception, I notice that you used the word banker and not bank;[4] but this I conceive does not alter the case in the least. With

[1] Edward B. Willetts, New York merchant; one of the sons of Samuel Willetts, founder of the hardware business of A. & S. Willetts, 303 Pearl Street, New York, which developed into a firm that at one time controlled 50 per cent of the whaling trade of the United States, as well as extensive Alaskan fur interests.

[2] Marine National Bank vs. National City Bank, 36 New York Superior Court (4 J & S.) pp. 470–81.

[3] Willetts's statement of the facts here is not too clear. He presumably meant to write 'returns it to the National City Bank'. The National City Bank refused to repay the amount involved, because the cheque had been certified, but the Courts found in favour of the Marine Bank. It was held that 'a bank, by certifying a check in the usual form, simply certifies to the genuineness of the signature of the drawer, and that he has funds sufficient to meet it, and engages that those funds will not be withdrawn from the bank by him: it does not warrant the genuineness of the body of the check as to payee or amount'.

[4] *Money and the Mechanism of Exchange*, p. 243, 'Certified Cheques . . . are really promissory notes of the banker.'

It is possible that Willetts was known to Thomas Jevons and had been approached by him about

you, I believe, all checks are instruments to bearer, or crossed for deposit at a bankers; but with us, checks, are as a rule, drawn to order requiring the endorsement and identification of the payee before payment. Since reading your book, I notice the Cheque Bank has closed its doors I think that this is to be regretted; for the idea, so far as I understand it, was an excellent one.[5] The reason given for the failure of this institution, was the want of sufficient capital to sustain it until the new idea should take root.

I am,

W. S. Jevons Esq.,   Very truly,
Manchester,   Yours,
England.   Edward B. Willetts

459.   W. S. JEVONS TO H. S. FOXWELL
       [RDF; LJP, 347]

36 Parsonage Road
Withington
25 Jany 76

Dear Foxwell

Thanks for the cheque for one guinea duly received.

Your account of the P.E. class at U.C.L. is certainly very discouraging. I never expected much, but could not have supposed there could be so poor a class.[1]

Last session I had in my day class of P.E. here 24 students in addition to an evening class of 42 held by a lecturer. This year I have 10 day students and an evening class held by myself of 54. I have also a fair class in Logic & philosophy of about 30 in addition to an evening class of logic held by a lecturer.

I am very well pleased with the first number of 'Mind' on the whole so far as I have read it. Pattison's[2] is a vigorous article. Venn's[3] is able and interesting but he much needs to be undeceived about Mill's logic.

I only heard of poor Mansel's death a week or so ago. I had never seen him, but regret his untimely end.

---

some of the questions raised by W. S. Jevons in Letter 385 above, p. 54; but there is no direct evidence of this and it seems more probable that Willetts had read the American edition of *Money* and queried this passage in an earlier letter which has not survived.

[5] Cf. below, Letter 478, p. 184.

[1] According to the Fees Books of the College only four students were enrolled for the class in Political Economy in 1875-6, but the number increased to twenty-three in 1876-7.

[2] Mark Pattison (1813-84), 'Philosophy at Oxford', *Mind*, 1 (1876) 82-97.

[3] John Venn (1834-83), 'Consistency and Real Inference', *Mind*, 1 (1876) 43-52.

Your news about Sidgwick[4] is quite news to me, and I am glad to hear it. Tho my acquaintance with him is quite recent I have conceived a great respect for Sidgwick in every way.

I think it likely that the vacancy in my professorship here will be advertised in a few weeks.

Believe me
Yours very faithfully
W. S. Jevons.

P.S. As Sidgwick has I believe a friend (brother?) likely to be a candidate[5] I should be glad if you wd take an opportunity of letting him know that the vacancy will soon be advertised.

460.   F. HINCKS[1] TO W. S. JEVONS

418 St. Antoine Street,
Montreal.
27th January, 1876.

Dear Sir,

I hope you will excuse the liberty which I take in addressing you though I have not the advantage of a personal acquaintance. Your name has long been familiar to me, not only from your writings, but because in early life I must have known some members of your family. If I am not mistaken you are a son of Mr. Thomas Jevons of Liverpool who married Miss Roscoe and if so I have been a guest both of your father and grandfather to whom my brothers the Rev. William and John Hincks were more intimately known. You in that case are uncle to Mr. Roscoe of Victoria B.C.[2] now a member of our Parliament with whom I have the pleasure of being acquainted. My object in troubling you with this letter is to ask your consideration of a pamphlet of mine[3] being a reprint of an

---

[4] This seems likely to have concerned Sidgwick's engagement in December 1875 to Eleanor Mildred Balfour (1845–1935), who succeeded Miss Clough as Principal of Newnham College, Cambridge, from 1892 to 1910. They were married the following April.

[5] The records of the University of Manchester concerning professorial appointments do not exist before 1898 and thus it is not possible to state the number of candidates for the Chair vacated by Jevons, nor whether a Sidgwick was among them. Cf. below, Letter 463, p. 164.

[1] Sir Francis Hincks (1807–85), Canadian statesman; emigrated to Canada from Ireland, 1832; founded the liberal newspaper *The Examiner*, 1839; elected to the legislative assembly of United Canada, 1841; prime minister, 1851–4; Governor of Barbados, 1855–62, and of British Guiana, 1861–9. Returned to Canada in 1869 and became finance minister in Sir John Macdonald's cabinet, from which he resigned in 1873; President of the City Bank of Montreal, 1873–9.

[2] Jevons's cousin, Francis James Roscoe. See Vol. I, p. 193, n. 6.

[3] 'The Bank of England and the Act of 1844', *Canadian Monthly and National Review*, 3 (1873) 177–88.

article which I contributed nearly 3 years ago to the Canadian "Monthly and National Review" published at Toronto in which I reviewed a pamphlet then newly published anonymously by Mr. Newmarch a very old acquaintance of mine and who must be well known to you. That pamphlet was entitled "The Bank of England a statement of its Constitution and of the principles and results of the act of 1844 with suggestions for amendments rendered necessary by altered circumstances."[4] It is more than probable that you are familiar with the pamphlet in question. The subject is one in which I have taken a deep interest since early life, and circumstances have led me to endeavour to give effect to my views. It is now 35 years since I entered the Canadian Parliament during the Government of the late Poulett Thomson (Lord Sydenham). In our session of 1840 he made an attempt to establish a Government Bank of Issue and I was Chairman of the Standing Committee on Banking and long and warmly supported the scheme which however was defeated by the influence of the Chartered Banks and the regular opposition – Lord Sydenham's death and other circumstances put an end to the hopes of those who shared his views and though several years in the Government at the head of the Finance Department I had no favourable opportunity of promoting my views. In 1855 I was appointed Governor of Barbados and in 1861 of British Guiana and only returned to Canada in 1869 when I again became Minister of Finance, and had then an opportunity of making a little progress. I succeeded in carrying a Dominion note out by which the Chartered Banks were prohibited from issuing notes under \$4 – thus giving the government the monopoly of the small note circulation \$1 and \$2. The government notes are a legal tender and although I could not carry out my views in their integrity by fixing a limit to the issue on government securities leaving all the issues over that to be based on gold in accordance with the Peel Act of 1844, yet there is practically a limit, and on the whole the Act works very well. The Govt. satisfied with the monopoly of the 1 and 2 dollar circulation does not try to compete with the Banks in the \$4, \$5, \$10 and \$20 circulation but issues large notes of \$1000, \$500 and \$100 and \$50. The large notes are never seen by the public but are kept as reserves by the chartered banks. The small notes vary very little—I am not without hope that in time the Banks will be prohibited from issuing notes under \$10 and that by degrees the entire circulation will fall into the hands of the Government. It was very gratifying to me after our failure in Canada in 1841 to find that Sir Robert Peel succeeded in England in giving effect to the same principle. I have never hesitated a moment since that Act passed in acknowledging its merits and I regretted very much that a

---

[4] Published in London in 1872.

gentleman of Mr. Newmarch's experience, and sound views should advocate what I feel assured you would concur with me in thinking a retrograde measure. I have lately had an opportunity of reading your last book "Money and the Mechanism of Exchange" and I read with the greatest pleasure your remark that the Act of 1844 is in your opinion as it is in mine "a monument of sound and skilful financial legislation" and again "the issue of paper representative money should continue to be practically in the hands of the Govt. or its agents acting under the strictest legislative control"–In the views propounded in your late work I entirely concur though I own I regret the publication of the chapter on "a Tabular Standard of Value" not because I dissent at all from the theory, but because I fear in the backward state of public opinion on all currency questions that it may distract the minds of controversialists. It is truly deplorable to witness the state of opinion in the United States – they might without difficulty have the best currency in the world. Their 'greenbacks' as the legal tender notes are called are only about 12% discount. By a gradual steady withdrawal they could in a few months bring them to pass with gold after which there would be no difficulty in reducing the state fraction so as to keep such a supply of gold in the treasury, as would render it impossible to create a difficulty. There is no institution analogous to the Bank of England in the U. States and the Banks all keep adequate reserves at hand. The trouble is that the National Banks are powerful in Congress and their policy is to compel the entire redemption of the greenbacks so as to give them a monopoly of the circulation – and mark the consequence. Instead of economising the gold, keeping merely enough for the redemption of the National Bank notes, the withdrawal of the greenbacks would leave the whole United States without a legal tender but gold so that in every town and city of the whole union stores of gold would have to be kept as Bank reserves – I have referred to the Bank of England and its peculiar position – I have always been of opinion that the true position of the B. of E. under the Act of 1844 (I mean of course the department of discount and deposit) would have been precisely that of the London and Westminster except so far as keeping the Govt. account made a difference. The other Banks should keep their own reserves and the Bank of England should not engage to carry the nation through these panics in order to do which it has had to violate the Bank Act. I fear however that the system can't be changed and that seems also to be the opinion of Mr. Bagehot. How then provide for the difficulty? Can't a way be found by which without violating any sound principle this can be effected? In the early part of this year a letter appeared in the 'Economist'[5] suggesting a new plan of issuing a Govt.

[5] *The Economist*, 27 February 1875, pp. 242–5. Hincks evidently made the common error of overlooking the New Year. The letter entitled 'A Plan for a Government Paper Currency', was

currency – Some obvious objections were pointed out to it by the Editor of the 'Economist' but I was not satisfied with his mode of disposing of the question and I wrote a letter for publication which I sent through my friend Sir John Rose a Director of the London and Westminster who is acquainted with Mr. Bagehot. The letter was not inserted as I had expected and I concluded that Mr. Bagehot did not choose to insert a letter advocating views that he thought unsound. During last summer I paid a visit of about three months to England and Sir John Rose then told me that Mr. Bagehot had been much pleased with my letter and thought my suggestions valuable but that he considered it better to wait for a suitable opportunity to publish the letter. He said likewise that he would like me to meet Mr. Bagehot and promised to arrange a meeting. I went soon after to the Continent and was travelling for about two months and was a very short time in London prior to my departure for my home in Montreal. Sir John Rose gave me a note of introduction to Mr. Bagehot but I failed to see him. I very much wish that you could have seen my letter to the 'Economist' of which I have no copy at least that I can lay my hands on. This scheme which I recommend and on which and in which I have implicit confidence bears some analogy to what you term the "Elastic limit" [6] provided by the Bank Act of the German Empire. This latter you say "it seems likely will work well and form an improvement on our method". I quite agree with you however that the fine or tax upon the excessive issue ought to be much more than 5 per cent and in this country should certainly not be less than 10%. My object was to provide 'ways and means' for enabling the Bank of England Issue Department *with perfect safety* to loan to the Banking Department at a high rate of interest to the extent of say ten millions which I am persuaded would be amply sufficient. It has made such loans on several occasions during crises but contrary to law and unfortunately there has been no certainty as to the power being given. I would authorise the loans to be made when the rate of interest was not less than— [7] The important feature of my scheme however was to strengthen the issue department so as to enable it in times of stringency to make loans on Govt. securities at a high rate of interest to the Banking Department. How then is this object to be accomplished? First I hold that an issue of £1 notes by the Bank of England on gold might safely be resorted to. The objection I have always heard stated is the in-

signed 'G'. Bagehot's editorial comments were published the following week in *The Economist*, 6 March 1875, pp. 270–2.

   [6] *Money and the Mechanism of Exchange*, p. 226: 'Observing . . . that the English Bank Charter Act has on several occasions been violated to prevent a panic, the German legislature has provided that more banknotes may be issued, provided that a tax of 5 per cent be paid thereon.'

   [7] In the original manuscript there is only a dash at this point.

creased danger of forgery. Here we issue notes of $1 (4/2d) and $2 (8/4d) as they do in the States, and with perfect safety. The small note issue could be a great element of strength in the case of difficulty. You will recollect that at the period of the last or preceding crisis there was a threat on the part of the Bankers to close the Bank of England (Banking Department) by presenting cheques. There must be a very large amount of Bank of England notes held as reserves. The Banking Department alone holds about 10 or 11 millions but no one can tell the amount held in London by Bankers and Capitalists. This is a source of weakness but the small notes would keep in circulation. I am very strongly of opinion that this would be the best and most economical mode of getting an additional gold reserve. Second. The Bank of England notes should be made as legal tender in Scotland and Ireland which would cause some five or six millions (I have not the exact figures by me but they are easily got) of gold to be transferred to the vaults of the Issue Department. Finally if all these plans were operated, I hold that it would be wise for the Govt. to pay to the Bank of England Issue department say £5,000,000 of its 15 millions of debt, so that the issues on security would only be 10 instead of 15 millions. This would be no inconvenience in ordinary times. However, the point that I urge is that by some means the Issue Department should be strengthened from 5 to 10 millions and that concurrently power should be given to the Issue Department to loan to an equal amount to the Banking Department when the rate of interest rose to 7 or 8 per cent. – I think 7 would be sufficient – I have given you I fear at too great length my ideas on this question though I would like you to have seen my letter to the Economist which was more carefully written than I am able to write this. As I am writing allow me to call your attention to your remarks on Canada [8] in your 8 chapter. You say that "in Canada there is an intricate confusion of monetary systems" that the monetary unit is a dollar but this is represented by Bank notes and not by any coin and that there are two different moneys of account "Halifax currency pound" and "Halifax Sterling Currency". It is true that we have no mint in Canada and I own that I see no occasion for going to the expense of one when all we should do would be to coin $5 and $2½ gold coins *exactly of the same value* as the corresponding coins of the U. States which are a legal tender as well as the sovereign at its corresponding value $4.86⅔. Our exchange on New York is *at par* or if at a slight premium, which at similar times is only enough to cover the very trifling expenses charged on transmitting gold. The Halifax currency has not existed for years. I myself introduced the decimal system more than 20 years ago and our currency is precisely the same as the U. States except that we have no inconvertible legal tender.

[8] *Money and the Mechanism of Exchange*, chap. VIII, section entitled 'Coin, Money of Account and Unit of Value'. In later editions Jevons altered the passage quoted by Hincks into the past tense.

We still allow chartered banks to issue notes redeemable on demand to the extent of their paid up capital. Of course although I am President of a chartered bank I am on principle opposed to such ideas and I believe them productive of unmitigated evil. At the very time when most of our Bankers contend that the circulation should increase, as it does in order to promote the movement of crops the tendency is by increasing the volume of money to cause a rise in this agricultural produce and to tempt people to give more than its legitimate value. However it is difficult in a country where money is scarce to persuade people to contract Bank issues and to leave the Banks to operate on their capital and deposits. I thought it worth while to mention this matter as I think you have not been correctly informed as to Canadian currency. There is a circumstance that occurred to me when reading some of your earlier chapters. I recollect many years ago say 25 to 30 that it was a common practice in the old Province of Lower Canada now Quebec for the farmers to make loans systematically in grain to be repaid in kind say after harvest with most usurious interest of course. I fear that I shall have exhausted your patience and with no further comment subscribe myself,

Your faithful servant,
F. Hincks.

461.   W. S. JEVONS TO R. H. INGLIS PALGRAVE
        [KCP]

36 Parsonage Road,
Withington,
Manchester.
2 Feb. 76.

My dear Palgrave,

Thanks for your letter. Your work will be very interesting to the financial world when it appears, but I can quite understand the amount of work which it requires.

I enclose a copy of a circular I am thinking of sending out.[1] I have not fully decided on doing it yet, and the papers must be regarded only as rough drafts. If you have any remarks to make upon them or corrections to suggest I should be extremely glad to have them either in a letter or marked on the forms themselves.

I do not know much about Indian Exchanges. Some time ago I received 2 or 3 circulars full of information on the subject from an Indian firm. The best of these I gave away, but if I can recover it and find the others I will send them.

---

[1] See below, Letter 464, p. 165.

Will a copy of a pamphlet by Henri Cernuschi[2] on Bi-metallic money (just published) and its bearings on monetary crises in Germany etc. be of service to you? It refers to the depreciation of silver and I have a spare copy. I have various publications relating to Indian currency which I could lend if you wished.

You will find some remarks on the drain of bullion to the East and tables of the amounts towards the end of my paper on the variation of Prices. Statistical Journal June 1865 pp. 305 etc.[3]

Thanking you for the trouble you took about my substitute lectures in London,

I am yours very faithfully
W. S. Jevons

462. J. G. GREENWOOD AND A. W. WARD[1] TO W. S. JEVONS

The Owens College,
Manchester
11th February 1876

Dear Sir,

The Senate, having been officially informed by the Council that you have accepted the Chair of Political Economy at University College, London and intend to resign the Chair you now hold in this College at the close of the present session, has requested us to express to you the deep regret with which it has received this information.

The members of the Senate are convinced that the College will lose in you a Professor whose ability and energy have signally helped to advance its progress, and whose literary achievements have shed a lustre upon its reputation—

They at the same time feel that they will themselves lose in you a colleague in whose judgment they have long been accustomed to place the utmost confidence, and in whose friendship they have at all times taken the sincerest pride. Trusting that your interest in the College will outlive your connexion with it, they heartily wish you a long enjoyment of

---

[2] Henri Cernuschi (1821–96), *La Monnaie Bimétallique*. Articles publiées dans *Le Siècle*, en Novembre et Decembre, 1875 (1876). Cf. Vol. V, Letter 686.

[3] Reprinted as No. III in *Investigations*, pp. 119–49.

[1] Sir Adolphus William Ward (1837–1924), Professor of History and English Language and Literature, Owens College, Manchester, 1866; Vice-Chancellor of the Victoria University of Manchester, 1886–90 and 1894–6.

the honours your achievements have already secured for you, and all prosperity in your new Chair and home.[2]

We are, Dear Sir
Yours faithfully
J. G. Greenwood
A. W. Ward

463.   W. S. JEVONS TO T. E. JEVONS
[LJN, 347–8]

Owens College, 16th February 1876

. . . There is a great deal I ought to write to you, but I have more letter writing to do than I like. Your American friends are evidently reading my book on *Money,* as I get long letters from different parts of the States and Canada requesting my perusal of pamphlets and books.

. . . I am glad to say that Herbert Stanley is growing very well, and is already an amusing little creature. He has not the beauty of your children, but there are great signs of intelligence and character . . .

My professorship in the college is now advertised, and a fair number of applications will probably be received. We have not yet taken any steps about a house, but I shall probably go to London at Easter for a week of house hunting.

I have been thinking much about your visit, and planning a scheme of action. . . . I will write again soon. At present I am filling up a half-hour at college, waiting for a concert of chamber music. . . .

[2] The following Resolution was enclosed with the letter:

The Owens College,
Manchester.

At a meeting of the Council held at the College on Friday the 7th January 1876.

Read

Letter from Prof W. S. Jevons dated 17th ult. giving notice of his intention to resign the Professorship which he now holds in the College, on the 29th September next

Resolved

That the Council have received with sincere regret Prof Jevons's resignation of the Chair of Logic and Mental & Moral Philosophy, and Political Economy.

They desire to express their great appreciation of the ability with which he has fulfilled the duties of a Professorship embracing subjects with so wide a range and each of so great importance, and of the advantage which the College has enjoyed in possessing a Professor so distinguished in these subjects; and they offer him their best wishes for his future welfare and prosperity.

True extract from minutes
J. Holme Nicholson
Registrar

464.   W. S. JEVONS TO R. H. INGLIS PALGRAVE
[KCP]

36, Parsonage Road,
Withington.
17 Feb. 76.

My dear Palgrave,

I thank you very much for your letter about my proposed Bankers'
circular. I find there is much difference of opinion among those I have
consulted as to the practicability of the scheme, but they all agree that it
should not be done in conjunction with a bank officer. I have therefore
come to the conclusion to throw it over for the present.[1] If I attempt the
thing at all it will be after my removal to London and when I have had
time and opportunity to go into the matter more deliberately. Perhaps
then I may hope for further advice from yourself.

Yours faithfully,
W. S. Jevons.

465.   W. LANGTON[1] TO W. S. JEVONS

Manchester and Salford Bank.[2]
Manchester, 19th February, 1876.

Dear Mr. Jevons, I enclose a few corrections for "Money" which I have
received from Canada.[3]

Believe me,
Yours ever faithfully,
W. Langton.

[1] It seems likely that Jevons delayed this proposed investigation into the volume of banking
transactions indefinitely. Similar research was eventually undertaken by a former student of his,
G. H. Pownall: see Vol. V, Letter 676, n. 2.

[1] William Langton (1803–81), son of a Liverpool merchant; turned to banking when his own
prospects of a career in the Russian trade were ended by war; chief cashier of Heywood's Bank,
Manchester, 1829–54; managing director of the Manchester and Salford Bank from 1854 until
forced to retire through blindness in 1876. He was one of the founders of the Manchester Statistical
Society and its first secretary; also President, 1867–9. He read many papers before it on social and
monetary questions.

[2] The Manchester and Salford Banking Company was founded in 1836. The prospectus
announced capital of one and a quarter million shares of £20: after the first year 25,210 shares were
taken up, representing a capital of £252,100. By 1878 the paid up capital amounted to £600,000,
with a Reserve Fund of £250,000. Premises were built at Mosley Street, Manchester, on the site of a
Unitarian chapel: in 1861 the bank moved to York Street. Under the terms of the 1844 Bank Act,
branches were opened first at Salford in 1862, and at Southport, Ormskirk, Lancaster, Hulme, St
Helens, Chorley, and in other districts of Manchester, between 1864 and 1868. The Manchester and
Salford Banking Company was incorporated in 1870 under the Companies Act, 1862, and in 1873

P.S. The currency of our colonies was evidently very much neglected formerly; an acquaintance of mine told me that he had found it necessary to issue copper tokens in his younger days in Jamaica, and I have a story of a tradesman in one of the Canadian ports, buying the copper off a ship's bottom and punching it into round pieces, which passed current under the common designation of "coppers."

Extract

(Professor Jevons's book on "Money" pp. 73, 74 relating to Money in Canada).

It is true that we have no national mint but it is not true that our circulation "consists of many species of foreign coins". Our beloved mother country kindly coins our silver for us and we circulate scarcely any other coinage. We have no gold coins of our own however, but bank notes engraved in our own Establishment at Montreal answer the purpose equally well. The monetary unit is a dollar, but a dollar consisting of 100 cents and having no connection whatever with 'fifty pence'. Our silver coins are fifty cent pieces or half dollars, 25 cent pieces or quarter dollars, 10 cent and 5 cent pieces, and then we have bronze cents (at least I believe they are what would be called bronze). But our copper coin is I admit very various, and when Ian and I were young we had collections of curious "coppers" as we loosely called them. As for Mr. Jevons's "Halifax Currency Pound" and "Halifax Sterling Currency", no doubt they existed as he says so, but they are abolished now and I do not recognise his description of them as anything I ever was acquainted with. Sir Francis Hincks was our Finance Minister at the time that American silver was sent out of the Country and our own coinage substituted. That is five years ago – not very long.

466.   W. S. JEVONS TO SIR ANTHONY MUSGRAVE

Withington
Manchester
21 Febr. 1876

My dear Sir,
    I beg to thank you for your interesting letter of 3rd December.[1] Your anecdote about Mills panegyric on his wife is both amusing & suggestive.

took over the business of Heywood Brothers and Co. It was one of the few joint-stock banks to enjoy steady prosperity for over fifty years, and in April 1890 was amalgamated with Williams Deacon and Co. Ltd. See L. H. Grindon, *Manchester Banks and Bankers: Historical, Biographical and Anecdotal* (Manchester, 1878) pp. 281–92.
    [3] There is nothing in the manuscript which would enable Langton's Canadian correspondent to be identified. Cf. above, Letter 460, p. 161.
    [1] The original manuscript of this letter does not appear to have survived.

I feel sure that your opinions about Mill's philosophy are right, though I have heard your criticisms of his pol. econ. rather strongly condemned. Great as my respect for Mill's straightforward & zealous character is, I fear that his intellect if good originally was ruined in youth. At any rate I find after long study that his Logic is an extraordinary tissue of self contradictions.

I am at present engaged in writing a careful critique of it which will surprise even you. The system of logic when carefully analysed is found to be a most illogical book, and the great respect in which it is held must arise from the fact that readers never suspect the fact and attribute all their perplexity to the profoundness of the writer, who leads them into endless difficulties.

It is impossible however in a letter to give you any adequate idea of the results of my examination. My difficulty is to put them in a form which will attract readers & induce a publisher to print them.

Your remarks about the possible competition of India are worthy of much attention here, but I do not fear foreign competition at present.

Believe me to remain
My dear Sir,
Yours faithfully,
W. Stanley Jevons

His Excell? Governor Musgrave
&c   &c

467.   W. B. HODGSON TO W. S. JEVONS

PRIVATE.   University of Edinburgh,
                                            25th February, 1876.

My dear Professor,
I hasten to inform you that the Senators have this day resolved to offer you the Honorary Degree of *LL.D.* [1] at the next graduation on 1st May. I have all the more pleasure in writing this, because it is not I that originated the proposal; so that it is due not at all to private friendship but to a general recognition of your scientific eminence.

You will receive one long and official letter on the subject. Meantime, I hope you will be my guest when you come to Edinburgh to receive your Diploma.

Many thanks for the circular regarding your present Chair.
Yours ever truly,
W. B. Hodgson.

[1] See below, Letter 471, p. 173.

468.   R. H. INGLIS PALGRAVE TO W. S. JEVONS

Yarmouth 11 March
1876

My dear Jevons,

Can you give me your opinion as to the comparative purchasing power of money towards the *close of the 17th Century* (say 1680) in England and at the present time – i.e. about 200 years ago. Was it then 3 times more than what it is now – I mean might I take 6/8^d then to have the purchasing power of 20/ = now – or was the difference greater.

I should be very glad if you will not mind answering this question – So many changes in value have taken place in recent years that one hardly knows what "authority" to quote, or to use, in the question – When you answer will you say whether you will mind my quoting you as the authority for my statement.

I enclose a paper of mine on the Bankers Reserves & the Bank of England,[1] which I do not think I have sent you – I remember you were interested by a previous paper of mine on the subject. I think that the question will now rest awhile, – it is best it should rather simmer gently, than be brought forward too fast – as it is an extremely difficult point to settle in practise*

Yours vy truly
R. H. Inglis Palgrave

469.   W. S. JEVONS TO R. H. INGLIS PALGRAVE
        [KCP]

The Owens College,
Manchester.
13 March 76.

My dear Palgrave,

I will look up the information I have without delay and form the best guess I can about the change of prices but I have never made any accurate calculations stretching so far back as 1680. I hardly think the change has been so great as 3 to 1 since then.

---

[1] Palgrave had written a major paper entitled 'Relation of the Banking Reserve of the Bank of England to the current Rate of Interest, and the causes which have led to the Higher Rates charged in Recent Years' in *JRSS*, 36 (1873) 529–64, but the paper referred to here was probably one of his shorter and more recent contributions to the *Bankers' Magazine* —either 'The Reserve of the Bank of England, and the Deposits of the London Bankers', 35 (1875) 869–74, or 'The Proposal to form a Banker's Reserve in London', 36 (1876) 129–34.

I have been carefully reading your articles from the Bankers' Magazine while on a little journey. With reference to that on the details of banking,[1] I wonder it did not occur to you and other bankers to suggest a small fixed charge for clerical labour, in addition to commission etc. What I should propose is a charge of one penny for every entry credit or debit in a customers' account. There would be no appreciable labour in counting the entries. You could count so many to a page of the ledger. The result would be that every person drawing a very small cheque say for 10s. would pay 1d when it was paid and the person paying it into his account would be charged one penny, making 2d altogether.

I agree with you that the Cheque Bank is familiarizing people with small cheques or rather I should say represents the growing familiarity and arises out of the need. I think bankers should encourage this practise* because they can always protect their silver from loss by a charge merely covering clerical labour. Of course 1d per entry may be too much or too little. Then the question would arise how agent banks should be remunerated for passing the cheques through their books.

Thanks for your former letter and the account of the proportion of cheques. It has my best attention though I am rather distracted by the question of houses in London.

Ever yours faithfully,
W. S. Jevons.

470. W. S. JEVONS TO R. H. INGLIS PALGRAVE
[KCP]

36, Parsonage Road,
Withington,
Manchester.
14 March 76.

My dear Palgrave,

I have made some calculations concerning prices as far as data are available. The results[1] will rather surprise you as showing that since 1730 there has been no rise of prices but rather a fall. From 1730 to 1785 I have taken the prices at Greenwich Hospital which you will find in MacCulloch's dictionary under the article "Prices." They form by far the

---

[1] 'Suggestions on details in Banking Business', *Bankers' Magazine*, 35 (1875) 941–7 and 36 (1876) 1–6. The second of these articles contained a discussion of the 'Cheque Bank' system of issuing certified cheques for fixed amounts.

[1] The results of modern research do not suggest that Jevons's conclusions here require any substantial modification, although the difficulties of such long-period comparisons of prices are well known. Cf. P. Deane and W. A. Cole, *British Economic Growth, 1688–1959*, second edition (Cambridge, 1969) pp. 12–18 and figure 7.

best series I have anywhere found. Comparing the prices of 15 articles in 1730 and 1785 I find the average ratio of change is a rise of 27 per cent.

From 1785 to 1865 my own tables are available – see Statistical Journal June 1865 p. 315[2] giving a fall of prices as 90 to 78 or by 13 or 14 per cent.

From 1865 to 1876 I take the aggregate Index number as given in the Economists Annual Review just published p. 37. This gives a fall of prices as 3575 to 2711 or by 24 per cent. Then I find the course to be as follows in proportional numbers

1730	–	100
1785	–	127
1865	–	110
1876	–	83

This would show a fall of prices of 17 per cent from 1730 to 1876 but I think that the Economist's index no. rather exaggerates the changes and I would not like to say that there is any actual fall. I believe that prices are nearly on a level with what they were in 1730.

These results though contrary to your expectations and to some extent to mine are quite confirmed by the price of corn which so many economists have considered the best standard of value. According to A. Smith the average price at Windsor from 1637 to 1700 was 51 shillings per quarter; in the ten years 1865–75 it was 54 shillings in the whole of England. From 1701 to 1764 it is true it was lower namely 40.6. In the ten years 1725–34 it was 40s. And though this gives a rise of prices 1730 to 1874 of some 30 per cent yet it is not surprising that corn should get a little decrease as compared with more manufactured articles.

So far as we can judge from the prices given in the Wealth of Nations the rise of prices due to the discovery of America was quite accomplished before the end of the 16th century. The general course of prices has since been rather downward than upward, with the exception of the enormous rise in the early part of the century due in my opinion to the immense derangements and displacement of metallic currency.

If you wish to do so you can state my opinion that there has probably been no great change in purchasing power between 1730 and the present time. The figures are for your own information as showing that the opinion is not formed without some data. The subject ought to be

---

[2] 'Variation of Prices and the Value of the Currency since 1782', *JRSS*, 28 (1865) 315.

carefully investigated but it involves so much labour that the government ought to provide funds for such inquiries.

Yours faithfully,
W. S. Jevons.

P.S. I have been for some time collecting data for a general inquiry into the course of prices but it really absorbs too much labour.

470A. W. S. JEVONS TO THE EDITOR OF THE *MANCHESTER GUARDIAN*[1]

THE PROSPECTS OF THE TELEGRAPH DEPARTMENT

Sir,

During the discussion on the present state of the Telegraph Department it has been frequently stated and repeated that the Telegraph Department is just in the position of the Post-office after the introduction of the penny rate. Such a statement can only be made by those who are quite unacquainted with the facts of the case. I will therefore ask you to allow me to put before your readers the following table, showing the net revenue of the Post-office before and after Sir Rowland Hill's reform, and that of the telegraphs as estimated by the Treasury Commissioners: —

NET REVENUE OR PROFIT

	Post-office	Telegraphs
	£	£
First year before reform ...	1,659,087 ...	—
First year after reform ...	500,789 ...	308,456
Second year after reform ...	561,249 ...	159,834
Third year after reform ...	600,641 ...	103,120
Fourth year after reform ...	640,217 ...	90,033
Fifth year after reform ...	719,957 ...	36,725

It is difficult to imagine a greater contrast than is thus shown between the rapid progress of the postal net revenue, concerning which there can be no doubt, and the serious decrease in the telegraph profits. The Postmaster General in his letter to the Treasury contests the estimate of

---

[1] Published in the issue of 22 March 1876.

the telegraph profits given above, and his own estimate of revenue and expenditure for the year 1875–6 shows net revenue amounting to £172,235, to set against a charge for interest on capital amounting to £309,669. Now even if we accept the department's own view of its accounts, it is impossible for a moment to compare the state of affairs with the postal branch after the penny postal reform. As the table shows, the postal net revenue (a true net revenue, not to be charged with any appreciable sum for interest) was never less than half a million, and within four years increased by more than £200,000.

I need not here repeat the reasons which I gave in the *Fortnightly Review* of December last[2] for thinking that the worse rather than the more cheerful view of the telegraph finances is the true one. It is easy to talk about closing the capital account; but how is this to be done? Already, if Mr. Goldsmid[3] is correct, more than a million has been spent on buildings used by the Telegraph Department but not counted in their capital account. In Manchester the department is obliged to provide new premises at a large cost. As traffic increases, as leases fall in, or new necessities arise, the same thing will no doubt have to be done in other places. Having once undertaken a great business it is impossible to avoid expenditure, and the greatest vigilance will be requisite to prevent a continuous loss to the country.

One word more. We are assured by the Postmaster General that the telegraph stations which do not pay are rapidly diminishing in number. I presume that by "paying" he means "paying the working expenses", probably the mere wages of the operators and messengers. Seeing that the department as a whole, including the traffic of the greatest towns, does not pay 3 per cent interest, it is out of the question that the remoter and smaller stations can really pay their total cost.

I am, &c.

W. Stanley Jevons.

Withington, March 20, 1876.

[2] See above, Letter 455, n. 4, p. 150. The article was reprinted in *Methods*, pp. 293–306.

[3] On 17 March 1876 Sir Julian Goldsmid (1838–96), M.P. for Rochester, 1870–80, moved a resolution for the setting up of a Select Committee to enquire into the management and organisation of the telegraph department, on the grounds that the original estimates produced to justify the purchase of the telegraph system by the Government had proved grossly inaccurate and that it was necessary to find means of reducing administrative costs. He specifically referred to the fact that 'not a penny, so far as I can find up to the present time, has been put down in the Telegraph capital account for the buildings that have been erected, many of them in consequence of the extension of the telegraph system . . .'. The motion was withdrawn after a suggestion by the Chancellor of the Exchequer that a Committee should be appointed to examine the future improvement of the system. *Hansard,* third series, CCXXVII (1876) 172–98, 224.

471. W. S. JEVONS TO HARRIET JEVONS
  [LJN, 352]

Bonaly, Colinton, N. B.
20th April 1876.

. . . Bonaly[1] is a charming place – I had no idea a professor could have so nice a place. . . . The ceremony went off very nicely on the whole. Professor Maclagan[2] made a speech laudatory of each LL.D., and said of me that the *Principles of Science* had put me on the same platform with Whewell and Mill.[3] The students received me pretty well, especially when he referred to the *Elementary Lessons,* at which they applauded, much to my amusement. Professor Masson[4] gave a very good address upon the arrangements of education in Scotland.

Hodgson says he is going to give up his professorship certainly; but I do not think Edinburgh would suit us, though Scotch professors have a nice position here. . . .

471A. W. S. JEVONS TO H. S. FOXWELL
  [RDF]

36 Parsonage Road
Withington
Manchester.
2 May 76.[1]

Dear Foxwell
  I enclose a paper[2] giving some account of a special dinner which the Political Economy Club are going to hold. Will you do me the pleasure of

---

[1] W. B. Hodgson's home, Bonaly Tower, formerly the residence of Lord Cockburn.

[2] [Sir] Andrew Douglas Maclagan (1812–1900), President of the Royal College of Surgeons, Edinburgh, 1859–61; Regius Professor of Forensic Medicine in the University of Edinburgh, 1862–97; President of the Royal College of Physicians, Edinburgh, 1884; knighted, 1886.

[3] On this occasion Maclagan was standing in for the Dean of the Faculty of Law. In presenting Jevons he also said that 'Professor Jevons' writings on political economy have been numerous, and most important, including as they do his great work on the theory of political economy, his work on the gold question, a very popular and readable treatise on money . . and . . . his work on coal.' *Edinburgh Courant,* 21 April 1876, p. 2.

[4] David Masson (1822–1907), Professor of English Literature at University College London, 1853–65; editor of *Macmillan's Magazine* 1858–65; Professor of Rhetoric and English Literature, University of Edinburgh, 1865–95; Historiographer Royal for Scotland, 1893–1907.

[1] This letter was written on the back of a circular giving details of the rules and membership of the Political Economy Club.

[2] This paper is no longer with the original manuscript.

dining at the club with me on that occasion? If you can come I will send you the formal ticket of invitation as soon as the tickets are ready.

Believe me

Yours very faithfully

W. S. Jevons.

471B.   W. S. JEVONS TO THE EDITOR OF *THE SPECTATOR*[1]

THE ALLEGED POISONING OF NATIVES IN QUEENSLAND

Sir, – As in your opinion, the English public are entirely incredulous about the wanton shooting and poisoning of the North-Australian aborigines, and as Mr. Chesson, of the Aborigines Protection Society, has come forward officially to deny the recent existence of such practices, you will, perhaps, allow me to adduce evidence which, if not conclusive, is sufficient to show that I have made no random statements.

My attention was first drawn to this matter by *viva voce* accounts received from a gentleman, since dead, who had recently returned from the wild life of the gold diggings and the new districts of Queensland. He described to me one case of extensive strychnine-poisoning, and gave me to understand that the shooting of "niggers" was an ordinary and understood thing. His statements have lain heavy on my mind, but I cannot undertake to produce them as evidence, and I, therefore, turn to printed statements.

I may express some surprise that the Aborigines Protection Society should derive their information about Queensland from Dr. Lang's book, written in 1861.[2] The colony was only constituted in 1859, and the

---

[1] Printed in the issue of 27 May 1876, pp. 679–80. On 29 April 1876 the *Spectator* had published an article criticising Jevons's 'Cruelty to Animals – a Study in Sociology', *Fortnightly Review*, 19 (1876) 671–84 (reprinted in *Methods*, pp. 217–35). In this he asserted 'that English society, though it runs wild about surrendering a fugitive slave, has never cared even to ascertain whether or not scores of the Australian natives are shot like kangaroos, or poisoned by strychnine, like the native dogs'. The *Spectator* argued that this apparent indifference arose from incredulity, and that if Jevons could produce evidence that such outrages had actually occurred 'there would be such an outbreak of British feeling as this generation has hardly witnessed'. This was followed on 20 May by the publication of a letter from F. W. Chesson, secretary of the Aborigines Protection Society, saying that they knew 'no facts tending to show the continued existence of these horrible practices'. After Jevons had replied in the letter printed here, Chesson wrote a further letter, published in the *Spectator* of 3 June, suggesting that even the evidence given by Jevons related to past rather than present conditions but also undertaking to investigate the matter fully.

[2] John Dunmore Lang, *Queensland, Australia; a highly eligible field for emigration, and the future cotton-field of Great Britain: with a disquisition on the origin, manners and customs of the Aborigines* (1861). Cf. Vol. II, Letter 94, n. 16, p. 248.

greater part of it was in 1861 a *terra incognita*. I beg to refer Mr. Chesson, in the first place, to a work called, "The Queen of the Colonies; or, Queensland as I Knew It; by an Eight-year Resident," published by Messrs. Sampson Low and Co. a few months ago.[3] On pp. 310–313 we read as follows:—

> "Any notice of the black fellows would be incomplete that said nothing as to their treatment by the whites. Here one would willingly draw a veil over the sad picture. But truth compels us to say that all the treachery and murder has not been on the side of the blacks. . . . As a rule, at the present day, the natives are not ill-treated. . . . But this was not always the case. . . . Before the era of separation, when the whites were very few, and the native tribes were in a great measure intact, there were deeds so black and diabolical committed as one almost shrinks from recounting. . . . On a 'run' in the Moreton-Bay district, a squatter found his cattle constantly speared, and often killed by the natives. . . . From time to time, some of them were shot when caught on the 'run' but still the evil was unabated. At length, altering his procedure, the squatter established friendly relations with the blacks, and finally gave them a 200 lb. bag of flour, in which he had mixed a quantity of arsenic or strychnine. . . . The poor creatures soon divided the flour, and one and all, making cakes of their portions, ate them without any suspicion. A dreadful scene followed. Some accounts say forty, others twice that number, soon lay dead in their camp. . . . For many years, on offering a present of flour to any black-fellow, one was met with the inquiry, 'Mackenzie sit down?' the name by which poison became universally known among them for many miles. The man who thus acted was never called in question for his conduct, the real facts being perhaps known to no one but himself, or through the reports of the blacks, who can give no evidence."

The writer then proceeds to give the stories of an old squatter, whose theory was that the blacks were to be destroyed, like native dogs or vermin. He described the shooting of a black "much in the same way one would speak of firing at a brace of partridges." The same squatter, being troubled by the depredations of two station blacks, resolved to punish them by strychnine, mixed with sugar:—

> "Calling them by name, he said, 'Here, you eatem sugar,' and gave first one and then the other his portion, which the poor fellows took and ate unsuspiciously. He then told them to go and fetch up the horses, and have a drink at the water-hole on their way. By-and-by he went out to have a look round, and near the water-hole lay one of the blacks, who, on seeing him approaching, cried out, 'Here, Missa—, you see em me. Cabona[very much] me directly buck-jump!' referring to the convulsions caused by the poison, and which he called 'buck-jumping'. Soon another paroxysm came on, in which he died."

[3] E. Thorne, *The Queen of the Colonies* (1876).

The writer goes on to state that he himself incurred odium by trying to protect the blacks in his neighbourhood from the superintendent of a neighbouring "run", who wished to shoot them. He explains that though there is theoretically as severe a penalty for the murder of a black as of a white man, "in isolated districts it would often be well-nigh impossible to adduce satisfactory evidence. But these are now, we believe, very exceptional cases."

To form some judgment how far this question is one of the past only, we must turn to Mr. E. B. Kennedy's book, "Four Years in Queensland," published in 1870 by Mr. Stanford. In pp. 70–73 is given what Mr. Kennedy describes as a "very truthful article," taken from the *Port Denison Times* of May, 1868. I make the following extracts:—

> "The Black question is daily assuming a more serious aspect in this part of Australia. . . . . . Our Government, with their usual short-sighted and miscalled economy, are still reducing the native police force, which is the only protection that the out-settlers have from the blacks, and which, instead of being reduced, ought to be trebled or quadrupled in strength. If this suicidal policy is persisted in, the inevitable result will be the adoption by the white settlers of a system of self-protection against the savages. It is scarcely necessary to say how much such a result is to be deprecated, not only on account of the blacks, of whom, for every one that is killed now, ten probably will suffer if the settlers take the matter into their own hands, but on account of the settlers themselves, over whom the demoralising effects of such a system will exert an influence for evil that it will be difficult to counter-balance."

After some remarks upon pseudo-philanthropists and missionaries, which I need not transcribe, the Port Denison editor concludes:—

> "If the settlers are forced into the necessity of taking upon themselves the responsibility of repelling the aggressions of the blacks, and of doing so in a clandestine and illegal manner, consequences the most deplorable are sure to ensue."

Of this, Mr. Kennedy, writing in 1869, remarks:— "The above gives a very good idea of the state of things at present." It is, of course, impossible for me to adduce satisfactory evidence as to the extent to which this "clandestine" war of extermination is proceeding at the present time. Neither gold-diggers nor squatters are likely to tell tales of what is done far up the country, until years are gone by, and the danger of a prosecution for murder is past.

I can only give my own impression, which is that if Mr. Chesson and the Aborigines Protection Society continue to rely upon Dr. Lang's book, and his statements about the year 1815, there will soon be no aborigines for them to protect. That a fierce private war of extermination is now proceeding in North Queensland, uncontrolled by Government, and conducted with little regard to anything but the safety of the English invaders, can hardly be doubted. The *Australian Sketcher* for February 19, 1876, now before me, gives a graphic illustration of a fight between diggers and blacks on the way to the Palmer Diggings, and mentions (p. 182) that a little while ago it was contemplated by the Chinese merchants at Cookstown to organise a regular Chinese force, to protect their countrymen against the blacks. It reads like a satire, – that Chinese merchants should think of organising a police force in British territory.

I feel sure that a little of the over-abundant sentiment spent in England upon a few fugitive slaves or imported Kanakas, might well be used to impress upon the Queensland Government the necessity of establishing an effective native police force. Private and clandestine warfare is sure to lead, in some cases, as the Port Denison editor clearly implies, to lamentable atrocities. – I am, Sir, &c.,

W. Stanley Jevons.

472.   W. S. JEVONS TO R. O. WILLIAMS
         [LJN, 352 – 3]

Withington,
Manchester, 29th June 1876

. . . Thanks for your letter of 2d May.[1] I am sorry I have not been able to reply to it sooner, having been obliged by considerations of health to give up all work as far as possible.

I quite agree with you that symbolical statements are calculated to deter ordinary readers from proceeding further, but it is necessary that the mathematical nature of a science should be stated nevertheless.

I contemplate undertaking, as soon as possible, a new work on political economy generally, in which a more broad and popular view of the theory will be given, and then I can, in any future edition of the *Theory*, give the symbolical and purely mathematical view more fully.[2]

I took the liberty of sending you a copy of my *Logic Primer* just published.

I am going abroad to-morrow for a tour of some length. . . .

[1] The original manuscript of this letter does not appear to have survived.
[2] The next work 'on political economy generally' which Jevons undertook was the *Primer of Political Economy*, which he wrote during the year 1877, but it seems more reasonable to regard this passage as a first reference to the *Principles of Economics*, which Jevons began only in 1880, after the second edition of *Theory of Political Economy* had been published without any fundamental change in the presentation of 'the symbolical and mathematical view'. Cf. Vol. V, Letters 582, 644 and 656, pp. 22, 94 and 107.

473.   DR KRANICHFELD[1] TO W. S. JEVONS

Berlin, am 8. Juli 1876
Brunnenstraße 30. N.

Hochgeehrter Herr.

Durch Ihre vortreffliche Schrift "Geld und Geldwerthe" über den Zweck
und die Organisation der von Herrn James Hertz[2] in London ins Leben
gerufenen "Checkbank" unterrichtet und von der wirthschaftlichen
Bedeutung derselben überzeugt, wandte ich mich an hiesige Bankiers,
um ihre weitere Entwicklung kennen zu lernen. Ich mußte die über-
raschende Beobachtung machen, daß die Bank diesen fast völlig
unbekannt geblieben war.

Das lebhafte Interesse, welches ich für die Sache hege und das
begreifliche Erstaunen, in welches mich die Thatsache, daß dieses
bewundernswerthe Unternehmen in meinem Vaterland so wenig
Beachtung gefunden hat, versetzt hat, mögen es entschuldbar erscheinen
lassen, wenn ich mir gestatte, mich an Sie mit der Bitte um geneigte
Auskunft über den weiteren Fortgang der Bank zu wenden. Fast möchte
ich fürchten, daß die Resultate derselben nicht so günstige gewesen seien
als sich mit Recht erwarten ließ.

Vielleicht haben Sie zugleich die Güte, von meiner Ansicht über die
Moglichkeit der Einführung eines entsprechenden Duplikats in
Deutschland Kenntniß zu nehmen und dieselbe einer gefalligen Beur-
theilung zu unterziehen.

Indem ich von der Ansicht ausgehe, daß Neuerungen, welche die Kasse
des Volkes als Operationsbasis haben, nur dann auf einen raschen und
sicheren Erfolg rechnen können, wenn sie *klar in die Augen springende*
Vortheile, mögen sie an sich noch so klein sein, bieten, glaube ich nicht,
daß die in Aussicht gestellte Bequemlichkeit und Erleichterung in
Abwicklung von Geldgeschäften, die Sicherheit des Geldverkehrs das
große Publikum zur Adoptierung des Checksystems bewegen werden, da
es diese Vortheile erst bei Anwendung desselben verstehen wird. Wohl
aber wird ein an sich unbedeutendes Moment in Deutschland den
Ausschlag geben. Es ist eine geringe Ersparnis auch bei den kleinsten
Geldsendungen. Die Checks sind in Deutschland ausdrücklich von der
Wechselstempelsteuer befreit. Während nur der niedrigste Satz bei einer
Postanweisung mit Bestellgeld 25 Pfennige beträgt, läßt sich der Check
für 1 Sgr[3]. resp. 5 Pfennige durch die Post befördern. Die Differenz ist

---

[1] It has not proved possible to trace any biographical information about Kranichfeld.

[2] James Hertz (d. 1881), London banker; Fellow of the London [later Royal] Statistical Society;
originator of the Cheque Bank and its first managing director, 1873–80. Cf. below, Letter 478,
p. 184.

[3] Presumably an abbreviation of 'Spargroschen'.

klein, aber bei der Sparsamkeit, zu welcher wir Deutschen gezwungen sind, ist der Vortheil doch groß genug, um erwarten zu lassen, daß er vom Publikum in umfassender Weise benutzt wird. Was die Bedeutung dieses Umstandes noch wesentlich erhöht, ist eine Erscheinung, die im Verkehrsleben immer deutlicher hervortritt. Es macht sich – veranlaßt durch die Unsolidität der kleineren Geschäftsleute und unterstützt durch das niedrige Postporto für Pakete – die Tendenz auf Seiten der Consumenten geltend, mit Übergehung der Zwischenhändler sich direkt an größere zuverlässige Geschäftshäuser resp. an die Fabrikanten selbst bei Bezug von Artikeln jeder Art zu wenden, eine Tendenz, die einerseits die rasche Einführung der Checks unterstützen wird, andrerseits selbst durch den dadurch erleichterten Geldverkehr gesteigert werden würde.

Nach meiner Ansicht würde die volkswirtschaftliche Bedeutung eines solchen Prozesses wesentlich eine pädagogische sein, indem das Publicum bei dieser auf einen bestimmten Verkehrspreis beschränkten Anwendung der Checks die Vortheile des ganzen Systems kennen lernen würde, so daß dann auch die weiteren Momente, welche für Einführung desselben sprechen, in Geltung treten könnten.

Eine Einrichtung der Londoner Checkbank scheint mir jedoch alle Vortheile wieder in Zweifel zu stellen. Herr James Hertz sucht, [?   ]⁴ richtig verstanden habe, den Clienten die Möglichkeit auf einen höheren Betrag als die hinterlegte Summe ausmacht, zu ziehen – dadurch abzuschneiden, daß er die Checks auf einen bestimmten Betrag ausstellt; er benimmt aber dadurch zugleich den Clienten die Freiheit über die hinterlegte Summe nach Willkühr in einzelnen Quoten zu verfügen; d.h. er zwingt sie für jeden vorkommenden Fall sich einen Check zu kaufen. Vielleicht ließe sich die Freiheit des Clienten dadurch wahren, daß demselben in der Höhe der hinterlegten Summe Marken auf bestimmte Beträge lautend ausgehändigt würden, die auf den Check in der Höhe der bezogenen Summe zu kleben wären. Es würde dadurch zwar die Form nicht aber das Wesen des Checks verändert.

Gestatten Sie den Ausdruck vorzüglicher Hochachtung, in welcher zeichnet

[?   ]
ergebenster
Dr. H. Kranichfeld.

---

⁴ Several words in the original manuscript have proved indecipherable.

474.   L. WALRAS TO W. S. JEVONS

Château de Glérolles, par
St Saphorin.
Vaud (Suisse)
11 août 1876[1]

Cher Monsieur,

J'ai reçu, il y a quelque temps, votre livre sur "La Monnaie et le Mécanisme de l'échange", que j'ai lu en entier avec le plus vif intérêt et qui m'a procuré presque à chaque page, le plaisir de me voir entièrement d'accord avec vous. Je vous ai envoyé moi-même, il y a trois semaines, les épreuves d'un Mémoire intitulé "Equations de la Production"[2] dont je serais bien heureux que la lecture vous causât la même satisfaction. Mais, avec tout cela, j'en suis encore à répondre à votre lettre du 14 février 1875.[3] Excusez, je vous prie, ce bien long retard. J'ai été élu, l'année dernière, recteur de notre académie, ce qui m'a occasioné un notable surcroît d'occupation; et j'ai été atteint, à la même époque, d'une affection nerveuse, ou, pour employer le terme exact, d'une névrose cérébro-spinale, qui ne m'a permis de faire que bien peu de choses en sus de mes travaux d'enseignement et d'administration. J'espère que le repos et l'air de la campagne, où je suis venu demeurer, me remettront peu à peu.

Votre lettre m'entretenait de la publicité que vous étiez en train de donner à votre brochure sur la méthode mathématique, des adhésions que vous receviez, spécialement de l'article publié par M. George Darwin dans la *Fortnightly Review*, et enfin de l'intention où vous étiez de soulever la question devant le Club d'économie politique de Londres et le Congrès de l'association britannique pour l'avancement des sciences. J'ai eu l'occasion de prendre connaissance de l'article de M. Darwin que j'ai

---

[1] The only differences between the original manuscript received by Jevons, and reproduced here, and the version published by Jaffé (*Walras Correspondence*, I, 503–4), based on the draft in Fonds Walras (FW I, 278), are as follows:

	Walras Correspondence	*Jevons Papers*
para 3	moi-même	moi-aussi
para 4	sous le régime de la libre concurrence en débarrassant cette théorie	en debarrassant cette théorie

A misprint at line 4 in paragraph 1 of the Jaffé version (p. 503), has resulted in the omission of the passage 'vous ai envoyé moi-même, il y a trois semaines, les épreuves d'un Mémoire intitulé . . .'.

[2] L. Walras, 'Equations de la Production', read before the Société Vaudoise des Sciences Naturelles on 19 January and 16 February 1876; first published in the *Bulletin* of the Society, Second Series, 14, no. 76, 395–430.

[3] Reproduced above, Letter 418, p. 102.

trouvé très remarquable. J'ai eu soin aussi de lire le compte-rendu du Congrès de Brighton dans le Times; mais je n'y ai pas trouvé de communication de vous sur le sujet. [4] J'attends la publication du volume annuel que nous recevons à la Bibliothèque de l'Académie pour être définitivement renseigné à cet égard.

A force de répondre à diverses objections de principe, j'en étais venu, moi-aussi, il y a déjà longtemps, à avoir dans la tête une démonstration *à priori* de la possibilité de l'application des mathématiques à l'économie politique. J'avais même jeté ce travail sur le papier. Je l'ai revu et terminé cet hiver, et j'ai cherché à le faire paraître dans quelque recueil français bien posé; mais je n'y ai point réussi. Les uns l'ont trouvé trop spécial, les autres pas assez. Je l'ai alors envoyé à M. Boccardo, de Gênes, en le priant de le lire et de voir s'il ne ferait pas un article bibliographique avantageux à sa *Biblioteca dell'Economista*. M. Boccardo, ayant été tout à fait de cet avis, a traduit lui-même le travail avec le plus grand soin et s'est chargé de le faire insérer dans le *Giornale degli Economisti*. Je vous en envoie aujourd'hui un exemplaire. [5] Vous y trouverez trois ou quatre pages sur votre ouvrage de 1871 que j'ai écrites en toute sincérité et que vous prendrez, je l'espère, en bonne part. L'article a été remarqué et je puis vous annoncer, moi aussi, que des lettres d'assentiment m'arrivent de bien des côtés et quelquefois même de très loin.

Toutefois comme, après tout, le meilleur moyen de prouver l'excellence de la méthode mathématique est d'en tirer des résultats importants, je me suis donné pour tâche de concentrer dans quatre Mémoires une théorie mathématique complète de la détermination 1° des prix des produits, 2° des prix des revenus producteurs (fermages, salaires, intérêts), 3° du taux du revenue net, et, par conséquent, du prix des capitaux producteurs, en débarrassant cette théorie de toute discussion pour la réduire à des éléments essentiels. Le premier de ces quatre Mémoires est celui qui a paru en 1874 et qui a provoqué votre première lettre. Les trois autres vont paraître cette année dans le *Bulletin de la société vaudoise des sciences naturelles*, [6] et je vous les ferai tenir exactement en temps et lieu. Les épreuves que vous avez déjà reçues sont celles du troisième.

[4] Walras appears to have confused the meeting of the National Association for the Promotion of Social Science, which was held at Brighton in 1875, with that of the British Association, which in that year took place in Bristol. Jevons, however, had not carried out his expressed intention of speaking on the mathematical method in economics either at the British Association or the Political Economy Club.

[5] 'Un nuovo ramo della matematica. Dell'applicazione delle matematiche all'economia politica', *Giornale degli Economisti*, 3 (1876) 1–40. For a fuller account of the origin and content of this article, see Jaffé, *Walras Correspondence*, I, 493.

[6] The second of these three memoirs was that referred to in n. 2 above; the other two published in vol. 14 (1876–7) were: 'Equations de l'échange', no. 76 pp. 367–94, and 'Equations de la capitalisation', no. 77. pp. 525–61. Cf. above, Letter 375, n. 2, p. 39.

Dans l'espoir, Cher Monsieur, que vous accueillerez mes excuses pour mon long silence, et que vous voudrez bien, au premier moment de loisir que vous aurez, me donner des nouvelles d'Angleterre, je vous envoie l'assurance de mes sentiments bien dévoués.

Léon Walras

475. W. S. JEVONS TO HARRIET JEVONS
      [LJN, 362]

University College,
3d October 1876.

. . . I have managed to get through the lecture without any conspicuous failure. The attendance was poor, and there was no liveliness worth speaking of, and no other speeches, simply a lecture. The humorous attempts answered very well, except that about the dog's idea of property, which failed.[1] I am glad the affair is over and not worse.

I saw the house yesterday, and was charmed with its position again, and with most other things relating to it. . . .

476. W. S. JEVONS TO L. WALRAS
      [FW]

6 October 1876

My dear Sir,

I much regret that your letter of 11 August has remained so long unanswered. It arrived while I was travelling for my health in Norway. Since returning I have been much engaged in arranging for my removal to London and have been obliged to avoid all work that I possibly could. I was very sorry to hear of your nervous malady. I dare say it is much the same as I have been suffering from during the summer, namely, congestion of the cerebellum and the upper part of the spine, combined with general nervous depression. I am however much better and hope that the comparative freedom from academic work which I shall in the future enjoy will enable me to write more than in the past.

---

[1] "I should not despair of tracing the action of the postulates of political economy among some of the more intelligent classes of animals. Dogs certainly have strong though perhaps limited ideas of property, as you will soon discover if you interfere between a dog and his bone." – 'The Future of Political Economy. Introductory Lecture at the opening of the Session 1876–77 at University College, London, Faculty of Arts and Laws', *Fortnightly Review*, 20 (1876) 617–31; reprinted in *Principles of Economics*, pp. 187–206. The quotation is from p. 197.

I gave the Introductory lecture of the Faculty of Arts and Laws at University College London last Tuesday,[1] and made as I hope due reference to your writings though the mathematical theory was only partially discussed. It is true that I did not carry out my intention of discussing the theory at the British Association last year. This year I have not been able to attend any such meetings.

I am much obliged by your sending me copies of the paper which you have recently published. They shall have my careful attention as soon as I am able to begin reading again.

Before going to Norway, if I recollect aright, I posted to you a copy of the French edition of my book on Money in which you will find a brief reference near the beginning to our theory of economy. My successor in Owens College, Professor Robert Adamson, has pointed my attention to the work of von Thünen,[2] translated into French by Wolkoff. It seems to be very scientific, but I have not read it yet.

My address after the 11th October will be

> The Chestnuts
> Branch Hill
> Hampstead Heath
> LONDON NW

When more at leisure I hope to write again at greater length.
In the meantime I beg to remain my dear Sir

> Yours very faithfully
> W. Stanley Jevons.

477. W. S. JEVONS TO MRS LUCY HUTTON
    [LJN, 364]

> University of London,
> Burlington Gardens, W.,
> 27th October 1876.

. . . Our house is still in a good deal of confusion, and I do not see how I can do much at it now for a week, as I have a large number, some 180 papers, to read for the B.A examination, which is now going on. We continue to be pleased with our house in most respects. The heath is charming, and entices me out in a morning for a ramble in a way quite different from Withington.

. . . My books are selling pretty well, 8000 copies of the *Logic Primer* in

---

[1] See above, Letter 475, p. 183.
[2] Johann Heinrich von Thünen (1783–1850), *Le Salaire naturel, et son rapport au taux de l'intérêt. Traduit de l'allemand par M. Wolkoff* (1857).

six months, and 3350 of the *Elementary Lessons* in the year.[1] We shall probably have a new edition of the *Principles of Science* in the spring if I can prepare it. . . .[2]

478.   W. S. JEVONS TO DR KRANICHFELD
       [WM]

2 The Chestnuts,
Branch Hill,
Hampstead,
LONDON, N.W.
10 Nov. 1876.

Herr Professor,
Dr. Kranichfeld.

Dear Sir,

When your esteemed letter of the 8th July[1] arrived in England I was abroad in Norway, where I remained for 6 or 7 weeks after that date, almost beyond the reach of the post. I believe that Mrs. Jevons informed you of this fact. Since returning I have been much distracted by business connected with my change of professorships, and the removal of my house to London. I therefore deferred answering your letter until I could do it at leisure and with some information.

A few weeks ago I posted to you some papers which would inform you of the liquidation of the original Cheque Bank,[2] and the transfer of its business to a new company. This Company is now vigorously pushing on the work, and agencies for the sale of cheques are opened at a great many shops, chiefly *stationers* in London and elsewhere. These agents sell *single cheques,* made payable to the purchaser or his order, and after being endorsed they can be passed from hand to hand. The lowest charge is 2d.

---

[1] Cf. Vol. III, Letter 336, n. 2, p. 240.

[2] The second edition of *The Principles of Science* did appear in 1877, but in the autumn; the Preface bears the date 'August 15, 1877'.

[1] See above, Letter 473, p. 178.

[2] The original Cheque Bank, founded in 1873, went into voluntary liquidation at the beginning of 1876 but through reconstruction under a new company, the Cheque Bank Ltd, its operations were enabled to continue without interruption. The object of its founder, James Hertz (cf. above, Letter 473, n. 2, p. 178) was twofold: to provide money transfer facilities for people of modest means more cheaply and conveniently than did the Post Office Money Order system, and to relieve the banks of small transactions. For a time the Bank operated successfully, through the agency system here described by Jevons, both in Britain and on the Continent, but its business declined as joint-stock banks lost their reluctance to handle small business and widespread forgery of its easily cashed cheques led to the final liquidation of the venture in 1901. See *Bankers' Magazine,* 1875–7 and 1901–2, *passim.*

for a cheque of £1 or less, but the charges, in spite of the penny stamp upon each cheque seem to be rather lower than those of the Post Office Money order system.

I have heard nothing more of the sale of books of cheques on a large scale; in the case of a large Manchester bank which acted as agent to the original company, the sale of such books of cheques was not great, and my impression is that the business will resolve itself mainly into the sale of single cheques in shops.

I am told that the transfer of the Bank's business having become well known to the public, occasioned some loss of custom which it will take time to recover.

I give you only my own impressions, and my impression now is that the Bank can only be profitable by acquiring a very large business. Now I am afraid that under such circumstances competition would arise. Other banks might begin the practice of selling single cheques, indeed it is done already to some extent. Then again there has been an inquiry into the money order Department of the Post Office, and the Government made known some 9 months ago in the House of Commons, that a modification of the money order system, and the introduction of the cheque system, was being considered.[3]

I cannot say therefore that the prospects of the Cheque Bank appear to me to be of a very encouraging kind. I described the Bank carefully in my Book on Money,[4] because I thought it a very interesting and ingenious experiment, and one showing what might be achieved by banking organization. I am sure, too, that either through the Cheque Bank, the Post Office or the Banking system generally, the use of cheques for small payments will be extended. The communication between England and the Colonies and foreign ports, and places frequented by travellers is so much increasing, that the use of cheques issued by one single well-known bank would be a great advantage, and I cannot help thinking that it is in distant payments that the cheque Bank will be most useful and successful.

I am not sufficiently acquainted with Germany to venture on any opinion as to the need of a similar bank there. So far as I can learn, the German post office is in some respects better organized than the English one, especially as regards the paying and collecting of money. I have hitherto hardly been in Germany at all, and my knowledge of the German language is unfortunately so small (in spite of frequent attempts to learn it) that I had to get a friend to translate your esteemed letter. You will thus see that my opinion about any German matter would be of no value.

[3] See below, Letter 502, p. 000.
[4] *Money and the Mechanism of Exchange*, chapter XXII, 'The Cheque Bank', pp. 291–9.

Your suggestion about affixing stamps to cheques to increase their value is very ingenious, but I can hardly form an opinion as to the practicability of the proposal, without the discussion of details. One good point about the cheque bank cheques is that they are indelibly marked as under a certain limit (one £ or under, two £ or under, and so on up to £10 or under). The possibility of fraud is thus very much restricted.

I enclose you two old cheques returned to me by Mr. Hertz, which will show you how they are drawn, and dealt with in the course of payment. They need not be returned.

> Believe me to be dear Sir,
> with much respect,
> Yours faithfully,
> W. Stanley Jevons.

479.   S. WILLIAMSON[1] TO W. S. JEVONS

> Copley,
> Neston,
> Cheshire.
> 11th November 1876.

Dear Sir,

I have your letter of the 9th – pardon my again obtruding myself on your time and attention. It is to ascertain the line of duty for myself that I wish to arrive at sound conclusions. I am thoroughly convinced we are theoretically right. You (I apprehended from ill health and overtaxed energies) cannot take up this question. Should I, thoroughly convinced as I am that we are *right,* give it up in despair – simply because the obstacles to accomplish *what is right* appear to be overwhelming?

Permit me to speak to India – Forty years ago she sent silver to England. Mr. Langley[2] of London told me so. I don't know the circumstances. Then she was not internationally indebted. *Now* she has to pay £15,000,000 at least in gold, every year in London. The current has certainly flowed towards India. But I do think a reverse current would be inevitable in the event of insufficient produce – or wretched prices for

---

[1] Stephen Williamson (1827–1903), Liverpool merchant and advocate of bimetallism; M.P. for St Andrews, 1880–85, Kilmarnock, 1886–95. He was senior partner in the firm of Balfour, Williamson & Co. from 1851 to 1901. See *Balfour, Williamson & Company, and Allied Firms: Memoirs of a Merchant House* (1929).

[2] Possibly Edward Langley, a supporter of bimetallism, who was later associated with Williamson in the International Monetary Standard Association, founded in London in 1882 to promote the adoption of the double standard. Langley presented a paper before the Manchester Statistical Society in 1879 (see Vol. V, Letter 586, n.1), twice reprinted from the Society's *Transactions* as *On the Silver Question* (Salford, 1879) and *The Silver and Double Standard Questions* (1881).

Surat, Cotton, Jute, Rice etc. – coupled with the *absolute obligation* to send her above £15,000,000 in any event. A strong outflow frequently happens from England. It might *now* occasionally happen from India. I think there is sorry likelihood of its occurring ere long.

I quite agree with you [that][3] it would be folly to introduce a gold standard into India. The very folly of this leads me to the Bimetallic system.[4] But if refused, gold must be permitted or rather adopted in India. India has £100,000,000 of gold hoarded & in ornaments now. Much of this might be usefully employed under the bimetallic system. I cannot see where there would be any "revolution" in adopting a Bimetallic system or rather that it would cost anything. In fact I argue for it to save India from possible financial ruin. Its adoption at $15\frac{1}{2}$ to 1 (the status quo) would bring comfort and greatly stimulate trade in many directions.

The Comstock Lode has 50% of gold, but gold is actually diminishing in supply yearly. Were it not for Comstock Lode it would be down to £17,000,000 per annum against £33,000,000 in 1852. If the world persists in demonetising silver, gold will inevitably rise in value very greatly – to the great detriment of commerce and of our mercantile and industrial enterprises. London bankers who sit upon their gold would of course profit; but it would be short sighted policy. They would in the long run lose by the restrictions, embarassments and panics, which for a long time would ensue from their blind policy.

Yours faithfully,
S. Williamson

Do kindly answer me!

The discarding of silver would so reduce the world "money" (gold only being wanted) that a perpetual scrimmage for it would be kept up, involving constant drains – ebbs and flows and a higher rate of discount perpetually harassing commerce and hindering the developement of the world's resources – and the interchange of commodities.

S.W.

---

[3] Omitted in the original manuscript.
[4] See Williamson, *India in its relation to the Silver Question* (Liverpool, 1876).

480.   W. S. JEVONS TO L. WALRAS
        [FW]

15 December 1876

A review of your book "Elements d'Economie Politique Pure etc."
appears in the Deutsche Allgemeine Polytechnische Zeitung for the 9
December 1876.[1]

If you have not seen it I shall be happy to send a copy. 15 Dec. 76
W. S. Jevons.

481.   L. WALRAS TO W. S. JEVONS
        [FW]

Lausanne 19X^e 1876.

Cher Monsieur,

Je reçois à l'instant à l'Académie votre aimable avis concernant
l'article de la Deutsche Allgemeine Polytechnische Zeitung. Je vous
remercie vivement et vous serais tout particulièrement obligé de vouloir
me communiquer la copie que vous m'offrez.

D'ici à peu de temps je vous enverrai plus d'épreuves.

Votre dévoué
Léon Walras

M. S. Jevons.

482.   W. S. JEVONS TO J. MILLS
        [LJN, 364–5]

2 The Chestnuts
Hampstead,
3d January 1877.

... My paper on 'Sun Spots and the Price of Corn' has not been
published, and in fact withdrawn, because I found, with subsequent
calculations, that the same data would give other periods of variation
equally well.[1] The method of averages adopted seems delusive in this

---

[1] *Deutsche Allgemeine Polytechnische Zeitung*, Heft 4 (1876) 589–91. This was the review by A.
Hildebrandt forecast in Jevons's letter to Walras of 14 February 1875; see above, Letter 418, p. 103.

[1] 'On the Influence of the Sun-Spot Period upon the Price of Corn', the second paper presented by
Jevons to Section F of the British Association at Bristol in 1875 (cf. above, Letter 439, p. 128). No.
abstract of the paper appeared (see *Report of the Forty-fifth Meeting of the British Association . . . 1875*,
Transactions . . . p. 217) but it was eventually published in *Investigations*, pp. 194–205. A footnote on
p. 194 makes clear that Jevons had himself decided to include this paper in *Investigations*, though
evidently did not write his intended 'Introductory Discussion' on it before his death. See also below,
Letter 538, p. 271.

case, and I hardly see any way of settling the matter conclusively. That the inquiry is far from being an absurd one is, however, shown by the remarkable fact since brought to view, that Sir William Herschel,[2] at the beginning of the century, tried to explain the variations in the price of corn by the sun spots. I send you the MS. as it was read at the British Association and partially reported. Please, however, do not allude to it, except you add that I regard the conclusions as neither proved nor disproved.

The organ has been quite successfully re-established, and seems to sound much better in this than in the former house. The tone comes out more and resounds about the house.[3]

I think we shall be charmed ·with Hampstead in the spring and summer,[4] but the recent weather has not been such as to develop the pleasures of the heath.

. . . The summer holiday and comparative relief from college work have been very beneficial to me, and I am now in pretty good working order. I am just engaged upon a new edition of the *Principles of Science*, and also upon a *Political Economy Primer*, to serve as a companion to my *Logic Primer*. I have not heard any concerts yet to compare with Halle's as a whole; but I have been repeatedly to the St. James' Hall popular concerts, where the chamber music is delightful. . . .

483. L. WALRAS TO W. S. JEVONS

Château de Glérolles par
St. Saphorin, Vaud (Suisse),
17 février 1877[1]

Cher Monsieur,

Je vous ai envoyé au commencement de la semaine un exemplaire de mon quatrième et dernier Mémoire. Je pense que vous avez bien gardé les trois autres; mais comme, au surplus, vous saurez assurément tirer bon

[2] Sir William Herschel (1738–1822), astronomer father of Sir John F. W. Herschel. He correctly conjectured the periodic occurrence of sun-spots, and tried to prove the hypothesis of a corresponding weather-cycle by showing that the price of wheat rose as the incidence of sun-spots fell towards its minimum. Cf. *Philosophical Transactions of the Royal Society*, 91 (1801) 265–318.

[3] Cf. Vol. I, p. 79, n. 3.

[4] The text of this letter was also published in TLJM, p. 338. The version printed there differs at this point, reading '. . . Hampstead in the spring and summer. Mrs. Jevons and I hope that in the livelier season you will find some opportunity of coming up with Mrs. Mills and staying with us. I do not think I shall revisit Manchester for some time to come, but I hope that some time or other I may revisit your delightful retreat at Bowdon. The summer holiday . . .'.

[1] In the version printed by Jaffé in *Walras Correspondence*, I, 531–2, this letter is dated '(26–27) février 1877'. This is the date added in pencil on the draft in Fonds Walras; presumably Walras did not put the date on the draft when the letter was sent, and later remembered it wrongly.

parti d'un double, je vous envoie encore aujourd'hui un exemplaire des quatre Mémoires réunis. Il m'en reste peu; cependant, j'en aurai bien un ou deux autres, s'il le fallait, à votre disposition.

Votre lettre du 6 octobre est sous mes yeux; et j'y vois que malheureusement nous nous sommes rencontrés aussi exactement en fait de maladie nerveuse qu'en fait de théorie mathématique de l'échange. Ce serait à croire que c'est la théorie de l'échange qui est la cause de la maladie. Mes symptômes sont identiquement ceux que vous me décrivez. Je ne sais comment vous vous êtes soigné; mais quant à moi, c'est la bromure de potassium qui calme le mieux mes congestions cérébrales, et ce sont les bains du lac, au bord duquel je demeure et les courses sur les monts qui apportent le plus de soulagement aux points douloureux de la nuque et de l'épine dorsale.

Vous m'annonciez dans cette même lettre votre "Introductory Lecture". J'ai su tout récemment qu'elle avait paru dans le numéro de novembre 1876 de la *Fortnightly Review* que je vais tâcher de me procurer. Quant aux travaux de Thünen, dont vous m'y parliez aussi, ce sont des tentatives que les Allemands paraissent considérer avec une certaine estime, bien qu'ils ne les imitent guère. Je les connaissais depuis longtemps, par les résumés et les traductions de M. Wolkoff;[2] mais je dois dire que je n'ai pas été assez heureux jusqu'ici pour y trouver quoi que ce soit à utiliser. Il est vrai que je les ai plutôt parcourus que lus, mais je doute, malgré tout, qu'il y ait grand'chose à y prendre.

Ayant jusqu'ici une idée à moi que je suivais, je ne lisais les auteurs occupés de recherches analogues que pour m'assurer qu'ils n'avaient pas pris ma voie. Quant à faire une lecture proprement dite de leurs ouvrages, ce qui, en pareille matière, veut dire une étude très approfondie, je ne m'y sens disposé qu'à présent que j'ai sur les points principaux de l'économie politique pure des conclusions bien claires et bien arrêtées. La première

---

Other differences between the version published in *Walras Correspondence* and that reproduced here from the Jevons Papers are as follows:

	Walras Correspondence	*Jevons Papers*
para 1	encore un ou deux	bien un ou deux
para 2	du lac, autour	du lac, au bord
para 3	les brouillons de	les traductions de
	M. Wolkoff	M. Wolkoff
para 4	et des Capitaux	et du capital
	du marché de ces services	du marché des services producteurs
	propriétaires,	propriétaires et
	capitalistes	capitalistes
	elles contiennent	elles contenaient

[2] Mathieu Wolkoff, *Précis d'économie politique rationelle* (1868); a resumé of von Thünen's theory of the 'natural wage' is given in Wolkoff's 'Notes du Chapitre XIV'.

que je ferai sera certainement celle de vos théories du *travail*, de la *rente* et du *capital*. Je les ai souvent parcourues déjà et il m'a toujours semblé que, sans fournir précisément la solution du problème de la détermination des prix des services producteurs, qui me préoccupait exclusivement et qu'il est impossible, selon moi de trouver en dehors de la conception du marché des services producteurs, de leur demand effective par les entrepreneurs, de leur offre effective par les travailleurs, propriétaires et capitalistes, elles contenaient toutefois des considérations extrêmement ingénieuses et tout à fait définitives à d'autres égards. C'est là un point dont il me tarde beaucoup de me rendre compte.

Recevez, cher Monsieur, l'assurance de mes sentiments de sincère attachement.

Léon Walras

484. W. S. JEVONS TO L. WALRAS
[FW;LJP, 366−7]

Hampstead, 28th February, 1877[1]

... I thank you much for sending me the copy of your four memoirs, which I have safely received. I am glad to see that you are proceeding with your inquiries, and have now found a theory of capitalisation. This appears to display all the originality and ingenuity which were so conspicuous in your previous memoirs. I am not myself much engaged at present upon political economy, being just now very busy in revising my book on the *Principles of Science* for a second edition, the first edition having been sold out. This work almost entirely prevents me from reading anything at present. After it is done I propose to complete my examination of John Stuart Mill's philosophy, in which I shall show that

---

[1] The only differences between the version published in LJ and that published by Jaffé based on the manuscript in Fonds Walras (FW ɪɪ, 538), are as follows:

	Letters and Journal	*Walras Correspondence*
para 1	found a theory	formed a theory
		Para. 2 begins at
		'I am not myself ...
para 2(3)	*Logic for Schools*	logic for schools
	Messrs. Macmillan	Messrs. MacMillan
		Para. 4 begins at
		'My introductory lecture ...
para 3(4)	*Fortnightly Review*	Fortnightly Review
	M. de Fortpertius	M. de Fontpertuis
	This, at least, is ...	This at least is ...

the logical value of Mill's writings has been much misunderstood, and that he is really a bad logician.[2]

I have the pleasure of sending you, by post, a copy of a small elementary work on *Logic for Schools*. Books of this sort are sold in large numbers in England and America. I am intending to prepare also an elementary book on political economy for Messrs. Macmillan.[3] My introductory lecture, printed in the *Fortnightly Review,* is about to be republished as a translation into French by M. de Fortpertius, in the *Journal des Economistes*[4] for March, where you will no doubt see it. This, at least, is what I am informed.

Some weeks ago I took the opportunity of reading Dupuit's[5] *Memoire de la Mesure de l'utilite des Travaux Publics, Annales des Ponts et Chaussees,* 1844,[6] which I had not previously seen. It is impossible not to allow that Dupuit had a very profound comprehension of the subject, and anticipated us as regards the fundamental ideas of utility. But he did not work his subject out, and did not reach a theory of exchange. It is extraordinary, too, what a small effect his publication had upon economists, most of whom were ignorant of its existence.

I hope that your health is now re-established, and that you are able to avoid excessive exertion. I am now comfortably situated at Hampstead, and having only few lectures at University College or other occupations, am able to give my time to repose or to literary work, as seems fit.

If you are ever coming to London, it would give me great pleasure to receive a visit from you here. If you have not been in England, there is something of interest here. I speak French *very badly,* but perhaps you speak English. In any case we would manage to discuss matters of common interest. At the end of June, however, I go to Norway, and may not return till the end of August. . . .

    [2] W. S. Jevons, 'John Stuart Mill's Philosophy Tested', *Contemporary Review,* 31 (1877) 167–82, 256–75; 32 (1878) 88–9.
    [3] The references here are to two small volumes which Jevons wrote for the 'Science Primers' series, edited by T. H. Huxley, H. E. Roscoe and Balfour Stewart, and published by Macmillan: *Logic,* first edition (1876) and *Political Economy,* first edition (1878).
    [4] W. S. Jevons, 'Le Passé et l'avenir de l'économie politique. Les méthodes. Les économistes contemporains. Le Political Economy club,' *Journal des Économistes,* third series, 45 (1877) 325–42.
    [5] A. J. Etienne-Juvenal Dupuit (1804–66), engineer and mathematician; Inspecteur-général des ponts et chaussées.
    [6] Second Series, VIII, 332–75.

485. W. S. JEVONS TO W. JACK
     [MA]

2 The Chestnuts,
West Heath,
Hampstead,
N.W.
28 March '77

Dear Jack,[1]

I have carefully read and considered the MS sketch and letter of Mr. Moffat sent me. I think it is out of the question that you should publish it at your risk at all. I cannot find that there is anything important and new. As far as I can judge from the abstract the book would be a rather discursive and probably tedious discussion of various points in political economy, all of which have been discussed already ad nauseam.

I dare say many worse books are published than Mr. Moffat[2] would make but I cannot recommend you to take part in one.

Whether you like or not to publish it on his account is a matter I need not trouble myself about.

I think the writer had better keep to his articles, for he seems to have a clear manner of expression and I am sorry he should throw his money away in a publication of the sort. The title he has chosen would alone condemn the thing, and unfortunately it seems to have little relation to the contents of the book, which is a weak point.

Yours faithfully,
W. S. Jevons

486. W. S. CHURCHILL[1] TO W. S. JEVONS

24 Birch Lane
Manchester
April 4. [1877]

My dear Sir,

I was much obliged for your card with your printed address which I have put so carefully by that it is as good as lost. However the Secretary of

---

[1] William Jack (1834–1924), who was with the firm of Macmillan & Co. from 1876 until 1879. Jack had been Inspector of Schools in South-West Scotland, 1860–6; Professor of Natural Philosophy at Owens College, Manchester, 1866–70, editor of the *Glasgow Herald*, 1870–6, and in 1879 became Professor of Mathematics at Glasgow University.

[2] The book referred to was almost certainly *The Economy of Consumption: an Omitted Chapter in Political Economy* by Robert Scott Moffat, which was published by Kegan Paul & Co. in 1878. The author professed himself a disciple of Malthus and adopted the latter's doctrine of under-consumption.

[1] William Smith Churchill (1826–1914), Manchester numismatist; donated a large collection of European coins to the Manchester Museum; founder member of the Lancashire and Cheshire Antiquarian Society, 1883; author of numerous papers published in the Society's *Transactions*.

the Statistical as is very proper has his facts better under command & so I am in a favourable position again to hold a short communion with you. You did not write me after your return from Norway but I thought that possibly you had not met with good success in your enquiries on my behalf and that your many engagements after your return would prevent you from informing me that you had not met with specimens that I should care to possess.

I know that very often it is difficult in the general circulation of a country to get good clear specimens of what we may desire. Money changers & bullion dealers are the best people to apply to and many do not care to trouble themselves much, & furthermore do not care for copper specimens at all.

I enclose you two Turkish notes for the present Sultan one for 5 Piasters or 5^d & 1 Piaster or 1^d Please add them to your collection of paper money, they have already depreciated at Constantinople cent per cent that is our 5^d would now be worth two of these pretty pink notes

I learn that the Merchant houses are so badly off for money to smooth small payments that they also issue notes for small sums which pass from hand to hand at full values. If you would like to have one or two of these I would gladly get them for you.

The lowest amount of note issued by late Sultan Abdul Asiz[2] was 10 Piasters.

A numismatical friend has given me particulars of two Swedish square pieces he has lately purchased for 40/ each & I give you the particulars thinking they might interest you.

I hope Mrs Jevons & your little boy are quite well & that you like Hampstead. Have you met Du Maurier[3] & his big St Bernard dog in their walks. I shall be glad to hear from you

believe me

Yours sincerely

W S Churchill

---

[2] Abdul Aziz, Sultan of Turkey, 1861–76.

[3] George Louis Palmella Busson du Maurier (1834–96), the artist, famous for his illustrations for *Punch*. He lived at New Grove House, Hampstead, from 1874 to 1895 and was a familiar figure in the neighbourhood, often accompanied by his St Bernard, 'Chang', which was frequently featured in his drawings.

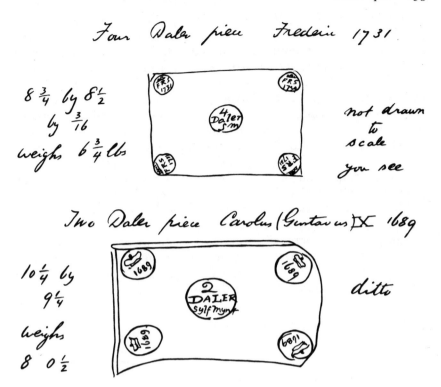

Four Daler piece Fredein 1731.

$8\frac{3}{4}$ by $8\frac{1}{2}$
by $\frac{3}{16}$
weighs $6\frac{3}{4}$ lbs

not drawn to scale you see

Two Daler piece Carolus (Gustavus IX 1689

$10\frac{1}{4}$ by $9\frac{1}{4}$
weighs
8 0 $\frac{1}{2}$

ditto

Curious that the early 2 Daler piece weighs more than the later 4 daler piece but Sweden had in the mean time passed through very much financial distress & disturbance & copper might be of a different value also.

487. L. WALRAS TO W. S. JEVONS

Château de Glérolles par
St. Saphorin Vaud (Suisse).
25 mai 1877.[1]

Cher Monsieur,
J'ai été empêché de répondre plus tôt à votre dernière aimable lettre par plusieurs circonstances de famille ou d'affaires et principalement par l'obligation que je me suis imposée de pousser l'impression de la seconde

[1] A number of minor differences between the original manuscript received by Jevons, and reproduced here, and the version published by Jaffé (*Walras Correspondence*, I, 534–5), based on the

partie de mes *Eléments d'Economie Politique pure* de façon à ce qu'elle soit terminée cet été. Mais je ne veux pas tarder plus longtemps à vous remercier de vos communications ainsi que de l'envoi de votre petit traité de logique. Je l'ai lu, et l'ai passé ensuite à mon éminent collègue le professeur Charles Secrétan.[2] Comme son autorité est considérable en ces matières, je suis heureux de pouvoir vous dire qu'il en a été aussi satisfait que moi, qu'il a beaucoup loué votre exposition de la méthode inductive, et trouvé dans votre jugement sur Bacon la marque d'un esprit vigoureux et indépendant. Sur quoi je lui ai assuré que c'était bien la tout justement ce que vos étiez en économie politique comme en philosophie.

Je n'hésite pas, du reste, à croire que la valeur de votre économie politique tient en grande partie à la supériorité de votre méthode philosophique; et je ne fais pas non plus difficulté de considérer avec vous M. J. S. Mill comme aussi pauvre logicien que médiocre économiste, malgré la peine incroyable qu'il se donne pour ne pas faire des démonstrations. Par exemple, je dois vous avouer que je ne suis pas de votre avis sur le mérite des Mémoires de M. Dupuit publiés en 1844 et 1849 dans les *Annales des Ponts et Chausées*.[3]

---

rough draft in Fonds Walras, are indicated below:

	Walras Correspondence	Jevons Papers
para 1	Votre communication	vos communications
para 1	que c'était bien tout justement	que c'était bien la tout justement
para 2	Je n'hésite pas donc	Je n'hésite pas, du reste
para 3	en propre sont les	en propre, ce sont les
para 3	de l'utilité de tous les autres produits	de l'utilité des autres produits
para 3	dont l'objet et le caractère	sur l'objet et le caractère
para 4	Le vice [profond]	Le vice principal
para 4	que la valeur	que si la valeur
para 5	de doses ou d'incréments	de doses et d'incréments.
para 5	sont réductibles en travail	soient réductibles en services personnels
para 5	pour se preter à l'expression de cette multiplicité	pour se preter à cette multiplicité
para 5	la détermination des prix et des produits et des services	la détermination des prix des produits et des services
para 5	C'est [pourquoi] il me semble	C'est à quoi il me semble
para 6	Or c'est justement	Or c'est tout justement
para 6	que je m'en applaudis	que je m'applaudis
para 6	que l'entente encore plus complète	qui une entente de plus en plus complète

[2] Charles Secrétan (1815–95), Professor of Philosophy at the Académie de Lausanne.

[3] 'De l'influence des péages sur l'utilité des voies de communication', *Annales des Ponts et Chausées*, 1849, no. 207, 2ᵉ, 170–248. For the reference to Dupuit's 1844 paper see above, Letter 484, p. 192.

En ce qui touche la détermination du prix dans le cas de monopole, M. Dupuit n'a fait que reproduire la théorie de M. Cournot. Les seules choses qui lui appartiennent en propre ce sont les observations relatives à la multiplicité possible des prix dans le même cas et son expression mathématique de l'utilité; mais celle-ci est radicalement inexacte. Cette théorie consiste à voir la mesure de l'utilité dans le sacrifice pécuniaire maximum que les consommateurs sont disposés à faire pour se procurer un produit, c'est-à-dire dans l'aire de la *courbe de demande*. Or, sans doute, ce sacrifice pécuniaire dépend, en partie, de l'utilité du produit; mais il dépend aussi, en partie, de l'utilité des autres produits; et il dépend aussi, en partie, de la quantité de richesse, évaluée en monnaie, que possède le consommateur. En termes précis, l'aire de la courbe de demande est *fonction* non seulement de l'utilité du produit à demander (exprimée par une courbe d'utilité), mais aussi de l'utilité des autres produits qui sont sur le marché (exprimée de la même manière), et aussi, enfin, des moyens du consommateur. En dernière analyse, la théorie de M. Dupuit me parâit consister dans une confusion complète de la courbe d'utilité et de la courbe de demande. C'est M. Cournot qui a trouvé celle-ci; c'est vous qui avez trouvé la première; et c'est moi qui ai trouvé comment il fallait tirer l'une de l'autre. Quant à M. Dupuit, je soutiens qu'il na'a rien à réclamer ici. En revanche, je vous indiquerai un bon article de lui sur l'objet et le caractère de l'économie politique pure dans le *Journal des Economistes* de juillet 1861.[4]

Puisque je fais tant que d'aborder les discussions scientifiques, il faut que je vous dise que j'ai récemment étudié à fond votre théorie de la rente, à propos de la réfutation, que je fais dans mon cours, et que je publie dans mes *Eléments,* de celle de Ricardo. Le vice principal de la théorie de Ricardo, comme aussi de celle de MacCulloch telle que vous la reproduisez résumée en quatre points,[5] c'est de reposer sur le principe que "le produit de la terre ne peut être indéfiniment accru, en proportion des *frais* (outlay)". En effet le principe ainsi énoncé ne serait vrai que si à des *frais* proportionnels correspondaient des *quantités* proportionnelles de services de capitaux et de services personnels, c'est-à-dire que si la valeur de ces services était constante; car autrement et si on admet que la valeur en question diminue, rien n'empêche qu'on puisse avoir un accroissement de produit proportionnel à l'accroissement de frais. Or, il est faux que la valeur des services de capitaux et services personnels soit constante, et

---

[4] A. J. Dupuit, 'Reponse à M. Dunoyer à propos de son rapport sur l'ouvrage intitulé *La Liberté Commerciale*', *Journal des Economistes*, second series, 31 (1861) 111–17.

[5] *T.P.E.*, first edition, p. 201. The second of the four points which Jevons quoted from McCulloch's edition of the *Wealth of Nations* read:

'2. That the produce of the land cannot, at an average, be increased in proportion to the outlay, but may be indefinitely increased in a less proportion.'

qu'il n'y ait, en conséquence, de rente que par l'effet d'une cherté croissante des produits agricoles. Il y a rente sans qu'il y ait enchérissement de cette sorte.

Vous évitez cette erreur en parlant, quant à vous, de *doses* ou d'incréments de capital et de travail, doses et incréments mesurés non par leur prix mais par leurs quantités. Et ainsi, le principe fondamental devient vrai. Mais, alors, reste à savoir s'il est susceptible d'être exprimé dans la forme mathématique que vous lui donnez, c'est-à-dire dans la forme d'une fonction décroissante d'une seule variable: Pl. J'avoue que je ne le crois pas: parce que je ne crois pas que les services de capitaux soient réductibles en services personnels,[6] et parce que le fussent-ils, ils ne le seraient pas en une seule espèce de travail. Il faut admettre nettement que les produits agricoles ou industriels résultent de la combinaison d'espèces multiples de services personnels, de services de capitaux et de services de terres, et chercher une forme mathématique qui soit assez large pour se prêter à cette multiplicité dans le problème de la détermination des prix des produits et des services producteurs. C'est [à quoi] il me semble que seuls mes *coefficients de production* réussissent.

J'aurais le plus vif désir de discuter avec vous ce point capital, et après y avoir bien réfléchi, je suis vivement tenté d'accepter l'offre séduisante que vous me faites, en allant moi-même vous porter mon ouvrage à la fin des vacances. Vous me dîtes que vous serez absent en juillet et août. Or c'est tout justement au commencement de septembre que j'espère avoir mon demi-volume imprimé; et j'irai fort probablement à cette époque à Paris pour le recommander à quelques revues et journaux, en même temps que je ferai à Chartres une visite à ma mere. Ce serait une occasion de pousser jusqu'à Londres et d'y faire votre connaissance. M. Secrétan me félicitait l'autre jour bien vivement de m'être rencontré scientifiquement avec un homme tel que vous; et je puis vous dire en toute sincérité que je m'applaudis tous les jours de cette rencontre. J'ai la conscience qu'elle ma donné tout d'abord une parfaite sérénité d'âme quant à la valeur de mes travaux; j'ai, de plus, la persuasion qu'elle a singulièrement hâté le

---

[6] *T.P.E.*, first edition, p. 206: 'The whole produce of a piece of land is x, the whole labour spent upon it is l; and x varies in some way as l varies, never decreasing when l increases. We may say, then, that x is a function of l; let us call it Pl.

While in the second edition of *T.P.E.* Jevons retained the assumption that increments of labour could be substituted for increments of capital, he altered the justification of it in a manner which, as Professor Jaffé has pointed out (*Walras Correspondence*, 1, pp. 537–8), seems to have been the result of Walras's criticism. In the first edition Jevons supported his use of this assumption by citing McCulloch's statement 'that as all capital was originally produced by labour, the application of additional capital is the application of additional labour. "Either the one phrase or the other may be used indiscriminately". ' In the second edition this was followed by the words: 'This doctrine is in itself altogether erroneous, but it will not be erroneous to assume as a mode of simplifying the problem that the increments of labour applied are equally assisted by capital. It is a separate and subsequent problem to determine how rent or interest arises when the same labour is assisted by different quantities of capital.' (p. 216)

résultat de ces efforts; je suis enfin convaincu qu' une entente de plus en plus complète avec vous me serait toujours aussi avantageuse sous tous ces rapports. Et, puisque, dans la haute situation que vous occupez, vous voulez bien me traiter en ami, je serai ravi, si rien ne vient m'en empêcher, d'accepter votre gracieuse invitation avec autant de simplicité et d'empressement que vous me l'avez faite.

Recevez, Cher Monsieur, l'expression de mes sentiments bien dévoués.

Léon Walras.

488. W. S. JEVONS TO J. MILLS
[LJN, 368–9]

Hampstead, 30th May 1877.

. . . Can I trouble you to let me have back the MS of my paper at the British Association, on 'Commercial Crises and Solar Spots?' I am working at the subject again, and am more convinced than ever that there is some connection; but it is a treacherous subject, and requires much care. I am not sure whether I have not found out the relation between the sun spots and the price of corn; but at present it is little more than a surmise.

I have been having a great feast of music lately, between Rubinstein, Wagner, and minor performances. Several hearings of Rubinstein[1] quite confirm the first impression that I gathered when I heard him in Manchester some years ago, namely, that he is one of the most extraordinary performers who ever lived – perhaps the most extraordinary. He realises one's ideal of musical creation more than I ever thought possible. I heard the Sonata, Op. 111 a few days ago.[2] Wagner also has given me some new sensations.[3]

We discuss the subject of periodic crises next Friday at the Political Economy Club.[4] . . .

[1] Anton Grigorevich Rubinstein (1830–94), was at this time almost better known as a pianist than as a composer, and was performing at the Crystal Palace.

[2] Jevons was probably referring to a recital given by Rubinstein at St James's Hall on 28 May 1877. The Programme included Beethoven's Sonata in C Minor, Op. 111 (*The Times*, 28 May 1877, p. 1).

[3] Richard Wagner (1813–83) gave a series of concerts of his own works, conducted by himself, at the Royal Albert Hall in May 1877 (*The Times*, 9 May 1877, p. 10; 22 May 1877, p. 9).

[4] On 1 June 1877 H. R. Grenfell proposed the question: 'To what extent is the present Stagnation of Trades exceptional, and in what respects does it present features similar to those of periodically-recurring Commercial depressions?' (*Political Economy Club, . . . List of Questions Discussed, 1872–1880*, III (1881) 61).

489.   F. GALTON[1] TO W. S. JEVONS

42 Rutland Gate,
May 31 / 77.

My dear Sir,

When you talked to me about Reversion last night, I did not express myself clearly so I write out now what I ought to have said, for the chance of your caring to read it.

I start with a "Pangenesis" theory of life, by supposing the germ to be an organised collection of a vast number of elements, of various descriptions, — just as one would observe in a great organised emigration from a parent country, to found a new colony, in which the various individuals would have various trades and capacities.[2]

Deviation, I suppose to be due to the presence of one particular class of elements in abnormal proportions (as regard number or quality,) in the germ. By abnormal I mean what is not the best proportion for the well being of the organised germ, either in excess or deficiency. Once more, I suppose descent to be such as is indicated in the enclosed diagram. First the germ g_I, then a development of it, G_I, then a lateral segregation from it to form sexual elements, that is to say the germs, of the next generation g_2, and lastly a continuation of development of G_I, to the adult stage A_I. g_2 goes through exactly the same process to form g_3, and so on.

Referring to the diagram, suppose an undue preponderance of some class of germ as represented by the crosses in g_I. This preponderance continues in G_I. Then when the segregation takes place from G_I to form g_2, there ensues a resistance to their admission in their previous large proportions. The number of applicants is greater than there is place for them, without crowding out others who by the hypothesis are most serviceable to the organisation of the germ. It is therefore clear that many of these over abundant applicants would be rejected. Now according to the typical law of reversion formulated in my paper,[3] the rejections would

---

[1] Sir Francis Galton (1822–1911), anthropologist. An enthusiastic supporter of the theories of his cousin, Charles Darwin, Galton from 1865 onwards was occupied with research into heredity and the measurement of inherited characterstics. Among his best known works were *Hereditary Genius* (1869), *English Men of Science, their Nature and Nurture* (1874), *Natural Inheritance* (1889). See his *Autobiography: Memories of my Life* (1908) and K. Pearson, *The Life, Letters and Labours of Francis Galton*, 3 vols (Cambridge, 1914–30).

[2] For details of the development of Galton's ideas and their influence on the study of human genetics, see P. Froggatt and N.C. Nevin, 'The "Law of Ancestral Heredity" and the Mendelian – Ancestrian Controversy in England, 1889–1906', *Journal of Medical Genetics*, 8 (1971) 1–36.

[3] 'Typical Laws of Heredity', *Nature*, 5, 12 and 19 April 1877, pp. 492–5, 512–14, 532–3. This paper was the text of a lecture delivered at the Royal Institution on 9 February 1877. It contained Galton's first published reference to the concept of 'reversion', to which he soon afterwards gave the now familiar name of regression. Cf. H. Westergaard, *Contributions to the History of Statistics* (1932) pp. 270–2.

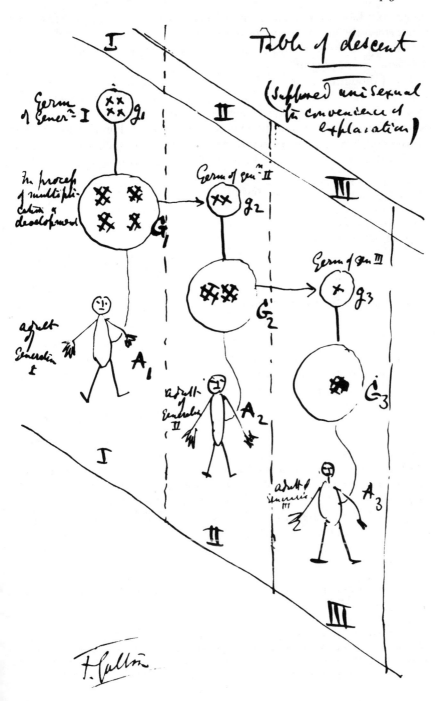

Table of descent

(supposed unisexual for convenience of explanation)

invariably bear a constant proportion to the *excess* of applicants; and conversely, the favor shown (probably during the course of development between g and G) would bear the same constant proportion to the deficiency of applicants.

I had thought that some classes of observations in Political Economy would run sufficiently parallel to this hypothesis to throw a useful light upon it. Thus the successive stages by which a period of accidental over production of any commodity reverts to one of normal production, would be analogous, and *if* it were found that an excess (x) which was reduced in the first year to $\frac{x}{n}$, became reduced in the second year to $\frac{x}{n^2}$ and in third year to $\frac{x}{n^3}$ and so on, the parallism* with typical law of reversion would be exact.

Pardon this by letter,

Very faithfully yours,
Francis Galton.

Professor Stanley Jevons, F.R.S.

490.   W. S. JEVONS TO J. MILLS
[TLJM, 339]

June 3, 1877
2 The Chestnuts, West Heath
Hampstead, N.W.

My dear Mills—

The discussion at the Political Economy Club would have amused rather than informed you. Grenfell's[1] opening was not impressive, but there was a very lively discussion, in which Villiers,[2] Edwin Chadwick, Harrison,[3] Newmarch, Fawcett, Courtenay,[4] Dilke[5] and myself took part. Most of what was said was off the point, and little corresponded with

[1] See Vol. V, Letter 730, n. 1.

[2] See Vol. I, p. 86, n. 5.

[3] Frederic Harrison (1831–1923), Professor of Jurisprudence, Constitutional and International Law, Council of Legal Education, 1877–89; President of the English Positivist Committee, 1880–1905.

[4] Presumably Leonard Henry Courtney. Cf. above, Letter 391, p. 66.

[5] Sir Charles Wentworth Dilke (1843–1911), second Baronet, Radical M.P. for Chelsea, 1868–86; Under-Secretary of the Foreign Office, 1880–2; President of the Local Government Board, 1882–5. Retired from public life, 1886, as a result of being cited in a divorce suit, but was returned to Parliament again in 1892 as Member for the Forest of Dean Division of Gloucestershire, until his death.

our views, but Courtenay and I upheld the periodic character. Courtenay takes a really scientific view of such matters.

I hope that next session you will visit us & join in one of our meetings, which are sometimes very interesting, though not always.

I am glad that my impressions of Rubinstein agree so well with those you yourself expressed.

Believe me, yours very faithfully,

W. S. J.

491.   B. STEWART TO W. S. JEVONS

Manchester, 5 June 1877.

Dear Jevons,

Many thanks for your Australian pamphlet[1] which I will read with interest. I do not think Strachey made out any case the other night.[2] He merely put into a numerical form what every one knew already, namely that in the case of rainfall periodic variations of whatever nature are probably small compared to non periodic ones.

The test with tropical barometers was quite fallacious and Strachey afterwards owned this.

The true test of the physical existence of a period whether small or large is its repetition. Of course it is possible to suppose that in another 64 years at Madras we may have results that will cancel those we now have but I think we can split up our present evidence so as to show a considerable tendency to repetition – we must of course always remember the limited amount of our evidence and the anomalous fluctuations that pertain to rainfall.

I have done this on the next page. Bear in mind that we may have a definite connection between rainfall and sun spot without the two maxima coinciding together.

---

[1] The context suggests that this may have been one of Jevons's early papers on meterology, possibly 'Some data concerning the Climate of Australia and New Zealand', a work of fifty-two pages, originally published in *Waugh's Australian Almanack for the year 1859*. See Vol. II, Letter 121, n. 3, pp. 340–1.

[2] Presumably a reference to the paper entitled 'On the alleged Correspondence of the Rainfall at Madras with the Sun-spot Period, and on the True Criterion of Periodicity in a series of Variable Quantities', read before the Royal Society on 31 May 1877 by Lieut - General Sir Richard Strachey F.R.S. (1817–1908), (*Proceedings of the Royal Society*, 26 (1878) 249–61). Strachey had a long and distinguished career in India as a soldier and administrator; in 1897 he was awarded the Royal Medal of the Royal Society. In collaboration with his brother, Sir John Strachey (1823–1907), he published *The Finances and Public Works of India* (1882) and was author of numerous scientific papers: he also invented instruments for taking meterological measurements.

Result of grouping 64 years observations into eleven yearly periods beginning with the first at 1813.

		1	2	3	4	5	6	7	8	9	10	11
A	1813 – 23)											
B	24 – 34)	49.1	49.2	58.3	50.9	50.4	54.4	52.9	45.2	37.0	49.2	35.0
C	35 – 45)											
D	46 – 56)											
E	57 – 67)											
F	68 – end)											

Of these $3+4+5+6+7$ may be regarded as maxima years.

Also $8+9+10+11$ as minima years

We have therefore

	Max years	Min years
Six cycles	53.4	41.6
A	54.7	50.8
B	51.3	34.7
C	54.3	47.5
D	53.7	39.6
E	42.6	41.2
F	63.8	29.3

thus the same behaviour is repeated in each. We have therefore I think a certain amount of evidence in favour of some connexion in fact we have as strong evidence as we could well expect.

I fear that other elements besides the sun influence the price of corn too much to permit of any result being obtained. Could you do nothing about the quality or wt. per bushel of the corn – Schuster[3] seems to have done something about the wine years.[4]

Yours very truly,
B. Stewart.

492. W. S. JEVONS TO A. MARSHALL[1]

2, The Chestnuts, West Heath,
Hampstead, N.W., June 23, 1877.

Dear Mr. Marshall,

I have just received your letter informing me that you have decided to

---

[3] Arthur Schuster. See Vol. V, Letter 572, n. 1.

[4] In the third part of an article entitled 'Suspected Relations between the Sun and Earth', published in *Nature*, 17 May 1877, pp. 45–7, Stewart referred to the fact that 'Dr. Arthur Schuster has found that the years of minimum sun-spots coincide very nearly with the good wine years in Germany . . .' and illustrated the statement with a table covering the years 1784 to 1868. He did not cite the source of Schuster's research. Cf. Vol. V, Letters 572 and 711. See also Schumpeter, *Business Cycles*, I, 165–6, n. 2; and *Investigations*, p. 231.

[1] This letter was printed with other testimonials accompanying Marshall's application for the Principalship of University College, Bristol.

apply for the posts of Principal of University College Bristol, and Professor of Political Economy. There can be no doubt that the College is to be congratulated on counting you among the candidates, but as you have many intimate friends who will speak of your remarkable fitness for the Principalship I will restrict myself to saying that in appointing you to the Professorship, they will add to their staff of Professors one of the most able and experienced teachers of Political Economy in England.

It is known to many how much attention you have bestowed, and how thorough have been your inquiries in certain branches of the science. Your forthcoming work on the theory of Foreign Trade is looked forward to with much interest by those acquainted with its contents, and will place you among the most original writers on the science.

I consider it superfluous to say more, for I cannot imagine that there is likely to be any other candidate comparable to you in fitness for the joint posts for which you are going to apply.

I am, yours very faithfully,

W. Stanley Jevons.

493. W. S. JEVONS TO L. WALRAS
[FW]

24 June 1877

My dear Sir,

I was much pleased to receive a little time ago your interesting letter. Your remarks upon the Memoirs of M. Dupuit, shall have my best attention, and I will on an early opportunity read the article in the Journal des Economistes which you mentioned.

I have been a good deal occupied for 6 or 8 months past in preparing a second edition of my larger logical work called "The Principles of Science," which is now all done except the preface.

I am glad that your friend Professor Charles Secretan likes some parts of my "Logic Primer." I have been preparing a companion volume, in the form of a "Primer of Political Economy," which is about half written.

Mr. George Darwin was speaking to me with interest of your last publication, the three memoirs. Have you sent copies of your publications to Mr. Francis Galton, F.R.S., of 42 Rutland Gate, London, S.W.? He is well fitted to appreciate them.

In a day or two I go on a tour in Denmark and Norway, as I previously informed you. After my return, *should my wife be in sufficiently good health,* I shall be most happy to welcome you here and show you a few of the interesting points of London, but September is a time of year when people are usually in the country, and nothing is going on. Still London remains where it is, and you may find some things of interest.

Please let me hear where you may be addressed in the early part of September. It will be pleasant to discuss various points of political Economy personally.

Believe me my dear Sir

Yours faithfully,

W. Stanley Jevons.

494.   W. S. JEVONS TO HARRIET JEVONS
[LJP, 369–70]

Hotel d'Angleterre,
Copenhagen, Tuesday, 3d July 1877.

My dearest,

It seems now a long time since I left England and we have seen a great deal. So far our tour has succeeded well in spite of an unfavourable beginning. At Hamburg Tom seemed to be unwell & showed disinclination for travelling. One night when we had taken our tickets & registered our luggage for Copenhagen, he suddenly said he could not go and as he seemed to be ill & tired I of course agreed to go back and we got our money & luggage back. I was afraid at first that it might be some illness coming on but it seems now to have been only indigestion.

We went by rail to Lübeck the next morning, & were interested by the quaint old town. Then at 4 p.m. we took the steamboat for Copenhagen, sleeping on board & getting in about 7 a.m.

We have been much pleased with Copenhagen which is a most lively interesting town. We have been about twice a day to the Museums & that of old Northern Antiquities is altogether excellent.

Soon after breakfast on Saturday we went to find Falbe Hansen, but he was not at his office & we only saw him later on for a few minutes. On Sunday morning he came with a friend Herr Madsen,[1] & took us to Thorwaldsen's Museum, & some other places & then to dine at a place some miles down the coast. There was a little misadventure, as the Danes were so busy talking that they forgot to land at the right place, & the steamboat appeared to be making off for Sweden. However a few miles further on it called at another dining place & we had a good dinner with them, partly walking & partly driving home. It seems that on Sundays almost everyone who can goes out to dine & amuse himself in the suburbs where there are numberless cafes & hotels & music saloons. Every night too we have spent at Tivoli, which is a great pleasure garden something like that we visited at Gothenburg but much larger. There are concerts with good music every evening, pantomimes, ballets, a great two storied

[1] See below, Letter 524, n. 2, p. 245.

merry go round many times as large as that at Hampstead, &c &c. All the people of the town go there, & on Sunday night there were 10000 or 15000 there.

Tom has shown much disinclination to go to Norway, & seems afraid of the constant travelling which wd be necessary as the time is short we have decided to go to Sweden instead & our address will be the *Grand Hotel Stockholm.*

I have been much pleased to get your letter written the day after I left. I telegraphed you yesterday but have had no answer yet.

Tom seems now to be perfectly well & much pleased with our journey so far. I am perfectly well also & up to much more than used to be the case.

There is much I might tell you but time is too short. We gave Falbe Hansen & his friend a dinner here yesterday at the table d'hote. This hotel is a very large handsome one & comfortable, but the charges are moderate being only some 10 or 12s. per day. I now think it would have been a great mistake to take Tom on a hurried visit to Norway, & of course I shall like the novelty of Stockholm.

Ever your affectionate Husband

W. S. Jevons

495.   W. S. JEVONS TO J. CLERK MAXWELL[1]

2, The Chestnuts,
West Heath,
Hampstead, N. W.
5 August 1877.[2]

Professor Clerk Maxwell
Dear Sir

Some remarks which I made at p. 438 vol. II of the Principles of Science[3] were criticized by my friend Professor Clifford.[4] I quoted from the works of Professor Tait & yourself, to the effect that Fouriers theory of the motion of heat as followed out by Sir W. Thomson leads to impossible

[1] James Clerk Maxwell (1831–79), physicist, chiefly noted for his treatise on electricity and magnetism (1873); Professor of Natural Philosophy at Marischal College, Aberdeen 1856–60, and at King's College, London, 1860–5; first Professor of Experimental Physics in the University of Cambridge. Cf. *Clerk Maxwell and Modern Physics*, edited by C. Domb (1963).

[2] The original manuscript of this letter is in the University Library, Cambridge.

[3] *The Principles of Science,* book VI, chap. XXXI, section entitled 'Hierarchy of Natural Laws' (Dover edition, 1958, p. 746).

[4] W. K. Clifford, 'The First and the Last Catastrophe', *Fortnightly Review,* 17 (1875) 465–84 (480). William Kingdon Clifford (1845–79), Professor of Applied Mathematics at University College London, 1871–8; one of the most distinguished mathematicians of his day, he died prematurely of a lung disease. Cf. below, Letter 528, p. 251.

results for a sufficiently great negative value of the time. Professor Clifford as you probably know objects that Thomson's calculations only treated of the conduction of heat, & you in your Theory of Heat say very carefully,

"Some other event besides ordinary conduction must have occurred since that date in order to produce the present state of things."

But this seems to leave it quite open to Clifford to say that the consolidation of a liquid, the condensation of a gas, or it might be the conflict of two planetary bodies is the event producing a state of temperature which could not have been produced by conduction.

But in your next sentence p. 245 you say "This is only one of the cases in which a consideration of the dissipation of energy leads to a determination of a superior limit of the observed order of things".

Not knowing what are the cases to which you refer, I am quite unable to form any idea whether they are subject to the objections already urged by Clifford. I should much like to know whether by "the observed order of things" you mean merely the present state of the planetary system for instance, or the present state of the Universe, not only in the present moment but also in the past, so far as our knowledge enables us to trace it back. Do you still think, in spite of Clifford's remarkable lecture, that our present science leads back to some point at which some event must have happened of a kind not explicable by *any part of the theory of heat* or of other parts of physical science?

I am just engaged in writing the preface to a second edition of my 'Principles of Science', in which I refer to Cliffords criticism. So far as I can possibly see, Clifford is right, & I am wrong, and I must simply retract this point. My error indeed is quite countenanced by what Professor Tait says in his Thermodynamics, & in his "Recent advances in Physical Science" he does not seem really to retract.

It is probable that you will be now unable to answer, this being vacation time, but for the mere chance that you are at home or accessible I write this, hoping that you will excuse the trouble I give you on the ground of the great importance and interest of the point in question.[5]

Believe me to remain
Yours faithfully
W. S. Jevons.

[5] To judge from the text of the Preface to the second edition of *The Principles of Science*, it seems probable that Jevons did not receive any reply from Clerk Maxwell before the second edition went to press. In the Preface, Jevons conceded Clifford's point but added 'assuming that I have erred, I should like to point out that I have erred in the best company'; after quoting Tait in support of this, he went on – 'I may add that Professor Clerk Maxwell's words seem to countenance the same view', giving the passage from p. 245 of Clerk Maxwell's *Theory of Heat* (1871) quoted in this letter.

496.   W. LANGTON TO W. S. JEVONS

Docklands
Ingatestone.
Septr 1877

Dear Mr Jevons —

Were the Bank of England to allow Interest on Deposits, she might attract to herself, no doubt, a considerable amount of loanable capital; but what would be the consequence?[1]

If she allowed interest, she must seek to make interest by investing. She would be therefore under the constant temptation to increase her lock-up, and to hold smaller balances in her coffers. All that she kept there would be held at a dead loss, and were she to be exposed to any pressure, such as we have seen in bygone times not unfrequently, where would she be? She is now made the keeper of all that the Bankers about her cannot or dare not lock up in Securities, because they feel it may be wanted from them at any moment. These balances the Bank Directors know to be precarious & therefore deserve no interest.

In times of difficulty there is a constant pressure to force securities upon the Bank of England & the Directors have had great difficulty in keeping in their till what is needful to prevent their own stoppage. The only way the Bank has of protecting herself in hard times is by selling Stock or raising loans upon it in the market, which by the absorption of notes makes the difficulties of the money market greater. – All her difficulties in such times would be aggravated had she more extensive deposits on which she paid interest, while the *proportion* of her reserves would naturally be diminished unless she could make up her mind to bear a very large loss of interest. She could certainly not make a profit *safely* if she allowed interest.—

I do not know if I have made my meaning clear. The Joint Stock Banks have I think been allowing too much interest. A great deal of capital has I

---

[1] In the absence of Jevons's letters to Langton, the stimulus which prompted Langton's varied comments on monetary policy and history in this and Letters 500, 502 and 505 below can only be a matter of conjecture. Here, however, Langton may have been reacting to the passage headed 'Remedy for the Sensitiveness of the Money Market' in Jevons's *Money*, chap. xxiv, pp. 322–4. At this period the problem of the limited size of cash reserves in London in relation to the rapidly growing liabilities of the banking system was much discussed and the 'Bagehot principle' of the Bank of England as lender of last resort was by no means universally accepted. In 1875 a scheme for the joint-stock banks to establish a common reserve independent of the Bank of England had been put forward; on this Jevons remarked that 'it matters little who holds the reserve, provided it actually does exist in the form of metal, and is not evaporated away by being placed at call, or deposited with other banks which make free use of it'. Earlier he wrote that 'as the Bank of England pays no interest upon the eight millions which it on the average of the last four years holds at the deposits of the London bankers, there seems to be no sufficient reason why the Bank should be allowed to make a profit out of so large a sum' – loc. cit., p. 322. Cf. *Bankers' Magazine*, 35 (1875) 13–18, 85–93; Fetter, *Development of British Monetary Orthodoxy*, pp. 272–5.

have no doubt been allured by them from the country to London, & their difficulty of employing it legitimately is shown by the bad debts they have made by taking Collie's spurious bills. [2]—

May not the former decennial periods of crises be shortening with changed circumstances? We have always seen some extraneous accompaniment of our panics.

In 1837 America was the weak point, beside the bad management of the Bank of England.

In 1847 we had an immense lock-up of floating capital in Railway works.

In 1857 the trade of the North of Europe was disorganised.

In 1866 the panic was premature in consequence of O, G & Co's fall. It would have been worse if the symptoms of inflation had gone on increasing into the following year.

Circumstances preceding the present year have kept back the *growth* of mischief. Beside what I told you of the curtailment of Bills, the collapse of the iron & coal trades came before its time, & we may perhaps therefore be spared a crisis this year, notwithstanding the doubtful prospects of the harvest.

Moreover this war[3] is preventing much trade that would otherwise have been carried on with the Levant on credit; and the great Indian trade has become one more of hand to mouth than it used to be when it throve on long bill transactions. Still were I in business I should watch narrowly the Bank returns & the manufacturers of cloth and yarns & seek to keep good reserves.

I think some of the London Bankers must have got a large stake in mortgages on Buildings, but this is not within my own knowledge.

Of course I need not remind you that the perils of certain great firms, averted within the last three years 1874–5 & 6, must not be spoken of.

Should you discover what Lord Bacon meant by the expression "common fund", pray let me know.

I have somewhere some old tracts on usury. They may perhaps assist in finding this out if I can lay my hands on them.

The word "mountebank" is Italian. I find *montambanco* or *montimbanco*. Plautus uses the word *trapezeta* for a Banker or usurer. [4] Its derivation is from the Greek word *Trapeza* – a table; and if I recall it rightly, the word *Trapesium* is used for a Bank in the charter of the Royal Bank of Scotland. [5]

Believe me

Yours ever truly

W. Langton

---

[2] In July 1875 Alexander Collie & Co., a firm of East India merchants in London and Manchester, failed with estimated liabilities of £3,000,000. 'This disaster had brought down a discount firm, and numerous suspensions followed in its wake.' – *Bankers' Magazine*, 35 (1875) 600.

PS. Since writing the above I have had a letter from a Bank Director & extract a passage which may interest you.

"We are passing through a very interesting period, both as regards the War & the money Market.

A few days or hours may bring news decisive of this year's campagne,* & may falsify the latest as well as earlier prophecies.

The period for very cheap money is I think gone by, & looking at the heavy grain imports before us, it may be relatively dear before we are well into the Winter.

I wish I could feel assured that Trade is really reviving or at least improving *sensibly*; but a bad Harvest and Strikes are not favorable* to recovery"——

497. W. S. JEVONS TO L. WALRAS
 [FW]

London, 3 September 1877

My dear Sir,

I have been thinking much of the visit which you were so kind as to say that you would pay me, and I am looking forward much to the pleasure of making your personal acquaintance. My wife's approaching accouchement has kept me for some time in a state of uncertainty and anxiety. It has now been safely accomplished and I have the pleasure of possessing a daughter[1] as well as a young son.

It seems very doubtful however whether Mrs. Jevons will during the next few weeks be strong and well enough to enable her to receive you here as we should like to do. Under these circumstances it has occurred to me that if you would extend your journey to London, and take up your quarters in any Hotel which may seem best to you, I shall be most happy to meet you in town and facilitate as far as I can your visits to the best sights in London. This is what we should call the "dead" season; all the people of consequence are away and many theatres and exhibitions are closed. There is still abundance in London to excite your interest, and I shall have great pleasure in spending several days, as far as my strength allows, in seeking with you the amusements of this large city.

If you are unacquainted with the London Hotels, I should recommend

---

[3] The conflict between Russia and Turkey: see below, Letter 508, n. 3, p. 225.

[4] In the plays of Plautus the word *trapezita* in the sense of 'money-changer' or 'banker' occurs a number of times, e.g. in *Captivi*, Act I, scene 2, line 193 – 'Quantillum argenti mi apud trapezitam siet'. T. Maccius Plautus, *Comedies,* edited by A. Ernout, 7 vols (Paris, 1957) tome II, p. 100.

[5] The word 'Trapesium' does *not* appear in the original Latin Charter of the Royal Bank of Scotland, 1727.

[1] Harriet Winefrid Jevons, born 26 August 1877; she died in April 1961.

you *not* to go to the Charing Cross Hotel, but take by preference *The grand Midland Hotel St. Pancras*, which is the newest and in some respects the best of all, and yet not expensive. As Hampstead is nearly an hour's journey from London, St. Pancras would be a more convenient position for a tourist.

Hoping to have the pleasure of making your acquaintance and to hear the day when you will arrive in London, I am

Yours very faithfully and respectfully,
W. S. Jevons.

497A.   W. S. JEVONS TO MADAME WALRAS[1]
[FW]

3 Sept 1877.
The Chestnuts,
Branch Hill,
Hampstead Heath
London, N. W.

I have addressed a letter to Monsieur le Professeur Léon Walras to the Chateau de Glérolles St. Saphorin.

W. Stanley Jevons.

498.   W. S. JEVONS TO W. H. HERFORD[1]

2, The Chestnuts,
West Heath,
Hampstead, N.W.
5 Sept. '77.

Dear Mr. Herford,

Pray keep the number of 'Mind'[2] until Miss Herford has read it, if you think she would like to do so. I have read your remarks with much interest and quite understand the objections you make. I do not pretend to set up the examination system as an ideally good or perfect method of

---

[1] Jevons wrote this note on a printed address card, after crossing out the text. It was addressed to Walras's mother, in Chartres. For biographical details of Louise-Aline Walras, see Jaffé, *Walras Correspondence*, 1, 83.

[1] William Henry Herford (1820–1908), educationist. Trained at Manchester New College, he became Unitarian Minister of Lancaster in 1848, but resigned in 1850 to take charge of one of the first schools in England run according to the principles of Froebel and Pestalozzi. From 1873 to 1885, Herford was the principal of Ladybarn House School, Fallowfield, Manchester.

[2] *Mind*, 2, no. 6 (April 1877), which contained Jevons's article 'Cram' at p. 193. Reprinted in *Methods*, pp. 82–100.

education, but merely that which is best for the majority of persons in the actual circumstances of the times. I do not think it the best especially for very clever and very dull persons but I do not believe we can do without it in the present state of affairs. I quite appreciate your wish to bring up the backward ones if possible and not leave them behind as a residuum. But the greater part of educational efforts could not be conducted on that principle, as it would involve the keeping back of the better and more able. You must not regard merely the good done to the individual, but also and even more the indirect good to the community through the cultivation of talent and ability. Your idea is partially analogous to that of the trades unions who think it unfair to the slow that the quick workman should beat him. They forget that it is not a question of the workmen only but of those who want their products. If the quick were kept back for the benefit of the slow, it would result in keeping back human affairs generally. Mine is not as you say an Aristocratic view of education; it is rather the true Republican, while your view tends towards Socialism. At the same time I am far from thinking that my view involves the actual neglect of the slow. As we have blind and deaf and dumb asylums and workhouses for paupers, which is really a concession towards Socialism, so the rigidity of the principle of competition and cumulation may properly be tempered by consideration towards those who might otherwise have the fate of the hindmost. As regards your question, perhaps a book called "How we are governed or the Crown the Senate and the Bench" might suit. It is by A Fonblanque Jun 2/6 published by Warne.[3] It is a popular book not of much profundity.—

Creasy's "Rise and Progress of the English Constitution", is considered a very good book.[4] Published by Bentley 7/6. 12th Ed. semi-popular. The Standard works are those of Sir T. Erskine May and Professor Stubbs,[5] but those are large stiff books.

Thanks for your congratulations. We are much pleased to have a girl both for ourselves and as a companion for Herbert. I am glad to say that Mrs. Jevons is progressing well and the infant is also getting on capitally. Little Herbert rules the house and it would have been a good thing for him if you had lived near to rule him. We regret leaving Withington on that account at least.

Yours very faithfully,
W. S. Jevons.

---

[3] Albany Fonblanque, Junior, *How we are governed or the Crown, the Senate and the Bench: A Handbook of the Constitution of Great Britain* (1858).

[4] Sir Edward Shepherd Creasy, *Rise and Progress of the English Constitution* (1853).

[5] Sir Thomas Erskine May, *The Constitutional History of England since the accession of George the Third, 1760–1860*, 2 vols (1861–3); William Stubbs, *The Constitutional History of England in its Origin and Development* (1866).

499.   L. WALRAS TO W. S. JEVONS

Ouchy sous Lausanne,
Maison Jomini.
6 septembre, 1877.

Cher Monsieur,

Je pense que vous devez être revenu de voyage. Pour moi, je vais m'y mettre demain, après avoir été fort absorbé jusqu'au dernier moment par la publication de mon second demi-volume d'*Eléments,* dont je vous envoie un exemplaire en même temps que la présente, et aussi quelque peu retardé[1] par la nécessité où je me suis trouvé de changer de domicile.

Ce que vous me dites, dans votre dernière lettre, de la santé de Madame Jevons m'aurait empêché de descendre chez vous, mais non d'aller vous voir et causer avec vous. Mais je crains fort que le temps ne me manque pour cette visite, en raison du petit nombre de semaines qui me restent d'ici à la fin de mes vacances, et du séjour que je dois faire chez ma mère. Mon adresse, jusqu'à fin 7bre, est chez Madame Walras à Chartres (Eure et Loir).

Recevez, Cher Monsieur, l'assurance de mes sentiments bien dévoués.

Léon Walras.

J'envoie mon ouvrage complet à M. Galton dont vous aviez la bonté de me donner l'adresse.   L.W.

Au moment même où j'allais fermer ma lettre, je reçois la vôtre du 3 ct. Tout ce que vous me dites, achève de me déterminer à remettre ma visite à quelque moment plus favorable. Ainsi, ne vous en préoccupez plus, je vous prie.

J'ai passé hier une excellente soirée avec M. le Prof. Quack, d'Utrecht, homme des plus distingués et des plus aimables (très mal nommé) et grand admirateur de votre ouvrage.   L.W.

500.   W. LANGTON TO W. S. JEVONS

Docklands
Ingatestone
21 Sep. 1877

My dear Sir,

Many thanks for your reference to the Dictionary of Political Economy[1] which I have ordered in order to study the articles you mention.

---

[1] In the version of this letter published by Jaffé (*Walras Correspondence,* 1, 540−1) from the draft in Fonds Walras, this phrase reads 'quelque peu en retard'. This is the only variation between the draft and the manuscript letter received by Jevons.

[1] H. D. Macleod, *A Dictionary of Political Economy* (1863) vol. 1. The article 'Bank' at p. 69 contains

Italy was the monied country of the Middleages. I think that Edwd 3^d – borrowed money to carry on his wars from the Florentine Merchants & never repaid them.

Royalty has frequently been short of money & no doubt the "common fund" mentioned by Bacon was a stock created to meet the exigencies of the State on some terms of which at present we lack the particulars or it might be referable to loans of Guilds or Corporations.

Under the head of Tontine in the Penny Cyclopedia[2] there are references to two books which may be useful, but which I have no opportunity of examining. One is the French "Encyclopedie" (Finance Division p. 704)[3] the other is Hamilton's "Hist. Public Revenue")[4] p 210—

The Tontine was not of course known to Lord Bacon but lotteries no doubt were, for there had been a state lottery so early as 1569. My Secretary, Mr Daniel, has turned up a fact which will be interesting to you in your researches respecting financial crises.—

In Novr 1696 "Bank Notes were discounted at 20 per cent and Government Tallies at 40, 50 & 60 per cent. which was no small inducement to the Court to listen to proposals of peace. Nor were the French in a better condition which made them equally pliable."[5]

Looking to the prospects of the present year, it is pretty certain that our own harvest is deficient, while across the Atlantic there is more than usual abundance. Our export trade in the United States being restricted, we shall have to remit much gold.[6] This will help them to improve their currency but may possibly impoverish the Bank of England. Watch carefully the difference between the "Other Deposits" & the "Other Securities". This affords the best barometric indication of commercial and financial prospects.

Yours faithfully

W. Langton

---

many references to the points raised by Langton in Letter 496 (above, p. 209) about the origins of the word. Thus Macleod explains that in Venice in 1171 a loan was raised by the state and known as the *Monte*, or joint-stock fund. 'The Bank of Venice was in reality the origin of the Funding System, or system of Public Debts; it did not for many centuries do any of what we call banking business. And this was the meaning of the word Bank when it was first introduced into England. Thus Bacon says – "Let it be no Bank, or Common Stock; but every man be master of his own money".'

[2] *The Penny Cyclopaedia of the Society for the Diffusion of Useful Knowledge*, xxv (1843) 41. Langton's secretary appears to have copied the ensuing references directly from this brief article on Tontines.

[3] *Encyclopédie Méthodique, Finances*, 3 vols (1784–7) III, 705–8.

[4] Presumably Robert Hamilton, *An Inquiry concerning the use and progress, the redemption and present state, and the management of the national debt of Great Britain* (Edinburgh, 1813).

[5] Cf. Clapham, *A History of the Bank of England*, I, 46–7.

[6] Cf. *The Economist*, 16 October 1877, vol. 35, p. 1177; D. C. Barrett, *The Greenbacks and Resumption of Specie Payments, 1862–1879* (Cambridge, Mass., 1931) p. 214.

501.   W. S. JEVONS TO HARRIET JEVONS[1]
   [LJN, 374]

Hampstead,
9th October 1877.

. . . My class came off rather well yesterday. The room was nearly full of students, including a good many ladies – several from last year's class.[2] If they all really join the class it will be a decidedly good one, but I cannot know at present. I gave a rather good lecture, although I felt much disinclined for it. . . .

502.   W. LANGTON TO W. S. JEVONS

Docklands,
Ingatestone.
12 Oct 1877.

Dear Mr. Jevons,

Thank you for your letter. It was my intention to follow up my communication to the "Financial Opinion" by another which has not hitherto been inserted and possibly may not be. – [1]

I cannot agree with the view which you take of the desirableness in adopting the Postmaster General's suggestion on the subject of money orders.[2]

[1] Mrs Jevons was at this time on a visit to her sister in Birkenhead.

[2] The number of students enrolled for Jevons's Political Economy class at University College London increased from 23 in 1876–7 to 30 in 1877–8. One of the lady students was Juliet Seebohm, daughter of Frederic Seebohm. (Information from Fees Books of University College London.)

[1] *Financial Opinion* was a short-lived journal which commenced publication on 28 February 1877 and discontinued on 27 June 1878. No signed contribution by William Langton appeared in it, but the issue of 27 September contained an article on 'The New Post-Office Bank Note' quoting various criticisms of it by 'an experienced correspondent' signing himself 'M'. A further article on Savings Banks, also signed 'M', appeared in the issue of 4 October 1877. The issue of 18 October contained a short paragraph on p. 9 headed 'The "Lock-up" of the Banks', quoting 'an esteemed correspondent'. The correspondent expressed doubt as to the ability of the Bank of England to act as lender of last resort if a sudden demand for gold should arise, but also remarked that 'the returns of the Bank of England used formerly to give us a most useful barometric index of coming waves and storms in the financial ocean'. The style and content of the paragraph resemble Letters 496 and 500 above and 505 below sufficiently closely to suggest that the 'esteemed correspondent' was Langton.

[2] Proposals were under discussion to institute a system of 'Postal Notes' to simplify the existing Money Orders service, which the Post Office found uneconomical. The most controversial aspects of the scheme, discussed here by Langton, concerned the proposals to permit orders to be purchased without a payee being named and to make orders cashable at any. Post Office. The *Report of the Committee of Inquiry into the Money Order System of the Post Office, into the Proposed Scheme of Post Office Notes* . . . 1877 (289) xxvii, 263, had been published on 25 June and was followed by the Post Office (Money Orders) Bill. The Bill was later withdrawn, owing to widespread opposition to what was regarded as constituting an unlimited small note issue by the Government, and the introduction of Postal Orders was delayed until 1881. See *Twenty-Third Report of the Postmaster General of the Post Office*, 1877 [C. 1863], xxvii, 201; Jevons, 'Postal Notes, Money Orders and Bank Cheques', *Contemporary Review*, 37 (1880) 150–61; reprinted in *Methods*, pp. 307–23.

He would alter the whole system of post office orders now in use wherein great precautions are used to prevent irregularities, by not placing the name and the recipient on the order and requiring him to name correctly the sender.

This is no doubt found to be troublesome; but surely some labour and even expense should not be begrudged for the sake of security; especially as it may be inferred that these orders are chiefly used by classes of people who are not wealthy.

The proposed new system of doing away with all such precautions and issuing orders from any Post office, payable at any other Post office and to any body is risky.—

There can be little doubt that such orders will be popular both with the post masters and the public; and their not having currency after a year, will prevent their taking the rank in the currency of the country of a small note circulation.

But how greatly will the risk of loss be increased! At present the public is advised not to send remittances in Postage Stamps as they are so apt to be purloined. The enclosure of such orders would be quite as easily detected and the temptation to theft would be equally great, as such stolen property would be equally easy of conversion into money if not easier since no licence such as is required for the sale of stamps would be necessary.

The loss by lapsed or *lost* orders now amounts to £6,000! What would it be under the proposed new regulations? Any gain to the revenue from such a source is not legitimate.

Believe me,

Dear Mr. Jevons

Yours truly

W. Langton.

503. W. S. JEVONS TO R. H. INGLIS PALGRAVE

2, The Chestnuts, West Heath,
Hampstead, N.W.
29 October 1877

Dear Palgrave,

Would you like to see my paper on the Silver Question[1] and the American currency read at the American Assoc. meeting with a view to

---

[1] The paper here referred to is Jevons's *The Silver Question*, which was read by Hamilton A. Hill, of Boston, before the American Social Science Association at Saratoga on 5 September 1877 and published as *The Silver Question: Papers by B. F. Nourse and Professor W. S. Jevons* (Boston, 1877). Palgrave accepted the paper and it was reprinted in the *Bankers' Magazine*, 37 (1877) 989–96. It appears as no. XII in *Investigations*, pp. 307–16.

printing it in the Bankers Magazine. It has been printed by various
newspapers in the U.S. but I have not seen any portions reprinted in
England nor any notice of it except an article in the Manchester
Guardian.

It would thus be new to the readers of the B. Magazine.

It is quite short.

Yours faithfully,
W. S. Jevons

504.   W. S. JEVONS TO A. MACMILLAN
       [MA]

2 The Chestnuts,
West Heath,
Hampstead,
N.W.
7th Nov. 1877.

Dear Macmillan,

I have been carefully considering the suggestion of an edition of the
Wealth of Nations which I made to you recently. [1] Having mentioned the
idea to several men able to judge they all welcome it as much as you and
Jack did.

It seems to me that the Wealth of Nations particularly requires
abridgement; it was from the first rather a collection of treatises and
digressions than a single connected whole, and large parts of the work are
either obsolete or of inferior interest.

Some rough calculations which I have made seem to show that the
whole text would make about 1100 pages uniform with the new ed. of my
Principles. [2] There must be great abridgement to make a text-book of
moderate size and price. I should probably retain little more than 1/3 of
the text say 400 pages and I would then occupy 200 pages at least with
supplementary notes and a historical introduction. These notes would be
mostly selected from the best writers on pol. econ. all of whom have
commented on parts of Smith. These notes would enable me to some
extent to fill up the gaps in Smiths doctrines and produce a kind of

---

[1] Jevons did proceed with this project for a 'students' (abridged) edition of the *Wealth of Nations*, but never completed it. The unfinished text is in the Jevons Papers and consists of a copy of one of the Strahan and Cadell editions of book I, chapters I–X, cut up and pasted on to foolscap sheets on which Jevons wrote his annotations. These are not continued beyond the early pages of chapter VI. There is also one page of manuscript on 'The General Character of the Wealth of Nations' and four pages headed 'Life of A. Smith'.

[2] This and the reference in para. 5 are to the *Principles of Science,* of which Macmillan was just producing the second edition.

classical textbook, which might well be accepted by any lecturer on pol. econ. as a safe basis for his course. I should endeavour to make the work neutral ground and while passing over doctrines which seem false, I would confine myself to presenting in the original language the best established facts of political economy.

I should propose to make the Introduction rather a prominent feature, and to write for it a new historical sketch of the science. There is nothing of the sort accessible to students.

I should like the form of the book to be uniform with the Principles. I would divide up the text into sections with Italic headings, and would present the illustrative notes in similar type so as to read uniform with the text, and avoid as far as possible a pie-bald appearance.

(The thought has occurred to me whether it might be worthwhile if you do set up 1/3 of the text to go on with it and produce also a complete text edition with the same historical introduction and merely brief footnotes. The same type might be made to do. (??)

I have been going about the book shops lately in search of editions of the W. of Nations, and have been surprised at meeting very few copies. They seem to be readily bought up, and MacCulloch's best edition sells at high prices.) [3]

Supposing you still like the idea of the textbook I should be glad to know what kind of terms you would propose. I might want some assistance in transcription, reading proofs and indexing. Any expenses of this sort you would I suppose take on your hands.

The Political Economy Primer is nearly done, but examinations interrupt me.

I send a few notes of suggestions as regards advertisements etc. which perhaps you will kindly look over.

I am,

Yours faithfully,

W. S. Jevons.

What is the maximum number of words you can allow me in a 7/6d text book? about 250,000.

---

[3] This does seem surprising since McCulloch's edition of the *Wealth of Nations* had appeared 'revised, corrected and improved' as late as 1863 and been reprinted in 1870 and 1872. Ward, Lock and Tyler put out a three-volume reprint of the 1812 edition in 1874 and again in 1877. See Bullock, *The Vanderblue Memorial Collection of Smithiana* (Kress Library Publication, no. 2, Boston, 1939) pp. 8 and 19.

505.   W. LANGTON TO W. S. JEVONS

Ingatestone 17 Nov 1877

Dear Mr. Jevons

I gather that very large operations have been taking place in American securities for transmission to the U.S.[1] The Telegraph gives the opportunity by the speedy advice of contracts and when they ensure a small profit the bonds are sent by post across the water.

This is another way in which the transmission of bullion may be checked as well as by the large importation into America of colonial products which will be paid for in a round about way.

Another movement too, I hear, is taking place which may affect the London money market – the uneasy state of political feeling in France is bringing French capital into this country.

The rise of the Bank rate has in former years speedily affected the exchanges – will it do so now?[2]

The great accumulation of loanable capital in other hands has made the Bank of England to hold a much less important position in the London money market than of old, and it may be in future more important to consider the grand total rather than the special strength or otherwise of the Bank of England.

Should her position become critical, we may possibly therefore find that she may be compelled – to raise her rate of discount much more than she would have had to do formerly in order to bring foreign gold into her coffers –

This season has many very abnormal features.

Believe me,

Yours faithfully,
Wm. Langton

[1] In October and November 1877 a considerable volume of U.S. bonds held in Europe were being 'called' by the United States Treasury, but earlier in the year there had been transfers resulting from a difference in the price of U.S. 4½ per cent bonds in London and New York. Cf. Barrett, *The Greenbacks and Resumption of Specie Payments, 1862–1879*, pp. 213–16.

[2] Bank rate had been raised to 5 per cent on 11 October 1877, without producing much immediate effect on the money market; see *The Economist*, 27 October 1877, vol. 35, pp. 1273–4.

The argument of the ensuing paragraphs of Langton's letter is very similar to that of the 'esteemed correspondent' of *Financial Opinion* on 18 October 1877: cf. above, Letter 502, n. 1, p.216.

506.   J. W. GLAISHER[1] TO W. S. JEVONS

Trinity College,
Cambridge.
1877 Nov. 22.

Dear Sir,

If you have no objection will you sign the enclosed certificate, for the Roy. Soc., of George Darwin?[2]

I know that Mr. Darwin would very much like to have your signature as when we were talking the matter over some time ago he spoke of you as one who he believed would be willing to sign, and whose support he should like to have.

The existing signatures represent exclusively mathematics, which is the subject that Mr. Darwin has almost entirely devoted himself to for some time.

If you sign the certificate I propose to send it in to the R.S. without obtaining any other signatures.

Believe me
Yours truly
J. W. Glaisher.

W. S. Jevons, Esq.,

507.   W. S. JEVONS TO T. E. JEVONS
[LJN, 375–6]

Hampstead,
16th December, 1877.

. . . Excuse economy of paper; I never waste a sheet.

I was pleased to get your letter last night, and this being Sunday evening (my letter-writing time), I answer at once.

Have you seen the *Contemporary Review*,[1] with my first attack on Mill? I am this evening finishing the proofs of the second article,[2] which will be stronger in evidence, though rather stiffer. It is a good thing bringing them out at intervals in a magazine and then republishing them. I am determined to go through with the matter, and upset Mill's logic altogether.

[1] James Whitbread Glaisher (1848–1928), Fellow of Trinity College, Cambridge, 1871–1928; Lecturer in Mathematics in the University of Cambridge, 1871–1901; President of the London Mathematical Society, 1884–6, and of the Royal Astronomical Society, 1886–8 and 1901–3.
[2] G. H. Darwin was elected F.R.S. in 1879.
[1] 'John Stuart Mill's Philosophy Tested', *Contemporary Review*, 31 (1877) 167–82.
[2] *Contemporary Review*, 31 (1878) 256–75.

I have not been going much to amusements of late, but took a holiday on Friday to visit the Cattle Show and Temple Bar before it is pulled down.[3]

Rather more than a week ago I had an interesting night at the Political Economy Club,[4] where I happened to sit next to an empty chair, and presently Gladstone came in and sat down next me. I reminded him of my name, when he at once talked about the *Principles*; and all through dinner, for some two hours, I had a long discussion with him, partly about Owens College, concerning which he made minute inquiries, but principally about legislative matters. He seemed desirous to discuss vaccination, and I am sorry to say he sticks to his idea that its value is not sufficiently proved to warrant making it compulsory. At any rate he considers the matter open to doubt. He argued that the vaccinators have changed their ground, and now think revaccination needful; and on my saying I would agree to compulsory revaccination if necessary he held that that would be absurd, and reduced the thing to an absurdity. When I mentioned his speech at the Adam Smith Centennial,[5] when he spoke against extending government, he rather gave in to some slight objections I made, and he would not object at all to compulsory vaccination if there were no doubt of its efficacy.

I was naturally much interested in an opportunity of judging of the style of reasoning of such a man as Gladstone in discussion. He was awfully wideawake, and picked you up quickly enough if you made the least slip, but I always regret that he had not a more scientific education.

Lord Granville was just opposite, and Lowe not far off, but I did not speak to them. Mundella[6] opened the debate on the causes of depression of trade, and made some rather pointed references to the *Coal Question*, which he seems to admire. The discussion turned chiefly to trades' unions, but I did not say anything. By the by, Gladstone spoke of a tax on coal, and was quite clear that if there were any such it should be on all coal raised, not merely exports, but he would no doubt oppose any tax at all. . . .

---

[3] The gate of the City of London, designed by Christopher Wren and erected at the east end of the Strand in 1670, was removed in 1878.

[4] On 7 December 1877 A. J. Mundella proposed the question: 'What are the conditions on which the manufacturing predominance of Britain depends, and is there any reason to think that they have been, or may be, endangered?' (*Political Economy Club . . . List of Questions Discussed, 1872–80*, III (1881) 61).

[5] Gladstone was in the chair on this occasion, 31 May 1876. Cf. Hutchison, *A Review of Economic Doctrines 1870–1929* (1953) chapter 1.

[6] Anthony John Mundella (1825–97), M.P. for Sheffield, 1868–97; President of the Board of Trade, 1886 and 1892–4. A pioneer in the establishment of arbitration and conciliation procedures in labour disputes, he established the Labour Department of the Board of Trade. See W. H. G. Armytage, *A. J. Mundella 1825–1897, the Liberal Background to the Labour Movement* (1951).

507A.   W. S. JEVONS TO H. S. FOXWELL
     [RDF]

address. $\left\{\begin{array}{l}\\\\\\\end{array}\right.$
2, The Chestnuts,
West Heath,
Hampstead, N.W.
21 January 1878

Dear Foxwell

I believe that you are sometimes in London now, and it would give me much pleasure if you would dine with me at the Political Economy Club next Friday week 1st Febr. as by enclosed paper.[1] If you can do so I hope that you will also go home with me afterwards & stay the night at Hampstead. There are many things I should like to discuss with you – especially my onslaught upon Mill, which I fear will not have your approval.

Believe me
Yours faithfully
W. S. Jevons.

507B.   W. S. JEVONS TO H. S. FOXWELL
     [RDF]

2, The Chestnuts,
West Heath,
Hampstead, N.W.
25 January 78.

Dear Foxwell

Please arrange to stay here the Saturday night as well as the Friday & that will give us an opportunity to talk over several matters of much interest to me.

Perhaps I might meet you at the Crystal Palace on Saturday afternoon, but that we can arrange when you are here.

If possible be in fair time 6.15 at the Club, but there is usually no difficulty about places for late comers, who often drop in half thro dinner.

The Restaurant is in *lower* Regent Street, where the German Reeds[1] used to be, and you enter by a door in a side street. If I am not at the door ask for the Pol Econ dinner room.

---

[1] This paper is no longer with the original manuscript.

[1] Thomas German Reed (1817–88), musician and entertainer, who began his career as musical director of the Haymarket Theatre, 1838–51. From 1856 he and his actress wife Priscilla (1818–95) performed operettas at the Gallery of Illustration in Regent Street: 'Mr and Mrs German Reed's Entertainment' became widely known.

F. Harrison will no doubt give a very good opening from his point of view but will need to be dropped upon.[2] Have a few remarks ready.

What a grand victory at the U. of L.[3]

But what a critical state of affairs in Parl^t. I hope it may result in a Dizzy fall, but who can tell.[4]

Yours faithfully,
W. S. Jevons.

No need to dress for the dinner.

508.   W. S. JEVONS TO W. VISSERING[1]
       [LJN, 376-8]

Hampstead, 8th February 1878

. . . I have sent you, by book post, a copy of the *Journal of the London Statistical Society* for December 1877, at p.664 of which you will find a brief notice of your important book on 'Chinese Currency.'[2] As this journal is in the possession of all the leading statisticians and economists, and is carefully indexed, it will, I hope, make your work somewhat known, as it deserves. I hope to have other occasions of bringing your valuable inquiries under the notice of English readers, though I am not just at present engaged in any writing in which it could be fitly done.

It has occurred to me to ask whether you could render me assistance in an inquiry of much importance, regarding the periodical recurrence of monetary crises during the eighteenth century. I find that considerable crises occurred in England in the years 1763, 1772, 1782 or 1783, and 1793, and I have discovered some indications of a crisis in 1753. These crises were simultaneous with like events in Holland, and it is of course

---

[2] On 1 February 1878 Frederic Harrison proposed the question: 'Is it consistent with the design and practice of Adam Smith, to treat the laws of Industry as an independent and abstract science?' (see *Political Economy Club . . . Questions Discussed, 1821–1920*, VI, 100).

[3] Presumably a reference to the decision to open its degrees to women. The University of London was the first British university to do so. See H. Hale Bellot, *University College London, 1826–1926* (1929) p. 372; Roach, *Public Examinations in England*, p. 259.

[4] On 23 January 1878 the Cabinet ordered the Mediterranean Fleet to steam through the Dardanelles to Constantinople and asked Parliament to vote £6 million for military purposes. A week later Russia granted Turkey an armistice. Derby and Carnarvon resigned over the decision, but Disraeli did not intend to make war, despite jingoist pressure, and remained in office. See Ensor, *England 1870–1914*, p. 48.

[1] Willem Vissering (1851–1931), son of Simon Vissering (1818–88), who was Professor of Political Economy at Leiden, 1850–79, and Minister of Finance of the Netherlands, 1879–81. Willem Vissering later became Secretary of the Board of Supervision of the Netherlands Railway Services.

[2] *JRSS*, 40 (1877) 664–6, notice of W. Vissering, *On Chinese Currency, Coin and Paper Money* (Leiden, 1877).

Holland which was the leading commercial nation at the time. Now, in regard to the theory of crises, it becomes most important to ascertain whether there were in Holland, in or about the years 1731–32 and 1741–42, any events at all corresponding to commercial crises or difficulties. This is the more interesting inasmuch as the great bubble of the South Sea Company occurred in the year 1720, so that I am not without hope of showing that from 1720 to the present time there has been a constant tendency to the periodical recurrence of these events.

Being unacquainted with the history of commercial affairs in Holland at the time, and being unable also to read Dutch, I feel great difficulty in pursuing the inquiry. If, however, you or M. d'Aulnis de Bourouill could point out to me any information on the subject, or indicate the works in which it might be found, you would render me the most important assistance.

Please give my sincere compliments to M. d'Aulnis de Bourouill when you have an opportunity.

P.S. – I write at a time of intense political anxiety. As you will learn from the newspapers, the House of Commons, this morning at 1 A.M., passed a vote of £6,000,000 for war purposes, after an excited debate of remarkable character. If the Russians should really occupy Constantinople the war party here will have it all their own way, and it is impossible to foresee the results. There is an uneasy feeling in England that we may be on the brink of a great, in fact a European, war.[3]

I am entirely opposed to the war party here; but there can be no doubt that if once involved in war there would be no difference of opinion as to the necessity of carrying it to a successful conclusion.

If Russia and Germany are determined upon aggression, then England will have to fight, as she has fought before.

We may have made many mistakes in diplomacy in past years, but it has been done in the sincere love of peace. There is a horror in most people here of spending blood or money in the defence of Turkey or in a wretched conflict like that in the Crimea, but of course Russia cannot be allowed to paralyse Europe as she has paralysed so large a part of Asia. I do not believe in the civilisation of Russia. It is a barbarous system of despotism, and it is surely inconsistent with the interests of humanity that such a Power should be permitted to extend herself much farther. . . .

[3] Russia and Turkey had been at war from 24 April 1877 to 31 January 1878, when the armistice of Adrianople was concluded after a series of Turkish defeats. Great Britain had remained neutral during the conflict on the understanding that her vital interests would be respected; among these was the navigation of the Straits and the sanctity of Constantinople. News that the Russians were occupying Constantinople a week after the armistice led to the vote of £6,000,000 referred to by Jevons and the ordering of the British fleet to the Straits. There was considerable support in Britain for a war against Russia, but Disraeli was not prepared to go to this length; on 19 February Russia undertook not to occupy Gallipoli on the understanding that Britain would not land forces in Turkey. Cf. Ensor, op. cit., pp. 40–54.

509.   R. ADAMSON[1] TO W. S. JEVONS

60 Parsonage Road,
11th February, 1878.

Dear Jevons,

I have been puzzling a good deal over the formula you give for rate of interest, and I am rather glad to learn from your last note that some other people have been in the same predicament. I expect my difficulty will be one you will be able to remove, at present I do not see my way out of it.

At first I felt inclined to accept the formula altogether but on trying to realise the meaning of 'rate of increase of the produce divided by the whole produce' I was a little shaken. You start with the view that the produce for equal amount of labour (I suppose you would include under this equal amount of capital) may be regarded as a function of the time. You then suppose the time t extended, and state the increment of produce as

$$f(t + \triangle t) - ft.$$

that is to say as I understand it the same expenditure of labour is continued through $t + \triangle t$. You then say the ratio of this increment of produce to increment of investment of capital will determine the rate of interest. So far there is no difficulty though I would merely suggest a doubt as to taking the *whole* increment of produce into consideration. Labour we may suppose under ordinary circumstances will always yield an increment over what is consumed in the time before the enjoyment of produce. It would rather seem to be the additional increment due to the employment of capital as an aid to labour that ought to influence interest. This by the way.

You now it appears to me make an altogether new assumption, viz. that at close of time t the produce $f(t)$ is realised and invested as capital. The investment of $f(t)$ capital for time $\triangle t$ will of course be as you state $f(t)\triangle t$, but this introduces an altogether new idea. Instead of an extended expenditure of the same amount of labour over $t + \triangle t$, you have now during $\triangle t$, labour assisted by all the capital $f(t)$. You cannot at all assume that the increment of produce due to this will be $f(t + \triangle t) - f(t)$.

You will see that my real difficulty is this: — I cannot see any method for expressing the amount of capital invested as a function of the time, while your formula absolutely requires that it should be so expressed.[2]

---

[1] Robert Adamson (1852–1902) succeeded Jevons as Professor of Philosophy and Political Economy at Owens College, Manchester. He gave up the Chair of Political Economy in 1882 but retained that of Philosophy until 1893 when he was appointed Professor of Logic and belles-lettres at the University of Aberdeen. In 1895 he moved to the Chair of Logic and Rhetoric at the University of Glasgow.

[2] Cf. below, Letter 513, p. 230.

I am not very clear as to whether you employ rate of interest to denote what is often called rate of profit, and this leads me to remark on what you say of profit (p. 259).[3] Part of your statement of course depends on what you say of the ultimate rate of wages. Your definition of this would apply exactly to the case of a labourer carrying on production with borrowed capital.[4] His remuneration would be the produce minus interest and say allowance for risk. The same applies to the entrepreneur. But is it well to apply the word wages to this variable remuneration. The entrepreneur no doubt receives part of the gain as compensation for personal exertion, but the amount so received cannot be regarded as proximately fixed in a manner corresponding to the price of labour. It seems to me impossible to regard the allowance for risk as a determinate quantity; I should be rather inclined to say that profit is mainly due to this element of risk. The entrepreneur has taken all the responsibility, and therefore the surplus after payment of labour and capital accrues to him. The only fixity about allowance for risk seems to be that the gains should on the average [be] a sufficient compensation for it, and that, if the risk in some employments is greater than in others, the rate of gain must be higher. In any other sense, I do not see how it equalises the results in different employments.

Although then I altogether agree with you in thinking that wages are ultimately determined by the productiveness of labour, or to take the entrepreneur's point of view, by the gain he anticipates from employing labour, yet it seems to me calculated to lead into ambiguity if we apply the same term to the price of labour when bought up by the entrepreneurs and to the surplus which would remain to a labourer employing borrowed capital. For the last Say's expression *profits de la classe ouvrière* seems to me the most appropriate.

There are one or two other points, rather of detail, on which I might say something, e.g. with regard to the construction of chapter on capital. Articles in the consumer's hands are they capital or not? You can undoubtedly find cases, for instance a man laying in a stock of wine, where it will be very difficult to draw the line, but I cannot see how you reconcile this opinion with your general view of capital. It would be far more in accordance with that view if you simply said that capital had been invested in these articles. Food, etc. is necessary for sustaining labourer when engaged in work, but it will not therefore follow that *all* food, etc. is discharging the same function and is therefore capital.

One other matter in which I have always felt great difficulty, though I

[3] *T.P.E.*, first edition; fourth edition, p. 270. Since Jevons here says that profit can be resolved 'into wages of superintendence, insurance against risk, and interest' it is difficult to see why Adamson was not clear as to whether Jevons 'employed rate of interest to denote . . . rate of profit'.

[4] Jevons's definition was: 'the wages of a working man are ultimately coincident with what he produces, after the deduction of rent, taxes, and the interest of capital' (loc. cit., p. 259).

cannot in short compass explain my reason fully enough, the little equation on p. 95, $\frac{dy}{dx} = \frac{y}{x}$.[5] You make use of this equation as if the x and y were really increments, whereas in fact they are not: they are portions *of* the total quantities given and received. I am not at all sure that your fundamental theorem as to the ratio of exchange would be affected were this equation put out of court.

But on this I must write you at some other time. Pray excuse the length of my letter, it is difficult to be short on these matters.

With best regards,

Yours very truly,
R. Adamson.

510.　W.S. JEVONS TO J. MILLS
　　　[LJN, 378]

Hampstead, 11th February 1878

. . . In a few weeks my *Political Economy Primer* will be out. I give a long chapter to Credit Cycles, which it occurs to me you may like to see before it is printed off. I therefore send you proof by book post. In a day or two the first proofs will have to be returned.

I thought it a good opportunity to disseminate your and my various ideas on the subject. The nature of the book does not admit of particular reference or discussion, but I hope you do not object to my introducing your name in a way which does not make you responsible for the statements.[1] If you have any remarks to make, they would be much valued if received in a day or two. I hope that the *Primer* will have a large circulation, say fifteen or twenty thousand copies a year.[2] I have now and then been going into the past history of crises with care, and am becoming more and more confident about the ten years' period. The matter is one difficult to establish from the paucity of information, but I believe I can detect an almost unbroken series of expansions of credit *pressures* or crises at approximate ten years' intervals since the South Sea Bubble of 1720, if not before. The physicists now reduce the sun-spot period to 10.23 years, so that the coincidence is as close as could be desired. . . .

[5] This equation also appears on p. 95 of *T.P.E.*, fourth edition.

[1] Jevons, *Political Economy* (Science Primers Series), chapter xiv, 'Credit Cycles', pp. 115–22. Cf. p. 120: 'Generally, a credit cycle, as Mr. John Mills of Manchester has called it, will last about ten years'.

[2] See Vol. III, Letter 336, n. 2, p. 240.

511. W. S. JEVONS TO J. MILLS
   [LJN, 378–9]

Hampstead, 14th February 1878.

. . . Thanks for your letters, also for the proofs and pamphlet. The latter seems very interesting as regards the letters of Gibbs, because he lets one a little into the arcana of the bank parlours . . .[1] I am quite aware that you insisted on the recurrence of these panics in spite of all kinds of casual incidents of the currency, etc. When I write more at freedom in the matter I shall bring it out clearly.

What I want to do now is to prove the matter empirically, by actual history of last century occurrences. Formerly I thought, judging from various statistics, that the interval 1720–63 was a blank; but it is not so. I have now got an important link in the year 1732, when there was a bubble, or at least what they called *stock-jobbing*. It was so bad that an Act to prevent its recurrence, if possible, was passed in 1734; and a contemporary writer compared the bubble with that of 1720, no doubt an exaggeration, but a significant one.

My impression is that the collapse of 1720 was premature, like that of 1873, and that about 1722 was the due time.

My evidence concerning 1742 is yet very slight, as also 1753, but I hope to find plenty of evidence in a little time.

1763 was a great crisis, as you no doubt know, and 1772, 1782, and 1793 were very distinct events. . . .

512. W. S. JEVONS TO J. D'AULNIS
   [LJN, 379–80]

Hampstead, 18th February 1878.

. . . I am very much pleased to hear of your appointment by the King as Professor of Political Economy at the University of Utrecht. I feel sure that the choice is a wise one, and that you are determined to advance the science of which you have made a study to so good a purpose. It will always give me great pleasure to hear of your success, and I hope that we may have, in due time, various economical works from your hand.

Since I wrote to M. Vissering, I have been engaged in following out the inquiry I mentioned to him, as regards recurrent commercial excitement, periods of activity, and depression of trade during the eighteenth century.

[1] Henry Hucks Gibbs, Baron Aldenham, *Correspondence between H. H. Gibbs and Sir Louis Mallet, on the Silver Question in its relation to India* (1877).

The information is very scanty, and I cannot make more than surmises at present, but I am inclined to believe that there were *small or great* crises in or about the years 1701, 1711, 1720, 1732, 1743, 1753, 1763, 1772, 1782, 1793, 1805, 1815, 1825, 1836, 1847, 1857, and 1866. The periodicity is remarkable, and the average length of the period is somewhere about 10.3 years, so nearly the same as the sun-spot period – which is variously estimated at 10.45 or 10.23 years – that there can hardly be a doubt about the connection of cause and effect.

About most of the crises there can be no doubt, but the earlier ones underlined are doubtful, and I am eagerly seeking information.

If they could be shown to extend to Holland, the fact would be most interesting. . . .

513.   R. ADAMSON TO W. S. JEVONS

60 Parsonage Road,
18th Feb. 1878.

Dear Jevons,

Your remarks about the dimensions of the quantities f t and ft seem to me correct, and I am quite satisfied by them.[1] On the other point, however, the expression ft.$\triangle$ t for increment of investment of capital, I am not clear. When reading over my letter to you I noticed that the expression 'same amount of labour and capital' might be misunderstood. I meant expenditure of either at the same rate, which is an assumption required by the problem. As a matter of course extending the time of expenditure of labour requires additional capital; the crucial question is, how are you to estimate what this additional amount is. You say 'it is capital which enables the labourer to defer realisation'. That is agreed upon, but it does not seem to me to entitle you to say that if the labourer defers realising ft at end of time t and defers it for time Δt the capital which enables him to do so is ft.$\triangle$ t. The amount of investment of capital would appear to me not to be measured by the amount of produce not realised x by the time during which it remains unrealised, but by the amount of capital expended during this time of deferring x by the time. In your other expression for investment of c Σpt. you have this very element in p̲ which is the amount of capital invested, not the produce due to investment.

At the end of time t the labourer certainly abstains from realising the

[1] In the first edition of *T.P.E.* the sections headed 'Dimension of Interest' and 'Peacock on the Dimensions of Interest' did not appear. These were added in the second edition (1879) apparently as a result of this correspondence with Adamson, as well as an earlier letter from G. H. Darwin (see above, Letter 365, p. 24).

produce ft, but is not the word *abstinence* used here in a sense somewhat different from that in which it is employed to denote the expenditure of capital in anticipation of its result? If the amount of abstinence for each interval of time were to be measured, not by the capital invested during that time, but by the produce which might have been realised at the close of the preceding interval, you would seem to me to require a much more complicated formula than Σpt.[2]

I sent to Edinburgh and inquired about W. R. Smith's paper.[3] I find it was not printed in the Transactions of the R.S.E. but in their *Proceedings*, vol. VI pp. 477–485, (Session 1868–9). Perhaps that is only an abstract of the paper. There is a 'note' by Smith on 'Bain's Theory of Euclid 1.4' in the *Proceedings* vol. VII, session 1869–70, pp. 176–9.

I have succeeded in getting Reusch's Systema Logicum[4] but have not had time yet to look into it. If there seems to be anything interesting I shall let you know. I am doing a little notice of Schröders Logik Kalkul for Mind:[5] the book seems rather ingenious. Have you Boole's Math. Analysis of Logic?[6] I had it once from the Edin. Univ. Lib. but since coming here I have not been able to procure a copy.

Yours very truly,
Robert Adamson.

514.   W. S. JEVONS TO J. MILLS
       [LJN, 380]

Hampstead, 20th February 1878.

. . . I now return the correspondence to Northwold. I have read Gibbs' letters with much interest . . . No doubt a judicious raising of the bank

---

[2] Cf. *T.P.E.*, first edition, pp. 224–5: 'Let p = amount of capital supposed to be invested instantaneously at any moment, let t = time elapsing before its result is enjoyed, also supposed to be instantaneous. Then p × t is the amount of investment and if the investment is repeated the sum of the quantities of the nature of p × t, or in the customary mode of expression Σ pt is the total amount of investment'.

It was probably in response to these criticisms of Adamson's that Jevons altered this in the second edition to read: 'Let$\triangle$p = amount of capital supposed to be invested in the time$\triangle$t; let ι = time elapsing before its result is enjoyed, the enjoyment taking place in an interval of time $\triangle$ t, which may be disregarded in comparison with t. Then t $\triangle$p is the amount of investment; and if the investment is repeated, the sum of the quantities of the nature of t $\triangle$p or, in the customary mode of expression, Σ t $\triangle$p is the total amount of investment'.

[3] William Robertson Smith, 'Mr. Mill's Theory of Geometrical Reasoning mathematically tested'. The text printed in the *Proceedings of the Royal Society of Edinburgh* appears to be a full revision.

[4] Johann Peter Reusch (d. 1758), *Die citate nach dem Systema Logicum* (Jena, 1734).

[5] R. Adamson, Critical notice of *Der Operations kreis des Logik kalkuls*, von Dr Ernest Schröder (Leipzig, 1877), *Mind*, 3 (1878) 252–5.

[6] G. Boole, *The Mathematical Analysis of Logic, being an essay towards a calculus of deductive reasoning* (1847).

rate in good time would do much to mitigate panics; but it would be requisite that bankers generally should learn to look ahead. Even the bank directors are now beginning to allow that there are tides in their accounts – a fact which Langton so clearly put twenty years ago.[1] It is only quite recently, I believe, that the idea has been recognised in the bank, and I believe we may look for a more intelligent treatment of such matters in future. Gibbs is, I suppose, one of the best.

I find it exceedingly difficult to procure information about the state of trade in the early part of last century; but I am gradually getting slight indications. The price of copper seems likely to be the best indication of the condition of credit, just as the price of iron is now the most subject to variation. I suspect that the periods of collapse are about as follows:—1711, 1720, 1732, 1743, 1753, 1763, 1772, 1782, 1793, 1805, 1815, 1825, 1836, 1847, 1857, 1866, 1873–77. The average interval is about 10.3 years. The sun-spot period is variously estimated but either 10.23 or 10.45 seems the favourite number now. You see that the South Sea Bubble was one of the series, but it broke somewhat prematurely. . . .

514A.   W. S. JEVONS TO H. S. FOXWELL
         [RDF]

2, The Chestnuts,
West Heath,
Hampstead, N.W.
24 Feb. 1878.

My dear Foxwell

Thanks for the syllabuses. They seem to be very well drawn up, and I like to know the tendencies which opinion is taking as shown by such courses.

I send you by book post a list of the Statistical Society. If after looking over it you wish still to be a member please let me know & name 2 or 3 members whom you wd like to sign the paper & then I will have you elected without delay.[1]

It has been proposed to make the Society partly a Pol. Economy society.

I am

Yours faithfully

W. S. Jevons.

---

[1] W. Langton, 'Observations on a table showing the balance of account between the Mercantile Public and the Bank of England', *Transactions of the Manchester Statistical Society*, 1857–8, p. 9. Reprinted as an appendix to the *Transactions of the Society*, 1875–6.

[1] Foxwell was elected Fellow of the Statistical Society on 19 March 1878. See *JRSS*, 41 (1878) 418.

515. W. S. JEVONS TO W. VISSERING
[LJN, 381]

Hampstead, 3d March 1878.

. . . I cannot enough thank you for your kindness in procuring the work on the Amsterdam Exchange, as also the pamphlet on the crisis of 1720. They contain exactly the kind of information which I need; and I expect to derive guidance from them, though I do not know Dutch. My English, joined to a slight knowledge of German and a few words of Danish, enable me to read a sentence here and there, and I have procured a dictionary to assist me.

The references are invaluable. I do not yet despair of finding some distinct information about depressions of trade intervening between 1721 and 1763, so as to complete the decennial series. In London there was said to be stock-jobbing in 1732 comparable with that of 1720, though this is obviously an exaggeration.

I am interested to perceive that the pamphlet on 1721 is by your father,[1] so that by good fortune I have the assistance of those perhaps the best qualified in any country to inform me.

I am interested in your remarks on the Chinese labour, and should like to discuss it with you, if you happen to visit London. It is too important and difficult a question to be answered in a few words.

We have a large Chinese library at University College, some 10,000 tracts collected by the Rev. Robert Morrison.[2] I suppose nobody ever looks at them. Indeed, in the close neighbourhood of the British Museum it is of little use.

I shall have the pleasure of sending you a copy of my new little book on *Political Economy*. . . .

516. H. FORSSELL[1] TO W. S. JEVONS

Dear Sir!
    If i dare to propose to you an exchange of portraits, it is because i suppose you might forgive an admirer of your writings his strong wish to

---

[1] Simon Vissering, 'Het Groote Tafereel', *De Gids*, Jaargang 1856 1, 643 – 84. Cf. A. H. Cole, *The Great Mirror of Folly (Het Groote Tafereel der Dwaascheid) An Economic Bibliographical Study*, Kress Library Publications, no. 6.

[2] Robert Morrison (1782–1834), founder of the Protestant missions in China and pioneer of Chinese studies. Translated the New Testament into Chinese, 1809–14, and completed a Chinese dictionary in 1823.

[1] Hans Forssell (1843–1901), Secretary of the Bank of Sweden; Minister of Finance, 1875. In matters of economic policy Forssell was an advocate of free trade and an opponent of private bank-note issues.

make your personal acquaintance as well as to fill a considerable want in a collection of portraits of modern economists that the benevolence of the respective authors has allowed me to get very complete. If you grant my request, i permit me to add the wish to get your name signed upon the card – in the same place as the mine upon this included [2] – together with datum.

  With great estimation

Your obedient servant,
Hans Forssell
Minister of Finance of Sweden.

Stockholm
18 $\frac{8}{3}$ 78.

517.   J. MARSHALL[1] TO W. S. JEVONS

8 Monkbridge Road,
Headingley, Leeds.
13th March 1878

My dear Sir,

  I found the diagrams ready for my inspection on Monday, and gladly availed myself of several of them. Among the rest was one showing the coalfields of the world, which I think will do very well: so that I shall not require the slides. I need not say, however, how heartily I am obliged to you for so kindly offering me them.

  There are one or two points in your treatment of the coal question that I expect I shall have occasion to express my dissent from: I don't quite know whether I ought to trouble you by mentioning them as I have no right to occupy your time, but if there is nothing in what I have to say, I shall not at all expect you to take the trouble to notice the matter further.

  My chief point is as to the 'Crucial figures' as you rightly call them – especially as to your deduced rate of increase. The difficulty comes out clearly enough in the calculation you made of 117.9 millions for 1871. As you notice in your second edition – the figures on which that calculation is based were erroneous – the numbers of 1861–2–3 being wrong by about 2 millions. You thus got 41 per cent as a decennial ratio,

---

  [2] The portrait which was apparently included with this letter is no longer among the Jevons Papers.

  [1] John Marshall had been appointed Professor of History at the Yorkshire College in 1877. These letters (see also below, Letter 518) were written during the preparation of *Coal: its History and Uses* (1878) of which Marshall was co-author with his colleagues Professors Green, Miall, Thorpe and Rücker. He contributed two chapters entitled 'The Coal Question' (pp. 292–349) in which he examined evidence supporting the calculations relating to the eventual exhaustion of Britain's coal reserves, with particular reference to Jevons's arguments, which he largely endorsed.

when the true numbers would have given you a higher ratio. Then you take one of these erroneous numbers, 83.6 millions for 1861 – as the basis of your decennial calculations – and as a result get a number for 1871 not greatly in excess of the actual amount. But it seems to me that so far from confirming your calculation of a decennial ratio of increase of 41 per cent, as you claimed in your speech at Bristol in 1875 that it did – the correctness of the result, one of the factors being wrong, shews that the other factor was wrong also. Had you not had erroneous data to start from, your calculations for 1871 would have been greatly in excess of the truth. The later returns seem further to show that the ratio of increase has been a rapidly decreasing one, even during such years of industrial activity as 1869–73.[2]

It seems to me further that in admitting as you do, that the 41 per cent rate of increase cannot long continue – you lay yourself open to the inquiry, how you know that the influences which in time would prevent its continuing are not now, and have not been for years in operation? If they have been, then apparently they are not incompatible with a very large industrial growth, and the fears entertained by you on the one hand as to the rapid exhaustion of our coal, and on the other as to the decadence of our material prosperity, would in that case lose part of this justification.

You will pardon the apparent bluntness of my statement: I desired to make my letter as brief as possible. Thanking you again,

I remain yours,

John Marshall.

518. J. MARSHALL TO W. S. JEVONS

Coal

8 Monkbridge Road,
Headingley, Leeds.
March 15th 1878

My dear Sir,

I must thank you again very heartily for your kindness to me in this business. I have had abundant reason in the course of my reading on the

---

[2] 'Such are the critical numbers of our inquiry' – *The Coal Question* (third edition, revised), pp. 265–72, contains the figures and argument here paraphrased by Marshall. The second edition of *The Coal Question* appeared in 1866 and Jevons produced no further revision of it during his lifetime, but the third edition, revised by A. W. Flux, contains a 'Note On the Realised Increase of Coal Consumption', pp. 279–84, in which Flux argued that the reduced rate of increase in the later years of the nineteenth century in fact constituted a proof of Jevons's arguments.

It is clear from Marshall's second letter, and from references made in his first chapter, that Jevons, in his reply, was able to satisfy Marshall as to the accuracy of his calculations. Confusion had evidently arisen as to whether the rate of increase calculated by Jevons was arithmetical or

subject to observe how grossly you have been misunderstood, and yet I fear I may have shown that I too have been apt to misinterpret you. I shall give my best attention to your letter which has cleared up matters for me very greatly in many points. I certainly was not aware that the earlier years also were incorrect: it seems very strange that Mr. Hunt should still continue to give us these inaccurate returns substantially as you have them up to 1860 – and the higher figures from 1861 onwards.

I have altered some of my calculations in accordance with this correction: but there still remains as it appears to me sufficient grounds for concluding that while on the whole period, as you show in your letter – your ratio 3.5 per cent is rather under than over the facts: yet this ratio is only apparently correct, because it is considerably under the ratio of increase in the earlier period and considerably below the ratio for the later. I have calculated the ratio of increase for all the decennial periods from each year successively since 1855 – and I find that for the six decennial periods – 1855–65: 56–66: and so on up to 60–70: there is an average decennial increase of 47.8 or about 4.2 per annum. The next six decennial periods – give an average decennial increase of 38.3, or about 3.4 per annum. Or again taking the three periods 1856–61: 1861–67: 1867–73: each of which begins and ends with a year of excess over both its predecessor and successor – and which do not touch at all on the late exceptional bad trade: I find – that the first period of 5 years gives a total increase of 24.8 p.c.: or 4.4 per annum the next – a period of 6 yrs. gives a total of 22.2 per cent: or 3.4 per ann: the last gives a total for the 6 yrs. of 21.5 p.c. or 3.3 per ann.

So far as the statistics go therefore, they seem to indicate that the rate of increase is decreasing, now this is just what one would expect to happen if the tendency of new economies to increase demand were approaching its limit, and some portion were beginning to expend itself in reducing the coal consumption. Of course the evidence of such a change is but small, you have convincingly shown that such has not been the effect up to the period of your book: but it is difficult to believe that under no circumstances could such a limit be reached, not of course a permanent one, but one sufficient to affect the relation between consumption of coal and production in the way of a gradual diminution of ratio.

And when one considers the utterly forced and fictitious character of much of the 'big trade' of 1866 to 1873 – fostered by swindling foreign

---

geometrical. Marshall confirmed the point on p. 316: 'Prof. Jevons . . . deduced from the returns of the years from 1854 to 1865, that the actual law of geometrical increase was on the average probably 3.5 per cent. per annum, equivalent to an increase of 41 per cent. in ten years, or 100 per cent. in a little over twenty years. His calculations received striking confirmation in 1871, when the actual production, 117,350,000 tons, differed only fractionally from the calculated amount 117,900,000. . . .'

loans – share companies and syndicates and the rest to a degree I believe unprecedented – I think it possible at least that the theory of a definitive limit to the demand of the world for manufactured goods – such as Mr. Mundella[1] discusses – may after all have some truth in it. Each revival of trade would then be fiercer and briefer – and the collapse more lengthened – till something like a permanent relation between production and the natural growth of demand had established itself again. No doubt there is great scope in the world yet – but I doubt if the 'pace can be forced' in the future as it has been during these last twenty years. We should in that case have a serious check put on our prosperity – but the check would be a world wide check – there would be nothing of that kind of check spoken of by you as likely to result from *comparative* scarcity of coals here, as compared with other countries. But this I know is but poor speculation at the best. I should be very glad to be permitted to quote your statement of the position you hold with which you have favoured me: it seems a very clear one.

I am

My dear Sir

Yours very sincerely,

John Marshall

Professor Jevons

518A. W. S. JEVONS TO H. S. FOXWELL
        [RDF] (postcard)

From
W. Stanley Jevons,
18 March 1878

2, The Chestnuts,
Branch Hill,
Hampstead, N.W.

Best thanks for the extract. It is just the sort of thing I want and I suspected there wd be speculation in 1710 or 1711, ten years previous to the great bubble of 1720. I must examine more closely into the subject.

---

[1] Cf. A. J. Mundella, 'What are the conditions on which the Commercial and Manufacturing Supremacy of Great Britain depend, and is there any reason to think they have been, or may be, endangered?', *JRSS* 12 (1878) 87–112.

519.   W. S. JEVONS TO W. JACK

[MA]

> 2 The Chestnuts,
> West Heath,
> Hampstead,
> N.W.
> 22 March 1878.

Dear Jack,

I enclose receipt for the fifty pounds as requested.

Finding that there are now only 31 copies of the Theory of Political Economy in stock and that the sale though naturally limited is steady, I propose that we should at once prepare for a new edition to be ready say in October next. I wish to revise the book carefully, add new sections, a bibliography of previous works of a same kind, and other matters which will make the contents probably from 30 to 50 per cent more than at present, the present contents of the text being about 58,000 words.

By using smaller type the size of the books need hardly be increased or at any rate need not exceed 300 pages.

I think we might very well raise the price to 10s. 6d., but this might be afterwards considered.

I should make a point of having the book stereotyped now, as life is not long enough to be often revising books. When if ever I accomplish my large book on Pol. Econ. I shall carefully exclude the mathematical statements so that this theory will always be needed to accompany it.

I find that I signed an agreement to the effect that all future editions of the "Theory" were to be on the half-profit – no risk – to – author system, so that this must I suppose be the basis, and having regard to the nature of the book it seems fair.

If Messrs. Macmillan agree to my proposal please send a copy of the Theory (a damaged one would do) for the revision.

> Yours faithfully,
> W. S. Jevons

519A.   W. S. JEVONS TO H. S. FOXWELL
    [RDF]

2, The Chestnuts,
West Heath,
Hampstead, N.W.
23 March 78.

Dear Foxwell

I shall be glad to tell you all I know about the Examinerships.[1] I hear rumours to the effect that Sully,[2] Robertson[3] & perhaps Adamson are applying for the Logic one. Robertson thinks Sully shd have it but if not wants it himself. Adamson consulted me a week or two ago, and I advised him to make an offer of his services with a view to future if not immediate appointment.

I have not heard of any candidates for the Pol. Econ. but doubtless there might be some fair ones. There are several reasons in favour of your applying for this; you have made pol. econ more your specialty; *in proportion to work*, it is much better paid, as there usually [are][4] only about 30 papers to read for the £30, & two papers to set. Whereas the Logic examiner has something like 300 papers to read for £80 besides setting 3 or 4 times as many exam papers. In fact there are three weeks hard work in the year for the logic examiner. Now as you seem to be heavily worked at present this is a consideration.

It seems to me that your well known position gives you an unquestionable claim, & as they have now and then had difficulty in getting good examiners in P.E. your election now or at all events at the next vacancy shd be a matter of certainty.

As regards your appln I think a simple statement of the experience you have had in Cambridge exams. & in lecturing on P.E. wd be almost sufficient, but the test[s] which you would get from Sidgwick, Marshall ought to settle the matter. I should be most happy to assist in any way I can, & shd be most pleased to have you for a colleague in the MA. But I

---

[1] For the M.A. degree in the University of London. Foxwell was appointed Examiner in Political Economy in the University in 1878 and was an examiner for the M.A. papers in Political Economy in the years 1879–83 and 1894–8 inclusive.

[2] James Sully (1824–1923), writer on psychology, formerly Lecturer in Education in the University of Cambridge; succeeded Croom Robertson as Grote Professor of the Philosophy of Mind and Logic in University College London from 1892. Author of numerous works including *Sensation and Intuition* (1874), *Outlines of Psychology* (1884) and *My Life and Friends* (1918). He and Jevons were neighbours in Hampstead and became close friends.

[3] George Croom Robertson (1842–92) was born and educated in Aberdeen. Professor of Logic and Mental Philosophy in University College London, 1866–92; member of the Metaphysical Society; editor of the journal *Mind* from 1876 until his death. His most notable work was his edition of Grote's *Aristotle* (1872) and he contributed numerous articles to various periodicals.

[4] Omitted in the original manuscript.

declined to give a test[1] to Adamson on the ground that an examiner had better not try to choose his co-examiner in the same subjects. The objection applies in a much less degree to your appln as the subject is different tho the examn[5] is the same (MA). I will therefore if you like give you a statement on hearing that you decide to go in.

The examiners in P.E. have too often been men inexperienced in teaching or crotchetty.* I think some of the senate are aware of this & might welcome a thoroughly experienced and impartial lecturer like yourself.

Would not Fawcett who is I suppose the outgoing examiner in [the] same subject give you a test[1], or is he too crotchetty?*

Yours &c
W. S. Jevons.

520.   W. S. JEVONS TO J. MILLS
    [LJN, 381–2]

Hampstead, 24th March 1878.

. . . The evidence of bubbles and crises in the eighteenth century is apparently of a slight and fragmentary character, but when put together will have much circumstantial strength. I have nothing but fragmentary notes as yet, and much searching will be necessary.

Only an hour or two ago I got valuable indications of the earliest bubble yet connected with the series from Mr. Cornelius Walford, [1] being the number of insurance companies started in the undermentioned years: –

1704	. . .	2	1712	. . .	20
1706	. . .	2	1714	. . .	6
1707	. . .	1	1715	. . .	1
1708	. . .	2	1716	. . .	2
1709	. . .	8	1717	. . .	4
1710	. . .	37	1719	. . .	6
1711	. . .	35	1720	. . .	52

This is very important, as it clearly puts the South Sea Bubble in the series, and puts one before it which I had previously suspected.

[5] Substituted for 'degree', deleted in the original manuscript.

[1] Cornelius Walford (1827–85), Director of the Accident Insurance Company, 1866–85; founder of the Colonial Assurance Corporation Ltd, 1867; manager of the New York Insurance Company for Europe, 1870. The list given here was partially published in Walford's *Insurance Cyclopaedia*, 5 vols (1871–8), article 'Gambling'. Cf. Jevons, 'Commercial Crises and Sun Spots', *Investigations*, p. 229.

Then there was a bubble in 1732 which, in the *Gentleman's Magazine*, is compared to that of 1720 (or rather 1721).[2]

In 1743 there was a general and great rise in the price of wool, attributed to stock-jobbing.

In 1753−54 there was a foreign drain and great scarcity of money; but I must search for more information. In 1763 there was a well-known Continental crisis, as also in 1773. About 1782 I have not much evidence yet; but 1792−93 was a great collapse, as you know. The difficulty of finding reliable information is very great. . . .

521.   W. S. JEVONS TO H. RYLETT[1]
       [LJN, 382−3]
                                        Hampstead, 24th March 1878.

. . . I thank you very warmly for writing out so much of my lectures and sending them to me.[2] It is interesting to read what purports to be a verbatim report, but which has, I fear, undergone some improvement in the process. It is well known how much of the oratory we read is due to the reporters.

As regards Shaw Lefevre's[3] address, I cannot understand so large a reduction of cattle and sheep, because there has been no fall in price of meat or other cause to make the holding less profitable; and rise in wages of labourers would not much affect stock-farming. Decrease of corn-land is easy to understand. . . .

I fear the transcription of the whole of the lectures will be a very long and tedious work, which I cannot venture to ask of you.

Excuse my delay in answering your letter; but I have had a good deal

---

[2] *Gentleman's Magazine*, 2 (1732) 616. The article examined newspaper criticism of the performance of the South Sea Company since 1720.

[1] Rev. Harold Rylett (1851−1936), Unitarian minister. A former student of Jevons's (see below, n. 2), he was educated at the Unitarian Home Missionary Board, and at Owens College, Manchester, 1874−7. His first pastorate was at Reading (1877−8), then he moved to Ireland, becoming minister of Moneyrea Non-Subscribing Presbyterian Church, Co. Down, from 1879 to 1884. During this period he took an active interest in Irish politics: he was strongly Liberal, favouring the Nationalist and Land League movements, and in 1881 stood unsuccessfully for one of the Co. Tyrone divisions. He held successive pastorates at Maidstone (1884−7), Dudley (1887−9), Hyde (1889−96), Bermondsey (1896−1900) and Tenterden (1904−29), and was also active in journalism and politics throughout his career; he became editor of *The New Age* from 1899 to 1907, and stood unsuccessfully as Liberal candidate at Burton on Trent in 1910. He returned to Ireland in 1930 to spend his retirement at Ballygowan, near Belfast. Cf. Vol. I, p. 49.

[2] Rylett attended Jevons's Political Economy class at Owens College in the session 1875−6. His transcript of the lectures is reproduced in Vol. VI.

[3] George John Shaw-Lefevre (1831−1928), Inaugural Address as President of the Statistical Society. See *JRSS*, 40 (1877) 509−30.

to do, and cannot work long at a time, so that when pressed I have to leave letters for a time.

I have been busy about the bringing out of the *Primer,* of which I think I sent you a copy. . . .

522.   W. S. JEVONS TO W. H. B. BREWER
        [LJN, 383]

2 The Chestnuts, Hampstead.
24th March 1878.

. . . I have now actually got a second edition of my *Theory of Political Economy* in hand, and want to have it out next October, few copies now remaining. In addition to a general revision, I wish to add a bibliography of books relating to the mathematical treatment of political economy. I have your letter, written some years since, [1] in reference to certain books, and shall find the trouble you then took valuable for my object. But it would greatly oblige me if you would just look over the books again at your leisure; and, after carefully writing down the title of each bibliographically, add a few remarks as to the contents and value, the note to vary from a single line to a page or two, according to your caprice or your estimate of the value of the book.

I suppose Macmillan has sent you a copy of my *Primer,* with the disinterested idea that you would immediately use your tyrannical powers to force it on the wretched pedagogues who tremble at your approach.

Seriously speaking, would there be any way of bringing the need of elementary teaching of political economy forward again? or would it not be better to leave Dr. Watts [2] and others to do that? Some people do not believe in primary teaching of political economy. . . . No one is more likely to judge well than yourself. What do you think? I feel both the great need and the difficulty, and have not committed myself to any strong opinion in the preface but rather quoted the opinions of the authorities. . . .

---

[1] See above, Letter 355, p. 8.

[2] John Watts (1818–87), Secretary to Owens College Extension Committee, Chairman of the Manchester Technical School and a member of Manchester School Board from 1870 until his death; author of popular economic texts such as *A Catechism of Wages and Capital*; President of the Manchester Statistical Society, 1873–5.

523.   R. LOWE TO W. S. JEVONS

March 24, 1878
34 Lowndes Square,
S.W.

My dear Sir,

I have delayed thanking you for your excellent little book on Political Economy till I had time to read it. I am happy to find that I am entitled to claim your authority on my side in the discussion which we had a fortnight ago.[1]

My contention was that a strike is a mistake and I find in page 66 "I have not the least doubt that strikes on the whole produce a dead loss of wages to those who strike and to many others—" 67 "The conclusion to which I come is that as a general rule a strike is an act of folly".[2]

Believe me with many thanks,

Very truly yours,
Robert Lowe.

Correspondence with Harald Westergaard, 1878

The ensuing letter, which begins without preamble of any kind as an 'Abstract of Mr. Madsen's paper' and ends with a reference to a day apparently spent with Jevons, seems to require some explanation.

On 10 March 1876 C. L. Madsen read a paper before the Nationaløkonomisk Forening at Copenhagen, 'On the Law of International Telegraph Traffic' (Den Sandsynlige Lov for den internationale Telegraftrafik). This was published in Danish in the same year, in French in 1877 and in English (by the Society of Telegraph Engineers) in 1878. In this latter year Madsen's theory – that there existed a mathematical relation between the volume of international

[1] It is not clear which discussion Lowe had in mind here. No debate on industrial unrest was held in the House of Commons during March 1878. One explanation is that he had misremembered the date of the last meeting of the Political Economy Club, held on 1 March 1878, at which Jevons had proposed the question: 'Are not those Economists who have expressed a qualified approval of Strikes, in some degree responsible for the disastrous Strikes now occurring?' (*Political Economy Club . . . Questions Discussed, 1821–1920*, VI (1921) 100). Alternatively, Lowe may have been referring to the discussion arising out of a paper presented to the Statistical Society on 19 February 1878 by A. J. Mundella, 'What are the Conditions in which the Commercial and Manufacturing Supremacy of Great Britain Depend, and is there any reason to think they have been, or may be, Endangered?' (*JRSS*, 41 (1878) 87–134), in which Jevons took part and which was largely concerned with the effects of industrial conflicts. The discussion was adjourned to 5 March 1878 although neither Jevons nor Lowe appears to have made any contribution on that date.

[2] *Primer of Political Economy*, chapter VIII, 'Trades-Unions', paragraph 51. The phrases quoted here by Lowe appeared in the 1878 edition of the *Primer* in heavy black type.

trade and the numbers of international telegrams – was strongly attacked by Harald Westergaard (then a young doctoral candidate) in a review in *Nationaløkonomisk Tidsskrift* (Bind xi, 103–15). To this Madsen replied, and Westergaard appears to have sent Jevons a translation both of his review and Madsen's answer. It is the abstract of the latter which forms the first part of Westergaard's letter of 28 March 1878.

The reference in the final paragraph of the letter to 'returning from the pleasant day' suggests that Westergaard had been visiting Jevons. There is no indication in *Letters and Journal* that Jevons was abroad in March 1878, but his wife states (p. 386) that he 'determined to take a few weeks' holiday on the continent in May and June' and went to France, Germany and Switzerland. An undated letter from Westergaard headed '2 Euston Square' opens with the words 'While you have been abroad I have been overlooking your political economy . . .' From this it may be inferred that Westergaard came to London in March 1878, met Jevons and discussed Madsen's theory with him, and remained there for some months, contacting Jevons again in June when he returned to England. Support for this theory comes from a passage in an obituary of Westergaard written by Professor Axel Nielsen in *Nationaløkonomisk Tidsskrift*, 1936, p. 393: '. . . in some notes left by Westergaard he mentions that Falbe-Hansen had given him Jevons's book, and that later, through his acquaintance with Jevons in England, he could draw his (Jevons) attention to an error, for which Jevons thanks him in the second edition of his book . . .' Westergaard is indeed referred to on p. xiii of the Preface to the second edition of *T.P.E.* On these grounds his undated letter is reproduced here along with others for July 1878 (see below, p. 254).

In the controversy between Westergaard and Madsen over the statistical analysis of international telegraph traffic Jevons appears to have been treated as something of an 'independent expert' by both parties; he had been introduced to Madsen by Falbe-Hansen during a visit to Copenhagen in July 1877[1] and Madsen's letter to Jevons of 14 March 1879 (Vol. V, Letter 587) makes clear that Jevons was in correspondence with him in February 1878. It has not proved possible to trace the letter to Madsen of 25 February 1878, but this may well have arisen out of Westergaard's critique of the 'Telegraph Law'.

Correspondence with Harold Wedergaard, 1878

[1] See above, Letter 494, p. 206.

524.   H. WESTERGAARD[1] TO W. S. JEVONS

March 28th 1878

Abstract of Mr. Madsens[2] paper: Den sandsynlige Lov && Svar til Hr Cand mag & polit H Westergaard.

After a short introduction Mr. Madsen proceeds to give a brief sketch of the development of his theory from 1859 to its present form. After this his paper runs thus (page 5): "In a trafic-law we are entitled to seek for something more than a guide for the statistician in establishing an estimate of the trafic considered. When the real, statistically proved, trafic has been dissolved in its several factors, we have means for ascertaining the mutual effect between any two among them; thus if we have succeeded in incorporating, for instance, the tax as a factor in the trafic-law, we are enabled to treat in an exact manner the real influence of a change of tax, which now is veiled by several other counteracting or co-operating forces. The international trafic is shown to be composed by several of those factors, which by and by will appear and among which besides the seven original factors some new elements already lay claim to our attention – But when thus all the cooperating elements in the whole international variation [or movement] are embodied in the law, I feel convinced, that, the regular order in the relation between the several

$$\frac{2 \quad 1}{}$$

branches of international trafic having been by and by more precised, we will at last arrive at definitions and results significant and interesting for the whole international trafic and for any direction of trafic. Among those elements I have already in the new treatises pointed out "the commercial organisation" and the "commercial centres of gravity" and probably new investigations will lead to new elements. Yet as a beginning, all factors are collected and included into the two capital factors: the coefficient and the commercial trafic, and the question is then, whether there in the form in which the law is now represented is a source for contradictions and inconsequences, as asserted by the reviewer, or whether the investigations are going on in a right direction, so that we from further investigations upon the base already given can expect fertile and harmonic results, which I hope to have proved and in the following will continue demonstrating". After this Mr. Madsen criticises my theoretic objection to the law. This I fear, that he has not quite

---

[1] Harald Ludvig Westergaard (1853–1936), Danish statistician, economist and social reformer, lecturer in political science and theory of statistics, University of Copenhagen, 1883; Professor of Political Science at Copenhagen, 1886–1924. Author of *Die Lehre von der Mortalitat und Morbilitat* (1882); *Die Grundzuge der Theorie der Statistik* (1890).

[2] Christian Ludvig Madsen (1827–99), telegraph and telephone engineer; began his career in the Danish Army and rose to the rank of Overkrigskommissar. He became the first Director of the telephone service in Copenhagen in 1880.

understood, as I have only stated, that the law cannot be a *necessary* law only a formula of interpolation. He objects to my examples, that no such case ever appeared in praxi and especially not in his tables, which lead to no contradiction because we almost always have approximately $\frac{v}{N} = \frac{v^1}{N^1}$ etc. But my objection was, that if any imaginable case gave a difference, even the slightest one, then the law could not be a necessary law.

After this again he proceeds to refute my objection to his "law of distance" pages 9−13. The principal objection was that this law was not proved to hold good for all countries, only for single groups of countries. Mr. Madsen states in his original papers that when the whole telegraphical connexion is the same, then a given value of U will produce a number of telegrams T which is in inverse proportion to the distance, and moreover, that this necessarily *must be* the case. To this I answered firstly that when the law concerning U was not necessary, the law for distance cannot be necessary, and moreover that we cannot ascertain the law statistically, because we have no means for numerical calculation of the telegraphical connexions between two countries. In fact Mr. Madsen himself does not find c directly but from the equation $T = \frac{c}{d} \cdot U$.

But when this is the case, we are not entitled to think, that c is a numerical expression for the whole status of telegraph. But as we have *two* unknown quantities c and d to be found from *one* equation $T = \frac{c}{d} \cdot U$ we have two possible alternatives: either that c always is constant, then the law of distance can properly be said to hold good, or that the law has only a formal existence as we can give d what value we please and afterwards find c from the equation $T = \frac{c}{d} \cdot U$.

To this Mr. Madsen (after having cited my words: "but if this is not the case that c is nearly constant, the law of distance has no existence at all") makes the following objections:

"According to the definition of the coefficient c, it includes all the geographical, telegraphical and remaining elements, which are contributing factors in the international trafic, for which the commercial factor forms the base. The coefficient c then shows the intensity or vivacity of the trafic of telegrams produced by a certain commercial operation. After a series of detailed investigations, the geographical element is separated from the coefficient − distance between the countries − and the law of distance made a subject for a series of minute considerations, and finally in "Recherches sur la loi etc" for a theoretical investigation, proving that the law of distance must hold good in all the steps of international communication. The coefficient c then is dissolved in the elements $\frac{c}{d}$, d is the distance, and c the progress in the telegrafic and commercial organisation and in the communication generally. Now we see the meaning by Mr. W's assertion, that c ought to be constant. Nothing less than total stagnation in the whole international trafic. The development of railways, steamroutes. . . . (some words omitted) . . all is in vain, c must be constant, neither progress nor retrogression –, and the international trafic of telegrams is not altered by the movement so important for the whole international life. Why? Is there no difference between the extremely bad and good management of the telegraph? . . . (half a page omitted) – I trust to have said enough for proving clearly and plainly, that c ought not to be and possibly cannot be constant" . . . After this some numerical calculations are performed, which I think are of no direct interest for the understanding of the scheme for the paper. He ends with the following passage: "The law of distance is the basis upon which this law of trafic, and any other too, must be built, and the results of this proof can be laid down in the following words . . . ," but when this is the case, that c neither ought to be, nor can be constant, then the law of distance exists."

To the objection, that c ought to be found directly or at least once for all, and that it afterwards was to be ascertained, whether this value would satisfy the equation $T = CU$, the author replies: "To this I cannot but answer: try to do so! This would, I fancy, be quite the same thing, as if we would have waited till we had invented exactly all the factors working in the steam engine before we constructed this mechanism. . . . In the law of trafic several elements are hidden, that only can be ascertained by experience, but then surely times will bring them into appearance and give them their proper place in the law." p. 14

The last page contains some concluding remarks – I cannot hope, that the translation is quite correct nor of course that the english language is good. For all mistakes as well as for the bad handwriting I ask your pardon.

While returning from the pleasant day last night it struck me that the price-problem[3] can be solved in the following way:
Any measure of prices must submit to the following equation

$$\frac{u_2}{u_1} = f\left(\frac{x_2}{x_1}, \frac{y_2}{y_1}, \ldots\right)$$

[3] As the subsequent argument makes clear, the 'price-problem' in question was the following: given a relationship between price-relatives, what is the implied relationship between the actual prices? For comment by Westergaard on Jevons's contribution to index-number technique, see his *Contributions to the History of Statistics* (1932) pp. 203–4, and *Grundzuge der Theorie der Statistik*, pp. 218–20.

u_2 and u_1 x_2 and x_1 y_2 and y_1 && being average prices and prices in two arbitrarily chosen moments. Therefore we may take two subsequent moments, and we shall have

$$\frac{u + du}{u} = f(\frac{x + dx}{x}, \frac{y + dy}{y}, \ldots)$$

or $\quad 1 + \dfrac{du}{u} = f(1, 1 \ldots) + \propto \dfrac{dx}{x} + \beta\dfrac{dy}{y} + \ldots$

from which $f(1,1..) = 1$ and:

$$\frac{du}{u} = \frac{\propto dx}{x} + \frac{\beta dy}{y} + \ldots$$

or $\qquad u = x^{\propto}y^{\beta} \ldots$

This equation includes the following one

$$n^2 = \sqrt[n]{x_1 x_2 \ldots x_n}$$

I am Sir
Your grateful and obedient
H. Westergaard

Mr. Professor W. Stanley Jevons

525. W. S. JEVONS TO W. JACK
[MA]

2 The Chestnuts,
West Heath,
Hampstead, N.W.
31 March 1878.

Dear Jack,

I quite agree to Messrs. Hoepli[1] translating and republishing my Political Economy Primer on the terms named. By the bye* they did the same with my Logic Primer without permission, but, when they send a cheque I will overlook the infraction of copyright.

The alterations in the Primer will only be a few words to correct blunders but I will not send corrections for a few weeks in case of more being discovered.

I am preparing Adam Smith as in the annexed form to allow of

[1] Ulrico Hoepli, publishers at Milan.

footnotes.[2] Will you kindly say before I do more whether the foolscap sheet thus arranged is convenient to the printer?

Yours,

W. S. Jevons

Dr. Jack.

526. W. S. JEVONS TO W. H. B. BREWER
[LJN, 384]

2 The Chestnuts,
3rd April, 1878.

. . . I now enclose your former letters, which contain many notes, but it would be a great convenience for me to have a brief account of each of the books you have in your possession. I enclose a paper which shows the form of entry in my bibliography. The subject grows upon me as I proceed. There are more books than you would suppose, and I find that the Memoirs of Dupuit[1] in the *Annales des Ponts et Chausées* are most luminous and valuable. Though he chiefly applied his ideas to the tolls, bridges, etc., he had a perfectly correct notion of the theory of value. It is curious how such writings come to be forgotten. . . .

527. W. S. JEVONS TO E. J. BROADFIELD
[LJN, 384–5]

Hampstead,
7th April, 1878.

. . . I was very sorry to hear from your last letter that you have so soon again had to bear another loss, and one less to be looked for.[1] Sometimes I think that I am wanting in the imagination which alone can enable us to enter into other people's feelings – so far, perhaps, but only so far I may not feel with you so acutely as I should do. If indeed for your sorrows to remind me of my own is sympathy, then no one could feel more. . . . Not long since, too, I lost a brother in New Zealand, who died suddenly and

[2] See above, Letter 504, n. 1, p. 218.
[1] For the references to Dupuit's memoirs, see above, Letter 484 and 487, pp. 192 and 197.
[1] It has not proved possible to trace any details of Broadfield's bereavement. His father had died in October 1876 (see LJ, p. 363), and it seems likely that Jevons was referring to the death of his younger brother.

all alone of another hopeless disease, under peculiarly touching circumstances. If any one has had cause to doubt the benevolent government of human affairs, it is I and my brothers and sisters; and yet nothing can eradicate from my mind the belief that there must be a brighter side to things, and that we do not see all. It may be very unscientific, and 'exact thinkers' like Mill may have proved the opposite. In that case I must consent to remain among the unscientific.

But to come to business. I should like to spend a night with you at Prestwich. I could go next Monday and be with you some time in the evening, if you should be disengaged and not disinclined for a *perfectly quiet* visit. I should probably go first to Birkenhead. Please let me know exactly what you wish. I might put off my visit for a week, or even till after Easter; but I should like nothing better than to have a few hours' talk with you when I do go.

I am much pleased with your few remarks on the Mill article. Some people seem to think that I am doing myself much harm by the articles; and I almost suspect some of them to mean that I have no straightforward purpose in writing as I do in the *Contemporary*. But the fact is my attack on Mill is as much a matter of the heart as the head; and I feel sure that, if I can succeed in convincing people of the groundless character of much of Mill's writings, the service to truth must be of an important character. Moreover, it is one so difficult to accomplish that I was warranted in accepting Strahan's offer, to insert some articles in the *Contemporary Review*. I do not always like the company I am in there; and yet, on the whole, their company is more congenial than that of the Comtists who reign in the *Fortnightly*. Mallock's article is an extraordinary production.[2]

I have three or four books of different sorts on hand, especially a new edition of the *Theory of Political Economy*, and I have worked myself a little below par, perhaps more than a little, so that a few days' rest will do me good. . . .

---

[2] William Hurrell Mallock (1849–1923), satirical writer, 'Positivism on an Island', *Contemporary Review*, 32 (1878) 1–28.

528. W. S. JEVONS TO W. JACK
[MA]

2 The Chestnuts,
West Heath,
Hampstead N.W.
13 April 1878

Dear Jack,

Your account of Brittain's[1] book sounds rather doubtful. I do not know anything about him. I suppose he is one of these people who want to bring about a reaction against Free trade, and to meddle with treaties. I see no sense in making treaties with 12 months notice. Better have no treaties at all. Without seeing the MS I certainly cannot advise you to publish and I ought not to advise you against it. If you like to send it I will look over it. The dedication to Sampson Lloyd is no recommendation, nor are 30 pages of tables.

Thanks for the returns about the Primer. I am sorry to hear of Clifford's critical state.[2]

I am,
Yours ever,
W. S. Jevons.

529. N. G. PIERSON TO W. S. JEVONS

Amsterdam, April, 13, 1878.

Dear Sir,

As my name is not wholly unknown to you – I once saw it mentioned in one of your speeches – I may venture perhaps to trouble you with a question.

I am making an inquiry into the history of banking-*policy*.[1] I wish to know, how and when the idea of correcting the exchanges by raising the rate of interest first presented itself. While reading Henry Thornton's[2]

---

[1] Frederick Brittain, *British Trade and Foreign Competition*. The work was published by Simpkin, Marshall & Co. in 1878. It was dedicated 'To Sampson S. Lloyd, Esq., M.P., President of the Associated Chambers of Commerce' and contained twenty-seven tables and four diagrams.

[2] W. K. Clifford had contracted tuberculosis in 1876; he died in 1879. Cf. above, Letter 495, n. 4, p. 207.

[1] This inquiry does not appear to have led to the publication of any specific work on banking policy by Pierson, but his *Leerboek Der Staathuishoudkunde* (Haarlem, 1896–1902), translated as *Principles of Economics*, did contain a long chapter on Banking in the Principal Countries, including a section on the development of British banking policy. Cf. below, Letter 535, n. 4, p. 267.

[2] Henry Thornton, *An Enquiry into the Nature and Effects of the Paper Credit of Great Britain* (1802) p. 93: 'It thus clearly appears that the Bank of England is placed, by the very nature of its institution, in a situation in which it may not be possible to avoid a temporary failure of the regularity of its cash payments.'

book of 1802 it struck me that this idea never entered into his mind, and as he strongly opposes the practice of refusing credit, he comes at last to a very despondent conclusion. (See page 93).

I did not even find the idea in Ricardo's works, nor in the Bullion Report, nor in the Parliamentary Reports till 1832. Only at that time the idea of governing the money market by raising the rate of interest seems to have taken hold of bank directors and political economists. This at least is the conclusion to which my researches led me but I should like to know your opinion on the subject and that is the reason why I take the liberty of addressing you this letter. Of course I do not mean to say that before 1832 the rate of interest has never been raised or lowered but my impression is, that this never has been done with a view of correcting the rates of exchange, the balance of payments.[3]

There is another thing which I should like to ask you. I saw in one of the Parliamentary papers, that about the year 1834 the Bank of England has addressed a petition to Government for being exempted of the Usury Laws. It must be interesting to read this petition. But has it ever been printed? I should like to know on what *grounds* the repeal of the Usury laws has been advocated by the Bank.[4]

I hope you will excuse the liberty, I allowed myself to take, and if ever I can be of any service to you, I hope you will as freely dispose of my service. I am a very constant reader of your books. That On Money for instance is always recommended by me to my students as the best existing on the subject. I have also engaged my friend Baron d'Aulnis – who to my great pleasure has lately been appointed to occupy the Chair of pol.Economy at Utrecht – to give an account of your theory of value. He has done it very ably. All this means, that your name *to me* is very familiar, and this perhaps may be an apology for my encroaching upon your time and troubling you with scientific questions.

I remain,
Dear Sir,
Your obedient,
N. G. Pierson.
Professor of Political Economy and Statistics, University of Amsterdam.

In the light of modern assessments of Thornton, Pierson's reading of his views seems an extremely narrow one. Cf. Sir John Hicks, 'Thornton's Paper Credit (1802)', no. 10 in his *Critical Essays in Monetary Theory* (1967) pp. 174–88.

[3] This was for the reason (apparently unknown to Pierson) that the Bank Charter Act of 1833 exempted the Bank of England from the operation of the Usury Laws in respect of bills of exchange with less than three months to run to maturity. See King, *History of the London Discount Market*; Cramp, *Opinion on Bank Rate 1822–60* (1962) pp. 1–8 and appendix B.

[4] See below, Letters 544A and 545, pp. 279 and 280.

530.   J. CONRAD[1] TO W. S. JEVONS

Sir,

Though personally a stranger to you, I beg to take the liberty of asking a favour which if granted, I trust, will much further the international co-operation of political economists and thereby the progress of political science.

Several of your writings are well known in Germany and much appreciated; but the libraries of our Universities show great incompleteness in foreign literature and especially in the periodical literature of Great Britain; and we have nothing to show us wheter we possess an author's works complete or not.

This is a Deficiency which I should like to fill up and as Editor of the Annals of Political Economy and Statistics (: Jahrbücher für National-ökonomie und Statistik founded by Professor Hildebrand[2] & published at Jena) I hope, with your kind assistance to be placed, in the position of doing so. I shall therefore be greatly obliged, if you will kindly send me a list of all your writings,[3] including those that have been published in periodicals that you place most importance upon, with just a few more added to show students of political economy the subjects treated therein in order that they may not be at fault, when wishing to select those which they feel special interest in.

I beg to address myself directly to you, the author, because this is the only way to enable me to give your readers a warranty of completeness and accuracy.

I may add that I intend to publish in the Annals a translation of such information as you may be kind enough to supply without any alteration of, or addition to it.

Later on, however my endeavour will be to give our readers a complete synopsis of some works separately.

Trusting to receive a favourable reply I remain

Sir

Your most obedt. Servt.

J. Conrad   Dr. Phil.

Ordinary Professor of Political Economy and Statistics at the University of Halle

Halle $18\frac{26}{VI}78$
Prussia

---

[1] Johannes E. Conrad (1839–1915), Professor of Political Economy at the University of Halle; editor of *Jahrbücher für Nationalökonomie und Statistik* from 1870 to 1915.

[2] Bruno Hildebrand (1812–78), Professor of Political Science at the University of Marburg, 1841–50; at Zürich and Berne, 1850–60; Professor of Political Economy at Jena, 1861–78. One of the 'older' generation of the German historical school.

[3] Jevons complied with this request and the list appeared later in 1878: 'Nationalökonomische

531. H. WESTERGAARD TO W. S. JEVONS

2 Euston Square,
London
[July 1878]

Dear Sir,

While you have been abroad I have been overlooking your "political economy" in the pleasant intention to find the largest possible amount of errors and objections. The following are the very few and unimportant remarks.—

As to the philosophical elements of the book I am at present very much puzzled with regard to the proper measure of pleasure and pain and similar questions, so here I am no judge at all. But as these questions do not touch the principal questions in your treatise on political economy, your object being only to state, that in the society all or most events come out exactly as if really pleasure and pain are to be measured in the way explained, it is of no consequence here, though of great general interest, how the human feelings really stand in relations to each other.

With regards to the economical elements I can hardly find anything to observe. This part of the book has always been of great use to me while studying political economy, containing the clearest notions and explanations I ever saw. Some slight alterations might perhaps be made, for instance, on page 129, where the ratio of exchange of gold and silver is mentioned,[1] and page 201 lines 4−6 which seem to me incorrect or rather misleading.[2]

The proposition in pages 175−177 seems true to me, only when the increases in the wages are computed to last for a long time.[3] There is here an element of future, which is very difficult to deal with properly.

In your observations on commercial statistics I totally agree with you that correct and complete tables·would be very useful, but it would be

---

Schriften von William Stanley Jevons', *Jahrbücher für Nationalökonomie und Statistik*, 30. Band (1878) 267−9.

[1] *T.P.E.*, first edition, p. 129, contained a reference to 'the extraordinary permanence of the ratio of exchange of gold and silver, which for several centuries past has never diverged much from 15 to 1'.

[2] In the chapter on the Theory of Rent Jevons had written:

'It is quite impossible that we could go on constantly increasing the yield of one farm without limit, otherwise we might feed the whole country upon a single farm. Yet there is no definite limit; for, by better and better culture we may always seem able to raise a little more.' It was the latter sentence which Westergaard characterised as misleading – rightly, since it introduces the idea of changes in technique into the usual diminishing returns example without making clear that a change of assumptions is occurring; nevertheless, the passage remained unaltered in later editions of *T.P.E.*

[3] The reference here is to Jevons's discussion of the choice between work and leisure – 'We may conclude, then, that English labourers enjoying little more than the necessaries of life, will work harder the less the produce; or, which is the same, will work less hard as the produce increases' (p. 176).

difficult to get people interested in these tables so as to make the sacrifices[2] necessary,[1] because no direct money advantage in connected with them as in case of sickness and mortality tables.

Passing now to the mathematical elements, I have also here only trifling remarks, and it might seem to you, that I had better not put them down but I do so to show you, how difficult it is for ordinary readers to find important objections to your theory. I really cannot see any objections to the theory of interest, it seems to me perfectly obvious and clear, and with regard to the other mathematical propositions I shall confine myself to some general observations. The chief problem in the book is a question of maximum and minimum.[4] Such problems occur in most sciences, where mathematics are applied. They are very frequent for instance in optics and the whole theory of statics and dynamics may be based upon these problems. It is the same with political economy. To get a certain amount of property with the least possible trouble, to buy the largest possible quantity of goods for a certain sum of money etc. these are the frequent and principal questions. And it may easily be shown that your equations always lead to the maximum or minimum required. The functions we make use of have, indeed certain general properties which enable us to show this. Thus taking the produce x (vide p. 205) of a certain sum of money spent in cultivating a piece of ground, the function x is always positive and increasing, $\frac{dx}{dl}$ positive and decreasing, at least from a certain point and $\frac{d^2x}{dl^2}$ is from this point constantly negative. The function x may be represented by the curve a b c d in the following diagram

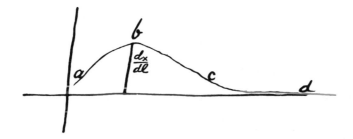

[4] In the Preface to the second edition of *T.P.E.* Jevons wrote:
'Two or three correspondents, especially Herr Harald Westergaard of Copenhagen, have pointed out that a little manipulation of the symbols, in accordance with the simple rules of the differential calculus, would often give results which I have laboriously argued out. The whole question is one of maxima and minima, the mathematical conditions of which are familiar to mathematicians. But, even if I were capable of presenting the subject in the concise symbolic style satisfactory to the taste of

Most of the functions have quite similar properties. Now if we take as an instance the case named in p. 205, the problem is how to spend a certain capital or labour (l) so as to raise the greatest possible produce (P). If we have three pieces of land, we have the equations:

$$P = x_1 + x_2 + x_3 = \text{Maximum}$$
$$l = l_1 + l_2 + l_3$$

from hence

$$dP = \frac{dx_1}{dl_1}dl_1 + \ldots + \frac{dx_3}{dl_3}dl_3 = 0$$

and

$$dl = dl_1 + dl_2 + dl_3 = 0$$

requiring that

$$\frac{dx_1}{dl_1} = \frac{dx_2}{dl_2} = \frac{dx_3}{dl_3} \quad (p.\ 206)$$

and the condition of maximum is

$$d^2P < 0$$

or

$$d^2P = \frac{d^2x_1}{dl_1^2}dl_1^2 + \ldots + \frac{dx_1}{dl_1}d^2l_1 \ldots < 0$$

but as we have at the same time

$$d^2l_1 + \ldots d^2l_3 = 0$$

we easily get

$$d^2P = \frac{d^2x_1}{dl_1^2}dl_1^2 + \ldots + \frac{d^2x_3}{dl_3^2}dl_3^2 < 0$$

This holds good if l_1 l_2 and l_3 are large enough,–or rather if l is large enough. But if this is not the case, we have the well known cases of discontinuity (vide for instance Todhunters Researches in The Calculus of Variations)[5] giving as one solution $l = l_1$ $l_2 = l_3 = 0$.

In the theory of utility we have similar problems. A person who is to

a practised mathematician, I should prefer in an essay of this kind to attain my results by a course of argument which is not only fundamentally true, but is clear and convincing to many readers who, like myself, are not skilful and professional mathematicians.'–pp. xii–xiii.

[5] Isaac Todhunter, *Researches in the Calculus of Variations, principally on the theory of Discontinuous Solutions* (1871).

buy different commodities, for a certain sum of money, at certain prices will try to manage so as to get the largest possible amounts of utility. Thus taking the case in p. 69, the question is to find the maximum of

$$u = u_1 + u_2 + u_3$$

while $\qquad S = x_1 + y_1 + z_1$.

The equations required are:

$$\frac{du_1}{dx_1} = \frac{du_2}{dy_1} = \frac{du_3}{dz_1}$$

and we have maximum because

$$d^2u = \frac{d^2u_1}{dx_1^2} dx_1^2 + \ldots + \frac{d^2u_3}{dz_1^2} dz_1^2 < 0.$$

There may be some extraordinary cases, in which we have to look out for other solutions. Thus $x_1 = y_1 = 0 \quad z_1 = S$ will give us:

$$du = \left(\frac{du_1}{dx_1} - \frac{du_3}{dz_1}\right) dx_1 + \left(\frac{du_2}{dy_1} - \frac{du_3}{dz_1}\right) dy_1$$

and as dx_1 and dy_1 must be positive for $x_1 = y_1 = 0$ we may have for these values $du < 0$ if $\dfrac{du_3}{dz_1}$ is greater than $\dfrac{du_1}{dx_1}$ and $\dfrac{du_2}{dy_1}$,

giving therefore a case of maximum (vide p. 70).

Supposing further, that a man has a quantity (a) of one commodity and nothing of another, and that the ratio of prices is fixed (k), he will try to get the greatest possible utility and we, therefore, must have:

$$u_{a-x} + v_y = \text{maximum}$$
and $\qquad y = kx$

The conditions are:

$$\frac{du}{dx} dx = \frac{dv}{dy} dy$$
and $\qquad dy = kdx$

whence follow the all important equations

$$\frac{\dfrac{du}{dx}}{\dfrac{dv}{dy}} = \frac{y}{x} = \frac{dy}{dx}$$

and it is easily shown that there is maximum.

The equation $\frac{y}{x} = \frac{dy}{dx}$ will always hold, for whatever the prices may be, the buyer will always try to get a maximum of utility out at these prices; and this equation again easily leads to the solution of all the remaining problems (for instance p. 104, 117 and 132 and the theory of labour with a few alterations). This is no improvement of your theory and you have clearly enough stated the maximum problem yourself, but it confirms the theory, that different ways lead to the same equation. I do not quite agree with you in your remarks on mathematical expectation etc. This theory may mean two different things: either that it is immoral to gamble and moral to insure, or that game produces pain, insurance pleasure. The first must certainly be wrong, for the theory has nothing to do with the morality of the feelings. And in the second case, the theory does not hold good for the average man considered in the political economy but rather for a good specimen of ideal mankind, for the fact is that many people do gamble and omit insuring, and that they enjoy themselves in doing so, even if they know the chances pretty well. It seems to me, that the mathematicians have been wrong in arbitrarily fixing as a measure of the feelings the probability multiplied by the utility (p.u). It seems to be a fact, and a very important one, indeed, that a few good chances in a certain trade add considerably more to the competition than the same amount of advantage uniformly distributed. This is for instance, the case in the diamond-fields and many other cases, but it is contradicted by the mathematical theory. This I stated a few years ago in our mathematical journal but as not entering much upon political economy but rather upon the theory of probabilities, I did not mention it in the bibliography.

These are the very few and trifling remarks I have found. Some of them may perhaps be useful to you, but in all cases I beg you to look upon this letter as a humble return for your great kindness to me during my stay here. If you find my explanation too short and indistinct, please to write to me under my address Copenhagen Nörregade 23.

Believe me,

Yours faithfully,

Harald Westergaard.

532. W. S. JEVONS TO L. WALRAS
[FW]

Hampstead, N.W.
9 July 1878

My dear Sir,

I send by book post three copies of a list of works on the mathematical theory of political Economy which I have lately drawn up, for the purpose expressed thereon of discovering all the writings which have been published on the subject.[1] I wish to give a complete Bibliography in a new edition of my "Theory".

Would it be possible for you to assist me, not only by naming any omitted works known to you, but also by procuring the republication of the list in the Journal des Economistes, the Italian Economista and other suitable publications, which are probably better known to you than to me.[2]

I dare say you will be somewhat surprised at the number of works already discovered. I hope to give a brief but impartial account of the progress of the theory in my new edition.

Believe me to be

Yours very faithfully,
W. Stanley Jevons.

533. L. WALRAS TO W. S. JEVONS
[FW]

Ouchy sous Lausanne,
13 juillet 1878[1]

Cher Monsieur,

J'ai reçu avant-hier votre lettre du 9 courant et les trois exemplaires de votre *Bibliographie des ouvrages d'application des mathématiques à l'économie politique*; et je profite d'un intervalle de quelques jours entre la fin de mes cours et le commencement de mes examens pour répondre [un peu] longuement, ayant plusieurs choses à vous dire.

Je vous dois en premier lieu un accusé de réception et des remerciements de votre traité élémentaire: *Political Economy*. Je l'ai parcouru et l'ai trouvé plein de choses excellentes; [mais j'ai regretté cependant que les

---

[1] Presumably these were the copies of the list published in *JRSS*, 41 (1878) 398–401; see below, Letter 543, n. 1, p. 277.

[2] The list appeared under the title 'Bibliographie des ouvrages relatifs à l'application des mathématiques à l'économie politique' in *Journal des Economistes*, (fourth series), 4 (1878) 470–7, with an introductory paragraph signed by Léon Walras, who also made a number of amendments and additions. See Jaffé, *Walras Correspondence*, 1, 569.

[1] The original manuscript of this letter is not now among the Jevons Papers. The text given here follows that in Jaffé, *Walras Correspondence*, 1, 570–2, based on the draft in Fonds Walras, FW 1, 278/10.

circonstances ne vous aient point amené à retarder sa publication. Vous auriez pu ainsi je crois introduire quelques modifications et quelques améliorations sur des points importants. Votre exposition de la loi de l'offre et de la demande n'a pas la rigueur que vos analyses mathématiques permettent aujourd'hui de lui donner. Il est bien vrai que la hausse du prix fait toujours diminuer la demande; mais il ne l'est pas qu'elle fait toujours augmenter l'offre.]² mais il y a aussi quelques points que j'aimerais bien discuter avec vous. Pour n'en citer que quelques-uns, je trouve une lacune considérable dans l'absence de la définition de l'*entrepreneur,* personne dont le rôle est de faire à la fois la demande des services producteurs et l'offre des produits et sans l'intervention duquel vous n'aurez jamais de détermination des fermages, des salaires et des intérêts.

Pour en revenir à présent à la bibliographie de l'économie politique mathématique, je vous dirai sincèrement que ce bon nombre des ouvrages, mémoires et articles compris dans votre liste ne m'a pas autant surpris que vous le croyez. Je les connaissais presque tous de titre, et j'en ai une bonne partie dans ma bibliothèque. J'en ai, de plus, quelques-uns que vous ne mentionnez pas, par exemple un *Traité des richesses* en 2 vol. in − 18°, édité à Londres et Lausanne en 1781 où les rapports de valeur entre marchandises échangées sont exprimés fort correctement en langage algébrique et qui me paraît devoir être placé tout en tête de la liste. Il est anonyme; mais on sait que l'auteur est un ingénieur français nommé Isnard qui fut membre du Tribunat et mourut en 1802 ou 1803. ³

Du moment où vous citez (et vous avez grandement raison) les economistes qui comme mon père, Mill et Rau, sans employer proprement les mathématiques, ont cru à la possibilité et à l'avantage de cet emploi, vous auriez à nommer Rossi, Cherbuliez, Molinari⁴ et quelques autres encore.

La mention très exacte que vous faites de l'ouvrage de mon père me fait supposer que vous en possédiez, pour le citer, un exemplaire. Dans le cas contraire, je'en mettrai un à votre disposition. J'en ai retrouvé quelques-uns à mon dernier voyage à Paris.

J'ai aussi entre les mains le tirage à part de 3 ou 4 articles de MM. Zanon, Errera et Zambelli⁵ sur une théorie de l'échange assez importante pour l'étude de la question.

---

² This passage was scored out in the draft and therefore presumably did not appear in the letter received by Jevons.

³ See W. Jaffé, 'A. N. Isnard, Progenitor of the Walrasian General Equilibrium Model', *History of Political Economy*, 1 (1969) 19−43.

⁴ No works by these authors were included in subsequent versions of the bibliography.

⁵ Jevons did include these articles in the bibliography, although, as Professor Jaffé says, none of them 'contains anything more than resumes of Léon Walras's theory of exchange, interlarded with laudatory remarks' (*Walras Correspondence*, 1, 410).

Pour ce qui me concerne plus spécialement, je crois qu'il y aurait lieu: 1° de faire figurer sur la liste notre *Correspondance* extraite du *Journal des Economistes,* distribué par moi à 150 exemplaires tirés à part, et qui fixe un point important de l'histoire de la science; 2° de séparer mes *Eléments d'économie politique pure* en 2 fascicules parus l'un en 1874, l'autre en 1877; 3° de placer l'ouvrage de M. d'Aulnis de Bourouill, qui me cite, après le mien; et 4° d'indiquer *la traduction italienne de mes 4 Mémoires parus cette année dans la Biblioteca dell' economista* sous le titre *Teoria matematica della Ricchezza sociale.*

M'autoriseriez-vous, en demandant à MM. Garnier et Errera la reproduction de votre nomenclature, à y faire les changements ci-dessus ou à les indiquer par une note?

J'apprends avec beaucoup de satisfaction que vous préparez la 2e édition de votre *Theory of Political Economy*; ce qui, pourtant, ne m'a pas trop étonné non plus, vu que, de mon côté, je me suis aperçu ces jours-ci, en examinant les comptes de mon éditeur, qu'il ne se passera pas fort longtemps avant que j'aie également à m'occuper de faire réimprimer mes *Eléments.* Le moment est donc venu de vous déclarer que je serais très disposé à traduire cet ouvrage en français. Lors de mon dernier voyage à Paris, il y a un an, j'en ai parlé à Melle Guillaumin à qui j'ai demandé si elle accepterait de faire cette traduction dans sa *Bibliothèque des sciences morales et politiques* et qui a paru y consentir.[6] C'est une collection d'ouvrages in–18 à 3 fr. ou 3 fr. 50 le volume, dans laquelle ont été publiés des ouvrages très distingués (entre autres La Liberté de Mill, traduction Dupont White). L'avantage qu'il y aurait dans cette combinaison c'est que l'ouvrage serait ainsi recommandé au public et que l'éditeur serait un peu plus intéressé à sa vente. Mais le profit pécuniaire serait probablement nul. Peut-être vaudrait-il mieux faire l'opération à nos frais et de moitié. Les frais d'impression ici seraient peu élevés et je n'ai nul doute que l'écoulement serait sinon rapide, au moins assuré. Voulez-vous être assez bon pour me répondre sur ce sujet?

Au cas où ma proposition vous agréerait, je vous demanderais de m'envoyer les bonnes feuilles de votre volume au fur et à mesure qu'elles seront tirées, et aussi de mettre de côté les bois des planches intercalées dans le texte, en ayant soin de faire faire ces bois de telle sorte qu'ils

[6] Walras did in fact make a translation of the second edition of *T.P.E.* but did not publish it. Since the publication of the *Walras Correspondence,* Professor Jaffé has located the manuscript of this translation. Cf. Jaffé, *Walras Correspondence,* I, 572, 645–7, 797–8.

On the death of her father Urbain Guillaumin in 1864, Melle Félicité Guillaumin (1829?–85) had taken charge of the publishing house which he founded and through which most of the major French economic works of the first half of the nineteenth century had appeared. Guillaumin also published the *Collection des principaux économistes* and the *Journal des Economistes.* Jevons's *Theory,* however, was not added to the *Bibliothèque des sciences morales et politiques*; the first French translation of it, by H. E. Barrault and M. Alfassa, was published by the house of Giard et Brière in 1909.

puissent servir pour une édition française in – 18 aussi bien que pour une édition anglaise in – 8°.

L'exposé *bref ét impartial* de principes de la théorie mathématique de la richesse sociale que vous me faites espérer aura pour moi le plus vif intérêt. Un tel morceau venu de vous sera tout à fait capital; car votre solution et votre autorité scientifique sont à l'heure qu'il est de premier ordre. Attachez—vous donc moins à la *brièveté* qu'à l'*impartialité*; ou pour mieux dire à votre impartialité. Et pour remplir celle-ci [ne perdez pas de vue] l'exactitude. Et pour cela, mettez-vous bien au courant de la question. J'appelle, à cet égard, toute votre attention sur la définition des *capitaux* et revenus ou services producteurs et consommables et sur celle de l'*entrepreneur* dont j'ai parlé plus haut et enfin sur celle du *crédit* considéré comme étant "la location des capitaux en marchandise ou monnaie". En dehors de ces définitions fondamentales, on est toujours dans la vieille [doctrine] et, au contraire, grâce à elles, on a la théorie complète et définitive de la détermination des prix de produits, des prix de revenus producteurs, du taux d'intérêt, et par conséquence du prix des capitaux producteurs. Et dès lors l'économie politique est renouvelée et fixée sur votre principe de l'utilité maximum comme l'a été l'astronomie sur le principe de l'attraction universelle.

Croyez-moi bien, cher Monsieur,

Tout à vous
Léon Walras

534.   W. S. JEVONS TO L. WALRAS
[FW]

16 July 1878[1]

My dear Sir

I write at once to say that I shall be much pleased if you will add to my bibliography, such works as you think proper, including of course your own in such way as you prefer. I had not got the Italian translation of your works and could not insert the title. I shall then hope that you will get it inserted in the *Journal des Economistes*. Answers might be returned to you at the Academy of Lausanne instead of the London Statistical Society if you like and you can send me the results. In short I shall be glad if you will treat the matter as our joint work.

If you can take similar measures as regards some Italian periodical I shall be obliged, but I will myself write shortly to Boccardo and perhaps Errera. However it would be well for you to do something also.

---

[1] A pencilled note by Walras appears under the date in the original manuscript, and reads 'ne répond pas sur l'ouvrage de mon père'. Cf. Jaffé, op. cit., I, 573.

I am already in correspondence with Prof. J. Conrad of Halle.[2] I hope he will reprint it in the Jahrbuch he edits but you might know of some other German publication which would reprint it. I think that the wide circulation of this list will forward the reception of the theory, apart from the information it leads to.

As regards my new edition I shall be delighted for you to translate and publish it chez Guillaumin[3] and I will give you every facility but the details may be discussed when I am a little nearer completion of the revision.

If you like and give me permission, I will reprint the correspondence from the Journal des Economistes in full, and also insert in the bibliography considerable extracts from your memoirs. I want to make it a kind of history of the subject. I am greatly pleased to hear that you are thinking of a new edition.

I agree with you about *entrepreneur*,[4] but must remedy the omission in some future work

Yours faithfully,
W. Stanley Jevons.

534A.   W. S. JEVONS TO N. G. PIERSON

2, The Chestnuts,
West Heath,
Hampstead, N. W.
4 August 1878.

Dear Sir

Though I fear I may have seemed to neglect your inquiries (in your letter of April 13th), I have not really forgotten the matter. I have been away from home travelling, & otherwise prevented by health from working much of late. Not seeing any chance of answering your queries

---

[2] See above, Letter 530, p. 253.

[3] See above, Letter 533, p. 261.

[4] In view of this statement by Jevons, it is curious to note that among the seventy-two chapters in the planned contents of his *Principles of Economics*, no chapter on the entrepreneur is included. There is, however, a brief note on the subject in the manuscript of the annotated edition of the *Wealth of Nations* in the Jevons Papers, (see above, Letter 504, p. 218). The note is appended to Smith's reference in book I, chapter VI to 'the profits of the undertaker' and reads—'French – Entrepreneur. It is to be regretted that this word has dropped out of the economist's vocabulary, owing to its sinister employment elsewhere. We need a name for the man who plans, organises, and finds the means for carrying on industry. Capitalist will not do, because though the undertaker ought to be a capitalist, it does not follow that the capitalist takes upon himself the labour of the entrepreneur. The name "promoter" might serve.'

Cf. also the brief remarks on entrepreneurial profits in Jevons's 1875–6 lecture course, Vol. VI.

satisfactorily myself, I put your letter into the hands of my friend Mr Hammond Chubb, [1] the Secretary of the Bank of England, and he kindly made some inquiries. But I am sorry to say that no new light can be thrown on the matter. Mr Chubb referred me back to the Report of 1832, especially to the evidence of Mr G. W. Norman Questions 2388 &c. You will see that in Q. 2392 Mr Norman distinctly says that for several years the Bank had looked narrowly to the state of the Foreign Exchanges. [2]

You will remember that previous to 1819 or 20 the state of things was different owing to the suspension of specie payments. In the Report of the Select Committee on the Bank resuming cash payments in 1819 you will find a great deal said about the Exchanges. Thus near the beginning of Mr Hardiman's [3] evidence he says distinctly that the foreign exchanges and the price of gold are principally affected by the amount of paper currency issued.

My opinion is that it would be impossible to decide definitely when the Bank directors began to look upon the rate of interest as governing the exchanges. The practice of such a body as the Court of Governors of the Bank of England is seldom guided by any fixed rules; & it would be difficult to say when particular modes of acting first originated. [4]

[1] Hammond Chubb (1830–1904), Secretary of the Bank of England from 1864 to 1894. He joined the Bank in 1847 on being nominated by a Director, William Cotton, having previously been a Clerk at the East and West India Dock House; served in various offices before being appointed Assistant Secretary in 1863.

[2] George Warde Norman (1793–1882), grandfather of Montague Norman; Director of the Bank of England, 1821–72; founder member of the Political Economy Club; Exchequer Bill Commissioner, 1831–42; Director of the Sun Insurance Co., 1830–64; pamphleteer on trade, currency and taxation.

Committee of Secrecy on the Bank of England Charter, Minutes of Evidence, *Parl. Papers*, 1832 (722) vi, p. 167:

'Q.2392. Do the Bank of England, in regulating the amount of their paper in circulation, have reference to the state of Foreign Exchanges? – The Bank, for several years, have always looked very narrowly at the state of the Foreign Exchanges. Since the principle which I have just mentioned has been adopted, the plan has been, under ordinary circumstances, to let the Public act upon the Bank, rather than the Bank upon the Public. Having fixed the amount of securities and treasure at about two-thirds and one-third, the drain is allowed to go on unchecked, unless some special occasion for interference should arise. The diminution of treasure is then accompanied by an equivalent diminution of circulation and deposits.'

The principle here referred to by Norman was that which has since come to be known as 'the Palmer rule'. While the statement made by Jevons is literally correct, Norman's replies to later questions made clear that he did not consider it necessary for the bank to take active steps to restrict credit when the exchanges became unfavourable.

[3] Although Jevons clearly wrote 'Hardiman' in the original manuscript, no one of that name gave evidence before the Committee on the Bank resuming cash payments in 1819. He was therefore presumably referring to William Haldimand (1784–1862), London merchant and philanthropist; Director of the Bank of England from 1809; advocate of the resumption of specie payments.

When Haldimand was examined on 17 February 1819 the fourth question put to him by Sir Robert Peel was 'You are understood to say, it is your opinion, that the foreign exchanges and the price of gold are principally affected by the amount of issue of paper currency?' To this Haldimand replied, 'That is my opinion.' Minutes of Evidence taken before the Secret Committee on the Expediency of the Bank resuming Cash Payments, *Parl. Papers*, 1819 (282) iii, p. 55.

Mr Chubb was unable to give me any clue to the Petition of the Bank against the usury laws, if such there were. I have never heard of such a petition, but the views of some of the chief governors may be learnt from the report of 1832 in the evidence of Norman, Glyn, & Lloyd. The evidence of Norman is especially distinct on this subject, Questions 2429–2432, 2446 &c &c. It may interest you to know that this Mr George W. Norman is still living at a great age, & I see him sometimes at the Political Economy club. But I cannot say whether he would remember anything about matters now.

I take the liberty of sending you a copy of a bibliographical list which may interest you. If you can suggest any alterations or additions thereto, I should esteem it a great favour to be informed at your convenience.

In the Report of 1819 evidence of 5 March 1819 you will find a good deal about the rate of discount at the Bank, but I do not know whether any of the answers exactly meet your inquiries.[5]

Much regretting the delay which has unfortunately occurred in answering your letter

I am Dear Sir

Yours very respectfully

W. Stanley Jevons.

Professor N. G. Pierson.

---

535.   N. G. PIERSON TO W. S. JEVONS

Baarn, Aug. 9th, 1878

Dear Sir,

I am very much obliged to you for the trouble you took in answering so fully to my letter. It is very curious that the Petition of the Bank of England on the Usury Laws should be entirely forgotten, for I am certain, that it has been presented, having seen it mentioned in one of the evidences. I cannot say where, just now, being at home, but I have marked the place.

Of course I am not acquainted with all the books named in the list you sent me, but I found two mistakes. Von Thünen, *Isolirte Staat* (1 vol., not 2) is mentioned twice and both times under a wrong date: The *Recherches* are merely a translation of the *Isolirte Staat*, which, if I am not mistaken (if you like it, I will inform you after consulting my notes) has been

---

[4] Modern writers date the start of Bank rate policy from 1833. Cf. Cramp, op. cit., p. 1, and above, Letter 529, n. 3. p. 252.

[5] Loc. cit., pp. 143-52. The witnesses examined on 5 March 1819 were George Dorrien, Charles Pole, Samuel Thornton and Jeremiah Harman, respectively Governor, Deputy Governor and directors of the Bank of England.

published in 1829. I am not sure, that Le Salaire Naturel is not a translation (of a part of the Book) also. If you possess Roscher's *Geschichte der Nationaloekonomie in Deutschland,* you will be able at once to decide these questions. At all events, Von Thünen[1] – Germany's Ricardo, the greatest economist it produced in the first half of this century! – ought not to be mentioned otherwise, I dare say, but[2] in the original edition. If you are not in possession of Roscher's book, please write to me again; at home, I would find at once all you want to know. It would not take me five minutes

Mathematical theories of political economy are not in vogue at present on the other side of the Rhine! Political Economy in Germany is in a sad condition as it appears to me. They write a good deal, but the historical part excepted, it does not tend very much to the advancement of our Science.

I see that you have given to the expression Mathem. method a certain extension, as you include also those books, where mathematics are used for illustrations. Perhaps my own Principles of pol. Ec. ought therefore to be included in your list, as I have tried to explain the theory of wages by a kind of mathematical exposition. I do not care for it at all, but if you wish to have your list complete, you might name my book, especially the *second* volume. The title is N. G. Pierson, Gronbeginselen der Staathuishoudkunde, Haarlem, 1875–6, in 2 vol. My illustrations are extremely simple, I divide, for instance the whole agricultural produce of a district in 8 parts, 1.2.3. etc.+ *Each* of these parts is obtained from *the same number of acres,* but the fertility of the soil being unequal, part 1 is so much larger than part 8. Now this illustrates how many workmen can find labour in this district at a given rate of wages; it shows also, that an increase of the number of labourers must lower this rate, as these people cannot find employment, unless land of inferior quality be cultivated; it proves equally that strikes can never be efficient. The same exposition may be used for *industrial* labour; very fertile land corresponding with industrial undertakings having peculiar advantages. "C'est simple comme bonjour" & merely illustrative of a well-known theory of Ricardo's.

I have read with special interest a beautiful article[3] of yours in an American Review (I forget which) on Bi-metallism. A friend of mine

---

[1] Pierson is here referring to *Recherches sur l'influence que le prix des grains, la richesse du sol, et les impôts exercent sur les systèmes de culture.* Traduit par Laverrière (1851). The first volume of von Thünen's *Der isolierte Staat in Beziehung auf Landwirtschaft und Nationalokonomie* was published in 1826, with a second edition in 1842. The first part of the second volume was published in 1850, and the remainder, together with a third volume edited from von Thünen's manuscripts by H. Schumacher, appeared in 1863.

[2] 'than' is crossed out here in the original manuscript.

[3] 'The Silver Question', *American Social Science Association* (Boston, 1877).

gave it to me and it has pleased me exceedingly. I entirely agree with your views on this subject.

I am, dear Sir,

Yours very respfy.

N. G. Pierson

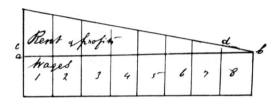

† See last page[4]

Suppose, labourers by a strike, should succeed in raising their wages to c−d. Then land No. 8 would no longer be cultivated and 1/8 less labourers wanted, etc.

536.   R. ADAMSON TO W. S. JEVONS

60 Parsonage Road,
Withington
14th August 1878.

Dear Jevons,

    I write to bring under your notice as soon as possible a very remarkable work on political economy which has just come into my hands. Some time ago I was attracted by a notice of it in a German History of P. E.[1] The historian said the author, Gossen,[2] tried to work out mathematically a theory of pleasure and pain. I advertised for the book but failed to get a

---

[4] This note was inserted by Pierson in the original manuscript and refers to the diagram reproduced above. A similar diagram appears in the English translation of Pierson's later book by A. A. Wotzel, *Principles of Economics* (1902), 1, 251.

[1] Gyula Kautz (1829–1909), *Theorie und Geschichte der National-Oekonomie* (Vienna, 1858–60) 1, 9. This reference is given by Jevons in the Preface to the second edition of *T.P.E.* (fourth edition, p. xxxii).

[2] Hermann Heinrich Gossen (1810–58), German civil servant. Tax assessor, first at Cologne, subsequently at Magdeburg and Erfurt; retired in 1847 and occupied himself first with a project of universal insurance, then with writing the book whose 'discovery' Adamson here recounts. Cf. L. Walras, 'Un Economiste Inconnu – Hermann Heinrich Gossen', *Journal des Economistes*, fourth series, 30 (1885) 68.

copy. A month ago I saw it advertised second-hand in Germany, ordered it, and have just received it. I will give you a brief sketch of the first portion, and I think you will acknowledge it is very remarkable.

The preface claims honours in P. E. for the author equal to those of Copernicus in Astronomy. This, however, may pass. It then goes on to say that mathematical treatment as the only sound one, is applied throughout, but out of consideration for the reader, the higher analysis will only be introduced where it is requisite to determine maxima and minima. The treatise then starts with the view of P. E. as the theory of pleasure, as the theory of the way in which for the individual and for society the maximum of pleasure may be realised with minimum of effort. The laws of pleasure are then stated   1. That increase of the same kind of enjoyment yields steadily diminishing satisfaction, up to the point of satiety   2. That a repeated enjoyment yields diminishing satisfaction, and on occasion of its repetition gives less pleasure than when first experienced. These laws are then exhibited geometrically, exactly in your manner. He then examines and expresses geometrically the condition that the total pleasure from one or several objects may be a maximum. This is done very elaborately, and in the course of it, he points out that the time of enjoyment varies continuously and accordingly employs differentiation to give his final result. He then introduces the word 'Werth', which, with strict accuracy, may be translated *utility*, points out that the magnitude of a *utility*, material or immaterial, is equal to the quantity of pleasure (Lebensgenuss) which it affords, and classifies objects of utility (1) as those which possess pleasure giving properties in themselves, (2) as those which only possess such property when in combination with other objects, (3) those which only serve as means towards production of pleasure giving objects. He is careful to point out that there is no absolute utility, that utility is entirely relative. He then gives, with full geometrical representation, the laws of utility.

1. That separate portions of the same pleasure-giving object have very different utility, and that, in general, for each man only a definite number of such portions has utility; any increase over this number is completely useless, but that the point of uselessness is only reached after the utility has gone through all the steps of magnitude.

2. When we increase the quantity of utility each new portion has less and less of it, until ultimately the point of inutility is reached.

Practical conclusion 'that each man should so distribute his labour that the final quantities of each pleasure-giving commodity should have for him equal utility.'

He then deals with labour, and starts with the proposition that the utility of any produced object must be estimated after deduction of the pains of labour required to produce it. He points out the variation of the pains of labour, exactly as you do, geometrically illustrates them, and concludes that we carry on labour so long as the utility of the object produced exceeds the pain of labour and up to the point at which these two quantities are equal.

Practical conclusion. Man should so distribute his labour that the utility of the last produced portion of commodity is equal to the pain of the last moment of labour. All this is done most elaborately. In pp. 80–90 he gives his theory of exchange. He points out that by exchange there is an enormous increase of utility, takes the case of single barter between A & B, each possessing commodity and inquires at what point exchange will cease so that the maximum of utility may have been gained. This point is reached when the utilities of the final portions of commodities possessed by the two parties are to each equal, i. e. to say A continues to give portions of his commodity, until the utility of the next portion to be given is exactly equal to the utility of the next portion of B's commodity which he would receive. The geometrical representation of this is naturally complicated. I have not looked through much more of the book, but I see he deduces the law of Rent in its most general acceptation, and works it out mathematically. Towards the latter part of the work, which is not a long one, he seems to get rather mystical, but I speak from very insufficient knowledge as yet.

I am far too busy with other matters to go into the thing at present therefore if you care to see the book I would let you have it at once. The full title is Entwicklung der Gesetze des menschlichen Verkehrs, und der daraus fliessenden Regeln fur menschliches Handeln, von Hermann Heinrich Gossen, Braunschweig, 1854, pp. 278. (Development of the laws of human commerce and of the consequent rules for human action – *Verkehrs* is sometimes used for communion or society and I am not sure in what sense Gossen intends it to be taken here.). The book seems to have attracted no attention in Germany.

I would have sent it to you at once had I been sure that you were at home.

With kind regards
Yours very truly
Robert Adamson

537.   L. WALRAS TO W. S. JEVONS[1]
    [FW]

Ouchy sous Lausanne,
17 août 1878

Cher Monsieur,

J'ai envoyé avant-hier à M. Joseph Garnier votre liste bibliographique après y avoir fait un certain nombre d'additions et de corrections relatives principalement à divers articles publiés dans le *Journal des Economistes* et dans le *Journal des Actuaires français*. Je suivrai cette affaire suivant vos recommendations.

Je vous donne bien volontiers la permission d'inscrire dans cette bibliographie des extraits aussi considérables que vous voudrez de mes Quatre mémoires. A cet effet, je vous envoie en même temps que la présente deux nouveaux exemplaires de ces mémoires: l'un de la traduction italienne très bien faite par M. Boccardo qui a paru dans sa *Biblioteca dell'Economista*; l'autre, en français, contenant les quelques changements que j'ai faits à l'occasion de cette traduction. Comme vous le verrez, j'ai mis la Préface en tête, donné des titres aux paragraphes, fait une table, rétabli deux passages importants et fait quelques menues corrections diverses. J'ai aussi modifié dans la figure 3 les courbes d'utilité. J'avais d'abord pris des lignes droites [afin] de déterminer exactement par le calcul la courbe de demande qui s'en déduit; mais je trouve, toute réflexion faite, qu'il vaut mieux n'avoir qu'une courbe de demande approximative et ne pas risquer de donner cette idée fausse que la rareté décroît toujours en raison inverse de la quantité possédée ou selon quelque loi simple analogue. Il me semble qu'avec ces légers perfectionnements, les Quatre Mémoires en question donnent bien, comme je l'ai voulu, une théorie mathématique condensée mais claire et satisfaisante de la richesse sociale. Vous me ferez d'autant plus de plaisir que vous en insérerez des extraits plus considérables, et même ma satisfaction serait complète si vous les traduisiez in-extenso. Pour ma part, je crois qu'une publication faite en anglais et en français qui contiendrait votre *Theory of Political Economy*, votre exposé des progrès de la méthode,[2] la bibliographie et enfin mes Quatre Mémoires serait plutôt d'un effet décisif, vu qu'elle fournirait la solution complète du problème de l'économie politique pure; et si je fais la traduction de votre livre, je tâcherai de la publier dans ces conditions.

Un incident qui a retardé ma révision de votre liste bibliographique et

---

[1] As with Walras to Jevons, 13 July 1878, the original manuscript of this letter is not now among the Jevons Papers, and the text given here follows that in Jaffé, *Walras Correspondence*, I, 573–4, based on the draft in Fonds Walras, FW I, 278/11.

[2] i.e. 'The Progress of the Mathematical Theory of Political Economy' (1874), reprinted in Vol. VII.

son envoi à M. Garnier a été une visite d'un ami de M. d'Aulnis de Bourouill qui a passé huit jours à côté de moi à l'Hôtel Beau Rivage, que j'ai promené dans nos environs et avec qui j'ai causé longuement et agréablement. Il me fait espérer la visite de M. d'Aulnis (actuellement, comme vous savez sans doute, professeur à Utrecht), pour le mois de septembre. Ne pourriez-vous songer vous-même à me faire un jour ou l'autre une visite semblable. Beau Rivage est un hôtel tout à fait confortable placé dans une situation magnifique; et notre lac est surtout admirable en automne. Nous l'admirerions tout en discutant les problèmes essentiels et fondamentaux d'une révolution de l'économie politique.

Je suis, Cher Monsieur, tout à vous.

Léon Walras

538. W. S. JEVONS TO T. E. JEVONS
[LJN, 387–8]

Manor House, Eastbourne,
21st August 1878.

. . . When your last letter arrived, I had just written to you, and our letters crossed. Another letter is now, however, due, and I write after spending a very pleasant week in comfortable quarters at Mr. Russell Scott's[1] country house at Eastbourne. It has suited us all very well, the boy being newly introduced to the beach with spade and bucket, and instructed in wading and paddling by myself. Harriet always enjoys the sea, and we have had some pleasant drives to Beachy Head, Pevensey Castle, etc.

After some ten days at home, we go for three weeks in September, to Derbyshire, where we have taken lodgings near Matlock, at a breezy farmhouse called Castle Top Farm, near Cromford. The hot weather which we have had lately has not agreed with me, and I have made up my mind to spend my summers in Norway as much as possible.

I did not feel well enough to go to the British Association at Dublin, but I sent a paper on the periodic recurrence of commercial crises, and their

---

[1] Russell Scott (1801–80), London businessman and philanthropist, brother-in-law and close friend of Harriet Jevons's father John Edward Taylor, the founder of the *Manchester Guardian* (cf. Vol. I, p. 47); father of Charles Prestwich Scott (1846–1932), distinguished editor of the paper from 1871 until his death. For details of the Scott–Taylor connection, see David Ayerst, *Guardian, Biography of a Newspaper* (1971). Russell Scott retired to live at the Manor House, Eastbourne, during the last five years of his life.

connection with the sun-spot period.[2] I do not know what they will do with it. Within the last few days I have had rather a disagreeable incident in the discovery, by Adamson of Owens College, of an unknown German book, by a man called Gossen, containing a theory of political economy apparently much like mine. There are, in fact, a whole series of books, hitherto quite unknown, even on the Continent, in which the principal ideas of my theory have been foreshadowed. I am, therefore, in the unfortunate position that the greater number of people think the theory nonsense, and do not understand it, and the rest discover that it is not new. I am getting on but slowly with the new edition, and altogether am rather at a standstill. . . .

539.   T. E. C. LESLIE[1] TO W. S. JEVONS

August 28, 1878

Dear Jevons,

I return with thanks your lecture. It came with the ragged corner which I have not ventured to treat, but it might be the better of a piece of paper gummed so as to keep it together.

The German book you refer to is unknown to me,[2] and not mentioned by Roscher in his History of German Pol. Economy.

I hope Ingram's address may be regularly published.[3] It was noticed in the Times,[4] & an article on it appeared as a leader in the Pall Mall, but still few people can have gathered what it really says.[5]

---

[2] 'On the Periodicity of Commercial Crises and its Physical Explanation,' presented to Section F on 19 August 1878. See *Report of the Forty-eighth Meeting of the British Association held at Dublin, in August 1878,* Transactions of Sections, pp. 666–7, where it was noted, 'In this paper the author took up again the inquiry into the relation between the solar spot period and commercial phenomena, which he had previously treated, but, as he now believes, unsuccessfully, at the Bristol meeting of the British Association . . .' See above, Letter 482. p. 188.

[1] Thomas Edward Cliffe Leslie (1825–82), Professor of Political Economy and Jurisprudence in Queen's College, Belfast, 1853–82; established a reputation as one of the leading advocates of the historical method in economics outside Germany, especially by his article 'On the Philosophical Method of Political Economy', *Hermathena* 4 (1876), reprinted in his *Essays in Political and Moral Philosophy* (1879).

[2] For details of Gossen's work see above, Letter 536, p. 267.

[3] John Kells Ingram, 'The Present Position and Prospects of Political Economy', Presidential address to Section F of the British Association at its Dublin meeting, 1878. This paper was published in the *Journal of the Statistical and Social Inquiry Society of Ireland,* 7 (1876–9) appendix, appeared separately as a pamphlet and was translated into a number of languages. For further details of Ingram's life and work, see Vol. V, Letter 672, n. 1.

[4] *The Times,* 17 August 1878, p. 10.

[5] 'Political Economy, New and Old', *Pall Mall Gazette,* 22 August 1878, p. 1:

'No subject claims the attention of statesmen and politicians more pressingly: but we are not quite sure whether the misgivings of the men of science assembled at Dublin have been quite the same as those of the youthful student of politics who is asked to recognize the last word of his calling as having been said in *laissez-faire.* To speak frankly, we believe that the natural philosophers have been

I shall probably get the blame of some scolding of Section F in an article on it in the Academy, [6] but this was entirely Appleton's doing. [7] I am by no means desirous of cutting off Section F and relegating it to the Social Science Association, which is ten times worse and less scientific. I had been a member for the last 16 years, but could stand it no longer and retired this year.

I hope the notice that you had a paper, or had one read for you on Crises will not interfere with its publication. [8] There is always a risk of that Although Morley [9] occasionally publishes lectures, he would be very apt to regard a paper as stale which had been read before the British Association and more or less reported. The lectures he publishes have generally been reported nowhere else and have had small publicity of any kind.

I should now be in the country but for this horrid rain which must be breaking the hearts of the farmers and the Chancellor of the Exchequer.

Very sincerely yours,

T. E. C. Leslie.

540.   W. S. JEVONS TO J. MILLS
       [LJN, 388]

2 The Chestnuts, West Heath,
Hampstead, N.W. 30th August, 1878

. . . Are we to have a crisis and collapse next October or not?

Accounts which are sent me show a large increase of bankruptcies in the first half of '78 compared with '77, and the recent unexpected pressure in the money market is very curious, and might seem to foreshadow a

frightened out of their wits by the ladies who flock to the Section of "Economic Science and Statistics" and who insist on reading papers and starting discussions which are not only not scientific but which savour of the singular antipathy to science for its own sake common to all the feminine movements of our day.'

[4] 'Mr. Ingram's Address to the Economic Section of the British Association at Dublin; *Academy*, 14 (1875) 191–2. The article described the Economic Section as 'a mere bear-garden for Members of Parliament and local quidnuncs', maintaining that its 'scientific character has been on a par with that of the Social Science Congress, or even lower'. It went on to suggest that the Section should be relegated 'bag and baggage' to the Social Science Congress: 'If its existence can be justified at all, it is only as Mr. Ingram has justified it, not so much by his pleadings as by the weighty character of his address at large.'

[7] Charles Edward Appleton (1841–79), Fellow of St John's College, Oxford, from 1864 until his death; editor of the *Academy*, 1869–79; a philosopher of Hegelian leanings.

[8] Jevons's paper, 'The Periodicity of Commercial Crises and its Physical Explanation' was, like Ingram's, published in the *Journal of the Statistical and Social Inquiry Society of Ireland*, 7 (1878) 334–42.

[9] John Morley, afterwards first Viscount Morley of Blackburn (1838–1923), statesman and man of letters, at this date editor of the *Fortnightly Review*, 1867–82.

greater pressure in October and November; in fact I think there must be such.

But, on the other hand, the occurrence of such numerous bankruptcies is what *often follows* a collapse, so that the real crisis might be placed in the autumn of 1877. The sun-spot theory, on the other hand, would lead me to expect the collapse in 1878.[1] My paper on the subject was, as you perhaps heard, read at the British Association at Dublin, but it has not yet been printed in full. I contemplate writing further on the subject soon. . . .

541.   HYDE CLARKE TO W. S. JEVONS

32 St. George's Square, S.W.

31st August, 1878.

My dear Sir,

Mr. Walford has the volume of misc, in which the article referred to is to be found, if at all.

There was a paper on Cycles in Herapath's Journal about 1837 or 1838, which contains an hypothesis for a selfworking variable cycle, but it has no reference to the cycle of crises.[1] Upon this I worked in the winter of 1846–7.[2]

I cannot find the diagrams in my collections of MSS and it is possible they were mislaid or lost during the transit of my library and collections to the east in 1859–66.

My results were obtained altogether by computations, as although many of us were struck by the ten yearly occurrence of these panics no

---

[1] 'The Periodicity of Commercial Crises and its Physical Explanation', *Journal of the Statistical and Social Inquiry Society of Ireland,* 7 (1878) 334–42; reprinted in *Investigations,* pp. 206–19.

In a Postscript to this paper, written in April 1882 (*Investigations,* p. 220), Jevons showed that the highest quarterly aggregate of bankruptices occurred in the first quarter of 1879, and so assigned the crisis to the autumn of 1878, 'a date which accords perfectly with the theory of periodicity maintained in these papers'. There was indeed a financial crisis of some magnitude at that date (cf. below, Letter 566, p. 304) so that Jevons was able to claim that his theory accorded well with facts. On the other hand, his paper of August 1878 began with the statement that 'the depression of trade . . . has now lasted for some four or five years'. Hence, as contemporary writers recognised, the autumn crisis of 1878 was not the typical liquidity crisis at the end of a boom (cf. *Bankers' Magazine,* 38 (1878) 923). But how this could be reconciled with a theory of the trade cycle, rather than of commercial crises alone, was a subject into which Jevons did not enter.

[1] *The Railway Magazine and Annals of Science,* edited by John Herapath, New Series, vols 1–6 (March 1836–August 1839). In vol. 5 (1838) 378, there is a paper entitled 'On the Mathematical Law of the Cycle, by a Correspondent', but this contains no more than vague generalisations about cycles in nature. I have been unable to trace any other paper in the volumes for 1837–8 which seems to fit Hyde Clarke's description [Editor].

[2] Hyde Clarke, *Physical Economy. A preliminary inquiry into the physical laws governing the periods of famines and panics* (1847). This pamphlet was originally published as an article in the *Railway Register* (1847).

known astronomical period would fit. I had a good chance of getting at such notions had they been known, being intimate with the late James T. Hackett,[3] a very fair mathematician and astronomical computer, who had been Secretary of the London Astrological Society, and whose inner craze was astrology and consequently periodicity.

In your paper you spoke about James Wilson recognising the decennial period.[4] There was nothing in that we all did that, we could not help it. The periodicity particularly struck all of us, who were writing on currency. The whole content of currency turned upon this condition. In 1836 and 1837 it necessarily affected my writing, as it did my seniors Thomas Joplin, Gilbert, Tooke, and so many others.

Of course the next period set the seal upon it and everybody aknowledged the coincidence.

It is not impossible that something may be found in the first Economist,[5] which was the organ of the banking interests and which was edited by Joplin and of which the editorship was offered to me by the bankers in 1837, but they afterwards determined to discontinue it.

Another possible channel is in the economical writings of John Rooke[6] (see Lonsdale's Cumberland Worthies)[7] He was the man who had a chief hand in Sir James Graham's free trade in Corn pamphlet,[8] as Sir James had in his. Many of his writings are wild, but containing striking and original thoughts. In 1836 he came in contact with me and some of his writings passed under my hand.

[3] James Thomas Hackett (1805–76), astrologer and mathematician; became a member of the London Astrological Society, 1826, and later secretary; reporter on *Herapath's Railway Journal* for nearly forty years; railway correspondent of *The Times*; author of *The Student's Assistant in Astronomy* (1836).

[4] Jevons's British Association paper, 'The Periodicity of Commercial Crises', contained the statement, 'It is well worthy of notice that nearly forty years ago (in 1840) Mr. James Wilson, the well-known founder of *The Economist* newspaper, published a small book, or large pamphlet, on "Fluctuations of Currency, Commerce and Manufactures; referable to the Corn Laws". Mr. Wilson speaks of "the frequent recurrence of periods of excitement and depression in the monetarial and commercial interests of the country", as if the idea of periods was familiar to him.' There is no specific reference to a decennial period. Cf. *Investigations*, p. 217.

[5] *The Economist, and Joint Stock Banker's Journal and General Commercial Chronicle*. Twenty-four numbers of this journal were published, from 15 April to 28 October 1837. Once again, a study of these numbers does not confirm Hyde Clarke's recollection. In fact the issue of 8 July 1837 contained the editorial dictum that 'our sudden and repeated passages from a highly flourishing to a ruinous condition are affected by no uncontrollable law of Nature' and this *Economist* found it unnecessary to look beyond the mismanagement of the Bank of England for an explanation of commercial panics.

[6] John Rooke (1780–1856), author of *An Inquiry into the Principles of National Wealth, illustrated by the Political Economy of the British Empire* (Edinburgh, 1824). Cf. E. R. A. Seligman, 'On Some Neglected British Economists', *Economic Journal*, 13 (1903) 511–14.

[7] Henry Lonsdale, *The Worthies of Cumberland*, 6 vols (1867–74).

[8] *Free trade in corn the real interest of the landlord, and the true policy of the state*. By a Cumberland landowner (1828). This pseudonymous pamphlet is attributed to Sir James Graham in *Halkett and Laing's Dictionary of anonymous and pseudonymous English Literature*, and to John Rooke in the *Catalogue of the Kress Library of Business and Economics, 1818–1848*, C. 2169.

Dr. Lonsdale says that Rooke was the originator of the west coast railway and of the opening up of Furness, and that he employed me but it was directly the reverse. Dr. Lonsdale promised to set this right in an after edition, but is dead.

John Herapath, who was a zealous physical mathematician, more than once talked with me of cosmical cycles, down to 1844, but he had no idea of any period affecting production, and exhibiting itself in economical results.

I cannot but think that at the present period of universal trade, we must limit ourselves to broad general results, rather than endeavour to disentangle the wet and dry periods affecting various crops, as wheat and wine.

With regard to tin, as my people were connected with the tin trade in the last century, I was always taught that it was a speculative trade worked by a monopoly. Therefore, I should be cautious how I relied upon it. It was in fact the Cornish combinations of tin smelters which laid the foundation for that of copper smelters, which in our time migrated to South Wales.

The tin trade was undoubtedly a regulated trade.

Yours faithfully,

Hyde Clarke.

Professor W. Stanley Jevons.

542.   A. FROUT DE FONTPERTUIS[1] TO W. S. JEVONS

Paris   31 août 1878

Cher Monsieur,

Je mets à la poste à votre adresse aujourdhui même: 1° un n° de *L'Economiste Français*, celui du 31 août – qui renferme mon appreciation de l'"Inaugural adress" du D.ʳ Ingram, et où je me suis beaucoup servi de votre "Inaugural Lecture" à l'université de Londres, jadis traduite par moi pour le *Journal des Economistes*;[2]

2° 1 Exemplaire de chacun des volumes que j'ai consacrés à l'Inde ainsi

---

[1] Adalbert Frout de Fontpertuis (b. 1825), French economist; joint author, with Clovis Lamarre (see below, n. 3) of *L'Inde britannique et l'Exposition de 1878* . . . (1878) and *La Chine et la Japon à l'Exposition de 1878* . . . (1878), as well as various other works published between 1857 and 1883.

[2] A. F. de Fontpertuis, 'Le Congrès de l'Association Britannique pour l'Avancement des Sciences', *L'Economiste Français*, 31 August 1878, pp. 263–7. De Fontpertuis gave an account of J. K. Ingram's address as President of the Political Economy Section and contrasted his views as to the nature of the science with those expressed by Jevons in his Inaugural Lecture at the University of London, delivered on 2 October 1876. This had been published in translation in the *Journal des Economistes*, 15 March 1877, pp. 325–42.

qu'a la Chine—Japon dans la collection intitulée Les pays étrangers à L'Exposition, dont M. Lamarre, [3] docteur—ès—lettres et administrateur de S^{te}. Barbe a eu l'initiative et pris la direction *suum cuique* et je serais bien aise si vous donnez suite à la bonne intention que vous me manifestiez dans le temps. Si j'ai bien compris vos paroles d'alors que vous fassiez cette part à M. Lamarre, qui est un très galant homme, en rendant compte ou en faisant rendre compte de mes deux petits volumes, dans quelque "periodical" anglais. Je ne vous cache pas, d'ailleurs, que je serais heureux et honoré à la fois de cette marque d'attention de votre part.

Permettez-moi de vous demander aussi de me faire savoir si vous avez bien reçu ces deux volumes. M. Cliffe Leslie à qui j'en avais adressé par la poste 1 exemplaire de chacun *et en deux fois* à quatre jours de distance m'informe, en effet, que les trois ne lui sont pourtant parvenus, ce que je regrette d'autant plus qu'on a été fort parcimonieux chez le librarie dans la distribution de ces malheureux bouquins.

Veuillez croire, cher Monsieur, à la sincère expression de mes meilleurs sentiments

Ad. F de Fontpertuis

29 boulevard Orléans.

543. J. E. CONRAD TO W. S. JEVONS

[September 1878]

Dear Sir!

Please excuse me for delaying so long to thank you for the list of your works, which you so kindly sent me. It is exactly what I wished and I delayed answering only because I intended to send at the same time the proof sheet of the translation which however I have not been able to do. But few English writers in our department are as much admired in Germany, as you are; so it gives me great pleasure to be able to publish a full catalogue of your works. [1]

The list of mathematical works I would like to publish, but I think, that I do not understand what class of writings you wish to collect, since many

---

[3] Clovis Lamarre, classicist; received a doctorate from the University of Dijon in 1863 for a thesis on the Roman Militia; Principal of the College de Sainte-Barbe an old and well known private secondary school, situated in the Latin Quarter; author of *Histoire de Sainte-Barbe, avec aperçu sur l'enseignement secondaire en France de 1860 à 1900* (1900) and a number of works on the 1878 Paris Exhibition. Cf. below, Letter 553, p. 287.

[1] A 'Bibliography of Works on the Mathematical Theory of Political Economy', not signed by Jevons but clearly prepared by him, had appeared in the *Journal of the Statistical Society* in June 1878, with a request for additions and corrections (*JRSS*, 41 (1878) 398–401). Jevons evidently asked Conrad to republish this when supplying the list of his own works.

of the Germans mentioned for example Lang, [2] Rau, Hagen [3] and English men like J. St. Mill have not used the mathemat. method as I understand it, that is, they have not used algebraic formulas. I fear that we do not understand one another. Do you merely mean the deductive method or the using of mathem. formulas? I will publish in the Nov. Heft of my Jahrbucher an Essay on the mathematical method by Bela Weisz [4] and I will send it to you and hope you will give me an explanation of your meaning.

Respectfully,

Prof. J. Conrad

Wildbad
im Wurtemberg [18]

544.   W. S. JEVONS TO H. S. FOXWELL
       [RDF; LJP, 388–9]

2, The Chestnuts,

West Heath,

Hampstead, N.W.

1 Sept 1878.

Dear Foxwell

Thanks for your suggestion about De Quincey's book [1] which I will look into. I always thought it was not worth reading but I dare say it was from a groundless prejudice against the writer.

A remarkable book has been discovered by Adamson. It is by Gossen of Brunswick pub^d in 1854, & in a remarkable manner anticipates the principal results of Walras & me. [2] No one seems ever to have heard of the book & not reading German I was of course quite ignorant of its existence. The Theory in question has in fact been independently discovered 3 or 4 times over & must be true.

Believe me

Your faithfully

W. S. Jevons.

[2] R. D. Theocharis in an article 'Joseph Lang and Macroeconomics', *Economica*, 25 (1958) 319, describes Lang as 'an obscure German whose principal work was published in Russia in 1811': i.e. *Grundlinien der politischen Arithmetik* (Kharkhov, 1811).

[3] Karl Heinrich Hagen (1785–1856), Professor of Political Science and Political Economy at Königsberg, 1811–49. References to Lang, Rau and Hagen were all included in the *JRSS* list.

[4] Béla Weisz, a teacher at the Commercial Academy and privat-dozent at the University of Budapest; author of *Der Einfluss des Agios auf den Aussenhandel* (Vienna, 1880), a pamphlet examining the effect of the premium on silver on the foreign trade of the Austro-Hungarian Empire.

[1] Thomas De Quincey (1785–1859), *The Logic of Political Economy* (1844). This work is included in Jevons's 'List of Mathematico-Economic Books' appended to the second edition of *T.P.E.*

[2] See above, Letter 536, p. 267.

544A.   W. S. JEVONS TO N. G. PIERSON

2, The Chestnuts,
West Heath,
Hampstead, N. W.
1 September 1878.

Dear Sir

During a recent visit to the British Museum I took the occasion to examine further concerning a petition of the Bank of England on the Usury Laws. I found that there is a *general Index* to all petitions presented to the House of Commons in the years 1833–52, contained in the Parliamentary Papers 1854–5, vol. LIV. In this were mentioned under the head of *Usury*

(1837).   For alteration of the law, John Crowther & 9,489 (signatures).
(1844)   ditto Patrick O Malley & 564 others.[1]

Unless then it was presented to the House of Commons before 1833 it could not exist, & if so, it w^d surely have been mentioned in the inquiry of 1832.

As regards the House of Lords Petitions which are distinct from those of the Commons, I found an index to them in the general index to the *Journals*. Between 1820 & 1837 were several petitions about Usury Laws, but none from the Bank of England. There was however an important one (apparently) from the Merchants, Bankers and Tradesmen of the city of London in 1829; one from the Chambers of Commerce of Manchester in 1831. Under the heading *Bank of England* & elsewhere in the indexes I could find no trace of the supposed petition. If you can give me a precise extract or statement regarding the petition I will gladly renew the search, but in the meantime I must assume that it does not exist. Is it possible that it is the Merchants & Bankers Petition of 1829 that you mean.

I am much obliged to you for your remarks and corrections concerning the list of books, which I take due note of. Any further corrections or remarks which you think proper to send at your convenience, will be of much value to me. I will gladly add your work to the list on the ground which you suggest.

A remarkable book by a German writer named Gossen, published at Brunswick in 1854 has just come to my knowledge for the first time. To a great extent it anticipates my Theory of Pol. Economy, but my want of knowledge of German prevented my ever hearing of the book before, nor do I find that any other economists are acquainted with it. The

---

[1] *Public Petitions Index*, 1854–5, LIV, 967.

coincidence is however very remarkable as regards the results especially, & goes far to prove the truth of the theory.

                    Believe me
                        Dear Sir
                            Yours faithfully
                                W. Stanley Jevons.
Professor N. G. Pierson.

I have a *duplicate* copy of the Report upon the Bank of England in 1832 which I would gladly present to you, if desired.

545.   N. G. PIERSON TO W. S. JEVONS
                                Amsterdam, Sept 9th, 78
Dear Sir,

I am at a loss to find a proper expression for the gratitude I owe you for the trouble you took on my behalf. Indeed you rendered me a great service in making these extensive researches. I see clearly that I must be wrong somehow, for if the Index you consulted does not mention the petition, it can hardly have been presented. According to my notes it ought to have been framed in 1834, but this cannot be. Unfortunately, and contrary to what I use to do, I did not mention my source in making this note. So I am inclined to suppose that either I made a mistake, or that the book I consulted made one. – You will oblige me very much by sending me the duplicate copy of the Report on the Bank of England, you speak of. It will be of great value to me.

I take a great interest in the history of economical theories and ideas. It seems to me that the study of this subject tends very much towards the advancement of our science and connects it with the history of human civilization, in general.

Gossen's book is wholly unknown to me. Roscher does not mention it in his very extensive History of political Economy in Germany. I never saw it quoted, but I will try to get it. It is very curious that such a remarkable work has remained wholly unknown even to a man like Prof. Roscher, who has read everything.

Shall we some time or other have the pleasure of seeing you in Holland? You would find many people here, to whom your name is as familiar as many a Dutch author, and who would be very happy to make your acquaintance.

With kind regards
                            Yours faithfully,
                            N. G. Pierson

546.   W. S. JEVONS TO J. MILLS
       [TLJM, 340]

September, 11, 1878.

Dear Mills,

Thanks for your answer to my former letter; it interested me much, and no one is likely to know better than yourself about the advent or otherwise of a crisis. But I am not quite sure whether a breakdown of credit in the ordinary sense is of the very essence of a crisis or rather a collapse. A general failure of profitable business may involve a breakdown of industry and an impossibility on the part of limited companies and others of paying their way. I will not attempt to put my idea clearly: indeed I do not clearly apprehend what I mean. But we shall see in the course of two months what happens.

I am,
Yours,
W. S. J.

547.   W. S. JEVONS TO L. WALRAS
       [FW]

Derbyshire, 15 September 1878[1]

My dear Sir,

Thanks for your letter, as also for the copies of printed memoirs which I am glad to have.

I am much obliged to you for giving me permission to extract and translate from your work as I think proper. It would have given me great

---

[1] In LJ, pp. 389–90, there appears the following extract from a letter of W. S. Jevons 'to L. Walras':

'Hampstead, 20th September 1878.

I shall pay careful attention to your remarks on my list of works on political economy. If I mention those which use only the geometrical method, I must be careful to point out the difference. I am sorry that my want of knowledge of German will prevent me from properly treating the German economists. I am now informed that there is an almost unknown work by Hermann Heinrich Gossen, published at Braunschweig in 1854, which to a great extent anticipates my theory. Of this work, however, a friend promises me an abstract for my new edition.'

As Professor Jaffé has pointed out (*Walras Correspondence*, I, 581) this presents something of a puzzle. No letter dated 20 September from Jevons now exists in Fonds Walras. It is possible, as Professor Jaffé notes, that it could have been lost when Mrs Jevons returned to Walras the packet of manuscript letters which he had lent her in 1883 to assist the preparation of LJ. On the other hand, a note by Aline Walras on the letter of Jevons dated 15 September 1878 identifies it as the one published in LJ.

Neither explanation seems wholly convincing. Walras's letter to Jevons of 17 August 1878 makes no mention of the geometrical method; in fact, this extract would fit very much better as a reply to d'Aulnis's letter of 25 September 1878. If this is what it was, however, Mrs Jevons must have mistaken both the addressee's name and the date. In the absence of the original manuscript, no firm conclusion is possible.

pleasure to translate the whole and join it to my own, but there are obstacles especially my own want of time for the work. I have a number of other publications in hand and I hardly know when I can complete the new edition, though I have done a good deal towards it. How would it do to insert the whole of *one* of your memoirs in the original French? In that case which would you think most suitable? I only throw out the suggestion being *uncertain* what I can do.

The matter has been rather complicated, too, by the discovery of a work, published at Brunswick Braunschweig in 1854, which contains many of the chief points of our theory clearly reasoned out. It is by Hermann Heinrich Gossen and is entitled somewhat as follows – Entwickelung der Gesetze der Menschlichen Verkehr (??).

The book seems to be totally unknown even in Germany, and as I do not read German I was absolutely ignorant of its existence. My successor Professor Adamson of Owens College found it mentioned in some history of political economy, not that of Roscher, who seemed ignorant of it I am told. Adamson is going to prepare me an abstract of the book from a copy which he accidentally procured. Hoping that you will still endeavour to procure the insertion of the list in the Journal des Econs.

I am

Yours faithfully

W. Stanley Jevons.

548.   J. D'AULNIS TO W. S. JEVONS

Utrecht 25 September 1878

Dear Sir,

With much interest I received a month ago the Bibliography of Works on the Mathematical Theory of Political Economy. Unhappily, the library of the University at Utrecht being as for economical works very incomplete, I am unable of controlling the mathematical theories, expounded in the greater part of the mentioned works. But I also fear that some of these works contain expositions, rather of graphical than of really mathematical nature. For example, J. Stuart Mill's chapters on International Trade and Value, and von Thünens "der Isolirte Staat" seem to have adopted the mathematical apparatus, more for illustrating discovered truths than for discovering yet unknown ones. However that seems me to be the peculiar character of true mathematics, that they conduce to new conclusions; do they not so, they seem me to be specimens of mere graphical method.

Would they, who wish to promote the mathematical method in pol. economy, not do well, – I venture to ask with the utmost modesty, – when distinguishing carefully graphical method of mathematical deduction? I believe to have found here and there objections against the usefulness of mathematical method, which in fact are directed against graphical figures. The well-known German economist W. Roscher (Geschichte der Nationalökonomik in Deutschland 1874) writes on the formula's of Rau (p. 860): "Er giebt zu dass sie (d.h. die algebraische und mathematische Darstellung) nichts Neues enthüllen, sondern blosz verdeutlichen und abkürzen kann", and about von Thünen: Auch Thünen selbst, wie es mir scheint, ist nicht eigentlich durch seine Algebra und differenzialrechnung zu seinen Entdeckungen gelangt. Vielmehr war ihm der schöpferische gedanke schon vorher gekommen, und die Mathematik hat ihm alsdann nur dazu gedient, seinen gesammten Erfahrungskreis, wohl gesichtet und geordnet, jenem Gedanken zu unterwerfen." Is it, against such observations, not necessary to point out that mathematical theories are of an essentially different character?

I am not aware of other mathematical writers on the subject, than of you Sir and of M. Walras. In my country Prof. N. G. Pierson (since a year this eminent man has joined at his office of director of the Bank at Amsterdam that of Professor in pol. ec. at the University of that city) has written a treatise of political economy (Grondbeginselen der Staathuishoudkunde, Haarlem, 1875) in two little volumes. In the second volume he has made much use of figures to show the relation between supply and prices (p. 57), between value of land produce and rent (pp. 85, 86, 91, 93) and between rent, interest and wages (p. 154, 156, 157). But after all, these figures are mere applications of graphical method,[1] and (however the writer was the first, who in 1873 directed my attention to your theories) the only, still important point of connexion between your figures and his, is his distinguishing *different* portions of the same commodity, and his observing the economical phenonema, caused by the variation of the independent variables, at the *last* or *final* portion. In that point, I am happy to notice this work has been greatly influenced by your discoveries.

Let me now, Sir, step to an other topic. An important branch of the British income tax will soon be studied by many Dutchmen. It is the schedule C by which is taxed the "Capital en portefeuille". The Dutch Minister of Finances (you would say the first Lord of the Treasury) has announced a Bill for taxing the interest of public and private Debt. It will be a partial income tax. The discussion on the proposal will be very tumultuous "intra et extra muros" of our parliament (Staten Generaal, états généraux). The opposition as well as the governmental party will frequently appeal to the experience, made in England. Yet, the working

---

[1] See above, Letter 535, p. 265.

of the Schedule C in England is here almost completely unknown.[2]

You would Sir, very much oblige me by indicating some good "Brochure" or treatise on that subject, and in all case, by giving your valuable opinion on the said Schedule. Does it not give rise to many frauds and injustices? The question is: by what manner can the administration know the income, yielded to any individual by his valuable papers? By what manner the information, given by the tax-payer himself, is controlled? What is the rational basis of taxation, when the tax payer is unwilling to give information? By giving me the explication or the information, which I allow meself to beg, you would enable me to take part in the coming discussion and to prove to my countrymen that the adherents of mathematical formulas in pol. economy can also have and say an opinion on practical subjects. It is by this conduct, I mean, we can give credit to our theories.

In the meantime I have the honour of sending you a copy of my Inaugural Speech on the Kathedersocialism.[3] And while I humbly beg pardon for the faults, which I may have made in writing a language, uncommon to me, I pray you to believe me,

dear Sir,

your most respectful,

J. d'Aulnis

549.   G. ROLLESTON[1] TO W. S. JEVONS

Oxford, Monday
Sept 30, 1878

Dear Sir,

Seeing your name down amongst those of the Librarians Association[2] members who are coming here, I venture to ask you to come to discuss at my house on Wednesday at 6.30 p.m. *en route* for the Museum Soirée my house being close to that Building.

Though I have not the advantage of your personal acquaintance, I have a very considerable one of acquaintance with your writings, and upon that acquaintance (which I value very much) I presume thus to write.

Yours very truly,

George Rolleston

---

[2] Schedule C of the United Kingdom Income Tax at this time included all incomes derived from dividends in the public funds and in foreign government securities. It had been introduced by Peel in 1842 at the time of the revival of the general income tax.

[3] *Het Katheder − socialisme* door Johan d'Aulnis de Bourouill.

[1] George Rolleston (1829−81), Fellow of Pembroke College, Oxford, 1851; physician to the British civil hospital at Smyrna, 1855, and in 1857 to the Radcliffe Infirmary, Oxford; Linacre Professor of Anatomy and Physiology in the University of Oxford, 1860.

[2] i.e. the Library Association, whose conference at Oxford Jevons was attending. Cf. LJ, p. 390.

550.   W. S. JEVONS TO HARRIET JEVONS
[LJN, 390]

Clarendon Hotel,
Oxford, 2d October 1878.

. . . We are having a pleasant meeting on the whole, and I find some friends among the librarians. . . . Mr. Coxe, the Bodleian librarian,[1] is a very pleasant old man, and we had rather a good meeting last night, after the dinner. At the Rector's dinner I sat next to Professor Max Müller,[2] whom I was glad to get acquainted with. To-night I am to dine with Professor Rolleston. I think, when I get home, I will begin to consider the question of a catalogue of my books. If we had cards printed, I think you could gradually get on with it, and ultimately there would be great use in it.

Oxford decidedly surpasses Cambridge in the number and beauty of the colleges. The new buildings, too, in some cases are very fine, especially Waterhouse's Balliol College,[3] which I admired very much before knowing what it was. . . .

I shall make a point of being at Paris on the night of the 4th.[4]

Does the 'boy' miss me? . . .

551.   W. S. JEVONS TO HARRIET JEVONS
[LJP, 390−1]

Clarendon Hotel Oxford
3 Oct 78

My dearest

We had a decidedly pleasant day here yesterday the members of the Assoc[n] becoming better acquainted with each other as far as I am concerned. We had a very lively dinner at Prof. Rolleston's with he and Rogers[1] who took the other end of the table being good hosts. The Soirée afterwards in the Museum was also pleasing owing to the beauty of the

[1] Henry Octavius Coxe (1811−81), palaeographer; sub-Chairman, 1838−60, and Librarian, 1860−81, Bodleian Library, Oxford.

[2] Friedrich Max-Müller (1823−1900), orientalist and philologist; born and educated in Germany, he came to England in 1846. Taylorian Professor of Modern European Languages in the University of Oxford, 1854−68; first Professor of Comparative Philology at Oxford, 1868−1900; Curator of the Bodleian Library, 1856−63 and 1881−94.

[3] Balliol College, Oxford, had been enlarged between 1854 and 1870 by replacing the east and south sides of the front Quadrangle with new buildings designed by Alfred Waterhouse. See H. W. Carless Davis, *A History of Balliol College* (Oxford, 1963).

[4] Jevons planned to visit the International Exposition there.

[1] Possibly J. E. Thorold Rogers. See Vol. III, Letter 196, n. 1, p. 47.

building which however was only very partially lighted up. In the afternoon we visited Balliol College Dr. Jowett[2] showing us over the new Hall & Chapel and the new reading Room established in the old dining Hall in addition to the old library. In the reading room I was naturally pleased to find two copies of the first Ed of the Principles[3] placed side by side. It is not often a library has two identical copies of a book of that sort ordered. As far as I can make out my Principles is really becoming the text book here, tho a student is not expected to read more than certain selected chapters. Dr. Malet[4] the librarian of Dublin University told me that it was formally adopted as the text book in Dublin, & when the other Universities follow we ought to have a steady sale for years to come. Two of the booksellers here have the second Ed. in their windows – Mill's reputation is said to be rapidly declining in Oxford, in fact they say he is almost overlooked in the examinations.

After Balliol we went to All Souls where there are fine libraries & where they gave us old ale & very good tea.

I am going to breakfast this morning with one of the secretaries of the Assoc[n] & must therefore close. I think I shall go to Dover this afternoon but have not yet looked out the trains.

Ever yours
W. S. Jevons.

P.S. 3 pm. I am going to London by the 4:10 pm train & then to Dover by the 8 20 or thereabouts.

I have some prospect of making important price lists discoveries in the Bodleian.

552.   T. C. HORSFALL[1] TO W. S. JEVONS

Holm Acre
Altrincham
Octr. 13. 1878.

Dear Sir,

I have only this evening read your paper in the "Contemporary Review" of this month.[2] You will be glad to hear that in Manchester and

---

[2] Benjamin Jowett (1817–93), Fellow of Balliol College, 1838; Master of Balliol, 1870–93; Regius Professor of Greek in the University of Oxford, 1855.

[3] W. S. Jevons, *The Principles of Science, A Treatise on Logic and Scientific Method* (1874).

[4] John Adam Malet (d. 1879), educated at Trinity College, Dublin; B.A. 1830; M.A. 1838; Librarian of the College from 1869 until his death; author of *A Catalogue of the Roman Silver Coins in the Library of Trinity College, Dublin* (1839).

[1] Thomas Coglan Horsfall (1841–1916), town-planning pioneer; President of the Manchester Art Museum and University Settlement; M.A. (Hon.) Victoria University, 1902; member of the Manchester Statistical Society and of the Manchester and Salford Sanitary Association; author of many papers and pamphlets on education, public health, housing and town planning.

Salford we are trying to do several of the things you recommend. I have long urged the manager of the Coffee Tavern to open a large hall, shaped like the Free Trade Hall, filled with small tables & chairs – large enough to hold two or three thousand people – in Ancoats or Miles Platting to have the best possible band every evening & to sell good coffee, tea, cocoa and fruit drinks. We have promise already of £2000 or thereabouts though the scheme has not been mentioned to many people. There will be some delay in getting the scheme carried out as Colvile[3] is opposed to Sunday opening which I am determined to have.

Messrs. E. Armitage & Sons have opened this summer a large playground in Pendleton, fitted up with swings, seesaws, & horizontal and parallel bars. Whenever I pass it I see dozens of children and young people playing there. To learn to play together without quarrelling is a most valuable kind of training. I have today been writing to the Mayor of Salford begging him to ask the Town council to form playgrounds partly at the cost of the rates partly from a fund to be raised by the richer residents to which I offer to give £250.

I send you some papers relating to a museum which we are trying to form in Manchester and shall form eventually though the panic which seems to be beginning will make our rate of progress very slow. I heartily wish London had not taken you from us. Your help would be very valuable for all our schemes.

I am, dear Sir,
Yours Truly
T. C. Horsfall.

Professor Stanley Jevons.

P. S. I send the smaller of the two pamphlets only for the sake of the last seven pages. The rest contains the matter which is in the larger pamphlet in an abbreviated form.

553. A. FROUT DE FONTPERTUIS TO W. S. JEVONS

Paris. 16 octobre 1878

Cher Monsieur,

J'ai reçu la notice en *épreuve* que vous avez bien voulu consacrer dans le Journal de la "Statistical Society" à mes petits livres "Le Japon et la

---

[2] 'Amusements of the People', *Contemporary Review*, 33 (1878) 498–513; reprinted in *Methods*, pp. 1–27.

[3] Charles Robert Colvile (1815–86), M.P. for South Derbyshire, 1841–59 and 1865–8; Sheriff of Derbyshire, 1874.

Chine" et "l'Inde Britannique", de la collection des *Pays étrangers à l'Exposition*.[1]

Je vous remercie très sincèrement des choses si aimables que vous y dites de moi et de mon talent, que vous me semblez bien un peu surfaire, et je vous serais obligé de me faire parvenir, en temps et lieu, si cela vous est possible, un exemplaire du no. du "Journal", qui renfermera la dite notice. Les appréciations et les témoignages d'un homme de votre haute valeur me sont précieux, et ils me consolent de certains déboires et de certains ennuis auxquels ma vie d'écriváin militant est parfois sujette.

J'ai vu sur la couverture de *la Revue Scientifique* que la maison Germer – Baillière avait fait traduire votre "Primer of Political Economy".[2] J'en avais montré l'exemplaire que vous m'aviez envoyé vous-même à M. Joseph Garnier, qui dirige le *Journal des Economistes* et quelque peu quoi qu' "in partibus" la librairie de Melle Guillaumin. Il me pria de le lui laisser, afin qu'il l'examinât; ce à quoi je consentis d'autant plus volontiers que je n'étais pas sans un secret espoir qu'il songerait à le faire traduire, tâche dont je me serais personnellement volontiers chargé moi-même. Mais, j'ai compris plus tard que par des raisons qui d'ailleurs m'étaient personnelles ni au livre ni à son auteur, cela ne rentrait pas dans ses intentions. Je lui ai alors redemandé votre "Pamphlet"; et il me répond invariablement qu'il me l'apportera lors de la première occasion. Par malheur, M. J. Garnier met si peu d'ordre dans ses papiers que j'ai tout lieu de craindre qu'on l'y retrouvera bien mais lorsqu'on fera son inventaire mortuaire, ce que je l'espère bien et de tout mon coeur n'aura pas lieu d'ici à longtemps encore. Je tiens cependant beaucoup à votre "Primer", d'autant que vous me l'aviez transmis avec une mention personnelle et je vous trouverais fort aimable de m'en faire parvenir un second exemplaire.

Veuillez agréer, cher Monsieur,

La nouvelle expression de mes meilleurs sentiments

Ad. F. de Fontpertuis

Je me suis aperçu – Mais sans doute vous vous en êtes aperçu vous-même aussi – que dans la dite épreuve on avait estropié mon double nom en écrivant d'une part *Front* au lieu de *Frout* et de l'autre *Fontpertius* au lieu de *Fontpertuis*.

---

[1] See above, Letter 542, n. 1, p. 276. In *JRSS*, 41 (1878) 561, there is a paragraph noticing these two works by Frout de Fontpertuis and Clovis Lamarre. The notice was unsigned but presumably written by Jevons.

[2] *L'Economie politique*, par W. Stanley Jevons, traduite par Henri Gravez, ingénieur, Paris, Librairie Germer Baillière et Cie, 1878.

554. L. WALRAS TO W. S. JEVONS
    [FW]

Ouchy sous Lausanne,
17 octobre 1878[1]

Cher Monsieur,

Vous ne trouverez pas encore votre Bibliographie dans le dernier numéro du *Journal des Economistes*. J'en ai corrigé les épreuves il y a six semaines; mais l'"*abondance des matières*", comme on dit, aura sans doute empêché à deux reprises de la faire passer. Quand j'étais au Collège, nous disions de la nourriture qu'on nous y donnait qu'elle était fort peu abondante et que, pour cette raison, elle n'était pas trop malsaine. Il en est, paraît-il, autrement au *Journal des Economistes*, les matières y sont aussi abondantes que détestables.

La découverte, dont vous me parlez, de l'ouvrage de Gossen est quelque chose de tout à fait important. Je me suis occupé immédiatement de faire chercher le volume en Allemagne; mais je n'ai pas encore réussi à me le procurer. Dès que je l'aurai entre les mains, je l'étudierai avec soin en le lisant avec un de mes collègues, professeur de mathématiques et sachant bien l'allemand. Nous verrons ensuite le parti à tirer de ce nouvel incident. Il sera grand si, comme vous le dites, l'ouvrage contient plusieurs des points principaux de notre théorie nettement établis. Pour ma part, je me fais une fête de consacrer à cet essai un article spécial et de révéler à ces Messieurs les allemands qui savent tout, un livre lumineux, publié chez eux et dont ils n'ont nulle connaissance.

Ne pensez-vous pas que la publication dans la *Bibliothèque scientifique internationale* de Germer-Bailliere d'un volume d'*Economie politique mathématique* et qui contiendrait cet ouvrage de Gossen s'il n'est pas trop considérable, le vôtre et mes quatre mémoires, serait favorable au progrès de la théorie nouvelle? Et ne seriez-vous pas, en raison du succès de votre beau livre sur la Monnaie, paru dans cette collection et arrivé, je crois, déjà à la 2e édition, en position de proposer la chose à cet éditeur? Je me chargerais de la traduction française; vous de faire ou de surveiller la traduction anglaise. Et il resterait à trouver un traducteur allemand pour votre *Theory* et mes *Mémoires*, ce qui ne me serait pas difficile. C'est une idée qui m'est venue et que je vous suggère un peu en l'air puisque je n'ai pas encore lu Gossen, mais dont nous reparlerons en temps et lieu.

M. d'Aulnis qui m'a écrit, me fait sérieusement espérer sa visite pour les vacances prochaines. Il la ferait, je crois, certainement, s'il avait la certitude de vous rencontrer ici. Pensez donc aussi, je vous prie, à ce

---

[1] This is another letter of which the original no longer survives in the Jevons Papers: so again the text here follows that in Jaffé, *Walras Correspondence*, I, 585, based on the draft in Fonds Walras, FW, 278/12.

projet d'un petit congrès où nous pourrions discuter ensemble bien des idées et arrêter peut-être quelques résolutions.

Je suis, Cher Monsieur, tout à vous

Léon Walras

555. W. S. JEVONS TO L. WALRAS
[FW]

Hampstead Heath London N.W.
31 October 1878

My dear Sir,

I thank you for your letter of 17th inst. and for the trouble which you are taking to insert the Bibliography in the *Journal des Economistes*. I hope you will succeed in getting it printed in the next month or two.

I do not get on much with my new edition, being much occupied in other studies and writings, but I hope soon to get to work at it, and get it ready for the press.

Having inquired from Messrs MacMillan, they agree to my increasing the bulk of the book if I think proper, and I hope to be able to reprint in the original French, with your permission, already kindly given, some parts of your Memoirs. As almost all educated Englishmen read French, it is better to leave your writings in your own French, not only to save the labour of translation but to ensure the accuracy of meaning. Moreover it would be unfeasible to improve upon the perspicuity and elegance of a French scientific work such as yours.

As to the International Series there has been only a single new volume issued in England for one or two years back and I doubt whether the English publishers would venture upon so scientific a subject as the theory of P.E. But it would be easy for you to ascertain whether the French publishers of the Series Messrs. Germer-Baillière et Cie regard your idea favourably.

How would it be if when my new edition is in print you were to publish a new edition of your work appending a translation of mine together with a translation of the Bibliography improved, abridged or varied as might be desirable. We might treat the new edition as in some degree a joint production.

It would have given me much pleasure to meet yourself as also Mr. D'Aulnis but I fear there is little chance of my getting so far as Lausanne at present. My college duties almost forbid it. Thanking you for your kind invitation I am

Yours faithfully
W. Stanley Jevons.

556. W. S. JEVONS TO T. E. JEVONS
[LJN, 391–2]

University of London,
Burlington Gardens, W.,
31st October 1878.

. . . As usual, I seize a vacant hour in the B. A. examination to answer your last letter. I have been much pleased to hear about your country retreat in the Adirondacks. . . . It must much resemble my Norwegian life, barring the shooting, and barring also the interest and variety that attends the travelling from inn to inn in Norway. We must go there on the next opportunity. As to my visiting America, the expense, length of voyage, heat of the climate, etc., render such a trip scarcely practicable.

I have now published my article on the Amusements of the People in the *Contemporary Review*. It is partly the outcome of our investigations in Denmark and elsewhere. I have not seen much notice of it in the press, though there have been several articles, I believe. Various friends have expressed themselves much pleased with it. The *Spectator* remarks that it is *trite*, which, perhaps, is a somewhat fair criticism. [1]

I have, as usual, got a series of books and articles on hand, all of which want writing immediately, and I sometimes feel desperate about ever getting them done. But the sale of the books is certainly encouraging; the *Principles* is soon to be in the third edition, and is adopted as a text-book at two or more universities.

I hope your family are all well and flourishing as much as ever. It is a blessing to have such fine healthy children. Ours are in capital health, so far, and both get on very well, except that they will quarrel and fight, even at their tender age.

We have now got into the thick of the normal sun-spot crisis, and when this is over, there will, I hope, be a rapid recovery of trade. [2] I trust you will have a harvest these next few years. . . .

---

[1] The *Spectator*, 5 October 1878, p. 1246:
'. . . a paper on "The Amusements of the People", by Mr. Stanley Jevons . . . strikes us as rather trite, except in its key-note, that the aristocracy are putting down popular amusement too rapidly. Mr. Jevons's advice to give the people music may be sound, but where is the evidence that the people wish for it, in place of more objectionable entertainment? Why, in fact, does not the people, if it would like music, subscribe its twopences, and have music?'

[2] Cf. below, Letter 558, p. 293 and Vol. V, Letter 636A.

557.   C. L. CORKRAN[1] TO W. S. JEVONS

28 Colveston Crescent N. E.

31 Oct[r] 1878

My dear Sir

Since I had the pleasure of meeting you at the Manor House Eastbourne, I have had the additional pleasure of reading your very valuable paper on Amusements for the people. I need hardly say how largely I concur in the views you have propounded, & the interesting illustrations you have given, drawn from your experiences abroad of the power of really good music to refine & amuse the people at one & the same time. Our efforts in London in this respect, are very fitful. Climate and distance have much to do as obstacles to open air concerts in the Metropolis. Some time ago, I broached to a very active Broad Church vicar the founding of a Recreation Society in the East of London to combine the scattered resources of individual societys, religious & otherwise, & to unite them as one body for that purpose of having systematic & efficient means of popular recreation, including of course good music & *illustrated* lectures & c. The suggestion, like many others fell through. But could not *you* do something in this way, based on the views you have published? Would it not be possible, even easy to combine & utilise a vast amount of musical & other talent for the ends you propose? It is a pity your excellent suggestions should drop through for want of practical effort to carry them into effect.

We shall have a gathering on Wednesday Evening next (see the enclosed)[2] & it would give us much pleasure to see you present. M[r] Laurence Scott[3] is giving me very valuable aid at the Mission.

Very faithfully yours

C. L. Corkran.

W. S. Jevons Esq.

---

[1] Charles Loftus Corkran (1813–1901), Unitarian minister; worked for the London Domestic Mission Society at the Spicer Street Mission in Spitalfields, 1848–79 (cf. Vol. I, pp. 68, n. 3, and 89, n. 4). A strong advocate of temperance, he spent the early part of his life and career in Ireland before moving to London and later Norwich where he worked for Unitarian newspapers.

[2] This 'enclosure' is no longer with the original manuscript.

[3] Lawrence Scott (1844–1930), Unitarian minister, third son of Russell Scott. Cf. above, Letter 538, n. 1, p. 271.

558. W. S. JEVONS TO T. E. JEVONS
[LJN, 392-3]

University of London,
Burlington Gardens,
14th November 1878.

. . . I was much pleased with your last cheerful letter, as it seems to show that you are all well and fairly prosperous. I hope business is better in New York than England, and that you have not sufferred from the late great fall in corn and cotton. In any case, I trust that there is a good time coming now that the normal crisis is past.

I have just written an article on crises, for *Nature*,[1] and if I can, will send you a copy; but the American post office is so badly managed that there is little inducement to send papers or books. I have never received the *Evening Post* you sent.

My theory of crises has the appearance of being a little too ingenious, and it requires some boldness to publish it without more evidence. But I have great confidence in its substantial truth, and when I have worked the thing out more, shall perhaps write an article for the *Princeton Review* on the subject, though when I can do it must remain uncertain.[2]

I am glad you approve my Amusements article. I intend, in the course of time, to treat a whole series of similar social subjects, but each article requires much consideration and reading, and I can only get on slowly. The press has not noticed the article much here, but I have heard of numbers of persons privately who read it with approbation.

About politics, I confess myself in a fog. Sometimes I think Beaconsfield deserves hanging, and at other times I rather admire his cool and daring assertion of British power. I prefer to leave *la haute politique* alone, as a subject which admits of no scientific treatment. I have enough to think and write about which I can somewhat understand, without troubling myself about things which I cannot understand.

I have just had a pleasant lunch at my little club in Savile Row[3] with

---

[1] 'Commercial Crises and Sun-Spots', *Nature*, 14 November 1878, pp. 33–7; reprinted in *Investigations*, pp. 221–35. This article was written shortly after the collapse of the City of Glasgow Bank on 2 October had precipitated a financial crisis. Although mostly concerned to point out the correspondence between earlier cycles and J. A. Broun's new estimate for the sun spot cycle of 10.45 years, Jevons did not fail to note that 'the present crisis is at least partly due to the involvement of the City of Glasgow Bank in the India trade, through the medium of some of their chief debtors. Thus the crisis of 1878 is clearly connected with the recent famines in India and China, and these famines are confidently attributed to solar disturbance' (loc. cit., p. 232). Cf. above, Letter 540, n. 1, and below, Letter 566.

[2] Cf. below, Letter 567, p. 304.

[3] Presumably the Scientific Club Cf. above, Letter 431, p. 116.

Harry Roscoe and Huggins[4] the astronomer. They are agitated by the supposed discovery of Lockyer that the elements can be decomposed. Harry has been going over the experiments with Lockyer at South Kensington, but is going to investigate the matter more at Manchester. My impression is, it is a mistake, and that Lockyer will have to draw in his horns, *mais nous verrons*.[5] . . .

559.   A. C. WOOTTON[1] TO W. S. JEVONS

Grove House,
Shacklewell Lane,
Stoke Newington
London.

Professor W. Stanley Jevons.   Nov. 15, 1878

Dear sir,

I read today with much interest your article in *Nature* on "Commercial Crises and Sun-spots".[2] In the chance that the following may be of use to you I send it.

I have in my library some old French magazines. In one of these

---

[4] Sir William Huggins (1824–1910), founder of the science of astrophysics; President of the Royal Astronomical Society, 1900–5. Of private means, he built his own observatory at Tulse Hill in 1855, from which he carried out studies of the physical constitution of the stars and planets.

[5] Investigations into the nature and evolution of matter were a major preoccupation of physicists and chemists from the early eighteen-seventies onwards, and during this period the foundations of twentieth-century developments were laid. The results of Lockyer's researches on this subject, though proved after his death to have been partially correct, found little support at this time among his fellow physicists. However, they were received more sympathetically by chemists, notably H. E. Roscoe, who gave him considerable material assistance. Important advances had been made in chemistry towards resolving the confusion surrounding concepts of elements, atoms and molecules and by this date many chemists had come to accept the atomic theory of matter.

Lockyer had begun spectroscopic experiments in the early years of the decade in the belief that the spectrum of each element should always have the same appearance. When this proved not to be the case, he examined the factors causing variation and concluded that if molecules could be broken up into atoms on heating, it followed that atoms in turn could be broken down at still higher temperatures. Roscoe and other friends of Lockyer were unhappy about the assumptions underlying this 'dissociation hypothesis'; nevertheless Lockyer determined to publish it. On 12 December 1878, before a packed and hostile meeting of the Royal Society, he presented his paper 'Researches in Spectrum Analysis in connexion with the Spectrum of the Sun. No VII: Discussion of the Working Hypothesis that the so-called Elements are Compound Bodies', *Proceedings of the Royal Society*, 28 (1879) 157–80.

Roscoe repeated Lockyer's experiments and found that some of his results had been based on impure samples, which tended to discredit Lockyer's evidence in the eyes of chemists. Jevons was therefore proved correct in the short term. Lockyer nevertheless did not 'draw in his horns' and continued to work on the dissociation hypothesis despite widespread opposition. For a full account of Lockyer's ideas on matter and their reception, see A. J. Meadows, *Science and Controversy* (1972) pp. 135–74.

[1] Alfred Charles Wootton (d. 1910), author of *The Chronicles of Pharmacy*, 2 vols (1910).

[2] See above, Letter 558, p. 293.

entitled "Nouvelles de la République des Lettres"[3] for October *1701* (one of the years which you query) I find a review of a work thus entitled "Mémoires pour le Rétablissement du Commerce en France. Redigés par le dr. Jean le Pelletier, ancien juge Consul" &c.[4] The work was probably published at Rouen. The review thus commences "L'auteur de cet ouvrage ne dissimule point le mauvais état où se trouve le Commerce en France, la diminution des revenus du Roi, et la misère des Peuples". The review goes on to say that he (the author) believes the revival of Commerce in France to be *not impossible* explains what he considers are the causes and suggests certain remedies.

If you wd. like to see this work – probably you have already examined it – I shall have pleasure in forwarding it.

With great respect, I remain dear sir,
Yours faithfully,
A. C. Wootton.

560. HYDE CLARKE TO W. S. JEVONS

32 St. George's Square, S.W.
18th Nov. 1878

My dear Sir,

In your able paper on Commercial Crises and Sunspots one thing that particularly strikes me is your recommendation that observatories shall be formed at various points.[1]

What has struck me as a great difficulty has been the apparent impossibility of predicting the epochs of maxima and minima. Looking however, to the altered conditions of our trade, which is now carried on all over the world, and particularly looking at the passage of the last great drought, it appears possible that we may by means such as you propose obtain a forecast.

At the present moment the tail of the drought prevents the recovery of trade in many producing and consuming countries of the world, and before reading your paper I had addressed a note to Nature, on this subject.[2]

[3] *Nouvelles de la République des lettres*: A review published in Amsterdam between 1684 and 1718, founded by Boyle and carried on by La Roque Barrin, Jacques Bernard and Jean Leclerc. Cf. Hatin, *Bibliographie Historique et Critique de la Presse Périodique Française* (1866) pp. 33–4.

[4] Jean le Pelletier, *Mémoires pour le rétablissement du commerce en France*, redigés par le Sr. Jean le Pelletier (163?–1701).

[1] 'Commercial Crises and Sun-Spots', Part 1 – 'Solar observatories ought to be established on the table-lands of Quito or Cuzco, in Cashmere, in Piazzie Smith's observatory on the Peak of Teneriffe, in Central Australia, or wherever else the sun can be observed most free from atmospheric opacity' – *Investigations*, p. 235. Cf. also Vol. V, Letter 652.

[2] Letter published in *Nature*, 21 November 1878, p. 53.

With regard to an observatory in Ecuador it is hopeless, but in Peru, although on account of financial embarrassments it cannot now be proposed, it may at some not distant date be realised. As to Cashmere the Indian government ought to look to this, but there is no more reliance on them, than on the tyrant in possession. The country ought never to have been placed in his clutches nor be left in them.

Would a station in the Cerro de Pasco be suitable for your purposes? If so something might perhaps be effected.

If you can avoid calling me Doctor I shall be glad, for I find that people are indisposed to treat me as a practical man if I am a Colonel or a Doctor.[3]

Yours faithfully,
Hyde Clarke

Professor W. Stanley Jevons.

561.   C. PIAZZI SMYTH[1] TO W. S. JEVONS

Royal Observatory
EDINBURGH

Nov. 18 1878

Dear Sir,

What a masterly paper you have contributed to last Week's Nature on the Sun-radiations question, as well for what it, the paper, sets forth in its, or your, own more special path of the history of mercantile mania, as for the jobation given to astronomers and meteorologists for attending to so many a trifle and leaving "the great eye and soul of all physical life" to vary unattended to through amounts of light and heat that would swallow up all that we receive of both from every other known source, both external and internal to the earth.

One of your remarks *particularly* struck me; viz. that Pouillet did not go on with his measures of the direct solar radiation after 1837–8, because he thought it a constant quantity.[2] That was exactly what Prof. J. D.

---

[3] In the paper cited Jevons had included a number of the points made in Hyde Clarke's letter to him of 31 August 1878 (see above, Letter 541, p. 274), referring several times to 'Dr Hyde Clarke'.

[1] Charles Piazzi Smyth (1819–1900), assistant at the Royal Observatory, Cape of Good Hope, 1835; Astronomer Royal for Scotland, 1845–88.

[2] 'Pouillet showed me long ago (1838) how the absolute heating power of the sun's rays might be accurately determined by his Pyrheliometer. . . . But I have never heard that his experiments have been repeated . . . I fancy that physicists still depend upon Pouillet's observations in 1837 and 1838 for one of the most important constants of the solar system . . . Pouillet indeed assumed that the heating power of the sun's rays is a constant quantity, which accounts for his not continuing the solar observations . . . ' Jevons, 'Commercial Crises and Sun-Spots', *Nature*, 14 November 1878, p. 36. Cf. also Vol. II, Letter 110, n. 10, p. 306.

Forbes[3] did, about the same time with the first four years of the earth thermometer observations at this Obs[y]. But fortunately I kept them up after he had done with them; and when there was a series of 33 consecutive years to look at, – behold, (in the Vol. which I beg your acceptance of per Messrs Williams and Norgate),[4] – what a regular undulation of 10 to 11 years thrice repeated![5] And they were merely earth-thermometers, very indirectly indeed giving a measure of the real radiation of the sun from moment to moment, or even month to month

I remain

Yours very truly

Piazzi Smyth

562.   W. S. JEVONS TO A. MACMILLAN
       [MA]

2 The Chestnuts,
West Heath,
Hampstead N.W.
1 Dec. 1878

Dear Mr. Macmillan,

I am desirous of learning whether you would undertake to publish the work of the *Index Society*[1] in which I am much interested. This Society, as you perhaps know has undertaken to provide indexes to a number of historical, scientific and other works which are in want of such means of reference and in several other ways to render literature as accessible and

[3] James David Forbes (1809–68), Scottish physicist; Professor of Natural Philosophy, University of Edinburgh, 1833–60; Principal of the United College, St Andrews, from 1860 until his death; carried out important research on glaciers and heat radiation; in 1837 began research with four earth-thermometers sunk into the rock at Calton Hill, Edinburgh.

[4] Edmund Sydney Williams (1817–91) and Frederick Norgate, booksellers at Henrietta Street, Covent Garden, and Edinburgh, 1843–91.

[5] On 7 April 1870 Piazzi Smyth had presented a paper 'On Supra-annual Cycles of Temperature in the Earth's Surface-Crust', before the Royal Society (*Proceedings*, 18 (1870) 311–12) in which he discussed the results of the earth-thermometer observations carried out in Edinburgh between 1837 and 1869. These showed a marked eleven-year cycle in earth temperatures which Smyth suggested might be connected with sun-spot activity. After further research he published an expanded version, 'Observations of the Earth-Thermometers at the Royal Observatory, Edinburgh, from January 1870 to September 1876; also, a Review of the whole series from their commencement in 1837 to their termination in 1876', *Astronomical Observations made at the Royal Observatory, Edinburgh . . . 1870–77* (Edinburgh, 1877), XIV, 643 ff.

[1] The Index Society, founded in 1878 with the object of preparing indexes for standard works; incorporated with the British Record Society in 1891.

The publication of the early work of the Society was not undertaken by Macmillan, but by Longmans and Co. According to the first *Annual Report of the Committee* (1879) Jevons had undertaken 'ultimately to prepare a Handbook to the Literature of Political Economy' for the Society – a task which he had apparently not begun at the time of his death.

useful as possible. The society has barely existed a year I think and yet has about 170 members at a guinea each, and we hope by degrees to become much stronger.

The first publication consists of a pamphlet by the energetic honorary secretary Mr. H. B. Wheatley[2] illustrating the work of the society. I send a copy by book-post, and you will find it contains a list of members and committee. You will find that Mr. Grove[3] is one of our members as also Mr. Hutt.[4] If it prospers as we hope, the society will be of immense benefit to literature.

The subscribers will of course receive copies of the works direct, but it is desired to offer them for sale also to the public at large, and the society much desire that you would agree to publish them on commission without any pecuniary risk on your part. I have discussed the matter somewhat with Dr. Jack, but would now like to know whether you would be willing to lend your assistance to the Society to the extent proposed. The details might readily be settled subsequently.

I get on slowly with Adam Smith, but am proposing to put the new edition of the "Theory of Pol Econ" in the printers hands after Christmas.

I am yours faithfully,

W. S. Jevons

563.   L. BODIO TO W. S. JEVONS

Ministero di agra. e commercio

Dear Sir,

Profr. Francis Walker,[1] in his recent Work on "Money" (Chap. XII, §1), treating of the relation of Token-Money to Standard-Money, refers [to][2] some considerations of Colonel Tomline M.P.[3] and Mr. Hubbard[4] on the question.

[2] Harry Benjamin Wheatley (1838–1917), Clerk to the Royal Society, 1861–79, and assistant to the Royal Society of Arts. One of the founders of the Early English Text Society; produced a complete edition of Samuel Pepys's *Journal*, 1893–7. The pamphlet referred to by Jevons was Wheatley's *What is an Index?*

[3] [Sir] George Grove (1820–90), editor of *Macmillan's Magazine* from 1867 to 1883; first Director of the Royal College of Music; editor of the *Dictionary of Music and Musicians*, 4 vols (1878–89).

[4] Possibly William Wyatt Hutt, who assisted in the preparation of the catalogue of manuscripts in the Cambridge University Library, 1856.

[1] Francis Amasa Walker (1840–97), Professor of Political Economy at the Sheffield Scientific School of Yale College, 1872; president of the Massachusetts Institute of Technology, 1881. Walker represented the United States at the International Monetary Conference in Paris in 1878 and this, together with the publication in the same year of his treatise *Money*, secured him an important place in monetary discussions in ensuing years.

[2] Omitted in the original manuscript.

[3] George Tomline (1812–89), commissioned in the Life Guards but bought himself out in 1836; M.P. for Sudbury, 1840–1, Shrewsbury, 1841–7 and 1852–68, and for Great Grimsby, 1868–74. Honorary Colonel of the Royal North Lincoln Militia from 1858 until his death.

For my study purposes, I would know precisely the different arguments exposed by Mr. Tomline in sustaining his assertions.

I should be very obliged to you, if you could suggest to me a publication in which I may find the text of Mr. Tomline's argument, quoted by Mr. Walker.[5]

Very faithfully,
L. Bodio
Rome 3 December 1878

P. S. I have forwarded to your adress* the Atlas of the "Monografia di Roma e Campagna Romana";[6] I will soon send you the text-book of the Monograph;

564. R. ADAMSON TO W. S. JEVONS

60 Parsonage road,
5th Dec. 1878.

Dear Jevons,

I have only now got time to write you about your 'sun spot' evidence. The matter seems to me very complicated, and I do not at all feel in a position to give any very definite opinion about it. One thing at least may be taken for granted; the meterological changes which are indicated by the variations of sun spots cannot be without influence on economic phenomena, & it is a natural inference that if these changes are periodic,

---

[4] John Gellibrand Hubbard, first Baron Addington (1805–89); M.P. for Buckingham, 1859–68, and City of London, 1874–87; writer on currency and tax questions.

[5] In the section of his book referred to by Bodio Walker discussed the complaint that 'the wealthy and well-to-do receive their incomes in the principal coin of the country which is of full weight and fineness, the poor are paid in coins which contain only a part, and perhaps a small part, of the metal which would be worth the sum for which they are made a tender by law. This complaint, sometimes heard among labourers, was recently given a wider hearing through Col Tomline . . . The answer of Mr Hubbard appears to be conclusive, so long as such billon or token money is not issued to excess. "It is quite true," says Mr Hubbard, "that silver, rather than gold, is the medium through which the wages of the labouring classes are paid but to show that the labouring classes are injured by the Mint regulations it must be demonstrated that the shilling they now receive commands a smaller quantity of the necessities of life than would a shilling coined as an integral measure of value."' (loc. cit. 219).

Walker here did not correctly present the position taken by Tomline, as stated in the latter's pamphlet. *A Free Mint: addressed to all Ratepayers and Working Men* (1871). Tomline was concerned, not with excess, but with deficiency of token coinage – 'Millions ask for work; work is plentiful, but coins to pay for it are scarce'. He sent silver bullion to the Mint, and when the Acting Master refused to coin it for him charged – 'You do a serious injury to poor men who are willing to work, for whom I can find employment, and whom I desire to pay in shillings and sovereigns' (*A Free Mint*, p. 8). Tomline's ideas about reducing unemployment by increasing the supply of token money drew sarcastic comment from Jevons in the preface to his own book on *Money* (p. vii).

[6] *Monografia statistica della Città di Roma e Campagna Romana, presentata all' Esposizione universale di Parigi 1878. Annesse – Carte topografiche, idrografiche e geologiche.*

then the effects will show *some* corresponding periodicity. Apart from the difficulty of stating what is the particular mode in which the one set of facts may be connected with the other – and here it seems to me somewhat hazardous to cast the Indian trade as specially influential – there now come forward the questions of fact: Have we accurately determined the sun spot series? Have we accurately determined the cycle of crises? Is there a definite correspondence between the two?

With regard to (1) I can say little. Let it be supposed that the determination is accurate, though as is evident from your figures, a very slight change in the period would soon bring out discrepancy between the spots & crises. With regard to (2) I should have liked to see from you, as probably you alone could give, a more exact statement than we yet have of what constitutes a crisis. Tooke, as you are aware denies that some of the commercial depressions ordinarily called crises, e.g. 1836, 39, can be so described,[1] and many have held that 1866 could not in any way be regarded as similar in kind to 1847 & 57.

You guard yourself, of course, by saying that crises are due to many causes, but still you appear to imply that the deep, widespreading commercial disturbances, *properly* called crises, are decennial.
I must say that as yet the evidence does not seem quite sufficient to support this, nor do I think that if these crises are definitely connected with the decennial sun spot periods, such evidence could be forthcoming. Unless the physical circumstances connected with these sun spots be of such overwhelming force as to outweigh the other factors in a crisis, I cannot think that in the long development of trade & with increasing organisation of commerce, the periods of fluctuation would remain identical. I should rather expect that they would show a tendency towards increase of length.

The comparative theory of crises, such eg. as I find very perfunctorily in Juglar,[2] & with more care in Max Wirth,[3] seems to disclose no invariable conditions, & it is I think quite remarkable that we should be able to trace no exact periodicity in the prices or quantities of corn. So far as I can judge the American crises resemble the English, but have special features. So with the continental.

[1] Tooke and Newmarch, *A History of Prices and of the State of the Circulation from 1792 to 1856,* 6 vols (1838–57) 1, 258–65.

[2] Clément Juglar (1819–1905), trained as a physician but turned to the study of political economy in 1848. In 1862 he published *Des Crises Commerciales et de leur Retour Périodique en France, en Angleterre et aux Etats Unis.* Adamson's comment seems to undervalue Juglar's work, which is now generally regarded as of fundamental importance in the evolution of ideas about the business cycle. Cf. Schumpeter, *History of Economic Analysis* (1954) pp. 1123–4.

[3] Max Wirth (1822–1900), *Geschichte der Handelskrisen* (Frankfurt-on-Main, 1858). Wirth's approach relied on classification of crises (into credit crises, capital crises, etc.) but contained little analysis.

(3)   As to the connexion between the two that must partly stand or fall with the determination of the crises, but there is one point I do not observe you say anything about. To what condition of the sun spots, maximum or minimum do the crises correspond? If these maxima & minima of spots follow a simple law, that is if there is only the cycle of 10 + years, the crises should always correspond with a max. or a min., but if there were some larger law, it might happen that a crisis (supposing these to be decennial strictly) should coincide with a max, while another coincides with a min. Is there any evidence on this point? Can you shew that a crisis always corr. to one definite state of the sun spots?

With regard to your historical evidence, I must say it is curious that during so large a part of the 18th century one sees no definite record of crises. Mere fluctuations of industry one must always find, but for real crises one would think record must cremain.

The periodicity of crises seems to have occurred to several writers in economics. Thus Juglar, who is very vague, entitles his book (1862) '*Des crises Comm. et leur Retour Périodique*' & I find Adolph Wagner[4] in the article *Krisen* in Rentsch's Handwörterbuch d. National Okonomie,[5] distinctly states that he holds them to be periodic & points to the English Crises as indicating a decennial period. He also refers to the German writer Schäffle,[6] whose essays I have not yet seen.

I should myself be inclined to say that it is hardly possible there should be no connexion whatever where coincidence is so remarkable, but such an opinion must be taken for what it is worth. It is extremely difficult even to frame an hypothesis as to the mode of connexion. Is anything known with regard to the general meteorological changes accompanying the sun-spots?

I am rejoicing at the prospect of a few days to myself, as the work has been very heavy this session.

Yours very truly,
R. Adamson.

[4] Adolph Heinrich Gotthilf Wagner (1835–1917), taught political economy at the Commercial Academy in Vienna, 1858–63; Commercial Academy, Hamburg, 1863–5; University of Dorpat, 1865–8; University of Freiburg, 1868–70; Professor at the University of Berlin, 1870; specialist in banking and currency and advocate of state socialism.

[5] Wagner published a number of articles in the *Handwörterbuch der Volkswirtschaftslehre* (Leipzig, 1864–6), a dictionary of political economy edited by Hermann Rentsch.

[6] Albert Schäffle (1831–1904), Professor of Political Economy at Tübingen, 1860 and at Vienna, 1868–71.

565.   M. FERRARIS[1] TO W. S. JEVONS

Clearing H.
    'Money'

11 Houghton Place,
Regent's Park, N.W.
Dec. 18th, 1878.

Sir,

I am in receipt of your favoured. Please, accept my best thanks for your kind invitation which I will be very honoured in accepting.

I enclose you the few notices of the Clearing House, which I spoke to you about. I am sorry that I have not been able to find the Debates of the Italian Senate at the British Museum, as they are not now in place. Being unwilling to delay longer my answer to you, I must limit myself with reproducing the following few lines of late Prof. Rota's[2] "Principii di Scienza Bancaria" (Principles of the Science of Banking).

With an offer of my respectful compliments, I am, Sir,
Yours faithfully,
Maggiorino Ferraris.

Prof. W. S. Jevons, M.A., F.R.S.

These are Prof. Rota's words:

"It was generally thought that the Clearing House was an english institution, but Mr. Scialoja in a speech in the Senate stated that this too, as many other banking institutions, originated from Italy". The Clearing House – as Mr. Scialoja stated – "is an old institution at Leghorn, and it existed already in Tuscany before having been transplanted in England. At Leghorn there are the so-called *Stanze di Liquidazione* (Rooms for Clearing) and from the description of the arrangements of these "Stanze di Liquidazione", as it has been given to me by one of the principal bankers of Tuscany, I had reason to persuade myself that the "Stanze di Liquidazione" of Leghorn work even better than the Clearing House of Lombard Street, where it has been introduced by a member of the family Corsi of Tuscany" (Debates of the Italian Senate, 1864, pag. 763–64).

To this passage Prof. Rota added the following note:

"I cannot believe that the *Stanze di Liquidazione* work *even better* than the Clearing House, and englishmen will not believe that a Corso of Tuscany be the founder of their renowned Clearing House, until at least documents are not [*sic*] produced to support fully this mere statement".

[1] Maggiorino Ferraris (1856–1929), Italian journalist and politician; editor of *Nuova Antologia*, 1897–1926; Minister of Posts and Telegraphs, 1893–6; Minister of Provisions in the short-lived Orlando government of 1919; Minister for reconstruction of liberated territories in the Facta government of 1922. Ferraris was a member of Jevons's political economy class at University College London in 1878–9.

[2] Pietro Rota (1846–75), Professor of Social Economy at the University of Genoa.

The late Mr. Scialoja,[3] formerly a Professor of Political Economy at Turin, was several times minister in Italy, and one of its most eminent financiers. He is the author of many of our Currency Laws, and was a member of the recent financial Committee of Egypt.

566.   W. S. JEVONS TO T. E. JEVONS

2 The Chestnuts
Branch Hill
Hampstead
NW.

When you have
new photos of your
children please
send copies.

22 Dec[r] 1878.
[*Please forward letter to
Mr Libbey*][1]

My dear Tom

After receiving your last letter I took an early opportunity to get two maps of Affganistan (?) which I posted to you a few days ago.[2] Accept them as my Christmas present. Harriet sends the enclosed photos – with our best love to Isabel & the children. I hope you are all well & cheerful this christmas. We are all quite well, I am glad to say, & my own health is quite remarkable, owing partly to a better comprehension of what I need.

We are enjoying a real winter at last and as there is a nice little pond at the lower end of the west heath I have had some delightful little skates. The pond being little known the company is comparatively select & includes a good many ladies who now skate in public without the least compunction. I can do an hour or two of skating very comfortably provided it is not every day; with a little too much I get very achy in the back. However I feel younger on the ice.

The Boy is delighted with the ice & snow, & is vainly trying to learn to slide. He takes kindly to snowballs also.

I have been working rather hard of late having now finished my second article on the Methods of Social Reform for the January Contemporary. It is on the need of a *State Parcel Post*.[3] Mr. Libbey of the *Princeton Review* has been very civil in sending me two barrels of beautiful American apples which we & some friends are enjoying much. I must send him an

---

[3] Antonio Scialoja (1817–77), Professor of Political Economy at Turin, 1846–8; Minister of Finance for Italy, 1865, and subsequently Minister of Public Instruction.

[1] See below, Letter 567, p. 304.

[2] The Afghan War of 1878–9, in which three British armies invaded Afghanistan because of the Amir Sher Ali's encouragement of a Russian Mission and refusal tor receive a British one, had begun on 21 November. See *The Times Register of Events in 1878*.

[3] 'A State Parcel Post', *Contemporary Review*, 34 (1879) 209–29; reprinted in *Methods*, pp. 324–52.

article soon on the Suns influence.⁴ I have been going carefully into the question of late & entertain no doubt about the sunspot theory of crises. It is a subject of entrancing interest & I must work it out.

Last night I went to hear Weber's Oberon⁵ at H Majestys Opera. There was some good music & pretty scenery, but the opera cannot be ranked among the best. It was too long & too stagy.

Hoping for a longer letter from you soon & with best wishes for a happy New Year

Your affect Brother
W. S. Jevons

Il va sans dire that the crisis here is a very serious one & it is not quite clear that we are at the end of it quite.⁶

567.   W. S. JEVONS TO J. M. LIBBEY¹
[NYPL]

2 The Chestnuts
West Heath,
Hampstead, N.W.
22 Dec. 1878.

Dear Mr. Libbey,

I have to thank you warmly for your kindness in sending me two barrels of American apples. They arrived a day or two ago in good order and are much appreciated.

Just at present I am very actively engaged in following out my sunspot theory of commercial fluctuations, of which the plot thickens by degrees. It is a most interesting and important subject and after studying commercial fluctuation for 20 years I begin (or seem to begin) to see light.

---

⁴ The unfinished manuscript of an article entitled 'The Solar Influence on Commerce' is among the Jevons Papers; from internal evidence it is clear that this was the article which Jevons intended to send to Libbey for the *Princeton Review*, but apparently never completed. See below, Vol. VII.

⁵ Friedrich von Weber (1786–1826). *Oberon,* his last opera, was first performed at Covent Garden on 12 April 1826.

⁶ The financial crisis which had begun on 2 October with the failure of the City of Glasgow Bank, appeared less intense in November, although there were some further failures; but on 7 December the West of England Bank failed unexpectedly and this gave a considerable shock to confidence. At the end of the year, however, conditions improved quickly and Bank Rate, which had been raised to 6 per cent on 17 October and reduced to 5 per cent in November, was further reduced to 4 per cent on 10 January 1879. Cf. *The Economist*, 15 March 1879, vol. 37, pp. 298–300; Rostow, *British Economy of the Nineteenth Century* (1948) pp. 187–8.

¹ Jonas Marsh Libbey (1857–1922), editor of the *Princeton Review*, 1877–85. Prepared report for the U.S. Government on industrial conditions in England, published in the *First Annual Report of the U.S. Commission of Labour* (1885).

I shall hope to be able to give you some new results after a few weeks time, under the title – "The Sun's Influence on Commerce", but in a matter of this sort it is impossible to make any engagement or to name any time definitely.

With kind regards and the compliments of the season, I am,

Yours faithfully,

W. S. Jevons.

Jonas M. Libbey, Esq.,
Princeton Review,
47 Park Avenue
New York.

568.   R. STRACHAN[1] TO W. S. JEVONS

23 Dec. 1878
11 Offord Road,
London N.

Sir,

In "Principles of Science" page 27 you state: "Abstract terms are strongly distinguished from general terms by possessing only one kind of meaning; for as they denote qualities there is *nothing* which they *cannot* in addition imply". Should not *cannot* be *can*?[2]

Let one take this opportunity of remarking upon your interesting paper in a late number of *Nature* upon the periodicity of crises, in relation to the sun-spot period. Holding as I do that the latter is not made out satisfactorily, *a priori* reasons for similar periods for magnetism, rainfall, temperature, atmospheric pressure crises, locusts seem wanting. Nevertheless, presuming that it is worth while to endeavour to trace a relation if any, I would suggest that you might with equal plausibility trace a cycle for the success attending the whale fishery, the Hudson's Bay Company's dividends &c. &c. I believe that statistics could be got for the annual value of the take of whales, in Dundee; and the annual financial statements of the Hudson's Bay Company could easily be procured I suppose.

---

[1] Richard Strachan (1835–1924) superintended the Instruments Division of the Meteorological Department of the Board of Trade, 1855–1900; editor of the *Meteorological Magazine,* 1864–6, and of the *Horological Journal* for several years; Fellow of the Royal Meteorological Society from 1865 until his death; author of numerous papers and articles, as well as a portable Meteorological Register, and *Basis of Evaporation. Temperature of the Sea around the British Isles* (1910).

[2] As the third edition of the *Principles of Science* which Jevons hoped to see (cf. above, Letter 556, p. 291) did not appear in his lifetime, this error went uncorrected.

Pray excuse my presumption but having thought over these matters I imagine the hint may not be altogether an idle one.

Faithfully Yours,

R. Strachan

Prof. W. S. Jevons,
    2 The Chestnuts,
        West Heath,
            Hampstead N.W.

569.   E. H. FULLER [1] TO W. S. JEVONS

Manchester, Dec. 28/78

Dear Sir,

Reading much in the papers about "hostile tariffs" and "reciprocity" it occurs to me that one effect of protection in foreign countries upon the welfare of our own has been overlooked – at least I do not remember to have heard or read any discussion upon it.

Are not those countries which impede or prevent the importation of commodities from this country obliged to sell us their products at lower prices than they would obtain if they accepted payment in the form most convenient to us? For instance do not America and Russia sell us corn more cheaply than they would do if they allowed us to pay in commodities? And do we not thereby obtain a real and substantial setoff to the loss of profit which their tariffs or prohibition cause us to undergo? I do not of course suppose that we are thereby fully compensated for that loss of profits, but submit that it is to a large extent counterbalanced.

It is highly probable that you have considered this point, and do not hold it of much account. In that case pray accept my apology for troubling you with my crude notions.

I am dear Sir,
    Yours truly,
        Edwd. H. Fuller.

W. S. Jevons, Esq., M.A.

[1] Edward Harrison Fuller (1824–88) carried on business in Manchester as an engraver to calico printers. He took an active part in the local government of Chorlton and Withington, and was a member of the Manchester Statistical Society.